Presented To
Cedar Mill Community Library

In memory
of
Ines Whipple

Manifest Destinations

Manifest Destinations

Cities and Tourists in the
Nineteenth-Century American West

J. Philip Gruen

University of Oklahoma Press : Norman

Library of Congress Cataloging-in-Publication Data

Gruen, J. Philip, 1969–
Manifest destinations : cities and tourists in the nineteenth-century
American West / J. Philip Gruen.
pages cm
Includes bibliographical references and index.
ISBN 978-0-8061-4488-7 (hardcover : alk. paper)
1. West (U.S.)—Description and travel.   2. West (U.S.)—History—1860–1890.
3. Tourism—West (U.S.)—History—19th century.   4. Travel writing—
West (U.S.)—History—19th century.   5. Cities and towns—
West (U.S.)—History—19th century.   I. Title.
F594.G776 2014
978'.02—dc23   2014001463

For my father and the memory of my mother

Contents

List of Illustrations   IX

Preface   XI

Introduction: Into an Unknown   3

1. Attraction: Modernity and the Metropolis   18

2. Promotion: Escape to the Picturesque   41

3. Confusion: Wonder, Turmoil, Awe, and Hell   70

4. Civilization: Architectural Art, Pretense, and Process   106

5. Cosmopolitanism: Editing and Revising Culture   157

Epilogue: Return to an Unknown   201

Notes   217

Bibliography   245

Index   271

Illustrations

MAP

Railways across the continent in 1871   8–9

FIGURES

Bird's-eye view of the transcontinental route 24

"Just Arrived in Chicago" 35

Union Stock Yards in Chicago 48

Bird's-eye view of Denver 56

Guided tours of Salt Lake City 68

Larimer Street, Denver, in 1880 86

Moving a house in San Francisco 93

Chicago River, looking west from the Wells Street Bridge 99

View of Salt Lake City 107

The Auditorium Building, Chicago 127

State Street, looking north from Madison Avenue, Chicago 129

Palace Hotel and Market Street, San Francisco 150

Breakdown of nationalities in Chicago   166

Second South Street, looking east from Main Street,
    Salt Lake City   181

Tourists in Chinatown, San Francisco   196

Spofford Street, San Francisco   211

Preface

The idea for this book began in the busy streets of Chicago's downtown Loop. In the mid-1990s, I worked as a driver and tour guide for the Chicago Trolley Company—at the time, a new "hop on, hop off" outfit featuring a fleet of vehicles loosely modeled on nineteenth-century streetcars. My job was to drive tourists around downtown, stopping at various points of interest and keeping passengers informed and entertained in the meanwhile. The company required drivers to maintain passenger safety, follow the route, and stay alert for important announcements over the radio. Company managers encouraged drivers to highlight various facts and figures associated with the city's notable attractions, but they did not dictate the precise content of the spoken tour.

This was preferable. I had recently pursued a handful of topics regarding Chicago's architecture during coursework in a master's program at the University of Illinois at Chicago, so I envisioned my job as an opportunity to share some of that knowledge. Given the city's reputation as the birthplace of the skyscraper, I assumed that the built environment would be a principal reason tourists chose to visit the city. The company even used the city's architecture to sell its services: the cover of its brochure in those years set a trolley against a backdrop of the Chicago skyline, and the printed map highlighted the various stops with cartoons of the nearest attractions, including the Sears (now Willis) Tower, the John Hancock Tower, and the Water Tower. Smaller print indicated that the trolley discharged passengers near the Board of Trade, the Wrigley Building, the Tribune Tower, Orchestra Hall, the Art Institute, and the Field Museum, among other points of interest. These sites held cultural, artistic, and historic appeal beyond their merits as architecture, but I hoped an architectural focus would set my tour apart.

It took little time, however, to discover that my long-winded explanation about the advent of steel-frame construction and my questioning of the traditional interpretation of the "Chicago School of Architecture" neither captivated nor amused—my hollow tip box provided evidence enough. While tourists did seem interested in the city's architecture, they also inquired about the weather, debated the quality of restaurants and hotels, commented on passersby, and wondered whether certain heavily promoted attractions merited visitation. While I drove, I frequently overheard surprising, often mundane, comments about the metropolis. Tourists seemed more interested in the everyday pulse of the city: cars and taxis darting in and out of traffic, crowds of pedestrians on the sidewalks, street performances, and the clatter of the elevated train. So, I spent several weeks changing the verbal content of the tour to highlight the ordinary and the everyday—with occasional, albeit feeble, attempts at humor. My tip box, meanwhile, began to fill.

Strange as it seemed, this made sense. Poignant moments from my own travels frequently involved unplanned, surprising, and occasionally unpleasant circumstances—not always that which accompanied the heavily advertised attractions or monumental works of architecture that initially sparked my trips. Other travelers' reports corroborated with mine. Family, friends, colleagues, and students spoke highly of well-known or well-promoted sites upon returning from trips but equally as often recounted stories about lodging, weather, food quality, street conditions, travel inconveniences, or other ordinary, often unexpected, circumstances that significantly shaped their impressions. Their encounters rarely matched the alluring photographs, advertisements, television specials, websites, or enticing articles featured in the travel section of the Sunday paper. I found this discrepancy intriguing.

When I entered a doctoral program in architecture at the University of California at Berkeley in the late 1990s, I began exploring the intersection of tourism, cities, culture, and the built environment through coursework and research projects. Material for such an investigation was readily available: San Francisco was just across the bay and, at the time, billed itself as the "World's Most Popular City."[1] Although the city's popularity ranking was clearly a marketing ploy for which convincing evidence would be impossible to obtain, certainly San Francisco was an internationally popular tourist destination. I wondered, broadly, what drew tourists to San Francisco in the late twentieth century, how important architecture was to tourists' experiences, and how tourists might characterize their visits overall.

To provide background for one seminar paper about late twentieth-century tourism in San Francisco, I considered it responsible first to offer a brief history of early tourism in that city, which I presumed was largely a post–World War II phenomenon. But when I stepped into the Bancroft Library on the Berkeley campus one afternoon, one archival source slowly revealed another and still another. A staggering number of late nineteenth-century guidebooks, souvenir view books, magazine articles, newspaper accounts, engravings, traveler narratives, diaries, and letters indicated a substantial tourist presence. Many travelers, I gradually realized, arrived in San Francisco as part of longer trips that included visitations to other cities in the American West, most notably Chicago, Salt Lake City, and Denver. The multitude of sources I found suggested that late nineteenth-century tourists—in their fascination and engagement with the everyday life of the metropolis—bore much in common to my own travel experiences and those of my trolley customers in downtown Chicago. I finished the seminar paper but remained excited about my discovery. There were so many stories embedded in the tourist experiences of the late nineteenth-century urban American West, and I wondered if anyone had told them.

As I embarked on this project, I quickly became aware of the plentiful secondary work regarding the settlement and promotion of the nineteenth-century American West. But I found little guidance when I attempted to cast my findings within a larger history of tourism and travel. At the time—around 1999—scholarship on tourism remained primarily within the fields of anthropology and literary theory, dominated by questions of authenticity and focused on the presentation of place by agencies and organizations rather than the reception of place by tourists.[2] Far fewer analyses focused upon urban tourism, and almost nothing discussed urban tourism in the late nineteenth-century American West.[3] What secondary literature did exist typically concentrated on elite, booster efforts to shape cities for visitors in ways that revealed the overall grandeur and sophistication of the urban environment. Tourists themselves had little agency in this process; one tacitly assumed they encountered cities in much the way that elites hoped they would.

I found this odd. If my own experiences and those of others were any indication, how was it possible that tourists visited only that which suggested urban grandeur and sophistication? Did not tourists encounter nonadvertised, random, and unexpected activity immediately upon arrival and then again at their places of lodging? Where did tourists dine, with whom did they travel, how did they move from place to place, and how did they manage the weather? Were they in good health? What did tourists make of the urban population? And what did their encounters reveal about cities, about urban tourism, about the American West?

Discovering and interpreting tourist encounters became far more difficult than I initially suspected. Guidebooks, view books, and souvenir albums to the American West offered the booster perspective, presenting cities as organized, beautiful, and convenient for tourist exploration. This was not surprising: boosters were not wont to focus upon any everyday urban characteristics that might reveal a less-than-refined city. But accounts, diaries, letters, and the occasional travel album compiled by western-bound travelers complicated the promotional characterization of western cities. Some tourists offered impressions that matched promotional rhetoric, but others recounted ordinary or unusual circumstances that rarely appeared in guidebooks—

many impressions of which depicted cities in less-than-complimentary ways. As I surveyed a wide range of sources, tourist experiences became almost unmanageably complex. Yet the complexity itself brought to light important perspectives on tourism, on cities, and on the late nineteenth-century American West.

Tourist encounters do not disclose themselves easily, however. Along with guidebooks, brochures, and bird's-eye views, hundreds—possibly thousands—of late nineteenth-century traveler narratives had been printed for the reading public. Yet many of these accounts read like extended urban advertisements, making it difficult to sort tourist experiences from pure boosterism.[4] Furthermore, the most vivid, lyrical, and oft-cited descriptions of western cities were narratives written by journalists, novelists, or paid correspondents, whose accounts appeared originally as separate articles in magazines or newspapers (such as *Harper's Weekly, Scribner's Monthly,* or London's *Daily Telegraph*) before being compiled and edited for publication. Those tourists who headed west with an intent to publish may have crafted their impressions specifically to appease publishers, investors, or advertisers; this often meant casting western cities as efficient places set within picturesque landscapes. Other visitors held financial interests in western land or property and served to benefit from any future tourism or settlement the publication and distribution of their recollections might induce. To encourage investment (and lure future visitors), they too portrayed urban environments of tranquility and grandeur, featuring cohesive populations contributing to economic prosperity. Did such accounts reveal tourist experiences, or were there ulterior motives at work?[5]

Further complicating the ability to extract experiences from primary accounts is that some visitors discussed western cities in ways that mirrored promotional materials. What appears to be an original impression from one traveler is, in certain instances, a series of paraphrased or borrowed passages from a guidebook or previously published traveler account. A few tourists acknowledged their sources, as did T. S. Hudson in his 1882 account, *A Scamper through America,* when he cited George Crofutt's *Overland Tourist and Pacific Coast Guide,* or George Augustus Sala, who mentioned both Charles Nordhoff's

California: For Health, Pleasure, and Residence and Henry T. Williams's *Pacific Tourist* in his lengthy 1886 travelogue entitled *America Revisited.* M. Dwinell's 1878 travel account acknowledged that he was indebted to "Crofut's" [*sic*] for "many statistics."[6] But most tourists did not cite particular influences, and one can only guess whether they described their own experiences or recalled western cities in ways they thought their reading audience might appreciate.

Although many traveler narratives underwent review and alteration before publication, the printed versions rarely exhibit consistency. A substantial number read nothing like promotional accounts, and several tourists claimed they composed their memoirs initially as letters or diary entries meant for family and friends—not for widespread publication. To dispel any likeness to guidebooks, tourists often stressed in their book's prefatory material that they had not edited or rewritten their observations; instead, they wrote in the manner of "first impressions." Henry Alworth Merewether, following his around-the-world journey in 1874, explained in *By Sea and by Land* that he wrote only what "I saw and heard myself, and copied from no guide books," while Henry Brainard Kent, in his 1890 *Graphic Sketches of the West,* claimed his work was "entirely independent of corporate interests."[7]

The accuracy of such claims notwithstanding, neither traveler narratives and guidebooks nor what travelers heard from others beforehand could entirely direct tourist experiences. Even if tourists read the same books, viewed the same images, and arrived with a similar set of expectations, the range of on-the-ground reactions overall do not ultimately map a clear, like-minded urban West. Promotional materials also could not determine when tourists chose to visit, where they slept, what they ate, or with whom they traveled, and they could not control the climate. Tourists remained culture bound, as well: their education, gender, age, health, religion, political beliefs, and places of origin played a role in shaping their preconceptions, their encounters, and their interpretation of those encounters.[8] Information acquired prior to traveling could not account for the entire range of life experiences tourists brought with them on their journeys, and it did not, and could not, prepare tourists for the everyday and often unexpected activity of the city.

Rather than accept the urban American West as it had been sold to them, tourists often recast it in their own terms. At times, they offered decidedly negative assessments of western cities and their constituent parts. When young traveler Ellen H. Walworth arrived in Salt Lake City by train from the Ogden, Utah, depot in April 1877, she wrote in her diary that the city "is not as pleasant a place as we had heard it was; with the exception of the Tabernacle, it looks to us like any other raw, Western town."[9] Her traveling group chose not to stay in the city, returning to Ogden to spend the night. What had she heard about Salt Lake City prior to her visit? Charles Savage's 1870 guidebook *Salt Lake City, and the Way Thither* offers one possibility—Savage was a Salt Lake City–based photographer and publisher who contributed broadly to the city's nineteenth-century tourist appeal through the publication of a number of guidebooks and souvenir view books. In Savage's description, the traveler approaching Salt Lake City by train from Ogden would find "scenery which combines the beautiful and the sublime—the loveliness of the Bay of Naples with the grand magnificence of the Swiss Alps." All those who travel, Savage claimed, will "agree to recognize the admirable skill with which the Mormon leaders have selected the site and developed the plan of their city."[10] But did they? Walworth's entry suggests nothing of the kind.

At other times, tourists reported their urban observations without obviously adhering to any preconceptions, their impressions echoing the booster presentation of western cities on one level—but deviating from it the next. F. W. Woodbury's promotional 1882 *Tourists' Guide Book to Denver* cited "Mr. Crofutt" and noted that "in point of richness, beauty, and the *style* of its private residences . . . [Denver] is not to be outdone by any city of five times its age." Among other attractions, Woodbury's guidebook added that the city has "many beautiful business blocks" as well as "20 or 30 church edifices."[11] Three years later, *Crofutt's Grip-Sack Guide of Colorado* similarly described Denver as a city "built principally of brick and stone" and featuring "broad" streets with a "natural hard gravel and clay pavement" and sidewalks "mostly laid with large flagging stone."[12] British tourist Henry W. Lucy, visiting in 1885, found Denver much to his liking overall, but offered equivocal impressions about the city's infrastructure and built environment. "There is nothing lacking to complete the handsomeness and desirability of Denver," he wrote. "The roads are broad and well made— terribly dusty when the wind blows," he added, "but that is not every day." Lucy found impressive Denver's rapid growth, its "clusters of handsome residences," and its abundance of churches and chapels. But he issued a word of caution about overdevelopment, noting that one particular chapel bore "a placard announcing that it is 'For rent.'"[13]

Moreover, there was also the occasional (if less frequent) circumstance that western cities appeared far *more* congenial than travelers expected. Robert Anderton Naylor, visiting Chicago along with the "Arts Society" group in 1893, expressed surprise at the "majestic buildings, thousands of high-class residences, and some of the finest hotels the world has ever seen"—despite warnings from others about Chicago's "shanty hotels" and a guarantee that he would "never get out of the place alive."[14] Attempting to judge what was accurate and what was hyperbole became difficult. The more that patterns emerged, the more that exceptions arose. It seemed disingenuous to broadly summarize encounters for the purpose of writing an easily digestible narrative; I wanted to tell a good story, but I did not wish to simplify a situation for which there were too many conflicting impressions.[15] If the stories emerging from this book seem not to provide definitive conclusions about how tourists experienced the urban American West, it is because those experiences resist a tidy explanation.

I could have been more selective, however; limiting the number and type of sources to provide a more airtight narrative. For example, I could have isolated traveler accounts to demonstrate how ethnic groups, nationalities, or classes understood a specific city at a defined point in time.[16] I also could have restricted my focus to the booster perspective, demonstrating the ways in which elites shaped the city for tourist consumption and ignored—or exploited—much of the local population. Those stories are acknowledged here, but they represent selective perspectives on tourism in the late nineteenth-century urban West. I have chosen also to include equivocating, inconclusive, and sometimes contradictory traveler accounts that exposed a messier, kaleidoscopic urban environment that often countered the booster view. Such accounts were neither the exception nor the rule, but their existence reveals a more everyday—if more complicated and diffi-cult to discern—urban West. Late nineteenth-century western cities were too big, too unwieldy, too ordinary, and too complex to fully shape for tourist consumption. *Manifest Destinations* permits this very complexity.

Indeed, many tourist encounters demonstrate resistance, however unintentional, to a more official city of boosters, publishers, planners, architects, cartographers, and other figures of authority, who directed tourists to specific sites or suggested they understand the urban envi-ronment in particular ways. In that sense, tourists resembled the ordi-nary "practitioners" of New York City whom French scholar Michel de Certeau imagined as he gazed down on the orderly grid of Manhattan from the observation deck of the World Trade Center. In an oft-cited chapter entitled "Walking in the City" in *The Practice of Everyday Life* (1984), de Certeau imagined those practitioners reimagining the city as they walked, wandered, and wove meaningful—and occasionally subversive—tapestries that defied the order and rationality of the city imposed by planners.[17] Tourists in the late nineteenth-century urban West did not seem particularly interested in subverting authority (or, at least, they did not indicate as much in their memoirs). But they did have the tendency to wander away from the proverbial beaten path of the guidebooks or to characterize the urban environment as loud or foul smelling—characterizations that defied cities' bucolic, static, and visually oriented presentation in promotional material. That material encouraged tourists to "see" the sights while, unsurprisingly, ignoring the unpleasant sounds and smells of cities. Illustrations depicted build-ings, monuments, and parks in their most flattering light and suggested optimal angles by which visitors might best view them.

Yet tourists did not interpret sights in a purely visual way if their bodies also brought them into proximity with sounds, smells, or other bodies from which they would have preferred to remain distant or apart—no matter their often privileged vantage point from the windows of an observation deck, hotel room, carriage, or railcar.[18] That tourists encountered the cities of the late nineteenth-century urban American West in ways extending beyond vision is perhaps obvious. Yet a growing literature on "corporeal" tourism acknowledging a sensory awareness of place has yet to dethrone the primacy of sight in tourism studies.[19]

Recognizing the role of the senses challenges my field of architectural history as well, where—despite recent methodological shifts—vision also continues to dominate, leading to aesthetics-oriented interpretations of the built environment. To imply (as this book does) that visitor experiences that speak to the use, function, temperature, context, smells, or sounds of the built environment should be considered along with vision counters object-based approaches to architectural analysis. Methods common among scholars in art and architectural history throughout much of the twentieth century championed individual architects, design intent, originality, patronage, materials, structure, beauty, building types, and systems of classification. Analyses privileged the finished product over the construction process, monumentality trumped the ordinary, and aesthetics mattered more than use or function. Such approaches historically separated architecture from culture and attempted to maintain the history of architecture as a distinct discipline with its own internal logic, thereby legitimizing the design professions and pushing to the periphery many fields from which architectural history frequently drew.[20]

Tourist encounters in late nineteenth-century western cities complicate this historiography. Tourists discussed hundreds of buildings, spaces, streets, and parks, but only on rare occasions did they concern themselves with designers, styles, or the architectural profession. They discussed aesthetics and materials but never in ways that once preoccupied the attention of architectural historians, whose opinions regarding such matters concentrated upon uniqueness or the ability for particular structures to represent particular styles or movements. Visitors infrequently described the built environment using the ana-

lytical terminology that would best locate buildings within an established canon of periods and styles; they drew their attention as much
to the everyday urbanism of commercial storefronts, industrial buildings, streets, residential dwellings—and the people using them—as to
major civic buildings, monuments, and palatial hotels. Tourist descriptions of "imposing" and "sombre-looking" edifices; the "marvelous
energy" of construction; or "enchanting," "whimsical," or "dismal"
collections of buildings offered more descriptive, colorful responses
that enmeshed architecture within a much larger physical—as well as
social, symbolic, and psychological—context for which no designer
could adequately plan. In effect, tourists read architecture as a part of
the cultural landscape—the methods and investigation for which have
significantly broadened the scope of inquiry for historians of the built
environment.[21]

Purists may dismiss tourist impressions of architecture as the collective imagination of an uneducated, fickle lot. Yet architecture is designed
for a far larger audience than the comparatively small number of people who are involved in its initial planning, design, and construction.
When one considers that most sites are encountered by thousands of
visitors for years after the initial planners, designers, and builders have
departed, the significance of visitor impressions must be understood as
crucial to the overall history of those sites. This book thus attempts to
raise tourists' impressions to a level equal to that of the most talented
designers, astute critics, or refined architectural connoisseurs.

This book also reveals the prevalence of tourism in the late
nineteenth-century urban American West. This is significant because
studies of tourism in the West during this period mostly have concerned tourists' engagement with the natural environment. Where cities appear, the focus has been upon specific areas or neighborhoods
within these cities, including Chicago's Loop and Union Stock Yards,
Salt Lake City's Temple Square, and San Francisco's Chinatown. This
book does discuss tourist encounters in those areas but reads them
within a larger urban context that included the nonpromoted, ordinary landscapes of streets, residences, industries, and people that helped
make cities significant to tourists' overall western encounters.

Given the widespread promotional emphasis on the western natural landscape, tourists might have anticipated a region of geological
wonders sprinkled with a few, mostly underdeveloped towns. Instead,
they discovered metropolitan areas with the uncertainties, refinement,
and excitement of eastern U.S. and European cities. Such characteristics were not necessarily unfamiliar to nineteenth-century visitors,
many of whom hailed from the urban American East or Europe. But
nestled within the spectacular natural settings of the West, the urban
landscape often appeared rather startling. Tourist encounters helped
elevate the presence of the urban West on the late nineteenth-century
world stage.

Before lifting the curtain, however, a few words about the book's
title: *Manifest Destinations.* In western cities, tourists could gain insight
into the alleged fulfillment of the notion of "manifest destiny," a phrase
attributed to American journalist and diplomat John Louis O'Sullivan
for his support of the annexation of Texas to the American Union
in 1845. Politicians later adopted this phrase to justify the expansion
of the American continent to include California, the Southwest, the
Oregon territory, and Alaska. As the idea of "manifest destiny" gained
popularity, it also came to mean the inevitability of bringing the Far
West into the European American fold under the mantle of civilization, freedom, democracy, and divine right. Manifest destiny had to
look and feel a certain way. The West had to be settled and tamed
to demonstrate European American ways of gentility and refinement.

But none of this was inevitable. American expansionism necessitated the brutal subjugation of the indigenous population and the
imposition of an unfamiliar religion, the transformation of the natural
landscape for profit and capital, the establishment of new laws, and difficult negotiations with foreign nations. To legitimize any such notion
of European American manifest destiny also required the settlement of
the land with a physical infrastructure and a permanent built environment. The various transcontinental railroads completed in the nineteenth century brought parts of the newly acquired territory within
convenient reach of the population centers of the eastern seaboard,
but most of the land traversed by the railroads was sparsely popu-

lated and predominantly uncultivated. Vast portions of the American West remained inaccessible; for most travelers, only maps indicated the regions within U.S. jurisdiction. Without the obvious appearance of European American control, how would tourists recognize that the alleged civilization, refinement, freedom, democracy, and divine right had been attained? Western cities provided the most evident clues. With their substantial populations, permanent buildings, civic organizations, businesses, industries, residential districts, transportation networks, religious edifices, parks, and entertainment venues, the urban West offered the ultimate measure for gauging whether manifest destiny had been achieved on the land.[22]

There is, however, something of an irony in the title, *Manifest Destinations.* With the possible exception of a few urban sites, western cities were not nineteenth-century tourist *destinations*—or at least they rarely provided the original impetus for tourist journeys. Cities became attractions, but the principal appeal of the American West throughout the late nineteenth century remained the wonders and wilds of the natural landscape. Yet if a refined European American cultural condition best characterized manifest destiny, then visitors would need to discover that condition where culture was most apparent: in the urban environment. There, manifest destiny never fully behaved in the refined ways that its champions had hoped, and tourist encounters helped expose its challenges. What tourists encountered instead was a destiny manifest as much in stately architecture and signs of economic and cultural progress as with ethnic and religious diversity, ordinary buildings, and the noise, unexpected activity, and the occasional disorder of everyday urban life.

Occasional (and frequent) disorder also characterized my extended journey through the wilds of research, writing, and editing, so I remain indebted to several people who helped *Manifest Destinations* reach its final destination as a book. The intellectual, experimental, and interdisciplinary climate at Berkeley provided an ideal setting for initially exploring tourism in a critical fashion, and I was fortunate to have Dell Upton's critique and example as this project moved from seminar paper into dissertation—and beyond. Upton's readings of cities and architecture still resonate with me; I hope only that I have done reasonable justice to his approach. Mary Ryan, Nezar AlSayyad, and Allan Pred also provided valuable critiques of the dissertation as members of my committee in the early 2000s, and their comments stayed relevant as I began revisions several years later. The teaching and scholarship of Bob Bruegmann, Peter Hales, and Mitchell Schwarzer helped generate an ability to engage the built environment with an analytical eye, and I consider myself lucky to have studied under them while pursuing my master's degree at the University of Illinois at Chicago in the mid-1990s. In ensuing years, travels with them into landscapes both real and imaginative contributed to this work in tangible and intangible ways.

I conducted much of the initial research for *Manifest Destinations* during a fellowship with the Smithsonian Institution's National Museum of American History and the Architectural History and Historic Preservation Division in Washington, D.C., in 2000–2001, where I enjoyed the assistance of numerous scholars. Charles McGovern, my advisor-in-residence, went above-and-beyond to provide rapid turnarounds on early chapter drafts, while Cynthia Field, Helena Wright, and Jeffrey Stine offered useful suggestions on incipient stages of this work. I also met Cam Cocks through Smithsonian connections, and to say that I have learned from her writing, insight, and advice during several stages of this project would be a vast understatement. My friend and colleague Sarah Kennel suggested the title "Manifest Destinations" during an informal conversation that year. It stuck.

I also extend my gratitude to other colleagues, archivists, and friends who alerted me to sources I may otherwise have overlooked; accepted papers for conference presentation; or helped me fine-tune ideas in direct or indirect ways. No doubt this list is incomplete, but I would be remiss if I did not at least mention Tamsen Anderson, Barbara Berglund, Tim Davis, Frank Goodyear, Paul Groth, Robin Higham, Clif Hood, Catie Knoebel, Dave Kojan, John Maciuika, Jean Mansavage, Hal Rothman, Mark Souther, Jessica Teisch, David Whittaker, and Aaron Wunsch. Brian Cannon graciously offered lodging during a

2007 award with the Charles Redd Center at Brigham Young University. Conversations with Ray Rast, in particular, have been especially enlightening over the years.

In the School of Design and Construction at Washington State University, where I have been teaching since 2003, I have benefitted from student discussions and projects during seminars on architecture, tourism, and travel. I have also enjoyed the support and camaraderie of several colleagues—particularly as we faced the challenges of organizing and delivering content on massive faculty-led undergraduate study tours in San Francisco, Chicago, Los Angeles, Phoenix, New York City, and Washington, D.C. Critical discussions and debates about architecture and tourism with my close friend and departmental colleague Ayad Rahmani—either in the office or on the streets of San Francisco—have informed my research, teaching, and scholarship in more ways than he will ever know. My colleague Jon Hegglund in the Department of English, meanwhile, helped me navigate through the labyrinths of tenure, and his steadfast friendship and discipline have taught me to keep the bar raised high—without sacrificing everything else.

This project remains heavily indebted to Matt Bokovoy, whose willingness to take a chance on an unseasoned scholar helped transform a dissertation into a book proposal—and then the early stages of a book. Jay Dew, acquisitions editor with the University of Oklahoma Press, offered steady encouragement and sage advice, while manuscript editor Stephanie Attia and copy editor Susan Harris guided the manuscript through the byzantine world of editing and publication in a timely and efficient manner—and taught me much in the process. Outside readers provided incisive feedback at different stages, compelling me to rethink my assumptions and sending me scurrying for new information. This book has benefited from all of their suggestions in ways too numerous to mention.

Finally, the unwavering support of my wife, Corinna Nicolaou, gave me the strength to keep going even when the manuscript languished. Juggling her own writing projects and adjusting to life in a remote corner of the world, Corinna inspired me by her example as much as by her words and warmth. My mother, Joan Gruen, did not live to see this in print, but her bright and adventuresome spirit still shines through every page. It is difficult to pinpoint, but my approach and treatment of the subject bears her influence. My father, Erich Gruen, read drafts of the manuscript several years ago and served as a consistent sounding board through the proposal, revision, and publication process. He never doubted my ability to complete this project yet no doubt will be relieved to see that I did. To find *Manifest Destinations* on his library shelves alongside the many books he has authored will, for me, make this journey complete.

Manifest Destinations

Introduction

Into an Unknown

Seventeen stories was high enough. Mable Treseder might have gone higher, but her mother and Mrs. Smith thought otherwise. Looking over the city from their seventeenth-floor perch provided temporary respite from the elevator journey upward, yet glancing directly below revealed only tiny individuals milling about the first floor. Treseder's companions became dizzy, so everyone returned to the ground level. But the descent offered no comfort to the Wisconsin-based group of tourists, evidently unaccustomed to heights and elevators. "It seemed as if the floor of the elevator was drawn from under our feet," the eighteen-year-old Treseder recalled in her diary, "and there we stood in midair." She gripped the railing, hoping for support, but "all was in vain. It seemed as if we were going to an unknown by an unknown route."[1]

Yet much was real. The city was Chicago, the year was 1893, and the Treseder party descended in one of several electric elevators inside the new Masonic Temple skyscraper, the world's tallest commercial building following its 1892 completion. At 302 feet and twenty stories, the spectacular edifice, designed by Daniel Hudson Burnham and John Wellborn Root, pierced Chicago's skyline and dazzled visitors with a lofty, glass-canopied atrium that exposed the building's various floors to view. To reach those floors, fourteen passenger elevators greeted

3

building-goers in a semicircular arrangement along the back wall, ready to hoist shoppers to the first ten floors of retail establishments, workers or clients to the next six levels of offices, Masonic members and officials to the upper four stories of meeting and ceremonial rooms, or tourists to the observation platform and conservatory. At the top, visitors had a choice: they could peer down into the atrium, or they could look out over a city notable for its explosive late nineteenth-century growth. For much of 1893, they also could cast their gazes eight miles to the south, where the World's Columbian Exposition fronted the lakefront and sprawled westward.[2]

Guidebooks published in anticipation of the exposition also encouraged visits to the city's technologically advanced downtown area, arguing for its sophistication and elegance amid Chicago's breakneck pace and seemingly unregulated commercial activity. Skyscrapers occupied a prominent role among the urban highlights, with the Masonic Temple a regular feature: guidebooks championed its soaring height and engineering achievements along with its rich materials and expansive atrium. John J. Flinn's massive *Chicago: The Marvelous City of the West*, published the year prior to the fair, was particularly effusive. Flinn dedicated nearly two pages of text to the Masonic Temple, boasting of the number, reach, and speed of its elevators, which run "from the basement to the attic" and make "a round trip every three minutes."[3]

Similar to many nineteenth-century guidebooks to Chicago, Flinn's description celebrated the Masonic Temple's dimensions, materials, and technological advancements but did not forecast visitor experiences. To advertise fourteen elevators running the full height of the building was one thing; to step onto those elevators and be lifted skyward was entirely another. Mable Treseder, her mother, and Mrs. Smith found the elevators as harrowing as they did fascinating; for this rural Wisconsin group of tourists, the visit to the Masonic Temple—indeed, their visit to Chicago itself—*became* that elevator ride. Flinn's guidebook may have celebrated the elevators' ability to complete a three-minute round trip from the "basement to the attic," but as far as Mable Treseder was concerned, her group plummeted "to an unknown by an unknown route." The rest of the city was little consolation for her, and she claimed to have hardly any idea "what to say of the city. It was worse than the confusion of tongues at the Tower of Babel. Humdrum noise and confusion existed all day and all night long."[4]

Mable Treseder was not alone. Other visitors had difficulty making sense of this bustling modern metropolis, with its new technologies, rising and diverse population, rapid pace, incessant clatter, and towering skyscrapers—even while they found it impressive and exhilarating. Chicago offered the most dramatic urban example in late nineteenth-century America, but cities further West—especially Denver, Salt Lake City, and San Francisco—held their share of uncertainty and obscurity for first-time visitors. In those cities, tourists encountered places undergoing massive upheavals that transformed them into major metropolises. Guidebooks and other tourist-oriented material mostly denied the ambiguity of those transformations in favor of achievements, progress, and efficiency, but tourists described the messiness of the everyday city as often as they noted and contemplated the monumental and progressive one. Modernizing cities, such as those that are the subject of this story, lent themselves neither consistently to clarity nor approval. Tourists marveled at their ingenuity, speed, and accomplishments but recoiled at their rapid construction, scoffed at their pretensions to grandeur, and thumbed their noses at their alleged civility—often all in the same visit. The urban American West appeared enigmatic, exciting, frightening, ordinary, refined, and uncouth: remarkable as well as dull, thoroughly unique on certain levels, but still, to some visitors, resembling cities elsewhere.

Try as they might, the women and men who made the westward journey (potential settlers, land speculators, spiritual leaders, social reformers, members of traveling delegations, dignitaries, novelists, poets, journalists, artists, architects, engineers, and occasional working-class visitors) struggled to understand the urban environment. Whether the visitors were esteemed, and often well-off—for example, authors or journalists on lengthy trips such as Helen Hunt Jackson, George Augustus Sala, and Caroline Churchill—or if they were lesser-known and middle- or working-class folks on shorter trips—such as Mable Treseder, Solomon Mead, and Banyer Clarkson—tourists encountered western cities in myriad ways that cannot be easily classified. They engaged in a dialectic between the production of the city and its consumption, between presentation and experience, and between promotion and encounter. One sometimes, but not always, informed the other.[5]

By the early 1870s, tourists certainly knew of western cities, and the largest of them provided attractions or interest that other urban areas could not match. Chicago's explosive growth lured some visitors before the Great Fire of 1871, but the aftermath of the fire and the rebuilding process drew curiosity seekers from everywhere. Farther west, in Salt Lake City, tourists could encounter a large and thriving Mormon population. And nowhere but in San Francisco could tourists find a tighter-knit or more populous Chinese community, at least on American soil. Whether the physical rise of Chicago against its seemingly boundless prairie and lake or the collision of humanity with the scenic mountain, bay, or ocean backdrops in Denver, Salt Lake City, or San Francisco, no major late nineteenth-century European or eastern American cities featured such a marked juxtaposition between urban life and the natural environment as did those in the West.

That tourists took a keen interest in western cities is unsurprising given those cities' striking presence in a region where little urban development existed prior to the 1860s. But it *is* surprising because nineteenth-century promotional materials mythologized the West for the overarching power of its allegedly untouched natural landscape and because scholarship about nineteenth-century western tourism also has approached the subject matter from a decidedly nonurban angle.[6] Within this picture, cities also appear as extensions of the natural landscape; words and illustrations depict bucolic places where the efficiency of business operations, architectural grandeur, or urban open space prevail over the complexity of their urban conditions. Contemporary tourist accounts complicate this picture, however. The natural landscape looms large in traveler experiences—even within the city—but tourists were fascinated with the radical transformation of the western environment into the urban, full as it was with the contradictions of the modern world. These were settings where any certainties stood on shaky ground; where the expectations of stability were, as with Mable Treseder's description of the elevator descent in the Masonic Temple, "drawn from under our feet."

This book addresses the discrepancy between promotional materials and tourist encounters between 1869 and 1893 in the four most-visited cities of the American West: Chicago, Denver, Salt Lake City, and San Francisco.[7] A handful of hardy tourists made their way westward prior to 1869, but the region first attracted significant numbers of pleasure travelers following that year's completion of the Union Pacific and Central Pacific railroads—together making the nation's first transcontinental link. With the railroad traversing the nation, wealthy visitors from the American eastern seaboard and Europe boarded the luxury sleeper cars attached to long-distance trains, allowing them to visit the American West in relative comfort and ease. So many well-to-do tourists made this trip that a late nineteenth-century western journey could be considered a late phase of the eighteenth-century Grand Tour of Europe—where travelers' edification rested not in their exposure to the ruins and monuments of Western antiquity but with their contemplation of vast, unusual, and forbidding landscapes suggesting episodes in geologic time.[8] The line of the transcontinental railroad, however, passed much closer to major western cities than to the most spectacular of the heavily promoted western natural wonders. Tourists stopped to explore.

Many late nineteenth-century tourists approached the West by rail from New York City, visiting Niagara Falls in upstate New York before making their way to Chicago—the latter widely considered a western city in the late nineteenth-century.[9] They stopped in Chicago before continuing further west, where short railroad branch lines or ferry trips made Denver, Salt Lake City, and San Francisco conveniently accessible. Less frequently, travelers approached the American West from the Pacific Ocean, arriving in San Francisco by boat as part of around-the-world voyages and then proceeding eastward along the Central and Union Pacific. Still others approached cities from rural areas on day trips; by the 1880s, these mostly wealthy tourists could—and did—arrive in major western cities via other transcontinental railroads.

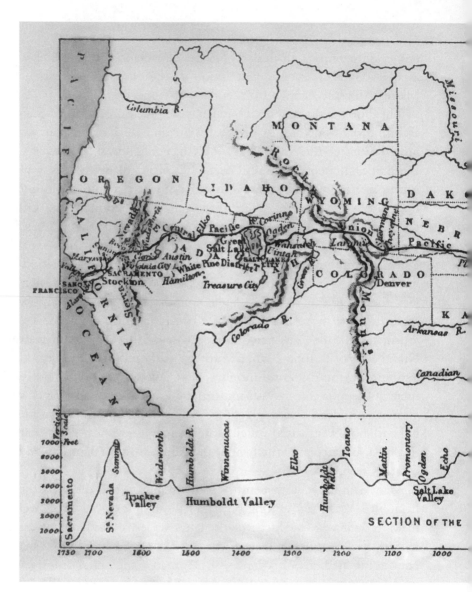

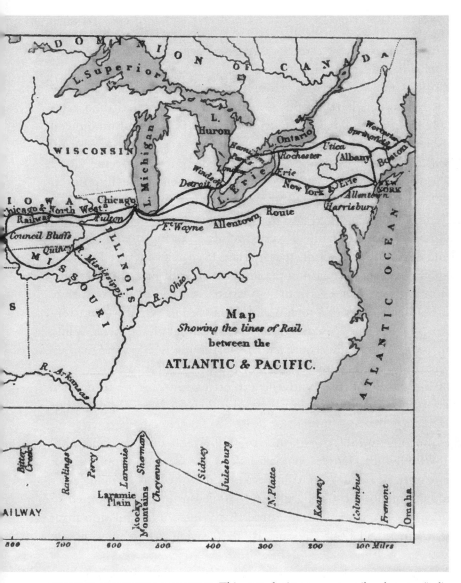

RAILWAYS ACROSS THE CONTINENT. This map depicts common railroad routes (indicated by heavy black lines) across the United States in 1871. Most routes converged in Chicago, and branch lines (not shown) brought tourists to Denver and Salt Lake City before reaching San Francisco. The cross section, below the map, shows elevation changes along the Union and Central Pacific route between Omaha and Sacramento—the stretch that marked the completion of the nation's first transcontinental railroad. (Source: W. F. Rae, *Westward by Rail,* frontispiece.)

Together, their visits gave tourists a presence in the late nineteenth-century urban West.

Visiting the West became more economically feasible for more classes of travelers by the mid-1880s, as railroads lowered their rates and the Boston-based Raymond and Whitcomb Company announced "personally-conducted" western excursions to rival those already offered by the well-established British-based company, Thomas Cook and Son.[10] When Chicago hosted the World's Columbian Exposition in 1893 and railroads engaged in a price war to lure visitors, tens of millions of tourists poured into that city from all corners of the developed world. Many continued westward after visiting the fair, leaving behind hundreds of accounts that marked 1893 as a watershed year for the gradual democratization of pleasure travel—just prior to a national economic depression.[11] As tourists visited cities along the way, they revealed the urbanity of a region and countered its popular characterization as a vast landscape filled only with natural phenomena. While visits to the West hardly abated after 1893, the 1869–93 period marked a significant period for urban tourism in the American West.

This era also coincided with the explosive growth of western cities. Chicago was already a substantial city in 1870 with 298,977 people but boasted more than one million by 1890. San Francisco had grown from 56,802 people in 1860 to almost 150,000 by 1870 and nearly 300,000 by 1890. Neither Denver nor Salt Lake City were as populous, but they featured an equally startling rate of growth: Denver held fewer than 5,000 people according to the 1870 census but mushroomed to 106,713 in 1890; Salt Lake City more than tripled its population from 1870, when it had 12,864 people, to 1890, when it contained nearly 45,000.[12]

Population growth in the American West neither drove nor sustained traveler interest in the region, but it required new buildings, services, and infrastructure to accommodate a rising population. Economic and cultural diversity, the presence of industries, the energy and visual clutter of commerce, the rattle of transportation, the residential districts spreading away from the downtown core, and ordinary as well as dilapidated buildings provided a curious, if sometimes disorienting, prospect for visitors—although many hailed originally from cities that featured these very characteristics. But such potentially troubling signs of modern urban growth provided only half the equation: tourists also could visit physical responses to haphazard development in the cities' parks, cemeteries, views, drives, and exquisite architecture. This juxtaposition of density and open space, of disorder and order, was also apparent in modernizing eastern and European cities but took on a magnified presence in the West because of the region's sparse population prior to the mid-nineteenth century and because western cities existed in spectacular natural settings so distant from tourists' points of origin.

Indeed, nineteenth-century magazines, guidebooks, dime novels, poetry, painting, photography, and many published accounts from previous travelers rhetorically and illustratively constructed the West for its incomparable natural beauty, on the one hand, and its "savage" natives and "wild" adventurers on the other. A variety of sources portrayed the American West in ways that denied the very realities of its urbanization, casting western cities largely as picturesque developments nestled within the grandeur of the open and wild landscape. These sources were in widespread circulation.

Set against that discursive backdrop, tourist encounters with western cities stood out in high relief. Upon arrival, tourists had to reconcile any preconceptions of tranquil environments with the realities of western urbanization and the circumstances of late nineteenth-century urban life. Whether "travelers," "tourists," "visitors," "health seekers," or "pleasure seekers" (as nineteenth-century guidebooks interchangeably referred to them), tourists also experienced western cities in a multisensory fashion, engaging in their sounds and smells as often as their sights.[13] Tourists encountered the built environment as part of the overall western urban fabric; they did not stand passively in front of individual buildings to contemplate their stately façades as the guidebooks and their illustrations seemed to recommend. The everyday activities inside and outside the buildings and the seemingly unsettled process of building construction captured tourists' attention as often as the completed designs did. There was always too much urban context in the way.

The ethnic, spiritual, and economic diversity of western cities did have an impact on tourists but not always in the positive, cosmopolitan ways conveyed in promotional materials and fostered by urban elites.[14] In Salt Lake City and San Francisco's Chinatown, promotional materials separated the Mormons and Chinese from the pulse of urban nineteenth-century American life, treating them as primitive or exotic attractions that represented deviance or a world free from the anxieties of the modern present.[15] This enabled the tourist literature to couch ethnic and spiritual diversity as cosmopolitan in a harmless and colorful fashion—no matter the actual circumstances of racial discrimination or attitudes of religious intolerance.

Yet tourist encounters with the Salt Lake City Mormons and the San Francisco Chinese, in particular, pushed the limits of such booster-inspired cosmopolitanism. Tourists typically maintained superior cultural and racial attitudes when they visited, but they also understood the instrumental contributions that Mormons and Chinese provided to the economic sustenance of the modern city. If a desire to escape the modern world for a utopian, preindustrial past inspired some tourist explorations, such utopias were difficult for tourists to maintain as they explored Salt Lake City or San Francisco's Chinatown—or anywhere else in the urban American West. Modernization and its effects offered poignant visitor experiences in late nineteenth-century western cities, even if they repelled as much as they attracted.

Modernization did not capture tourist attention uniformly over the twenty-four-year period from 1869 to 1893, however. From the completion of the transcontinental railroad in 1869 into the early 1880s, visitors more commonly reserved their most visceral reactions for the technological and engineering processes transforming western cities, many of which they encountered firsthand. In traveler accounts of the 1870s, for example, much attention focused upon waterworks systems, tunnels, bridges, telegraph lines, grain elevators, industrial processes, rail transportation, and houses being moved through western streets to accommodate urban growth and development. By the mid-1880s, tourists seemed to direct less attention to the power of engineering, industry, or transportation—their declining interest perhaps aided by a heightened awareness of the adverse effects of industrialization on health and a growing dissatisfaction with unfair labor practices and federal oversubsidization of the railroads.[16] One finds tourists commenting more often upon the physical changes that modernization contributed to western cities, some of which led to urban beautification in the form of hotels, parks, roads, views, and the aesthetics of a handful of new downtown buildings—including Chicago's skyscrapers. By the 1890s, and certainly by 1893 with the enormous output of tourist material produced in conjunction with the World's Columbian Exposition, one can point to a burgeoning tourist industry that emphasized beautification and high culture in western cities.[17]

Yet consistency among tourist accounts is difficult to discern, and many nonpastoral physical manifestations of the modernizing world continued to captivate visitors throughout the late nineteenth century—no matter the form. Tourists pointed to completed buildings in the early 1870s, for example, while occasionally marveling at the processes of modernization in the early 1890s. Factory tours remained popular in America, machinery exhibits dominated world's fairs and drew huge crowds, and the nighttime electrical illumination of the cityscape fascinated the traveling public well into the twentieth century.[18] The interior organization, height, and technological innovations of Chicago's skyscrapers, meanwhile, captivated tourists in the 1880s and early 1890s, just as the mechanical sorting operations of Chicago's massive grain elevators did in the 1870s. In that case, the building types had changed, but the curiosity with western efficiency, scale, and ingenuity had not.

As western cities continued to expand in population and density into the 1890s, elites and civic officials worked feverishly to arrange those cities as organized, rational places, and promotional literature increasingly ordered the urban environment into discrete sites to better direct tourist experiences. Tourists—whether because of heightened promotion, cheaper railroad rates, or a more organized tourist industry with a greater number of traveler services—grew in numbers as well. But identifying tourist patterns or encounters is difficult. To do so might make for a cohesive narrative, but it cannot easily be sustained. If there is a cohesive story to be told about tourist encounters in the late nineteenth-century urban American West, that story is one that highlights a *lack* of cohesion. It is a story that understands tourists as active and discerning agents and reads western cities as complex, diverse, and extraordinary—as well as ordinary—places immersed in a modernizing world. And to tell that story, this book is organized thematically rather than chronologically, with discussion of each of the four major late nineteenth-century western cities (Chicago, Denver, Salt Lake City, and San Francisco) sprinkled throughout. Examples from those cities are generally introduced in that order in each chapter, so as to mirror the visiting sequence as tourists headed West. But it is not to suggest that all tourists visited them in that sequence—or even that they visited all of those cities.

In fact, cities were not the principal draw in the nineteenth-century American West, a point acknowledged in chapter 1, "Attraction: Modernity and the Metropolis." Luring travelers westward, in general, was the much-publicized and highly romanticized natural landscape, punctuated with spectacular natural features, "savage" natives, and wild, open spaces. Yet cities became attractions for tourists upon arrival, filled as they were with the shocks and collisions of a modernizing late nineteenth-century world in a region so distant from tourists' points of origin. Modernization was not always an *attractive* prospect for tourists; to be sure, smoke, noise, and crowds offered little to be desired. But the processes of modernization rendered western cities as energetic, active, and diverse places, which travelers could not—and typically did not—ignore. Modern, urban encounters elevated cities' importance in the tourist imagination of the late nineteenth-century American West.

Still, tourist material tried to defuse modernity by shaping western cities as manicured extensions of the natural landscape. Chapter 2, "Promotion: Escape to the Picturesque," shows how tourist literature, illustrations, and photography sold western cities as "winter resorts" and "pleasure gardens," much as they did the natural environment.

Through both word and image, booster material abstracted everyday urban life, rendered any urban strife to a harmless past, and depicted cities and their constituent parts—especially their parks, drives, cemeteries, and view spots—as pastoral, romantic, and orderly. Even if tourists remained in the heart of western cities, guidebooks directed them to contemplate their urban surroundings in passive ways, thus encouraging them to escape the city.

Tourists did not always heed their advice. Chapter 3, "Confusion: Wonder, Turmoil, Awe, and Hell," delves into tourist accounts to reveal that western cities were far more—and far less—than late nineteenth-century pastoral retreats from the modern world. What they *were*, however, remained somewhat perplexing. While tourists occasionally marveled at the urban West and seemed perfect spokespeople for the celebratory, promotional descriptions in booster material, their accounts often discussed a series of other aspects that guidebooks avoided: from the messy, disorganized process of arrival to industrial processes that transformed the urban West into a less-than-appealing, sometimes appalling, environment. Tourists also filled their accounts with the everyday sounds and smells of the urban West, muddying the otherwise grandiose, visually oriented presentation in the tourist literature and demonstrating the multisensory nature of tourist experiences. Tourist accounts revealed Chicago, Denver, Salt Lake City, and San Francisco as complicated, complex places—spectacular in certain respects but at times repulsive and thoroughly unremarkable, much like modernizing cities elsewhere. Western cities were a number of things to tourists in the late nineteenth century, but easy to read they were not.

Urban elites, however, intended for visitors to read western cities as stately, civilized documents. In the nineteenth century, the degree to which cities exhibited a civilized existence relied, at least in part, upon the existence of cultural institutions and major public and private buildings whose designs drew from a long Western architectural tradition in style and materials—themes highlighted in chapter 4, "Civilization: Architectural Art, Pretense, and Process." Booster publications hoped tourists would regard the presence of such buildings as indicative of the West's refinement and civility, indicating the region's ability to maintain pace with Europe and the eastern American seaboard. Yet tourists only occasionally concerned themselves with matters of design; instead they turned their attention to the construction process and rarely ignored the everyday human activity inside or outside the buildings, thereby reading architecture as part of the western cultural landscape—not as style. If civilization existed in the tourists' understanding of the late nineteenth-century urban West, the culture of buildings, not their designs, made a larger impact.

But for boosters and urban elites, the spiritually and ethnically diverse peoples of the West had to be ordered in such a way as to ensure the cosmopolitanism of the urban environment: people needed to be understood as working together to achieve urban prosperity or—like the Chinese of San Francisco—they were left out of the discussion, cast aside as exotic "other." These issues highlight chapter 5, "Cosmopolitanism: Editing and Revising Culture." Tourist experiences, however, often rendered such organization moot; some western people were unique to tourists in their ethnic or spiritual makeup, but they resisted any rational ordering. Salt Lake City's Mormons and San Francisco's Chinese typically surprised wary visitors with their work ethic and dedication, but tourists interpreted them neither as part of a spiritual- or color-blind wave of urban progress nor solely as sideshow, exotic attractions set apart both geographically and imaginatively from the cosmopolitan city. Instead, tourists offered mixed impressions of western peoples and in so doing denied the elite cosmopolitan vision of the western city.

Such inconsistencies and equivocations make it difficult to summarize tourist encounters in the late nineteenth-century urban American West. I faced similar challenges when I loosely re-traced the transcontinental route in the summer of 2013 and attempted, unsuccessfully, to make sense of my own encounters—a trip I discuss in the epilogue. In their inexplicability, my experiences may have mirrored more closely those of late nineteenth-century tourists than I originally thought. Indeed, the range of accounts from the nineteenth-century past demonstrates a multiplicity of visions that revealed western cities as neither fully civilized nor entirely uncouth but a little of both—and much else between. Tourist impressions do, however, document the trials of urban expansion and capture the overall energy, complexity, and confusion of western cities even as promotional materials worked to temper urban growth by emphasizing monumentality, efficiency, and tranquility. Similar to the experience in the Masonic Temple for Mable Treseder and her companions, late nineteenth-century western cities offered little certainty or reassurance. Tourists ventured into an unknown.

CHAPTER 1

Attraction

Modernity and the Metropolis

In the early 1890s, when *New York Tribune* journalist Julian Ralph first considered writing a book about his western travels, he envisioned it as a "description of certain new States at the close of the nineteenth century." But the constant increase in population and the "rapid and bewildering changes" he had encountered during his travels compelled Ralph to reconsider his approach. It would be impossible for a book published in the early 1890s, he thought, to account for the American West at "the actual close of the century." So constant were the changes that he assumed his book already would have faded into the annals of history.[1]

In Ralph's estimation, no region of America better demonstrated the "energy" and "boldness" of the nation more than the West. Similar to many nineteenth-century narratives that included the region, Ralph's book, eventually published in 1893 as *Our Great West: A Study of the Present Conditions and Future Possibilities of the New Commonwealths and Capitals of the United States*, guided the reader over mountains, through valleys, and across plains—the vast, majestic, and heavily promoted western landscape that helped transform the region into a nineteenth-century visitor destination. Julian Ralph was one of thousands of travelers who ventured westward in the late nineteenth century and wrote or compiled a narrative about the journey from separate articles, letters, or diary entries.[2] Like them, he devoted much of his discussion to the natural environment.

But Ralph was careful not to depict the West as an uncultivated land roamed by cowboys, Indians, and wild game, an impression, he wrote, made "most famous in literature by Parkman, Irving, and Lewis and Clarke [sic]." Ralph boasted that his was the "first comprehensive book" to say little about these characteristics, which, by the late nineteenth century, he found either unimportant or inconsequential to the broader picture of western development. He declared that his would not be another myth regarding the open frontier and the "wild West."[3] Instead, he would concentrate upon the rise of the western metropolis and the "modern conveniences" of the cities, including electric lighting, elevators, and new modes of street transportation. This modern West included hotels, "fine" churches, "extraordinary" schools, "beautiful" theaters, and diverse and industrious residents.[4] For Ralph, modernity had transformed western cities into attractions.

The urban West also attracted French economist Paul de Rousiers during his 1890 visit. If one was to understand American character, Rousiers thought, the urban West offered the most accurate barometer. "There," he wrote in his 1892 book *American Life*, "can be seen very clearly the causes of its rapid developments still in action; there can be watched the elements at work which have combined to make America what she is; there, consequently, is to be found the key of the whole social system." To show American life "in its true light," Rousiers added, one must "describe this Far West where it is to be seen struggling with all the difficulties of savage nature, and also profiting by all the resources of a virgin soil."[5] Western cities appealed to Rousiers because they permitted direct encounters with the transformation of the "virgin soil" into the raw materials of American life. They provided a close-up look at a popular nineteenth-century understanding of the American character: one that favored speed, profit, and efficiency over refinement, tradition, and the past. This was reason enough for tourist investigation.

To be sure, some tourists were hired specifically to act as correspondents and report specifically on such matters. Ralph, for example, worked for *Harper's Magazine* when he toured the United States in 1891–92, while the French government sent Rousiers to report on American industrial and labor conditions. As professional writers and learned cultural critics writing for large audiences, they sought to identify particular characteristics that distinguished places from one another.[6] Yet the processes actively transforming a landscape embedded in myths of the open frontier captivated many travelers who came West in the late nineteenth century. Western cities found a central place in their narratives.

Modernity was not, however, always *attractive*. Ralph, for example, marveled at the collision of the human-made and the natural in environments far distant from the population centers of the eastern American seaboard and Europe. But he also noted the consequences of this collision: crowds, pollution, environmental destruction, and a maelstrom of ethnicities, cultural traditions, and spiritual beliefs seemingly tossed together in an unfamiliar setting. Rousiers, meanwhile, continually returned to the irony of major manufacturing operations creating urban pollution, noise, and inequality while providing the capital enabling ostentatious architecture, high-end commercial establishments, and elegant parks.[7] What modernity *was,* exactly, could not easily be explained by Ralph, Rousiers, or anybody else living through the dramatic transformations of the nineteenth century. But the "bewildering changes" merited more than passing reference in their narratives, and for many tourists, such changes characterized the late nineteenth-century urban American West. This chapter briefly highlights some of the modern developments that transformed the urban West while contending that they helped turn cities into tourist attractions—even if cities themselves rarely attracted tourists westward in the late nineteenth century.

MODERNIZATION AND THE WEST

Changes to the urban environment, bewildering though they may have been, were by no means unique to the American West. They were part of a larger modernization process that had transformed a number of European and American cities in the late eighteenth century and throughout the nineteenth century—changes that made cities into attractions and captivated visitors. The modernization of cities such as Paris, London, New York, and Philadelphia occurred earlier than those of the American West, as did that of Buffalo, Pittsburgh, Louisville, and Cincinnati—cities comprising an earlier, antebellum "West." Most nineteenth-century travelers, however, headed westward to explore the natural environment or to investigate life in the interior. Arriving in bustling western cities thus always seemed to constitute something of a surprise. Approaching the once far-western city of Cincinnati, Ohio, by steamboat at night in the 1830s, for example, writer Harriet Martineau was struck by the glare of the furnaces and the sparks from the factory chimneys.[8]

Industry was but one part of the modernization process. What the factories produced—the consumer goods that circulated on an unprecedented scale in the nineteenth century—also helped to usher in a new, modern world. There were also the *effects* of industry on cities and the human condition, including overcrowding (due largely to the movement of massive waves of people from the countryside into the city), repressive labor practices, and pollution. These processes and their effects—this modern world—set human subjects adrift; a world, according to Karl Marx and Friedrich Engels, that created "everlasting uncertainty and agitation."[9] The social consequences of modernization underscored an enduring myth: the idea that new technologies, opportunity, and urban growth had improved social conditions, broken down class barriers, and made the privileges of urban life accessible to all. The modern world, however, was not so liberating.[10]

Tourists, however, were neither likely to ponder the long-term consequences of modernization on the human condition that consumed the attention of some contemporary social critics nor to consider that their encounters did little to resolve deeper tensions that remained in western cities after they left. Tourists occasionally empathized with the plight of those who were shut out from the munificence of modernization but—perhaps because they benefitted from the modern technologies that brought them West—appeared more interested in reporting on urban conditions and generalizing about the character of western cities than pontificating on the social consequences of modernity. Although they were more than likely familiar with the growth and consequences of urbanization in European and American eastern seaboard cities, their reports nonetheless expressed intrigue with the density, production, and diversity of cities so far westward from their points of origin. The urban West thus began to emerge as distinctive in many travel narratives.

Tourists also read cities as characteristically western depending upon their distance from cities more familiar to them; the landscape in which the cities were set; the spaciousness of the urban environment; the spirit of individualism; the desire for profit; and the intensity of cultural diversity.[11] Tourists seemed unconcerned about whether specific meridian lines indicated a transition from East to West, from Middle West to West, or from the West to the "Far West"—geographical aspects that have been the subject of much scholarly debate.[12] They probably did not know that the American West was the most urbanized part of the United States, but based on their frequent writing about crowds and density, it may have seemed to them that western cities were busier than those elsewhere. In fact, by 1890, Chicago and San Francisco were two of the ten most populated cities in America, and the ratio of urban dwellers to rural dwellers in the West far outstripped that of the East (where rural areas were more densely settled).[13] Set as they were into a landscape mythologized for its overabundance of natural wonders, natives, and expansive space, western cities stood out.

The density of cities underscores the West's explosive urban growth. Chicago's growth was most explosive; its role as a processing center for the lumber, grain, and livestock from its hinterlands was known internationally and of considerable interest to late nineteenth-century visitors.[14] Cyrus McCormick opened a factory for the production of grain harvesters in Chicago in 1847, and the wheat harvesting process was quickly revolutionized on nearby prairie farms. In 1848, goods and foodstuffs began flowing along the Illinois and Michigan Canal, and the first of the Chicago-area railroads, the Galena and Chicago Union, made its inaugural run westward out of the city. Both transportation networks facilitated the shipment of agricultural products to Chicago and simultaneously to the rest of the world, linking Chicago and its hinterland, via the Great Lakes system, to America's eastern seaboard and to Europe.[15] The introduction of massive steam-powered grain elevators along the banks of the Chicago River by the late 1840s and 1850s provided a convenient method for dealers to weigh and sort grain for pricing and distribution. Boats transporting lumber cut from the forests of Michigan, Wisconsin, and Minnesota plied the Chicago River as they made their way to the city's lumberyards. The machine shops of Pullman, just south of the city, produced the nation's largest stock of luxury rail cars—those soon to carry many tourists westward on their transcontinental journeys. By the 1860s, several factories, including the enormous meat-processing plants that comprised Chicago's vast Union Stock Yards, poured smoke into the sky and filth and pollution into the south branch of the Chicago River. But for first-time visitors in the 1870s, 1880s, and 1890s, Chicago's rampant commercial speculation, speed, noise, and industrial prowess still seemed sudden, new, and fascinating. Certainly it did to Paul Rousiers: "Chicago, to which we must always return . . . sums up all the characteristics of a great Western city."[16]

Not everyone returned to Chicago. For many tourists, visiting once was enough. But Chicago never failed to elicit a reaction, as it laid bare modernity (or, at the very least, industrial growth) in the most explicit of ways. No city in the late nineteenth-century American West came close to the pace of development in Chicago, but modernity was apparent in other western cities following their earlier periods of settlement. Salt Lake City initially attracted Mormon emigrants as a safe haven to practice their beliefs following years of persecution elsewhere in the country. Once the earliest settlers overcame a cricket infestation that devastated ripening crops in 1848, steady numbers of people began arriving in the Salt Lake Valley. Denver and San Francisco urbanized in the 1850s and 1860s, respectively, as gateways, ports, and distribution centers for gold-mining operations.

These developments set the stage for substantial modernization programs that transformed western cities from upstart towns into major

industrial metropolises in the 1870s and 1880s. Mechanized transportation, automated factories, and the production and circulation of consumer goods lured thousands of migrants from rural or impoverished parts of the country and world with the promise of economic opportunities, social mobility, religious freedom, and a higher quality of life. Opportunity and entertainment attracted those who imagined cities as more promising and exciting than where they were, and scores of new settlers quickly urbanized the West. The urbanization process also transformed western cities into places of potential tourist intrigue.

Until railroad lines extended westward, however, only the most hardy tourists would dare venture an overland journey. While railroads reached Chicago from the East as early as 1852 via the Michigan Central and Michigan Southern, it was not until the completion of the Central Pacific and Union Pacific railroads in 1869 that tourists came within convenient reach of other western cities. By 1870, tourists could make the nine-hundred-mile trip from New York to Chicago on the New York Central in just two days.[17] From Chicago, the greater West beckoned. Once the Denver Pacific and Kansas Pacific railroads completed branch lines to Denver in 1870 and, that same year, when the Utah Central railroad extended a line from the transcontinental depot in Ogden to Salt Lake City (replacing what William Robertson and W. F. Robertson described as a "horrible" stage ride when they visited in 1869), tourists began to appear in those cities with some frequency.[18] At the far western edge of the North American continent, ferry and steamer lines departing from Sacramento and, by 1876, from Oakland carried Central Pacific travelers conveniently to San Francisco. In 1874, New Yorker John Codman estimated that the entire

BIRD'S-EYE VIEW OF THE TRANSCONTINENTAL ROUTE. This forced perspective bird's-eye of the transcontinental route suggests that the nineteenth-century American West began in Chicago (lower right) and that cities would loom as large in the traveler imagination as the wonders of nature. Modernizing Chicago, Denver, Salt Lake City, and San Francisco are each depicted here with accompanying skylines, nestled within, or near, the landscapes of dramatic beauty traversed by the railroads. (Source: Charles Nordhoff, *California: For Health, Pleasure, and Residence,* p. 60. Courtesy of http://cprr.org/Museum/Books/Calif_Nordhoff_1872.html.)

cross-country journey from New York to San Francisco, if all connections were made, would take exactly six days, twenty-two hours, and thirty-five minutes—at a cost of $139.50.[19]

Modernization alone did not draw tourists to western cities, but it facilitated visitor access and offered some interesting prospects for firsthand encounters, including the assembly-line operations at Chicago's Union Stock Yards, Denver's breweries and smelters, the busy transactions at Salt Lake City's Zion's Co-operative Mercantile Institution (ZCMI), and active San Francisco docks with ships filled with opportunistic Chinese from distant Asian ports. Liverpool-based visitor W. G. Marshall apparently spent just one day sightseeing in Chicago during his late 1870s visit to America yet made sure to visit the waterworks, the stockyards, and two "immense grain elevators," while peppering his seventeen-page account of "wonderful Chicago" with mind-numbing statistics about the city's industrial productivity.[20] Tourists also could encounter those people for which particular western cities had achieved attention on a national and international level; most notably, Salt Lake City's Mormons and San Francisco's Chinese. For many visitors, the opportunity to encounter supposedly immoral cultural practices and unorthodox spiritual beliefs on American land provided an urban attraction; to discover this cultural and spiritual diversity juxtaposed with industries and commerce in landscapes so distant from places of tourist origin heightened their interest. A bourgeoning tourist industry of sorts appeared in nineteenth-century western cities in response to modern urban development, as well. In Chicago, personal guides were available to direct tourists through the stockyards to highlight the supposed efficiency of animal slaughter (and, presumably, to suggest the city's overall efficiency and modernity). In Salt Lake City and San Francisco, non-Mormon and non-Chinese guides, respectively, were prepared to escort visitors through the alleged mysteries or labyrinths of the Mormon and Chinese built environment.[21]

Yet urban boosters and other elites desired to counteract western exceptionalism. They wished instead to bring western cities up to par with the older cities of Europe and the eastern American seaboard in order to promote the urban West to potential settlers—including tourists—as settings of dignity and high culture. In this respect, western cities stood at a significant disadvantage. Relative to settlements in Europe in particular, those in the West appeared "instantly" in the mid-nineteenth century and had not attained levels of refinement characteristic of more established urban environments.[22] Older European cities, such as London, Paris, Venice, Florence, Rome, and Athens, had long featured aspects that lured tourists, whether legacies of royalty, revolution, religion, democracy, or power—best exemplified in art and architecture whose designs or styles suggested epochal shifts or the supposed beginnings of Western civilization. These cities had captured traveler attention for pilgrimage or study at least since the eighteenth century, although tourist visitations had been limited primarily to British gentry traveling overland during the Grand Tour of Italy and France. Yet they remained the standard bearers for all things refined and cultured to the traveling public, and by the mid-nineteenth century, tourists—many of whom participated in Thomas Cook excursions—had become commonplace in Europe.[23]

American cities, comparatively newer and with fewer historical attractions capturing traveler interest, struggled to measure up. In 1799, French traveler F. A. F. de La Rochefoucauld-Liancourt declared that American cities were "exactly those on which the traveller has least to remark."[24] Yet throughout the nineteenth century, the cities of New York, Philadelphia, Boston, Washington, D.C., Baltimore, Pittsburgh, Cincinnati, St. Louis, New Orleans, and Charleston welcomed a steady stream of visitors, as tourists came both to investigate the origins of the American republic and to witness its incipient growth. Cities of the American West, meanwhile, could not lay claim to the longer European-American settlement history of cities in the East, Midwest, and South. But cities of the eastern seaboard and Europe had experienced periods of significant expansion and upheaval at an earlier time, and they plodded along in relative comparison to the rapidly expanding late nineteenth-century cities of the American West. Western cities held their own in activity and ethnic diversity, and by the late nineteenth century, they had become places about which travelers had *plenty* to remark. For French journalist and author Léon Paul Blouet, who traveled around the United States in the 1880s under the pen name of Max O'Rell, the "busy western cities" made Philadelphia— the nation's second-largest city for most of the nineteenth century— appear "slow, even monotonous."[25]

In the minds of boosters, however, expansion and upheaval did not always paint western cities in the most venerable light; modernization did not, in itself, transform cities into uplifting attractions. Indeed, the emerging metropolis may have instilled what German social theorist Georg Simmel termed the "blasé outlook." Ruminating about the metropolis in his 1903 essay, "The Metropolis and Mental Life," Simmel contended that the intensification of stimuli, brought about by an increased circulation of commodities and an obsession with punctuality and quantification in the city, generated emotional detachment—and thus alienation. To retain a sense of self, Simmel argued that modern urban individuals were compelled to turn inward and develop a "blasé" attitude to combat the impersonality of the metropolis.[26] Although Simmel did not discuss tourism and his essay focused upon no city in particular, one presumes that the rational, calculating modern city he describes would be hard-pressed to attract tourists.

Boosters favored modernization to the extent that it highlighted urban efficiency and commercial success and allowed for western cities to develop cultural institutions and places of sophistication and repose: banks, hotels, religious edifices, parks, landscaped cemeteries, well-paved roads, and zoological gardens. From a booster perspective, modernization meant progress and therefore brought western cities closer to the urban model of Europe and the American East. No matter how far-fetched their assessments, boosters compared Chicago to New York or Paris; Denver to Chicago; and San Francisco to Paris. They pitted San Francisco's Market Street, a major avenue marching diagonally from the visitors' point of arrival at the Ferry Building, against Paris's Champs Elysées and Boulevard des Italiens. Active commerce spurred them to judge Chicago's State Street, Denver's Larimer Street, and San Francisco's Market and Montgomery Streets against New York's Broadway and London's Regent Street.[27] Even single business establishments drew these sorts of comparisons. An advertisement for the Col. A. Andrews "Diamond Palace" in the 1882 *Guide Book and Street Manual of San Francisco, California* proclaimed that visiting "San Francisco without seeing the Diamond Palace would be like visiting Europe without seeing Paris."[28] Who knew?

So commonplace were such proclamations that by 1898, the publication *Denver: By Pen and Picture* prominently featured, without any equivocation, a statement from Western Union Telegraph Company's president William Orton announcing that the "four great cities of this continent are to be New York, Chicago, Denver, and San Francisco."[29] Although the likelihood that Western Union served to benefit from further settlement or investment in western cities is apparent, the inclusion of Orton's remark in the prefatory material to an illustrated book about Denver indicates that boosters hoped this upstart western city—if not also Chicago and San Francisco—would rank among the most sophisticated places on earth. Whether such books had any success elevating western cities to such standards is impossible to judge. As it was, tourists found it difficult to make one-to-one connections to eastern and European cities, aside from identifying buildings whose façades and plans recalled established architectural styles.

WILD MYTHS

Making western-bound tourists aware—or interested in—cities at all provided a challenge in itself. The majority of visitors came from urban areas and headed West to experience its natural landscape and the people and activities commonly associated with it. Tourists were principally inspired by a widespread popular perception that set the region in an earlier time when settlement amounted to isolated skirmishes on an unsettled frontier and when spectacular mountains, deserts, canyons, forests, lakes, rivers, and wild animals offered the dominant impression. Cities found little place in this picture; where they did, urban boosters worked to transform them into extensions of the natural landscape. Tourist encounters with the unchecked energy and activity of western cities threatened the otherwise genteel picture booster publications wished to convey—no matter how carefully boosters attempted to shape modernization as progress.

Tourists' attraction to, or with, western cities—at any level—competed with a pervasive myth that shaped the West, its cities, its landscape, and its people as wild, untamed, and uncivilized. On the one hand, popular literature and imagery portrayed the West as a lawless place characterized by rowdy miners and roaming bands of "savage" Native Americans. This legend persisted throughout the nineteenth century and into the twentieth century, although by the 1890s most western towns had moved well beyond their supposedly unsettled frontier days and nearly all Native Americans had been either decimated or removed to government-allotted reservations. A somewhat more romantic characterization comprised another myth, linking western people with the natural environment. From that viewpoint, the dramatic western landscape was punctuated by lofty, snow-capped mountains, wide-open spaces, and vast, haunting deserts that marked a truly Wild West. Living beings found a home in this view only in the most colorful of fashions, with Native Americans portrayed as brave warriors and noble savages, and wild animals, such as bison, rendered in harmony with the majestic landscape—even if most of the bison also had been exterminated by the 1890s. Neither picture accurately characterized the conditions of the frontier nor highlighted the western urban environment.

A variety of media fueled the spread of the uncivilized, rowdy portrayal of the Wild West and lessened the likelihood that potential travelers would find much to capture their attention in large, nineteenth-century western cities. Artists such as Frederic Remington and Charles Russell depicted troubling western conditions and, among other subjects, battles between European Americans and Native Americans; dime novels and engravings regularly featured in magazines such as *Harper's Weekly, Frank Leslie's Illustrated Newspaper*, and, following 1887, *Scribner's Magazine* brought this characterization to a broad public. Traveling entertainer William "Buffalo Bill" Cody also instilled into the popular consciousness an assumption that urbanization in the West amounted to small, hastily built towns where shootouts marked the order of the day. Cody blurred the lines between myth and reality by hiring real cowboys and Native Americans to perform reenactments of physical confrontations once experienced on the landscape, and many tourists headed West expecting versions of the events acted out on Cody's stage. These stories reached beyond the American West. Cody's show played to packed houses in England in 1886 and then in western Europe between 1889 and 1892, and Karl May's books on the western backwoods hero "Old Shatterhand" became bestsellers in Germany.[30]

Popular literature and imagery shaped the American West—natural or urban—so often as a lawless place that it threatened to inhibit settlement and visitation, and booster literature worked to counteract this impression. Charles Nordhoff's promotional 1873 account, *California: For Health, Pleasure, and Residence,* noted the widespread reach of this view: "California," he wrote, "is to most Eastern people still a land of big beets and pumpkins, of rough miners, of pistols, bowie-knives, abundant fruit, queer wines, high prices—full of discomforts, and abounding in dangers to the peaceful traveler." Nordhoff instead attempted to assuage travelers' fears. In San Francisco, he stressed the city's fine dining, excellent hotels, "honest" and "intelligent" people, and "unequaled" pleasure roads.[31] The perception of danger proved difficult to shake, however, and many tourists carried it westward. British adventurer Isabella Lucy Bird encountered nothing especially unusual while visiting Denver during her six months traveling through the Colorado Rockies on horseback in 1873, but a popular image of Denver as a wild, uncouth city prevailed. This portrayal was prominent enough, anyway, that Bird deemed it necessary to explain that shooting affrays in the Denver streets no longer occurred, and "one no longer sees men dangling to the lampposts when one looks out in the morning."[32] More than ten years later, the unruly West still lingered in the tourist imagination. During an 1880s visit to Chicago, British traveler Emily Pfeiffer imagined "dangerous"-looking men in the Chicago streets, with "a bowie knife not far off, and of wild experiences in the background." She considered Chicagoans "the true heirs of the Indians who existed on the same ground but yesterday in a state of perpetual warfare."[33]

An equally prominent characterization depicted the West as an open, awe-inspiring natural landscape, with Native Americans and wild animals roaming freely, albeit inconsequentially, within it. Contemporary artists contributed significantly to this picture, and cities were virtually nonexistent. The landscape paintings of Thomas Moran and Albert Bierstadt, depicting the grandeur and sublimity of the western natural environment, received heavy exposure at home and abroad. Their work appeared frequently in newspapers and magazines, bringing the western natural environment into thousands of living rooms. Guidebooks facilitated the dissemination of the wild, natural West: Thomas Cook and Son's 1884 *Cook's California Excursions* promised California-bound tourists with glimpses of "the odd villages of prairie-dogs that stick up their heads like porpoises along a steamer's track" and sometimes "glimpses of herds of buffalo still lingering on their favorite pastures."[34] Earlier in the nineteenth century, novelists and artists such as Washington Irving, James Fenimore Cooper, and George Catlin romanticized the American West with their presentation of Native Americans as still-extant reminders of a proud, yet slowly expiring, people. Their books and paintings remained popular during the late nineteenth century, even as U.S. federal policy mandated Natives' systematic elimination from the landscape.[35]

Historian Frederick Jackson Turner's much-debated "Frontier Thesis," formulated in 1893, also celebrated the power of the natural landscape. For Turner, the openness and ruggedness of the West, not its cities, laid the foundation for the "dominant individualism" of the American character. The urbanization of the West signaled Turner's final frontier, but it merited only a passing reference in his essay—and cities of the Middle West, not the Far West, received that momentary attention. For the most part, however, the spaces between and beyond cities marked Turner's West: previously unsettled and untamed wilderness that, through gradual settlement, transformed "Old World" Europeans into "New World" Americans.[36] The collective total of such characterizations makes it possible that western-bound tourists expected to discover Native American warriors on horseback, galloping along in tribal regalia, with wild scenery providing a stunning backdrop.

Yet to encounter Natives in their tribal settings or to visit the most spectacular of natural wonders, late nineteenth-century western-bound tourists, traveling by railroad, were required to head well off the beaten track. Cities, conversely, existed along or near the principal routes of travel, and tourists were bound to discover them. The convenience, provisions, and familiarity of a city often came as a welcome respite to tourists after the inconveniences of long-distance railroad travel. Such inconveniences included tight living conditions with strangers, tipping for services, and shared bathrooms—even for the wealthy traveling in well-equipped Pullman extra-fare cars, which doubled as sleepers. Western cities thus became de facto destinations for transcontinental trips, as the long and often uncomfortable railroad journey left few tourists eager to board another train or enter a carriage heading deep into the wilderness.[37] Cities provided their own appeal, as well.

The grandeur of Yosemite drew English visitor Charles Beadle to California in 1887, as it did countless others in the late nineteenth century. But the majority of nineteenth-century travelers intending to visit Yosemite arrived first in San Francisco. Traveling to Yosemite, 150 miles from San Francisco, involved an arduous overnight trip via train and horseback with no guarantee of luxurious accommodations upon arrival. In the 1870s, round trips to Yosemite from San Francisco typically required an additional ten days, and some tourists had neither the time nor the patience for such an excursion.[38] Beadle, however, intended to make the trek, but not without first exploring San Francisco. "On reaching San Francisco we went to the banker's to get some money, and to the agents to make arrangements for visiting the Yosemite Valley," he recalled. Yet the city beckoned. "We took a steam rope-tram to the end of a long street running on to high ground, and then walked to a hill overlooking the town, harbour, and ocean, so that we might see where we were and find our way about."[39]

Access to other highly promoted western destinations also proved cumbersome, resulting in still-longer urban stays for tourists. The Geysers in Sonoma County, California, necessitated a lengthy day trip from San Francisco over difficult roads, typically requiring overnight accommodations. The Hotel del Monte in Monterey, California, which attracted thousands of nineteenth-century visitors, fronted Monterey Bay some ninety miles south of San Francisco.[40] The right-of-way for the Central Pacific and Union Pacific railroads remained considerably distant from the most extraordinary of western natural wonders and nowhere near the heavily promoted resort accommodations in the immediate vicinity of various western hot springs. The geological oddities of Yellowstone, meanwhile, remained out of public reach until the completion of the Park Branch Line of the Northern Pacific Railroad in 1883 between Livingston and Cinnabar, Montana; while the Grand Canyon remained virtually inaccessible to tourists until the Atchison, Topeka, and Santa Fe Railroad completed a line running north from Flagstaff, Arizona, in 1901.[41]

ENCOUNTERING CITIES

Had tourists wished to avoid western cities altogether, an encounter with urban manufacturing, factories, engineering, and modern technology was still, to a large extent, unavoidable. Upon arrival in major western cities, the train depots, wharves, and warehouses alone provided quick doses of modernization to every arriving traveler. As it was, the transcontinental railroad started or stopped directly in a number of smallish cities en route, including Omaha, Cheyenne, Ogden, Reno, Sacramento, and Oakland, and connections to the major cities of Denver, Salt Lake City, and San Francisco via branch lines or ferries did not consume large expenditures of time. At some of these urban layovers, tourists either had to step off the train to transfer to another line or willingly choose to alight in order to secure meals before another lengthy stretch of track.

In Chicago, tourists intending to make their way across the continent had little choice but to encounter the city streets, for trains heading either toward Council Bluffs, Iowa, and Omaha, Nebraska (and the Union Pacific line), or to New York and points east departed from different locations in the downtown Loop. Tourists passing through Chicago had to find means of ground transportation to get from one

"JUST ARRIVED IN CHICAGO." A tourist leans out of a moving carriage and looks up to gauge the height of Chicago's skyscrapers in this drawing that appeared on the front page of the *Chicago Tribune* on July 12, 1892. Tourists found exhilarating the density, scale, and energy of Chicago's downtown Loop—and its fame was international. The *Tribune* caption read: "Just Arrived in Chicago—Trying to See the Tops of Buildings." (Reproduced from Arnold Lewis, *An Early Encounter with Tomorrow*, p. 145.)

station to the other, compelling them to traverse the heart of the city. Even those travelers who came to attend the 1893 world's exposition inevitably came into contact with the vibrancy and din of downtown. The exposure that travelers would have with Chicago as a whole worried journalist and pastor Washington Gladden, who in 1892 implored city officials to ensure the safety of the hundreds of thousands of visitors set to attend the fair. "Chicago is burning to show us her tall buildings and big parks," he wrote in an open letter to *Century Magazine*. "It is a thousand times more important that she show us a city well governed."[42] A *thousand* times? Given the international fame of Chicago's tall buildings alone, one assumes that encountering the city's "tall buildings" and "big parks" were at least of equal importance to visitors—if not more—as their safety.

In fact, tens of thousands of tourists willingly ventured into western cities in the late nineteenth century, not just because the railroad journey made it unavoidable or convenient. Many rail tourists transferred to the Denver Pacific Railroad at Cheyenne, Wyoming, to reach Denver, a city that attracted visitors because of its proximity to the resort hotels and springs in the nearby Rocky Mountains—but that nearly always captured tourists' attention once they arrived. According to Colorado booster Ernest Ingersoll, by the 1880s five hundred people per day entered the state of Colorado, and nine-tenths of them stopped in Denver.[43] Countless numbers of rail travelers also descended into Salt Lake City, desiring insight into Mormons and Mormonism. San Francisco's nineteenth-century tourist popularity is underscored by an 1883 guidebook, accompanying a personally conducted tour of Colorado and California, noting the array of attractions in the "wonderful" city. The guidebook highlighted San Francisco's "palatial residences," the "swarming inhabitants of the Chinese Quarter," and the "beautifully situated" Cliff House and thought it "wise to allow each member of the party to be a free agent during his stay in San Francisco."[44]

Was it so wise? If promotional materials could not effectively cloak the effects of modernization as progress or frame them in a way that brought supposedly earlier modes of existence to the fore, they usually ignored them altogether—perhaps because of their deleterious ramifications on the aesthetic and cultural environment. In western cities, tourists often remarked on the alterations to the physical and cultural landscape brought about by the modernization process, but they did not offer unilaterally positive impressions. Many accounts were ambivalent, and some were downright negative. Walt Whitman visited Denver in 1879, marveling at the city's "fine" and "well-laid out" streets, remarking on its "tall storehouses of stone or iron, and windows of plate-glass," while observing "plenty of people," "business," and "modernness." Yet he explained that the city featured "a certain racy wild smack, all its own." Denver's transformation seemed not to excite Whitman so much as to puzzle him.[45] San Francisco left tourists with equally as many contrasting, and sometimes conflicting, impressions. In the late nineteenth century, Robert Louis Stevenson, with the ruthless "justice" administered by the Vigilance Committee in the 1850s still on his mind, described San Francisco as a "city of contrasts," characterized by "extremes of wealth and poverty, apathy and excitement, the conveniences of civilization and the red justice of Judge Lynch."[46]

Modernization was everywhere apparent in the late nineteenth-century city, and its consequences could be as devastating as they were liberating: unprecedented pollution, racial discrimination, and isolating anonymity followed in the wake of massive urban change. Despite a smattering of economic success stories, most newly arrived settlers and immigrants struggled to make ends meet in the industrializing metropolis. Some discovered new opportunities, but those who moved from the country to the city usually found themselves in difficult conditions and subjected to extreme forms of dislocation.[47] Bulging late nineteenth-century cities also faced problems of inadequate or deteriorating infrastructure and the threat and occasional reality of waterborne diseases such as cholera, dysentery, and typhoid fever. Most new immigrants suffered from poverty and lived in substandard housing in the expanding and overcrowded slums—if they found housing at all. Difficult and lengthy working conditions, the mechanization of factory work, nativism, and the frequent suppression of unions led to further unrest. Two of the most dramatic examples of turmoil in late nineteenth-century America occurred in the urban West: Chicago's 1886 Haymarket Affair, whose violent circumstances and aftermath punctuated a gaping chasm between labor and capital that plagued industrializing America; and the rise of the Workingman's Party in San Francisco, whose objection to Chinese workers stealing jobs they believed rightfully belonged to European Americans led to the federally ratified Chinese Exclusion Act of 1882. Unchecked urban growth also spurred quick and routinely shoddy construction, and fires spread regularly over the late nineteenth-century western cityscape.

Most tourists spent little time considering the social ramifications of such developments, but they did react viscerally to the happenings around them, allowing events to stand for themselves and refraining from elaborate analyses. Although Emily Pfeiffer's impressions did not represent the majority, she had little positive to say about western cities during her 1880s visit. Even the city of San Francisco, so widely advertised as a picturesque hamlet gracing a series of hills overlooking a sparkling bay and the mighty Pacific Ocean, did not appeal to her. "None which I have yet seen of the much-vaunted cities of the Far West has, in my eyes, justified its claim to beauty—nor is San Francisco an exception," she wrote. "Each of them has an interest of its own for the traveller, if even it should in some cases be one of repulsion."[48]

A substantial body of nineteenth-century literature that characterized modernizing cities as repulsive, disorienting, and hazardous may have contributed to negative tourist interpretations of the urban West. Most travelers read as voraciously as they wrote, likely aware of an antiurban sentiment that proliferated among poets, novelists, journalists, scientists, reformers, and religious leaders of the day. Reform-minded tracts exposing the horrific living conditions for the poor and destitute in specific areas of industrializing cities reached a large reading public, including Andrew Mearns's 1883 work, *The Bitter Cry of Outcast London*, focusing upon conditions in London's East End, and Jacob Riis's 1890 publication, *How the Other Half Lives*, depicting life in New York's tenements. A wide body of fiction and poetry also played a role in shaping Victorian-era cities as seething metropolises and hotbeds of contagion where an impersonal capitalist machine stripped away human individuality and subjectivity. A number of mid- to late nineteenth-century literary figures including Charles Dickens, Edgar Allen Poe, Herman Melville, Theodore Dreiser, Joaquin Miller, Henry James, William Dean Howells, and to a lesser extent and slightly earlier, James Fenimore Cooper, Ralph Waldo Emerson, and Nathaniel Hawthorne contributed to this sensibility.[49] Many tourists could have—and likely did—read works by these authors prior to their western journeys. But rarely would such views color the entirety of visitor impressions, for tourists infrequently restricted themselves to just one area of western cities and did not assume that conditions in Victorian London were identical to, say, those in San Francisco. Furthermore, this impression of Victorian cities—principally those of Europe and the American eastern seaboard—did little to dissuade tourists from exploring the urban West. It may instead have helped lure them.

What tourists discovered in western cities was often less sensational than the specters of doom conveyed in such literature—and more pro- saic and less orderly than that for which urban boosters hoped. Instead of connecting Chicago's streets to the refined settings of Parisian bou- levards, in the mid-1870s British visitor Harry Jones made parallels to the more haphazard commercial activity of London's Pall Mall and Cheapside. For Ohio-based tourist Emma Adams in 1888, San Fran- cisco's growth and expansion reminded her not of European cities or those of the American eastern seaboard but of Chicago.[50]

This did not mean that western cities lacked careful planning and foresight—their wide and lengthy streets, awaiting future development, attested to the optimism of land speculators and planners.[51] Yet such perpetual speculation and hubris, to many visitors, suggested potential failure and hinted at monotony as often as they indicated the stabil- ity and grandeur for which their boosters hoped. In Chicago, urban expansion could extend indefinitely south, north, west or up; perhaps only Lake Michigan prevented the city from expanding eastward. It was only a slight exaggeration when Friedrich Wilhelm Heinrich Zehme, writing of Chicago's relentless spread, explained in his 1882 diary that one "can travel for five hours without being able to cross the city."[52] In the early 1870s, British traveler Rose Kingsley passed through Denver on her way to Colorado Springs and, noting Denver's sudden appear- ance on the land, remarked that it "looks as if it had been dropped out of the clouds accidentally, by some one who meant to carry it further on, but got tired, and let it fall anywhere." Denver's promise of future growth seemed even more evident. Kingsley visited a sandy hill that claimed to be the "public park of Denver" but declared that it "must be seen, like many other things in the West, by the eye of faith; as at present the road is a rough, sandy track."[53]

The very roughness was telling; tourists' firsthand encounters with western cities revealed active, expanding places that muddied the West's popular reputation for natural scenery and shocked travelers who expected western cities to be little more than stopovers on the way to more spectacular environments. That which revealed the modern- ization of Chicago, Denver, Salt Lake City, and San Francisco—from skyscrapers, electricity, and factories to the polyglot of cultures and belief systems—drew tourists' attention and, set as they were within largely unfamiliar yet stunning landscapes, helped mark those cities as characteristically western. Modernity did not always meet with widespread tourist comprehension or approval, but it made the urban West no less of an attraction.

CHAPTER 2

Promotion

Escape to the Picturesque

Sue A. Pike Sanders glanced from the window as her train approached the city of Denver on the morning of July 27, 1886. Like many travelers, Sanders had learned of the city as a "fountain of youth," where an ideal climate promised to restore the afflicted back to health. Much to her dismay, a large cemetery came into view. Was this really Denver? To uphold the city's reputation as a weather-perfect sanitarium, she thought the railroad might change its right-of-way or, alternatively, the city might consider relocating the cemetery altogether. After all, she recalled, "we have almost learned to think that people never die in Denver."[1] Sanders wrote in a tongue-in-cheek manner, of course. But her impressions speak to a popular late nineteenth-century notion of western cities as places where temperate climates and spectacular natural settings trumped the everyday life of the metropolis.

The promise of pleasant weather and improved health might have drawn tourists westward, but urban boosters assumed that such characteristics alone would neither sustain visitor interest nor encourage permanent settlement or investment.[2] In keeping with a general theme of health and the outdoors, guidebooks, pamphlets, brochures, magazine articles, illustrations, and some travel narratives shaped western cities as resort destinations. They turned to characteristics and leisure activities more closely associated with the pleasures of the natural environment: parks, drives, view spots, and excursions to the city's nineteenth-century edges, including carriage drives along Chicago's Lake Shore Drive; the Rocky Mountains seen from Denver's City Park; the view of Salt Lake City from Ensign Peak; and Seal Rocks and the Pacific Ocean from the perspective of San Francisco's Cliff House. In this way, promotional materials indirectly encouraged tourists to escape the city altogether.

This was strategic. Urban boosters—who typically comprised the city elites (editors, publishers, local chambers of commerce, land speculators, and commercial clubs, but also journalists)—considered the everyday, modern nineteenth-century world of industry, commerce, and technological advancement a necessary evil, indispensable for urban economic health. But they did not consider such a world suitable for visitors unless it could be designed in such a way to appear orderly, prosperous, and progressive. In the late nineteenth-century American West, the urban environment had to blend seamlessly into a natural one; cities had to cohere with a pervasive image of the West as a natural playground. Literature and imagery promoting the West constructed cities as picturesque, highlighting their natural attributes, sorting their built environment into discrete sites, emphasizing institutions of high culture, and minimizing street life. They intended for tourists to perceive western cities as cultivated places comparable to those in Europe or the East Coast, and they hoped visitors would thus read westerners as sophisticated people.

This chapter suggests that promotional material rendered western cities as picturesque environments. The picturesque is not necessarily meant in a landscape design sense (where circuitous, rustic pathways marked principal thoroughfares); instead, tourist literature cast western cities, their parts, and their histories as places to be viewed, contemplated, or appreciated from a safe distance—literally and figuratively. By focusing on natural attributes and encouraging tourists to escape the city, promotional materials depicted the urban West in its best light while essentially denying its very modernity.

SELLING THE NATURAL ENVIRONMENT

The rapidly developing western cities of Chicago, Denver, Salt Lake City, and San Francisco existed within, or near, dramatic natural landscapes, giving artists and writers ample opportunity to make connections between culture and nature for the potential traveler. In promotional materials, descriptions and imagery set human achievements in stone and steel in concert with the natural environment, making the modern West appear more familiar and less threatening. Guidebooks promised western-bound tourists excellent weather, plentiful springs, and the elimination of sicknesses more common to residents of colder climates and dense urban environments—without the use of risky medical procedures frequently advertised in the press.

Widely circulated guidebooks and handbooks such as Charles Nordhoff's 1873 *California: For Health, Pleasure, and Residence*, Benjamin C. Truman's 1874 *Semi-Tropical California: Its Climate, Healthfulness, Productiveness, and Scenery*, and Samuel Solly's 1875 *Manitou, Colorado, U.S.A.; Its Mineral Waters and Climate* gave potential tourists and settlers a healthy dose of the benefits awaiting them in the American West. Along with reports on climate, such publications advertised the grand resort hotels built within splendid landscapes and around natural springs, such as the Antlers Hotel in Colorado Springs, Colorado, and the Hotel del Monte in Monterey, California, promising their restorative powers for weakened dispositions.[3] Their campaigns were effective: they pulled tourists away from the main line of the transcontinental railroad, and the exquisite resort hotels never lacked for patients or visitors.

Promotional materials encouraged travelers to perceive the entire West, including its cities, as a health resort par excellence. This included Chicago, whose volatile and often miserable weather could be made to seem advantageous if promotional tracts used statistics to their advantage. A. N. Marquis and Company's *Ready Reference Guide to Chicago and the World's Columbian Exposition* advised European visitors, in particular, to "note that the mean average of temperature is much lower than that of the same latitude in Europe." The guidebook claimed that Chicago's climate "is healthful and invigorating" because "prevailing winds" help "keep the city remarkably free from malarial diseases."[4] The presentation of Denver's climate as ideal, meanwhile, presumably led Sue Sanders to believe its residents might live forever.

Yet a pleasant climate, plentiful mineral springs, and resort hotels were not that which set the West apart. Tourist literature instead seized upon the natural landscape, which writers and artists shaped as awesome, spectacular, and occasionally terrifying—aspects of the philosophical sublime established by philosophers Immanuel Kant and Edmund Burke in the late eighteenth century and early nineteenth centuries, and characteristics that could arouse spiritual feelings upon encounter. By the mid-nineteenth century, the notion of the sublime had entered popular discourse; certainly it had when Henry T. Williams declared that the "grandest of American scenery" awaited western-bound travelers in the opening line of his massive *The Pacific Tourist*, which began publication in 1876 and sold more than one hundred thousand copies in its first year. With the completion of the transcontinental railroad, Williams claimed that the "glorious views of mountain grandeur" at Yellowstone and Yosemite now presented themselves conveniently to the visitor, and the "sublimities" of the Rocky Mountains, the Sierra Nevadas, and the "canons" of Utah had become accessible.[5]

The Pacific Tourist was among the more popular of such guidebooks, but an enormous array of printed matter sold the nineteenth-century American West as a sublime landscape punctuated by natural wonders. Few guidebooks failed to advertise the grandeur of Yosemite and, following the completion of the Northern Pacific Railway, Yellowstone as the most remarkable examples of western natural landscapes, and some of them, such as E. M. Jenkins's 1883 *An Excursion to Colorado, California and the Yosemite Valley*, dedicated entire chapters or sections to those areas.[6] They highlighted other unique geological and natural phenomena as well, including Colorado's Garden of the Gods, the Geysers near Calistoga, California, and the Calaveras Big Trees in the foothills of California's Sierra Nevada range. Meanwhile, paintings, stereographs, and engravings intended for mass distribution unveiled the thrilling prospects of an untouched region with abundant wildlife and vast, open spaces.

Late nineteenth-century promotional materials also enticed tourists by promising them encounters with "America's Switzerland" in the mountain ranges of the West, even though the term had been used previously to lure visitors to New Hampshire's White Mountains and New York's Catskills. The use of this term for the western United States, however, also helped advance a nationalist impulse that was more logically associated with the American West than with the less naturally dramatic American East: boosters could claim that the Rocky Mountains and Sierra Nevadas rivaled, if not surpassed, the Swiss Alps in overall grandeur. If American cities had not attained nineteenth-century levels of refinement believed to characterize such places as London or Paris, the American West at least featured a natural landscape with which Europe—or the American East—could not compete.[7] Regardless of location, an economic rationale also spurred the promotion of *America's* Switzerland, for boosters encouraged tourists to spend their vacations, and their money, in America—not Europe. In the presentation of the nineteenth-century West in text and image, "America's Switzerland" could not be constructed into a manicured playground for the well-to-do; it was instead a sublime landscape of primeval force. Few tourists, however, wished to be thrust fully into the teeth of uncontrollable landscapes. Even if such landscapes had the ability to generate spiritual feelings, travelers needed to be protected from danger. The transcontinental railroad journey through the wilds of the West, with special excursions to the most extraordinary examples of the natural environment, brought tourists closer to nature but—with sleeper cars, resorts, lodging, and meals—also provided them with some measure of comfort and safety.

CONSTRUCTING THE URBAN PICTURESQUE

Promotional materials and physical design shaped the urban American West in this general fashion, as well. If the wilds of the natural landscape could be made more comfortable for tourists through railroads

and resorts, the wilds of the *urban* landscape might be similarly constructed. With their parks, boulevards, and viewpoints, cities—and the
tourist literature that promoted them—folded the urban environment
into the natural in ways that allowed both to peacefully coexist, transforming the urban American West for leisurely exploration and passive
contemplation. Most western cities already existed within, or near,
spectacular natural settings, so boosters and tourists could more easily
make connections between the natural and the urban, between nature
and culture. Promotional materials played up the connection between
the natural environment of the West and its alteration by humankind
to decided advantage.

The appeal of western cities as natural phenomena drew upon
a long-standing tourist desire to seek out the natural environment
for measure, study, and appreciation, dating back at least to the
Enlightenment of the early seventeenth century. The desire to sort,
organize, and understand natural phenomena during the Enlightenment later merged with an eighteenth-century imperative, inspired
by theories of the picturesque, to design the natural environment in
ways that generated associative feelings of tranquility, calm, or nostalgia. If such landscapes did not exist in nature, then perhaps they could
be crafted by humankind—whether through poetry, painting, or gardens. The more that nature could resemble art, as Joseph Addison once
declared in the *Spectator* in 1712, the more pleasing it could become.[8]
The implication was that experiencing nature for its beauty and art
might lead to refinement and ultimately improve individual and collective morality.

Shaping the entirety of modernizing western cities—with their
noises, dirt, ethnic strife, and discord—into "art" would be a monumental task, but in the West, with the natural landscape already such a
prominent, preexisting feature, parts of the urban environment could
be physically designed this way. Tourist literature also countered the
chaos and illegibility of the city by focusing on its pastoral attributes
and discursively organizing it into definable spaces and patterns. Writers, artists, and publishers of tourist literature presented cities from
the perspective of the bird's-eye view, transforming the clamor of the

streets or the clusters of ships in harbors or rivers into progress and efficiency. They essentially zoned western cities into separate areas—downtown here, suburbs there, industries here, commercial zone there, residential districts elsewhere. Out of the chaos, illegibility, and disorder of nineteenth-century urbanization, promotional materials crafted "readable" western cities, resembling vast gardens with buildings and neighborhoods set as sculptures within them.[9] In promotional materials, western cities emerged as places where calm reigned over chaos, order over disorder, rationality over irrationality.

Not all western cities could be constructed so conveniently, however—not in their early years, anyway. No matter how persuasive the booster literature, western cities needed to mature beyond their initial settlement period before speculators or city leaders could shape them for pleasure and relaxation. In the 1860s and 1870s, the first urban western guidebooks modeled themselves on the "strangers' guides" available for eastern cities since the early part of the nineteenth century. Strangers' guides provided new arrivals or tourists with essential urban information; for example, the addresses of city and county offices, the locations of fire alarm boxes, and timetables for streetcars and ferries. Tourist attractions, such as they were, typically fell under general headings such as "Principal Hotels" or "Public Buildings," with nothing particularly descriptive about them beyond their locations. Aside from advertisements, rarely did illustrations of city attractions accompany their listings.[10]

By the 1880s, promotional literature for western cities did include more buildings and areas that may have held tourist intrigue, but the majority existed in tight urban contexts surrounded by a number of nonmonumental, ordinary structures. Many others were mingled with, or near, structures of industrial or technological prowess. Industrial areas presented a messy and undignified appearance, however, and did not convey the refinement that city leaders wished to champion. Guidebooks only advertised industries or factories if they could be presented as models of efficiency or as aesthetically pleasing, such as illustrations depicting the atmospheric effects of factory smoke. The 1891–92 edition of *King's Handbook of the United States* offers just one

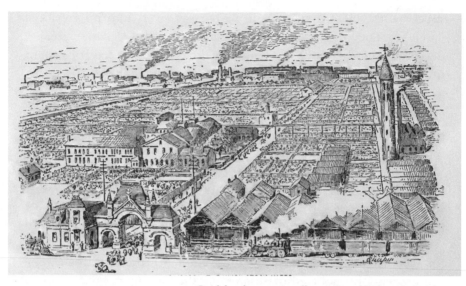

UNION STOCK YARDS IN CHICAGO. Guidebooks occasionally promoted industry or technology in nineteenth-century western cities but always described them in ways that made them appear rational or efficient. Chicago's Union Stock Yards are rendered from above in *King's Handbook of the United States* (1892), thereby depicting them as orderly and too distant to detect the horrific scenes of animal slaughter. Visitors who toured the stockyards usually offered rather different impressions. (Source: M. F. Sweetser, *King's Handbook of the United States*, p. 212. Courtesy of Internet Archive, http://archive.org/details/kingshandbookofu00swee.)

of many examples: in Chicago, the handbook noted the Union Stock Yards for their overall size, cost of construction, and profit; it did not highlight the packing houses for their brutality in animal slaughter but for their "modern appliances of wonderful ingenuity."[11] An accompanying illustration depicted the organization and precision of the operation.

Illustrations of late nineteenth-century western cities printed in guidebooks, souvenir view books, magazines, and newspapers typically worked with text to create the appearance of a pastoral, orderly urban environment. Most of these illustrations began as single photographs available for purchase. Noted photographers William Henry Jackson, Charles R. Savage, Eadweard Muybridge, Carleton Watkins, and Isaiah West Taber maintained portrait studios in western cities they helped publicize—Jackson in Denver, Savage in Salt Lake City, and Muybridge, Watkins, and Taber in San Francisco. Jackson, Watkins, and Muybridge, in particular, shot single- or multiple-plate aerial views or urban panoramas and sold them at their studios. Their studios also operated as souvenir shops, selling guidebooks and view books as well as stereographs and photographs. Although the natural wonders of the American West dominated the pictorial focus of these souvenirs (both Watkins and Taber, for example, promoted their studios by advertising their views of "Pacific Coast Scenery"), urban views appeared as well.[12] British traveler Emily Faithfull revealed that she purchased city views at Taber's studio when visiting San Francisco in the 1880s.[13]

How was the city typically portrayed in these views? As with other promotional images, photographers and, at times, city leaders who commissioned urban photography chose to present the urban West at its most idealized. This often meant vantage points requiring special access and under atmospheric conditions providing the best possible light. Railroad magnate Mark Hopkins commissioned Eadweard Muybridge, for example, to shoot his 1877 and 1888 San Francisco panoramas from the tower atop his Nob Hill mansion, and Muybridge advertised the 1877 panorama by noting that the "day selected for its execution was remarkable for the clearness of the atmosphere."[14] Moreover, photographers shot urban panoramas from high enough above the city so they could render the otherwise potentially messy human activity insignificant. In this respect, photographers crafted idealized images of the otherwise disorderly nineteenth-century cities—they rendered the city picturesque.[15]

Urban photographic panoramas remained prohibitively expensive to anyone but the wealthy, however, and even single photographic prints were costly in the late nineteenth century. But publishers reduced costs by hiring illustrators, lithographers, engravers, or woodcut artists to redraw, trace, or etch selected photographs onto paper, stone, tin plates, or wood and prepare them for mass production.[16] They also hired artists or lithographers to craft original interpretations of *urbs in horto* (the city in the garden) for their publications. Moreover, tourists could purchase stereographs, which were smaller, less expensive, and more durable than photographs. Already by the 1870s, a number of companies produced stereographs and made them available nation-wide by mail and door-to-door sales, allowing potential tourists to purchase images of the West and view them from the comfort of their living rooms.[17] Similar to the accompanying text in the tourist lit-erature, publishers hoped the presentation of the city as picturesque would imaginatively stamp out conflicts and erase the otherwise messy aspects of everyday life in the nineteenth-century urban West.[18]

Bird's-eye views offered another variation on this theme; they ren-dered western cities picturesque by virtue of their aerial perspectives alone. These views necessarily flattered, and flattened, the city—the city nearly always appeared in concert with the landscape with the view-point too high to reveal the troubling aspects of nineteenth-century urban life. Although magazine editors, guidebook publishers, entrepre-neurs, and other urban boosters often commissioned bird's-eye views to attract settlers and tourists, the artists made certain choices, just as did all illustrators, engravers, and lithographers who redrew original art-work for mass production. Bird's-eye views commonly featured ships, railroads, and other industries set against backdrops of soaring moun-tain peaks, fantastic cloud formations, shimmering sunsets, or limitless expanses of water—depending upon the particular geography.[19] They occasionally distorted the perspective to emphasize particular features that best demonstrated the cities' refinement or their promise of future growth, such as exaggerating building scale to highlight the presence of urban institutions. At times, bird's-eye views included an arrange-ment of prominent building façades around the edges of the print. Artists produced staggering numbers of urban bird's-eye views in the late nineteenth century; their idyllic perspectives allowed potential visitors to imagine ideal cities free from social tensions, ripe for invest-ment, and filled with promise.

Publishers, photographers, city leaders, and urban elites could not simply advertise the image of a natural, organized playground to poten-tial visitors. Western cities also had to physically demonstrate the ideal juxtaposition of nature and culture they promoted. Landscape architects offered assistance: they helped reshape the natural environment with design ideas that drew upon the antebellum rural cemetery and the English picturesque garden. The parks, boulevards, and cemeteries with their carefully placed trees, foliage, walkways, knolls, ponds, lakes, bridges, steps, benches, and follies were considered uplifting spaces for anyone who encountered them, and they were in concert with contemporary versions of gentility and refinement. As pastoral respites from city life, these spaces not only provided retreats for residents but in promotional materials became tourist escapes or excursions—even if they existed close to the heart of the city.

American urban parks designed in the English manner did not first appear in the West, however. Along the American eastern seaboard, municipal authorities and planners had earlier authorized the construction of new parks, boulevards, and cemeteries to provide antidotes to the industrial city and to create landscapes from which lower- and middle-class residents could cultivate a refined existence. In New York and Boston, for example, landscape architects such as Frederick Law Olmsted and Calvert Vaux offered picturesque designs intended to counter the supposed evils of urban commerce and their effects: advertising, gambling, swearing, and otherwise improper behavior. Together with urban elites, nineteenth-century designers hoped the new parks would provide suitable alternatives to the chaotic and competitive life of the commercial metropolis, offering versions of urban harmony in settings tucked away from the ordinary bustle of the nineteenth-century city.[20]

Western elites and planners applied a similar philosophy for park design. Guidebooks featured urban parks among the cities' best tourist diversions—in many cases, discussing parks, roads, and views before architecture and other urban highlights and describing these environments in language that could have been applied equally to English garden design. Announcing the roads built into San Francisco's Golden Gate Park, John S. Hittell's 1888 *Guide Book to San Francisco* noted that designers worked with the contours of the landscape, allowing roads to "wind about, with gentle ascents and descents, as well as level stretches, and obtain a succession of pleasing landscapes."[21] Guidebooks also presented the new boulevards and pleasure drives as urban escapes, even if those roads ran close to the city center. Such an escape could be literal: following these roads to their end, tourists could wind up in the city's largely underdeveloped nineteenth-century suburbs, which guidebooks also sold as excursions into the rural countryside.

GARDEN CITIES OF THE WEST

In the case of Chicago, the natural landscape itself had to be countered through design. According to Louis J. Schneyer's 1892 *Illustrated Hand Book and Guide to Chicago and the World's Columbian Exposition,* the alteration of the landscape was of particular urgency, for the "monotonously flat prairie" boasted little in the way of natural "scenic charms." Yet the landscape could be improved by "pleasant and beautiful" parks.[22] Chicago's frenetic late nineteenth-century growth necessitated more healthy open space and parkland, while its endless pursuit of wealth suggested to some critics that the city also lacked morality. By 1893, A. N. Marquis and Company's *Ready Reference Guide* deemed Chicago's parks so important to combat this reputation that it encouraged tourists to set aside a full day to visit the "leading" ones.[23]

City leaders hired noted landscape architects Olmsted, Vaux, and H. W. S. Cleveland to provide some of these designs, and—together with Chicago-based designers such as William le Baron Jenney—they responded with over two thousand acres of parklands and boulevards featuring artificial lakes, islands, pathways, drives, rambles, rustic bridges, fountains, monuments, bandstands, and sculptures. Through their landscape interventions, the designers intended to counter the monotony of the prairie; to offer places of passive contemplation, refinement, and leisurely recreation; and, according to Schneyer's handbook, to provide relief from Chicago's noisy, active streets and the wanton commercial pursuit of the "almighty dollar.[24] While an ambitious plan to link the entire system of parks via connecting boulevards never quite materialized, many individual parks did. These included Lincoln Park, Washington Park, Douglas Park, Garfield Park, Humboldt Park, Gage Park, and Jackson Park—the last of which, designed by Olmsted, emerged as the buildings and spaces of the World's Columbian Exposition rose to its west. Nineteenth-century guidebooks highlighted Lincoln Park more than the others, because its zoological garden, palm house, and many knolls and pathways existed within reasonable proximity to downtown. Yet promotional sources also boasted of the park system's unparalleled extent, which they contended no other American city could match. The parks contributed to Chicago's nineteenth-century moniker as America's "Garden City," although this characterization remained at odds with the realities of the downtown Loop.[25]

The notion of Chicago as the Garden City also relied upon a selection of highly landscaped boulevards, many of which connected to the new parks. One souvenir view book to the world's fair recommended that visitors stroll the boulevards to see their beds of flowers and "stately foliage plants" offering "a most pleasing and restful change for the eye"—presumably after observing the business-oriented activity in the city center.[26] The carriage drives flanking a decorative pedestrian-oriented median along Drexel Boulevard received the lion's share of promotional attention, but guidebooks encouraged tourists to frequent Lake Shore Drive and Oakwood and Grand Boulevards as well. An itinerary for the 1888 Raymond and Whitcomb three-week summer tour to Yellowstone incorporated a one-day stop in Chicago, where "no programme of action" was planned but the accompanying brochure noted that the stopover would be at a time "when the parks are especially inviting." It encouraged tourists to spread out from the Loop and visit the "very elaborate" park system, including the "South Parks," some six or seven miles from downtown, accessible via Grand and Drexel Boulevards.[27] Schneyer's guidebook, moreover, dedicated two and a half pages to Chicago's boulevards and parks, while the city's "public buildings," which were far more accessible and of which there were far more, merited slightly more than a page.[28]

Guidebooks also encouraged visits to the city's edges, including Graceland Cemetery in the Lake View Township and the suburban enclave of Evanston with its Northwestern University campus—both north of the city. Those guidebooks published after 1883 regularly featured the model company town of Pullman, Illinois—the center of railroad sleeper car production in early 1880s America. With its factories, arcade, clock tower, hotel, and the varied designs of its residential dwellings, guidebooks championed Pullman not only for the efficiency of its industrial operations but also for the supposedly class-blind moral order and improved worker behavior the plan, organization, and architecture hoped to inspire—as if Pullman itself was a small city in a garden. Some ten thousand foreign tourists reportedly visited Pullman in 1893 alone, when special trains were extended to the town from the site of the World's Columbian Exposition. Late nineteenth-century Chicago may have garnered international attention for its extraordinary rate of growth, its recovery from the fire, and the tall buildings in the Loop, but the printed media selling Chicago to the world treated the tranquility and order of its open spaces, parks, and outlying areas with nearly equal reverence.[29]

More easily marketed as "garden cities" or "urban pleasure resorts" were western urban environments with less overall energy, more spectacular natural surroundings, and more temperate climates than loud, busy, dirty, and alternately frigid and humid Chicago. Denver was one example. Late nineteenth-century guidebooks and illustrations of Colorado and Denver celebrated those resort-like qualities that depicted Denver at its most refined: its crisp atmosphere, its views, its parks, and its elegant residential districts. They generally buried information about the city center. Only brochures published for investment purposes or to otherwise promote the business community lavished greater attention on the activity within the city itself.[30]

Within municipal boundaries, Denver-area guidebooks highlighted the 320-acre City Park, established in the early 1880s, and, by the 1890s, South Park, Berkeley Lake, and Sloan Lake, as well as a series of "magnificent drives" through the city's residential districts.[31] Baedeker's 1893 guidebook to the United States suggested that tourists ride electric tramways to see the "fine residences" in the city's Capitol Hill district but also recommended traveling as far as Aurora, some six miles east, to visit more of these residences. A handful of sources also encouraged tourists to leave the city limits and visit Porter's Mineral Baths and Springs in North Denver.[32] The civic improvements to

Denver since the rough edges of its early settlement period inspired booster W. G. M. Stone to contend that tourists would be "astonished" to discover the "magical touch of civilization" some six hundred miles west of the Missouri River. For Stone, the city provided a refined mix of culture and nature: not only did it include "beautiful homes," "banks," and "wealthy corporations," but they were set among "miles of beautiful streets, shaded by grateful foliage." Stone argued that the city "in all that it is and promises to be, is more wonderful than mountain peak or canon."[33]

Few promotional materials elevated Denver's "improvements" above the region's natural landscape, however. Even the title of Stone's 1892 publication—*The Colorado Hand-Book: Denver and Its Outings*—hinted that the city's greatest asset was its natural setting and its "outings." In guidebooks and illustrations, Denver's significance relied more on its proximity to the Rocky Mountains and the towns and resorts at their feet or nestled within them. Most tourist material regarding Colorado spent fewer pages promoting its largest city than it did the resort areas of Colorado Springs and Manitou Springs south of the city or the smaller mining towns such as Georgetown, Leadville, Cripple Creek, Central City, and Silverton in the mountains. The red rock formations near Colorado Springs dubbed the "Garden of the Gods" alone garnered more promotional attention than Denver. More often than not, tourist materials sold Denver as a pleasant stop en route to the Rockies—a perfect blend of the natural and human made with a "healthful" climate and sweeping views of the mountains.[34]

Denver "occupies a series of plateaus, facing the mountains, and commanding a grand and beautiful view," D. Appleton and Company's 1888 *Hand Book of Winter Resorts* announced before describing the city itself. "Through the clear mountain atmosphere may be seen Pike's and Long's Peaks, and the snow-capped range extending more than 200 miles."[35] The city was approximately fifteen miles from the foothills of the mountains and not in their shadow—hardly "face to face with the Titanic wall of the Rocky Mountains" as *King's Handbook of the United States* claimed in 1891–92—but this never stopped promotional materials from exaggerating their proximity to one another.[36]

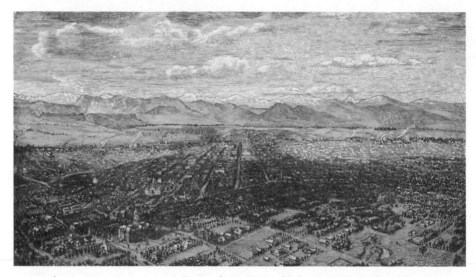

BIRD'S-EYE VIEW OF DENVER. Tourist literature and imagery promoted western cities such as Denver as gardens and health resorts—more for their settings or proximity to natural wonders than for their urban attractions. The Rocky Mountains were advertised as Denver's biggest features, but they were a bit too distant to be easily accessed or clearly seen by visitors. This bird's-eye perspective, however, permits the Rockies to appear closer than they actually were. (Source: Stanley Wood, *Over the Range to the Golden Gate*, p. 6. Courtesy of Internet Archive, http://archive.org/details/overrangegoldeng00wood.)

Apparently to accentuate the crisp atmospheric conditions that make distant objects seem much closer than they actually are, photographer William Chamberlain chose to shoot his 1870s Denver panorama for his "Rocky Mountain Scenery" series from them. From *that* distance, however, Denver appeared as little more than irrigation and farmland.[37] So widespread was the promotion of the city's rarefied air, however, that a number of travel accounts repeated the same, probably apocryphal, story about a man who thought he could walk from his Denver hotel to the Rockies one morning before breakfast. Having walked several miles across farmland with the mountains seemingly no closer than they were before, when he came to a tiny irrigation ditch, he presumed it was a wide river and stripped off his clothes to swim across.[38]

Guidebook publishers and city boosters also had an easy time portraying Salt Lake City as a garden city and a resort destination. One guidebook, published by the Denver and Rio Grande Railroad, argued that Salt Lake City's setting at the foot of the dramatic Wasatch Mountain range made it "one of the most beautifully located cities on this continent" and boasted of its "elements of beauty in such variety and of such superior character as are not to be found in any other one city in America."[39] While the Mormons, their practices, and their places of worship in Temple Square received the bulk of promotional attention, the "elements of beauty" regularly featured in Salt Lake City guidebooks included the city's 10-square-acre plan and 132-foot-wide streets (based on the "plat of Zion" stipulated by Mormon founder, Joseph Smith, for the earlier settlement of Independence, Missouri), the trees lining those streets, the foliage surrounding its residences, and the clear, swiftly flowing streams of mountain water used both for drinking and irrigation running through open channels along the street edges.[40]

To divert tourist attention away from whatever preconceived negative impressions they may have held about the Mormons, guidebooks focused on the settlers' ability to make an otherwise remote and desolate wilderness blossom like the proverbial rose. Williams's *Pacific Tourist* encouraged visitors to hire a carriage and drive up and down the wide city streets to "see the wilderness of fruit groves and gardens" and listed the city's various springs foremost among the city's sights, which he recommended tourists visit shortly after securing a place to sleep.[41] Other guidebooks extolled the city's "salubrious" and "bracing" climate as perfect for invalids and "ideal" for settlers.[42]

Guidebooks to Salt Lake City, to Utah, or to the West also directed tourists to Liberty Park and Calder's Farm south of the city; Warm Sulphur Springs and Beck's Hot Springs to the north; and to specific attractions in the Wasatch Mountains, such as City Creek Cañon and Big and Little Cottonwood Canyons, where summer visitors could delight in cool mountain streams and luxuriant foliage.[43] They also encouraged tourists to visit the nearby Great Salt Lake—the "Dead Sea of America"—although they recommended tourists do so in comfortable surroundings at either the Lake Park Bathing Resort, the Pavilion at Garfield Beach, or, by 1893, the Saltair resort. As with Denver, a cursory glance at promotional materials for nineteenth-century Salt Lake City reveals an emphasis on its setting and the activities visitors might undertake in that setting: beyond the few monumental buildings for Mormon worship and leadership and a handful of downtown hotels and institutions, the built environment proved less significant than the natural.[44]

Boosters shaped late nineteenth-century San Francisco in a similar fashion, despite its unique history, social conditions, and geography. In promotional materials, San Francisco appeared as a "picturesquely situated" city; a "pleasure resort district" with a "hundred hills, some of them crowned with palaces."[45] They contended that no city in the American West could compete with San Francisco's dramatic location on the edge of the continent, its steep and rocky terrain, its backdrop of ocean and bay, or the variety of attractions placed within its landscape. As with other cities in the American West, to depict the city in its best light, San Francisco tourist literature focused upon getting people away from the business district and the urban population. Mary Cone's promotional account pushed tourists immediately to the city's edges: "Your first ride will probably be to the Cliff House to see the seals and the Pacific Ocean," she instructed tourists, encouraging them to visit Lone Mountain Cemetery along the way. "If you have not seen the Pacific Ocean before," she continued, "that will be the great attraction—the grand sight for which you most care."[46] Whether tourists truly did *most* care for a view of the Pacific Ocean is debatable, but San Francisco's Cliff House ranked among the city's most heavily advertised nineteenth-century sites because sea lions (which guidebooks routinely referred to as seals) relaxed on rocks visible from the Cliff House balcony. At any given moment, hundreds of barking sea lions could be observed jockeying for position on these rocks. Many publications identified the largest and strongest of the sea lions by name, whether "Ben Butler" in the 1870s or "General Sherman" in the 1880s.

It took several years following initial settlement before San Francisco guidebooks cast the city as a pleasure resort and directed tourists to its scenic attractions. The city's rush to urbanization in the 1850s and 1860s left the downtown area mostly without the hotels and institutions that elites considered keys to civilized society, let alone much open space or greenery. Apparently little existed to inspire the citizens to a more moral and just city, and booster rhetoric only could do so much. The ocean and sea lions existed as natural attractions, but the city initially developed along the bay and the harbor, facing eastward. This made the ocean more than six miles distant from the city's first area of settlement, and sand dunes created significant barriers for convenient access via land. As early as the mid-1850s, citizens and boosters began to clamor for a public park to provide scenery and moral uplift; a grand park, according to the *San Francisco Chronicle* in 1855, would "do more in preventing dissipation and vice than half the sermons preached, half the moral lectures and teachings to children and to men."[47]

Golden Gate Park resulted from this civic imperative, although its distance from the city center required the extension of tram lines, new carriage roads, and sophisticated engineering by state engineer William Hammond Hall. City officials hired Olmsted to provide the overall design in 1874, and presumably the moral uplift as well. In the English garden design tradition (and similar to his parks elsewhere), Olmsted designed artificial lakes, islands, a bandstand, an iron suspension bridge, a large glass conservatory, rustic benches, monuments, statues, fountains, and beds of flowers. Together, they helped the park contrast markedly from the urban environment.

Promotional materials immediately elevated Golden Gate Park among San Francisco's premier tourist attractions, although city officials intended it as an antidote to modern urban conditions and most of it also existed well beyond the nineteenth-century municipal boundaries. Yet the park was as artificially constructed as the city, for Hall and Olmsted had to thoroughly reshape the existing natural landscape to make it function effectively. The final product for this urban "pleasure ground" allowed tourists to view hills within the park and, from certain perspectives, to see the Pacific Ocean in the distance.[48] The combination of the artificial and the natural at Golden Gate Park impressed British tourist James Fullarton Muirhead, who visited in the early 1890s. Muirhead thought the design spoke "to our admiration of nature" but also to a "sense of respectful awe for the transforming energy of man."[49]

By the end of the nineteenth century, San Francisco boosters proclaimed that the city contained more parks than any city in the nation. Many of those parks were rather small, however, and few were set aside as tranquil spaces for passive contemplation.[50] In the tourist literature, though, they all became parks or "pleasure grounds," including Woodward's Gardens along the southern edge of the city—a horticultural and zoological amusement area with a zoo, fossils, an aquarium, rare plants, a pavilion for musical and theatrical performances, a gymnasium, a library, and a restaurant. Adolph Sutro's private estate and grounds opened to the public as "Sutro Heights" in 1883 and, with its parapet overlooking the Cliff House and Seal Rocks, emerged as part of the tourist itinerary.[51] San Francisco guidebooks regularly heralded day trips to escape the city as well: to the Farallon Islands, Sausalito, Mare Island, the Napa Valley, Alameda, the new state university at Berkeley, and especially to Oakland—the "city of homes." With ferries running hourly, they encouraged tourists to travel across the bay and enjoy Oakland's abundant evergreen oaks, orchards, vineyards, parks, and gardens that sprouted in a city with an even more favorable climate than San Francisco.[52]

ABOVE THE CITY

Yet to thoroughly envision western cities as pleasure resorts or gardens, promotional materials encouraged tourists to rise above them. In the American West, elevated perspectives physically lifted the tourists out of the city's grasp and rendered the whole city picturesque. They allowed expansive natural features such as Lake Michigan, the Rocky Mountains, the Great Salt Lake, the Wasatch Mountains, the San Francisco Bay, and the Pacific Ocean to come into sharper focus, while simultaneously minimizing the intensity and activity of the streets, blocks, and buildings of the city. For those cities with a preexisting landscape of hills or mountains, guidebooks directed tourists to particular viewpoints, such as San Francisco's Telegraph Hill or Salt Lake City's Ensign Peak. Otherwise, observatories atop the cities' tallest buildings or structures provided viable alternatives. Similar to the way in which an artist's bird's-eye view or a photographic panorama characterized the urban environment, elevated natural perspectives and observatories permitted tourists to gaze upon western cities without having to participate in their everyday life. Such vantage points distorted activity on the streets, erased social conflict and unrest, transformed tourists from active urban participants into passive viewers, and rendered cities as romantic, cohesive documents.[53]

Given the flat landscape of the prairie, however, tourists seeking elevated vantage points in Chicago had little option but to scale that city's tallest structures. In the 1870s and early 1880s, the best views could be obtained either from atop the Illinois Central Railroad grain-storage facility along the Chicago River, or from the water tower that survived the 1871 fire. British visitor Thomas Greenwood, having seen the view from the water tower, recommended in the early 1880s that tourists ascend its spiral staircase to gain a "splendid" perspective on "Chicago Lake [sic] and surrounding country."[54] For those seeking better views of the downtown area, by the mid-1880s and into the 1890s, tourists had higher alternatives: the tower atop the Auditorium Building, the lookout balcony two-thirds of the way up the three-hundred-foot-tall Board of Trade, the twelfth floor of the Tacoma Building, or the roof gardens atop the Grand Northern Hotel and the Masonic Temple. From perspectives such as these, visitors remained at a remove from the city while existing in the heart of it; even the smoke from Chicago industries could be rendered aesthetically pleasing from such heights.[55]

The largely flat landscape of Denver did not lend itself to preexisting natural observation points either. The Rocky Mountains were too far away to allow for clear views over the city, although this did not prevent nearly all published views of Denver's skyline from including the Rockies as a backdrop. With the mountains outpacing Denver as nineteenth-century tourist attractions, most promotional sources instead focused on the view of the Rockies from within the city, rather than the view of the city from the Rockies. Guidebooks disagreed about how much of the mountain range was visible from Denver and the best spot from which to view them, however. Sue Sanders claimed to have traveled via streetcar out of the city just to catch a glimpse of Pike's Peak in 1886, although J. J. Upchurch recalled having Pike's Peak pointed out to him from the dome of the courthouse when he visited Denver a year earlier. The nine-story Equitable Building apparently offered spectacular views of the Rockies when it was completed in 1892, but it could not bring tourists much closer to them.[56]

Salt Lake City, however, featured hills and the steep Wasatch Range in close enough proximity to provide tourists with spectacular, nearly aerial, views. Guidebooks stressed the dramatic views of the city and valley from Ensign Peak just north of downtown but also urged tourists to view the city from Fort Douglas, three miles to the east. By the 1890s, for a ten-cent admission fee, tourists also could gaze down upon the city from the newly constructed "tourist's tower" on Prospect Hill. Charles Savage's *Views of Utah and Tourists' Guide* encouraged them to use field glasses or telescopes for a "fine view" over the city.[57]

San Francisco's hills also provided excellent natural opportunities for aerial views of the city and its surroundings, although entrepreneurs capitalized on the topography by erecting a fanciful, castellated observatory atop Telegraph Hill. Tourists visited Nob Hill and Russian Hill for views of the city and surroundings, but promotional materials also highlighted the parapet at Sutro Heights and some hills within Golden Gate Park for views focusing predominantly on water and the natural landscape. The wire-rope cable cars brought tourists to a few of these spots within the city, providing dramatic views while simultaneously encouraging visitors to inspect their mechanical operations.[58] Yet promotional materials were less wont to emphasize mechanization alone than to demonstrate how technology worked in concert with the beautiful natural surroundings. To fully construct cities as pleasure resorts for tourists, technological innovations and modernization had to be rhetorically shaped in such a way to eliminate their harmful effects.

USING THE PAST

Promotional materials also transformed western cities by turning to the past. If wire-rope transit and skeletal steel frames represented advances in mechanization and appeared on an urban scale initially in the American West, booster publications generally subsumed these technological innovations under an overall presentation that emphasized a continuity with, and nostalgia for, the history of these places. "In order that the visitor may thoroughly appreciate the magnitude of the Chicago of the present," began John J. Flinn's massive, 632-page 1892 encyclopedia and guide prepared in advance of the world's fair, "perhaps it would be well enough to take a glance at the Chicago of the past."[59] By turning to the past, promotional materials also could boast that western cities contained a patina of age that critics from Europe and the American eastern seaboard thought lacking. In the face of constant change, boosters may have wished that visitors seek solace in a stable history.[60]

Turning to the past had particular promotional advantages, for it had long motivated tourist travel through Europe. For the eighteenth-century British elite, this meant traveling on the Grand Tour to visit those ruins from antiquity that seemed best to convey the foundations of Western civilization. A venerable European history motivated nineteenth-century tourists as well, even in the rapidly industrializing countries of England and France.[61] Compared with Europe, however, America featured little in the way of an established historical tradition—or at least any tradition easily recognizable by European Americans. In the spheres of high culture in which most nineteenth-century tourists traveled, critics deemed America devoid of history, or at least devoid of traditions in literature, music, or the arts—the products of refinement. Could America, and the American West in particular, be provided with a history?

The American West did have a lengthy cultural history, of course, but the Native American past remained, at best, poorly understood, and, at worst, ignored; the European American settlement of the West, meanwhile, was still too new in the late nineteenth century to have established any long-standing traditions. Until the last years of the

nineteenth century, many of the monumental Native American architectural ruins, particularly in the American Southwest, lacked railroad
connections and remained virtually inaccessible for travelers. With
contemporary Native Americans regarded by many European Americans as savage, primitive, and unsophisticated, there was no chance that
the physical reminders of their ancestors would be treated as part of a
U.S. history.

Instead, nineteenth-century guidebooks to western cities turned to
the earliest stages of European American settlement, when newcomers
had to confront directly the hazards of the natural environment for
survival. To reverse preconceptions about the urban West as devoid of
tradition, guidebooks included whatever history they could—provided
that it demonstrated progress or told stories of the tribulations suffered
by hardy pioneers, missionaries, or conquistadors that had since been
overcome along the path to progress. This was the case even if the city
had existed for a limited time and its early history—fraught with fires,
natural disasters, ethnic and racial discrimination, or the emergence of
vigilante law—would not typically be worthy of celebration. Anything
potentially troubling about the past could be thus overcome and relegated to the annals of history. Promotional materials used the past as a
device to underscore the authority and advancement of the present.

"How incredible it seems," declares the 1892 *Chicago Illustrated*, a souvenir book printed for world's fair attendees, "that within the memory
of those now living, the great city that can now welcome to its hos-
pitalities the hosts of the world, a few years back was a mere hamlet."
Chicago's "hamlet" or village days were at least sixty years earlier, but
tourist literature cared little about accuracy so long as it could employ
the past to underscore the progress made since that time. The *Checker-
Board Guide to Chicago*, published for world's fair visitors, served much
the same purpose: it stated emphatically that no human achievement
could possibly match the transformation of "a dismal swamp, in the
midst of a trackless desert" into "one of the mightiest and grandest
cities on the globe."[62] Although the guidebooks to Chicago rarely discussed the city's initial home site erected by Jean Baptiste Pointe du
Sable, a Haitian settler of African and French descent, they usually

mentioned the seventeenth-century explorations of French Canadian explorers Louis Joliet and Pere Jacques Marquette and rarely missed an opportunity to discuss the city's phoenixlike rise from the ashes of the Great Fire of 1871. Highlighting the transformation of the landscape and the recovery from the fire made the past far more palatable for contemporary visitors.

Promotional sources constructed the past in other western cities in a similar fashion. To highlight the conversion of the Salt Lake City landscape into a garden paradise, guidebooks told and retold the difficulties of Mormon emigration and struggles for survival in the nearly inhospitable conditions of the Salt Lake Valley. Late nineteenth-century sources promoting Denver and San Francisco, meanwhile, discussed the lawlessness and haphazard urban conditions in the early years surrounding the gold rushes. This enabled them to illuminate the presence of urban institutions, infrastructure, and maturity of the cities in the present—even if they were still fraught with considerable discord. After beginning with a passage about the geography, Lippincott's 1892 San Francisco guide noted that three fires in 1850 swept away the original wooden structures of the city but that today "many large and costly buildings have been erected; and marble, granite, and terra-cotta are coming into extensive use, with interior frames of iron and steel."[63] By introducing tourists to western cities in this way, guidebooks effectively reduced the difficulties of earlier periods to a harmless nostalgia.[64]

The urban American West changed rapidly throughout the late nineteenth century for several reasons, but promotional materials neither celebrated change nor encouraged tourists to experience it—unless the physical embodiments of change, from destruction to construction, could be shaped in such a way to appear progressive or relegated to the historical record. What was built one day could become expendable, altered, or rebuilt the next; it was nearly impossible to render western cities picturesque under these circumstances. In San Francisco, fires and earthquakes frequently threatened and destroyed parts of the city, while humans and machines regularly altered its landscape.[65] Denver also suffered fires, particularly in the early years of settlement, and according to one local newspaper in 1872 the city kept "tearing down and build-ing up."[66] Nineteenth-century Chicago received international acclaim for its construction (and reconstruction) projects, whether rebuilding efforts after the fire, erection of skyscrapers in the 1880s and 1890s, or, earlier in the 1850s and 1860s, lifting buildings throughout downtown to meet raised streets covering a new sewer system. Yet promotional materials discussed such changes in the past tense, even if they were ongoing. They advertised stability over change; they presumed visitors would prefer reading about a completed city than one consistently reinventing itself.

The effects of urban change—much like urban disorder and the mundane—also could be mitigated through imagery. Photographs, for example, offered an especially useful medium for providing the rapidly modernizing late nineteenth-century western cities with an age and stability well beyond their years, even if this meant ignoring change altogether. Contemporary photos became part of the historical record as soon as they appeared in guidebooks or souvenir view books; they arrested change and heightened the sense of nostalgia.[67] Change was so constant in the earliest years of European American settlement that the *Alta California* newspaper urged 1850s San Francisco visitors to return home with daguerreotypes reminding them of the city's vari-ous stages of growth. Because of immigration and the persistent threat of fires, the newspaper thought San Francisco would not be recogniz-able in the near future.[68]

The same could have been said for Chicago, which *was* practically unrecognizable after the 1871 fire. Henry Alworth Merewether, visit-ing Chicago just two years after the conflagration, was not particularly interested in reliving the fire—he wished only to purchase photo-graphs of the city's newly erected "fine buildings." But he found only images of the fire ruins and of Athens.[69] That images of Chicago's destruction and Athens—and presumably of the ruins of Greek tem-ples on the Acropolis—amounted to the sum total of souvenirs for a tourist two years after the fire may not have been coincidental. Boost-ers consistently sought to elevate cities in the American West to the traditions, grandeur, and sophistication of the Old World, which occasionally resulted in promoting Europe *over* America.

So important was it that tourists be swept away to distant times and places that entertainment panoramas (large, circular landscape paintings inside rounded buildings dedicated to their display) usually depicted attractions or events in history that had little or nothing to do with the cities in which they were displayed. If they did their job, these panoramas could temporarily catapult visitors from the modernizing cities of the present to the glories of the past.[70] In conjunction with the 1893 World's Columbian Exposition, Chicago guidebooks recommended that tourists take advantage of the various panoramas in specific downtown buildings, including the "original" panorama of the Battle of Gettysburg and others of Niagara Falls and Jerusalem. Only a panorama depicting the 1871 fire had anything to do specifically with Chicago, but memorializing the fire through imagery offered further testament to the city's desire to highlight its troubled past to emphasize its victorious present.[71]

San Francisco featured panoramas as well, but none of San Francisco itself. In the 1880s, the "polygonal" building at Mason and Eddy Streets featured a panorama depicting the 1815 Battle of Waterloo, replete with real soil, grass, buttercups, trees, and shrubs. C. P. Heininger's 1880 *Historical Souvenir of San Francisco* waxed eloquently about the display because of the apparent difficulty of distinguishing between the three-dimensional space of the room and the illusionistic space of the painting. In this case, Heininger's guidebook did not focus on the subject of the panorama—a battle of unspeakable carnage that resulted in Napoleon's abdication as commander general of the French Army—but focused on the notion of escape instead, promising visitors they would be met with a "continuous landscape" with "beautiful fields and woodlands with hills and valleys" that seemed to stretch as "far as the eye can reach." Heininger insisted that tourists visit the panorama in person because it was an "impossibility" to offer a comprehensive account in the space of the publication and because "words can no more adequately describe it than words can portray the grand harmonies of Mendelssohn and Wagner."[72] If the cities displaying panoramas themselves lacked history, tradition, or places of retreat, the construction of entire buildings dedicated to scenes of distant localities or historical events indicates a belief that tourist encounters required such escapes in order for tourists to perceive cities in a positive light.

By the last decade of the nineteenth century, private tour companies in western cities also capitalized on the past. In the early 1890s, Salt Lake City tourists could purportedly visit that past by riding in a forty-person capacity passenger coach operated by the Grant Brothers Livery & Transfer Company. An advertisement for that company in the 1893 edition of *The Mormon Metropolis: An Illustrated Guide to Salt Lake City* attempted to entice tourists with its "native born guides" who "intelligently" provided "historical facts."[73] Intelligence

GRANT BROS'.
LIVERY & TRANSFER CO.

Furnish Tourists with native born guides to explain points of interest.

They can do so intelligently and give historical facts.

WE ARE NOT IN BUSINESS FOR A DAY.

We treat you so that you will take pleasure in recommending your friends to us. Do not fail to see that your order is placed with us when you visit Salt Lake City.

Grant Bros'. Livery and Transfer Co.

B. F. GRANT, MGR.   ※   Telephone 211.

GUIDED TOURS OF SALT LAKE CITY. The Grant Bros.' Livery and Transfer Company was one of several businesses offering tours in late nineteenth-century Salt Lake City. Many of these outfits attempted to correct any misinformation visitors may have heard about the city or the Mormons; apparently, providing "historical facts" was one way to set the record straight. (Source: *The Mormon Metropolis*, 1893.)

or historical accuracy notwithstanding, tour guides hoped to tap into an apparent visitor thirst for history—no matter the content of that history. One individual, Joseph C. Kingsbury, promoted his Salt Lake City tours by claiming to be among the pioneers who settled Salt Lake Valley in the late 1840s and by promising to inform tourists about that experience.[74]

Much as the realities of everyday urban life had to be masked by the creation of open spaces and rendered tranquil in words and pictures, history, too, had to be shaped as appealing and safe. When a difficult past could be made to seem harmless, boosters must have assumed the city itself would rise in visitor estimation. If the city could be made to blend seamlessly with the natural environment, even better—a potentially easier prospect in the American West, given the grandeur of the natural setting. As it was, most tourists journeyed westward in the late nineteenth century to encounter the wonders of the natural landscape, but in the cities "nature" had to be tamed and controlled, and promotional materials accentuated the physical alterations that provided this idyllic blend of nature and culture. Whether tourists encountered the urban West as an ideal blend of the natural and the urban, however, is another matter altogether.

CHAPTER 3

Confusion

Wonder, Turmoil, Awe, and Hell

In 1876, Scottish journalist and traveler John Leng visited Chicago to assess its progress since the 1871 fire. Similar to many late nineteenth-century Chicago visitors, Leng noted the rebuilding efforts and the "miles of streets" that seemed "crowded, busy, and bustling." He pointed to the "abounding signs of life and energy in the people" and expressed wonder that the "magnificent business streets" could have been rebuilt in such a short time.[1]

To obtain a panoramic view of the city's pulse, productivity, and promise, Leng climbed the largest and tallest grain elevator lining the banks of the Chicago River. But the machinery and processes of grain sorting inside the structure captured Leng's attention during his ascent. Stunned by the twenty-three shafts emptying five hundred cars of two hundred thousand bushels per day and loading river- and lake-bound vessels with sixty thousand bushels in two to three hours, Leng's narrative turned toward the abstract. Numbers, pounds, and horsepower marked his prose; the total effect of the "B" Central elevator, powered by a "splendid steam engine," seemed a complicated "labyrinth of bins and spouts." To Leng, the grain elevator resembled a city unto itself—perhaps a microcosm of the city of Chicago spreading out below: fast, efficient, extensive, powerful, astonishing, busy, loud, and complex. Just a few short years after a devastating fire, Chicago appeared to Leng as a technological marvel, filled with commercial promise.[2] But it was confusing.

Indeed, Chicago and other late nineteenth-century cities of the American West did not unfold with tremendous clarity. Shock, horror, and disgust at the noise, crowds, construction, industry, traffic, and swelling populations as frequently characterized tourist experiences as did their wonder and awe at urban technological achievements. Try as promotional sources might to shape cities as gardens or pleasure resorts or to present urbanization as indicative of progress, what many tourists encountered instead sent them recoiling in terror and fear. At their most persuasive, such sources could suggest places to visit, but they could neither order the everyday life of the metropolis nor entirely dictate tourist encounters. The urban West was too unwieldy, too unpredictable, too complicated, and too confusing to be fully manufactured for the tourist.

Although tourists were not subjected to the bureaucratic regulation and hegemonic power structures that monitored and controlled the lives of residents in late nineteenth-century industrializing cities, they often consciously or unconsciously resisted the carefully constructed visions of travel laid out by the tourist literature. Tourist experiences countered the booster vision of the urban West; they mapped an alternative western city that sometimes differed geographically and frequently differed emotionally and psychologically from that which urban elites hoped. With some exceptions, tourist encounters bled across the pages of constructed visibility crafted by promotional materials. Tourists became their own agents in the city.[3]

While they did visit the highly promoted attractions, tourists also immersed themselves in the less-orchestrated, interstitial, and everyday aspects of western cities: crowds, ethnic diversity, industrial districts, vehicular traffic, and the seemingly endless extension of residential development along undifferentiated street grids beyond the city center. Once on the streets, the legibility of the city visible in lithographic bird's-eye views and in engravings reproduced in souvenir view books lost focus. Not all was visible, either, although promotional materials focused upon how tourists should "see" the urban environment.

Diaries, letters, and traveler's accounts reveal that tourists consumed the city in a multisensory fashion, encompassing the visible within an invisible multisensory landscape of sound, smell, touch, and, occasionally, taste.[4] This chapter demonstrates that tourists engaged in the complex and occasionally paradoxical nature of modern life: the excitement and grandeur of the western city as well as its difficulties and despair. The urban American West struck tourists as extraordinary and shocking, sophisticated and primitive, placid and noisy, overwhelming and dull, fragrant and noisome, and much else in between.

THE URBAN SUBLIME

Chicago, for one, could not be experienced in a strictly visual manner. Beyond the pleasures and excitement of the urban environment, some travelers noted the stench of rotting garbage in city alleys, the grime and soot permeating the atmosphere, a general clamor in the streets, and the squeals of animals in the stockyards. Combined with the shock of a dilapidated, repetitive, or unfamiliar built environment, Chicago could be downright unpleasant. When Norwegian traveler Hjalmar Holand arrived in April 1884 as a teenager looking for work, his memories of the beautiful Oslo suburbs led him directly toward Chicago's edges. But he found no solace there. "There were no hills or lakes," he recalled, "no woods or wandering streams. Instead I passed countless blocks of small houses on both sides with a rough, unpaved lane between. Eventually the houses became scattered, and finally I was far out on a poorly drained flat without a tree in sight." A week later Holand tried again, this time setting out to the north. He claimed to have discovered "precisely the same conditions," aside from "a large, filthy-looking barn, surrounded by enormous manure piles."[5] Few tourists shunned the center entirely and headed straight to its edges, but Holand's account reveals a western city far messier than the manicured city portrayed in guidebooks, lithographs, engravings, photographs, and panoramas.

Lofty expectations about the rationally ordered "garden cities" of the American West often found themselves at odds with on-the-ground tourist experiences. At first, San Francisco appeared to be every-thing British traveler William F. Rae expected when, in the 1870s, he approached the "enchanting" city from Sacramento aboard a steamer. For Rae, the "fairy-like spectacle" of San Francisco was "such a city as Aladdin might have ordered the genii to create in order to astonish and dazzle the spectator." But from a perspective within the city, Rae's initial enchantment met the reality of the modernizing metropolis. "I had supposed San Francisco to be a second Liverpool," he wrote, presumably referring to the city's potential as a busy world port. Gaz-ing down toward the smoke-belching factories, however, he was "not prepared to find that it was also a second Birmingham."[6] Discrepan-cies between expectation and encounter also affected Phil Robinson, who arrived in San Francisco at the conclusion of a transcontinental journey in the early 1880s. Evidently inundated with accounts of the city's beauty, Robinson nonetheless found the city to be "disorderly, breathless with haste, unkempt."[7]

The activity of western cities intensified for tourists relative to places they had previously visited, as well. Following a visit to what he described as the leisurely, slow pace of Asia, DeWitt C. Bridges landed in San Francisco in May 1882 and was immediately struck by "huge volumes of smoke" pouring forth from "hundreds of smoke-stacks of the various manufacturing enterprises." Together with "street cars, innumerable cabs, hacks, drays and buggies" that "keep up a deafening racket," Bridges thought the "busy mart" of San Francisco marked a "wondrous contrast" with the "quiet, slow-going nationals of the East."[8] The contrast to Asia may have appeared "wondrous" to Bridges, but the smoke, noise, and activity of San Francisco presented a more troubling image. To Bostonian Susie Clark in 1890, the city of Oakland, across the bay from San Francisco, seemed "tree-embowered, garden-fringed, flower-crowned." But, she wrote, a "cloud of smoke which is seldom lifted hangs above San Francisco."[9] Was the city "enchanted"—as so much of the tourist literature claimed—or some-thing entirely else?

The complexities and contradictions of modernity marked indus-trializing cities everywhere—crystallized in the physical landscape, perhaps, by filthy-looking barns not terribly far from splendid down-town hotels and by the surface appearance of grandeur and harmony that, upon closer inspection, often splintered into a cacophonous array. Yet cities of the American West loomed especially large in the tourist imagination because promotional materials highlighted them for their clarity, organization, and the beauty of their natural surroundings.[10] Unlike cities in Europe and the American East, western cities pro-vided a surprising level of activity within a spectacular or otherwise prominent natural landscape, and few tourists were prepared for this activity so far from other centers of population. The collision of urban development and modern life within, or near, dramatic natural settings helped render western cities unique.

It also made them sublime. Guided tours, luxurious resort hotels, and large crowds of visitors at many of the most spectacular of western natural wonders, particularly Yellowstone and Yosemite, kept tourists—willingly or not—at a remove from the heavily promoted sublimity of the landscape that lured so many of them westward.[11] Yet fewer filters separated tourists from the raw, uncontrollable power of the western urban environment, particularly given its dramatic juxtaposition with nature and despite the attempt by promotional materials to accentuate the urban picturesque. In the cities, tourists more readily experienced the often contrasting emotions of terror, awe, and wonder—char-acteristics of the sublime that eluded them in a pure, unadulterated natural environment to which they could not easily gain access. This was not only the case in Chicago, where the relentless grid, towering skyscrapers, and frenetic urban life met the blue sheet of Lake Michi-gan, but also the circumstance in Denver, with the Rocky Mountain peaks providing a backdrop for the "Queen City of the Plains"; in Salt Lake City, where the Wasatch Mountains loomed over the "Mormon Metropolis"; and in San Francisco, where the density of buildings and street life clashed with a hilly topography, a sparkling bay, and a vast ocean. The sublime became urban.[12]

The railroad journey westward provided tourists with a taste of the sublime, prior to what would become a greater clash between nature and technology in western cities. The transcontinental railroad itself was a prominent representative of the sublime for nineteenth-century tourists, not merely for its power and strength but also for its right-of-way, which demonstrated the construction and engineering challenges that were overcome in difficult terrain. Some tourists noted the sublime directly in their narratives: as the Central Pacific twisted its way through the Sierra Nevada Mountains in the 1870s, for example, American traveler Benjamin F. Taylor expressed "awe, admiration, and sublimity" at the collision of nature and the machine in the treacherous landscape. Despite "ravines that sink away to China like a man falling in a nightmare," he wrote confidently that the "train pursues its assured way like a comet."[13] The sublime was most effective if one ultimately awoke from those sinking nightmares. Terror and fear were considered characteristics of the sublime, but one wished only for so many of them.

Mining offered a similar prospect, and the occasional tourist did veer from the conventional path of travel to explore the western mining landscape in remote locations. This included visiting gold, silver, and mercury mines, quartz-crushing mills, tunnels, and water flumes in towns such as Leadville, Cripple Creek, Central City, Black Hawk, and Georgetown in Colorado, Virginia City in Nevada, and New Almaden in California.[14] Active mining landscapes in the nineteenth-century West were not necessarily scenic attractions, however, and visiting a mine could be dangerous. Although railroads offered special excursions to visit some of the most active mines and mining towns, there were few amenities to accommodate tourists. To some degree, this brought tourists closer to the sublime.

Western cities featured more comforts to shield tourists from danger, dirt, and difficulty, but guidebooks, parks, and comfortable hotels never could protect visitors completely. Besides, several tourists desired to follow the process of mineral extraction in the wilderness to the finished product, so they fanned out to the urban edges and visited factories, lumber yards, stockyards, smelters, mints, and mills of all sorts. Such operations captivated tourists with their precision and exactitude but occasionally overwhelmed them with their speed, extent, and repetition. As early as 1870, Denver was still a small town with fewer than five thousand people when Walt Whitman marveled at the new smelters erected on the city's edge—"the biggest and most improv'd ones, for the precious metals, in the world." He noted their ability to transform raw minerals into gold coins, and pointed out the "long rows of vats, pans, cover'd by bubbling-boiling water, and fill'd with pure silver, four or five inches thick, many thousand dollars worth in a pan."[15] Thomson McElrath, traveling with journalists in the winter of 1893, found nothing in Salt Lake City so intriguing as the "spectacle" of flames shooting from pipes leading from natural gas wells outside the city. These were even more spectacular to McElrath because his party did not visit the wells until dark.[16] Evidence of landscape trans-formation was everywhere in the mineral-rich American West: in the wilderness, at the urban edge, and deep inside the rapidly expanding cities.

That western cities struck tourists as sublime also coheres with a triumphant narrative associating technological ingenuity with Ameri-can achievement and growth—and one that was physically apparent as tourists crossed the American continent on the railroad. For travelers attempting to gauge American progress, the ability for machines to conquer the western terrain not only demonstrated the ability to har-ness and control the natural environment but also a technical know-how necessary to establish and sustain developments in America's newly annexed territories. Many tourists read the otherwise violent clashes between technology and nature as indicative of America's abil-ity to transform the landscape for societal benefit, binding otherwise disparate citizens into a more cohesive democracy. Understood this way, the intersections between technology and nature could appear harmonious—even beautiful—to those who encountered them.[17] They also helped to make manifest destiny visible on the land, and they brought jobs, wealth, and prosperity. Most tourists cared not a whit about environmental destruction. After all, the transformation of the natural landscape through machine technology helped make western cities possible. And it facilitated tourism.

But it also brought pollution, noise, competition, ethnic strife, dis-crimination, and anonymity to the urban West, transforming otherwise pastoral landscapes into complex, seething metropolises.[18] Western cities startled and surprised those who expected a more rational, orderly intersection of mechanization and nature in the urban environment, and the effects of landscape transformation—from factory smoke to building construction—often were less aesthetically pleasing within dense urban conditions than they might have been as isolated examples in the wilderness. The contemporary conditions of western cities shook tourists from the comfort zone of the Pullman sleeper car and the pervasive depiction of the region as a natural paradise dotted by garden-like cities. Reality could be confusing.

NEARLY TERRIFIC, TUMULTUOUS CITIES

It also could be unsettling, particularly in Chicago—a city that offered travelers a multitude of contrasting sensations and extremes that upended their traditional frames of reference. A number of writers could not find adequate vocabulary to describe the city, resorting instead to hyperbole and exaggeration in an attempt to capture its essence.[19] In many cases, visitors found no essence. For Phil Robinson, stopping in Chicago from England in the mid-1880s, Chicago—the "central wonder of the States!"—seemed "nearly *terrific*," but its "real significance" was "almost appalling." He was continually shocked at the contrasts of the city, especially the penchant for municipal authorities to champion grand boulevards while neglecting Chicago's streets and sidewalks—littered as they were, Robinson noted, with orange peels and banana skins.[20]

Yet the inability to capture Chicago in words began even before tourists set foot in the city. As rail travelers arrived, more than a few mentioned a pallor of darkness and gloom hovering over a skyline marked by massive factories and smoke. This was not the Chicago of the bird's-eye view, with its tidy grid and efficient order. This was the worm's-eye view from ground level: disorganized, jumbled, and decidedly unpicturesque—a sharp contrast from the rural landscape through which tourists had traversed prior to arrival. Martindale C. Ward visited Chicago at the time of the world's fair, arriving in the morning and noting a "host of factories, workshops, and smoke" that reminded him of "London at its worst," while his compatriot Robert Anderton Naylor declared that the railroad approach was simply "dangerous" on account of the numerous at-grade crossings.[21] French visitor L. de Cotton characterized the moment of arrival as "painful" compared to the relative calmness of the landscape passed along his journey from the East Coast. "I felt an instinctive need to glance behind," he wrote, "and something cold pressed my heart. Oh! What an awful city!"[22] Most tourists still found the arrival by rail exhilarating, if disheartening—the contrast between the hinterland and the city left an indelible imprint.

Chicago-bound tourists likely would have known about the railroad's crucial role for the city's growth; by 1869, Chicago was the undisputed rail leader with more stations and transfer points than any city in the nation, and the tourist literature boldly proclaimed its prominence in this regard.[23] The dominance of rail was everywhere visible in late nineteenth-century Chicago. Tracks and rail yards clustered together on the outskirts of the business district bringing goods and people to the rising city; the passenger terminals occupied large sites closer to center of town; and some of the grandest hotels were owned and operated by rail companies. By 1882, cable cars had begun to replace horse cars and omnibuses as the principal mode of intra-urban transportation, and their tracks stretched throughout downtown and beyond. Electric streetcars followed in 1890, and the elevated train opened its first line between 12th Street and Jackson Park, the site of the World's Columbian Exposition, in 1892.[24]

Since most late nineteenth-century travelers arrived by rail, the railroad terminals themselves were tourists' first physical encounters with Chicago. The city was an important hub: several long-distance trains began and ended in the city, connecting Chicago to all corners of the continent. But all travelers had to alight, whether or not they were continuing on a transcontinental journey. To catch another train, they had to walk or hire carriages to take them to a different station in another area of town, thus bringing them into the busy Chicago streets.[25] For a preview of the urban environment, tourists need not have left the stations. They remarked on the complexity of the rail yards, the dizzying array of railway stations and connections, the masses of people moving every which way, and porters and hacks shouting their services to potential customers. For the vast majority of tourists who came from the East, such multisensory experiences marked their initial exposure to the American West.

For sheer noise and commotion, the conclusion of the lengthy western-bound transcontinental railroad journey in Oakland and the ferry trip across the bay to San Francisco competed with the Chicago arrival sequence.[26] Guidebooks sold Oakland as a "city of homes" and one of San Francisco's "suburban retreats," yet only those tourists who made a separate trip to Oakland discovered whatever pastoral attributes that city possessed. Most tourists, however, never set foot beyond the railroad right-of-way, encountering Oakland purely as a transfer point from railroad to ferry. From the train windows, tourists encountered a disheveled industrial corridor crowded with tracks and signals before they arrived at the combination railway and ferry depot at the Oakland Mole. They exited the train and transferred to enormous passenger ferries designed to carry them across the bay to San Francisco, which they shared with local traffic and commuters. The palatial size of the ferries impressed many tourists, but they found their noise, the "continuously ringing" bell, and the local crowds distressing.[27] Contrasts and confusion, again, offered the dominant impression.

The view *from* the ferry approaching the reputedly beautiful city of San Francisco was not much better. Gazing toward the city, E. R. Hendrix complained of "heavy mists" and "dismal fog" hanging over the irregular hills in a late 1870s fall or winter, failing to give San Francisco a "prepossessing appearance." Following a transoceanic trip, sailing through the Golden Gate did not offer the visitor a warmer welcome. New Zealand–based traveler W. T. Locke Travers noted that the picturesque appearance of the city on its hills vanished as his ship approached. Along the waterfront, all Travers saw were the "extensive warehouses, wharf-sheds and other unsightly buildings, which mask any general view of the city."[28] For many travelers, arriving in San Francisco was disappointing.

The situation was further complicated as tourists stepped ashore at San Francisco's ferry building. There, clusters of wagons, horse cars, streetcars, cable cars, and hotel runners thrust themselves upon disembarking, and unsuspecting, travelers, for local hotel entrepreneurs suspected that many tourists would arrive without prearranged lodging.[29] Hotels thus employed "hawkers" or "touters" to lure tourists into waiting carriages; their drivers prepared to transport visitors to particular accommodations should their services be desired. Those services were notoriously competitive. "As soon as the doors open and the public surges toward the exit, there is a hellish din that could give a nervous person an attack," wrote Russian physician Nicholas Russel during his 1891 California trip. "Like a flock of vultures, this mob throws itself on its victims and literally tears apart the indecisive people, fighting over them among each other."[30] The tourist literature did not prepare visitors for the San Francisco arrival process. Yet that process, emerging directly from the commerce and rampant economic competition of the modern city, made an indelible mark. Nineteenth-century travelers reserved some of their most descriptive prose for these experiences.

In many cases, it was not a confusing process so much as a miserable one—exacerbated by the fact that it marked the last stretch of the transcontinental journey for so many travelers. Mary Rhodes Carbutt, in the late 1880s, was first kept nearly an hour at the Oakland terminus because of a delay in transferring the luggage from the train to the ferry. Later, she was deposited on a "tumble-down, dirty platform" in front of the ferry building, after which she moved through "shabby wooden buildings amongst a crowd of screaming, hustling hotel-touters, who knocked us down and trampled upon us and tore us to pieces."[31] The swarms of people at the ferry building marked an immediate contrast with the city's promotion as a tranquil pleasure resort, and this situation persisted throughout the late nineteenth century. When Scottish travelers William Robertson and W. F. Robertson arrived at the San Francisco dock as early as 1869, shortly after the completion of the transcontinental railroad yet before the completion of the ferry building, they described a "drove of hyenas in the shape of hotel touters, who yelled at the unfortunate passengers as they landed in a most demonical manner." The Scots claimed to have been "assailed" by "a perfect Babel of voices" and their "baggage seized by dozens of these pestilential fellows."[32]

This level of activity decreased only slightly as tourists moved into the streets of western cities from the ports, ferry terminals, or railroad depots. On the streets, tourists encountered the vitality that accompanied everyday urban life in the late nineteenth-century American West. The speed and rattle of street transportation created much of this activity, which, in the late nineteenth century, included carriages, omnibuses, horse cars, streetcars, and, in San Francisco and Chicago, cable cars—an array of transportation options available just steps from the arrival terminals, and about which travelers typically remarked even if they spent little time in western cities. Guidebooks did not always include the cable cars among San Francisco's principal nineteenth-century attractions, yet some tourists sought out the cars moving up and down the hills on a continuously moving cable beneath the streets. They commented on their efficiency, but, in some cases, tourists noted their fear of this new mode of public transport. British visitor W. Henry Barneby found the "endless rope" cars to be "quite a feature" of the city in the early 1880s, explaining that they "ascend and descend a series of hills in the most charmingly quiet manner, without any noise or shaking."[33] Mary Rhodes Carbutt understood the value of cable cars in San Francisco's precipitous topography, but felt "less charmed with them" overall. Far from enjoying a pleasant ride, she could only envision the potential for catastrophe as she rode "in a car that dashed like lightning down an incline much too steep for horse cars." She knew that the "slightest mistake" on the part of drivers approaching at right angles "would dash the two cars into each other."[34] The cable cars were not the tourist attraction they would become in the twentieth century.

Streetcars also traversed the late nineteenth-century streets of San Francisco—British tourist W. G. Marshall claimed to have counted thirty-eight of them at one time crowding the "handsomely built (but villainously paved)" Market Street—and they competed with cable cars, carriages, wagons, and pedestrians.[35] They, too, met with mixed visitor reactions. During an 1875 summer visit, John Reynolds found comfort in the stream of streetcars that passed his temporary lodgings, about a mile and a half from the center of town. In a letter to his mother, he wrote that he felt "decidedly lonesome," but "in the midst of the sights and sounds of the busy city, street cars pass the house every 10 minutes. . . . I never saw as many street cars almost every main street has them and always full too—this is surely a very busy city."[36] Street transportation in San Francisco did not necessarily comfort Susie Clark on her personally conducted Raymond and Whitcomb cross-country tour in 1890, but they colored her impressions of the city as a spirited, yet "tumultuous," and "wide-awake" place. If one was to look out of a hotel window in the middle of the night, she explained, one would see "stores open, houses brilliantly lighted, cable cars with alarm bells whizzing by, merry strollers whistling under our window, strains of distant music in the air, and the same features of activity that belong to daylight."[37] Tourists could not agree about whether street transportation provided efficiency, reassurance, or fear, but it did provide a somewhat unexpected level of activity in a city heavily advertised for its bucolic charm and natural splendor.

Transportation did not drive this activity; it facilitated an already thriving commercial culture that dominated late nineteenth-century western cities. This was the case already by 1869 in San Francisco, when Harvey Rice visited and wrote that the "business streets, from morning till night, are crowded with passing drays, and men stepping on each other's heels, and jostling elbows at every angle, as if life were at stake."[38] In the late 1870s, British visitor Alfred Falk considered San Francisco's streets "fine" and "handsome" but noted that the traffic is "very great" which reminded him, in this respect, of parts of London.[39] For Mary Wills, touring San Francisco in the late 1880s, everyone seemed to be "in a hurry," and Henry Lucy, in 1885, found San Franciscans so caught up in the pursuit of wealth that they were "too busy even to drive with great regularity through the park out to the beach."[40] The activity was overhead as much as it was on the ground and underfoot: James Aitken, walking out of the Occidental Hotel in 1881, credited his Scottish heritage for requiring him to check the skies for potentially inclement weather. Yet he only noticed the extensive number of telegraph wires that facilitated business in the upstart city. To Aitken, it seemed as if a "large net" had been thrown over the city, as wires crossed each other "in every conceivable direction."[41]

Except for elite European travelers, who considered the pursuit of wealth in America indicative of a lack of refinement, most tourists spent less time criticizing the often frenetic urban activity on moral grounds and more time caught up in the activity itself. Thomas Dewar, a British traveler who visited Chicago at the time of the world's fair, chastised his fellow Brits for their inability to fully grasp the life of the American city. "The folks who in our country would try and make out a decent weekly salary by denouncing such things," he wrote, "are either bundled on one side in the frantic rush, or lose the power of speech; or else they get excited, and join themselves in the mad helter-skelter race after the 'almighty dollar.'"[42]

Rush hour itself provided a heavy dose of this "helter-skelter race," and many tourists quickly found themselves immersed in it. Samuel Smiles's son encountered a lively scene in the San Francisco streets in 1871, claiming that it had been "a long time" since he had seen "such a bustle of traffic as presented itself in the streets of San Francisco. The whole place seemed to be alive." He recalled "foot passengers" who "jostled each other" and observed that "drays and waggons were rolling about; business men were clustered together in some streets . . . with all the accompaniments of noise, and bustle, and turmoil, of a city full of life and traffic."[43] On an early May morning some twenty years later, Nicholas Russel explained that "San Francisco was already on its feet." He wrote of "stuffed" cable cars running "like chains" along the city streets, and many carts and wagons "delivering milk, vegetables, dry goods, and other groceries." At the height of the rush, he equated the city's noise and traffic with that of New York and London.[44]

Salt Lake City, too, struck visitor Matthew Johnson, perhaps in the late 1880s, with a "very animated" appearance in the afternoons, with the intersection of Main and Temple Streets "thronged with the wealthy and fashionable."[45] Yet the city, so commonly extolled for its tranquility, impeccable planning, and allegedly crystal-clear streams of water running along the street edges for irrigation and drinking, to many visitors resembled a busy, sometimes unpleasant, market town. Trying to relax in front of the Walker House, one anonymous English visitor in 1887 was disturbed by "continually passing" mule-drawn streetcars and produce-laden "country carts," heading to and from the Zion's Cooperative Mercantile Institution and the Tithing House along Main Street.[46] The growing commercial activity, coupled with the city's lack of an adequate water-distribution system or sewer system, also wreaked havoc on the freshwater channels.[47] For many tourists, those channels failed to live up to expectations. Already by the early 1870s, Welsh visitor Henry Alworth Merewether claimed that the "grandeur of these natural aqueducts had been exaggerated." Rather than clear streams, he noted water "flowing dirtily along."[48] They had not much improved when Iza Duffus Hardy visited Salt Lake City in the early 1880s. Hardy felt deceived by the promotion of the water channels as "beautiful bubbling Tennysonian brooks wherein little fishes frolicked." Instead, they "did not come up to our anticipations. One of the party, I regret to say, in her disappointment termed them 'gutters.'"[49]

Urban encounters sometimes left tourists with confused impressions of Salt Lake City. Edward Pierrepont, who offered mostly positive impressions of the city during an 1883 visit, nonetheless found it necessary to add that at night the city "is by no means free from the vices of other cities of its size."[50] Morris Phillips visited in 1891 and found Salt Lake City crowded because of a Mormon conference and complained of packed hotels with an insufficient number of waiters. His hotel experiences undoubtedly contributed to his impression of the city as a whole. "Salt Lake," he wrote, "must be miserable as a place of residence. In wet weather the mud in the streets is from six inches to two feet deep, and in dry weather the dust is intolerable."[51] Numerous nineteenth-century travelers complained about Salt Lake City weather; depending upon the season in which they arrived, it was either a complaint about the intolerable dust and brutal heat, or exasperation at too much snow or mud.[52]

Denver's reputation for a healthy climate and well-laid-out streets, meanwhile, did not consistently translate into orderly behavior or repose. For a city whose late nineteenth-century economic well-being relied so heavily upon the plentiful, yet volatile, yields of nearby mines, anything transporting money provided a potential target. Daniel Pidgeon, during his early 1880s visit, stood nearby while two men attempted to "attack" a tram car on Larimer Street and make off with its cash box, while the train conductor fired shots from his revolver. Underscoring the apparent regularity of such disorder in the Denver streets, Pidgeon found only a mention of the incident in the next day's newspaper—but no analysis.[53] Many visitors parroted the promotional rhetoric about Denver's refinement by the late 1880s, but Henry Lucy made a point of adding that just three days prior to his arrival a "gentleman" was accosted in the "broad and pleasant streets."[54] Julian Ralph, traveling around the country in the early 1890s, noted how the "night side" of Denver—with its smoke and expectoration-filled gambling "hells" populated by "rough men"—reminded him that, despite the city's many admirable characteristics, it still featured the uncouth tendencies of a dense mining community.[55] Perhaps Denver's tranquility was exaggerated.

Enough visitors provided accounts of Denver's business, commotion, and vice to reveal that the city—advanced as it may have been beyond its early years as a frontier settlement—was not the splendid, peaceful place that promotional sources indicated. Although the city's nineteenth-century popularity was due to its proximity to the Rocky Mountains, the minerals extracted from those mountains returned to the Denver streets in the form of mining speculation and crowds of single men—enough for William Bickham, a journalist from Dayton, Ohio, to note in 1879 that visitors would immediately understand Denver's economic role. "The commercial streets," he wrote, "are thronged with traders from the mountains, with miners and cattle drivers."[56] W. G. Marshall, visiting from England in 1879 on a return trip from San Francisco, also noted that in Denver everybody seemed "on the move, as if everybody had something to do."[57] Denver sustained this energy through the next decade, as well. Osmun Johnson, visiting in

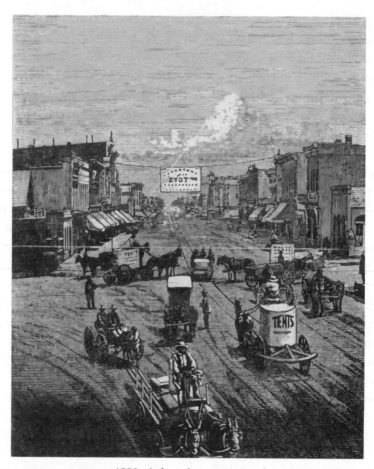

LARIMER STREET, DENVER, IN 1880. At least three carriages advertising "tents" reveal Denver's crucial role as an outfitter for mining camps in the Rocky Mountains, while the hanging sign over Larimer Street, viewed backward, apparently directs potential customers to a toy store. Denver was far more active—and considerably more ordinary—than its usual characterization as a pleasant stopover near the mountains might suggest. (Source: W. G. Marshall, *Through America*, p. 403. Courtesy of Internet Archive, http://archive.org/details/americathroughor00marsrich.)

1887, noted the increasing numbers of rail lines converging in the city and surmised that this would create a situation that would "help swell the traffic of an already busy city."[58] Denver, similar to other western cities, was a complicated place full of the complexities and contradictions of modern life.

But no western city exhibited those contradictions as much as Chicago. Tourists never could reconcile the promotion of the city as an efficient, orderly place with the fast-paced, sometimes chaotic, realities on the ground. German tourist Nicolaus Mohr, passing briefly through Chicago in 1883, noted big, wide streets, surging with life and excitement, lined by "powerful" buildings. But he also found the streets entirely lacking in comfort, with blackening walls and horrible pavement.[59] Chicago was confusing enough that tourist accounts reveal all sorts of conflicting impressions—sometimes within the same paragraph or sentence. Occasionally, tourists interpreted Chicago's never-ending pace as generative of progress. For example, there were select Europeans who read the city's pace as emblematic of capitalist excess and the demise of civilization, and many 1893 visitors' negative impressions of downtown were accentuated by its contrast to the order and sophistication of the World's Columbian Exposition. But most tourists routinely commented on Chicago's pulse without drawing conclusions about what that pulse might suggest about the city's, or America's, place in world culture.[60]

MOVEMENT, ANXIETY, AND UPHEAVAL

Urban transportation contributed significantly to tourist experiences in Chicago as it did in San Francisco but infrequently as a symbol of efficiency and progress. At times, transportation facilitated tourist views of the city. London-based visitor Harry Jones expected the worst when his train approached Chicago in the mid-1870s, not long after the fire, and a "black cloud hung over the flat land ahead." He found his expectations "far exceeded" when he gazed out toward Lake Michigan and noted "its sea-like horizon, studded with sails and streaked with steamer-smoke." But this visual respite would be short-lived. Once he left the rail station and stepped into the streets of Chicago, an unyielding, mechanistic city had unfolded before an "astonished" Jones: one "with great stone and brick-built houses, six storeys high, roaring streets as broad as Pall Mall, brimful of strong life, crowded with grand plate-glass-windowed shops, and a tide of men pouring along their sides like the endless processions on the pavements in Cheapside."[61] The Great Fire of 1871 seemed not to have slowed down the procession of people in Chicago, as the business district rose again and the tide of men—and women—pouring along the streets only temporarily abated.

At other times, the transportation itself characterized tourist encounters in Chicago. The speed and clatter of Chicago's streetcars created anxiety for New York–based journalist Julian Ralph in 1891, as they did for numerous city residents, who protested the speed limit increase to eight or nine miles per hour—apparently a leading cause of accidents.[62] "They go in trains of two cars each," he wrote of the Chicago cars, whose speed was nearly three miles per hour faster than those in New York City, "and with such a racket of gong-ringing and such a grinding and whir of grip-wheels as to make a modern vestibuled train seem a waste of the opportunities for noise."[63] Where streetcar and cable car lines did not extend, horses and wheeled vehicles did—leaving no Chicago street free from the din of transportation. The traffic created such a racket that office workers occasionally shut their windows to muffle the sounds of horses and carriages rumbling over the granite-block street paving.[64]

The concern over modern transportation and the new, perhaps involuntary, social circumstances that emerged may have created even greater anxiety among nineteenth-century Chicago visitors. The elevated railway worried Robert Anderton Naylor in 1893 during the exposition, not only because he imagined the horrible catastrophe that would result "should the brake fail to slacken speed, or the driver forget to apply it" but also because of an unfortunate personal encounter with hordes of people boarding the train from the world's fair platform. The on-the-ground city transport also instilled fear. Mme Léon Grandin found no comfort in the lack of regulations at street crossings in the city, where carriages and people moved about at will with no concern for moving streetcars. "Only a bell on the front of the locomotive," she wrote, "warned the pedestrians to take care."[65] And the streetcar route terrified Italian author and playwright Giuseppe Giacosa, who also visited Chicago during the time of the fair and rode the line that plunged under the Chicago River via the LaSalle Street tunnel. As the train approached the river, it slowly dropped into the tunnel—for Giacosa, equivalent to a descent into the underworld. As darkness enveloped the train, Giacosa quickly became afraid of the "diverse and unknown men" in the pitch-black car. He could not help but worry about the situation that might result should the other end of the tunnel be closed.[66]

In the tourist imagination, the pace of transportation mirrored the pulse of humanity in western city streets; that is, until the crowds grew so large that any movement at all became difficult. The rush of activity in the Chicago Loop did at times result in a crush of humanity, especially during rush hour when everything grinded to a halt and the otherwise wide streets became "uncomfortably crowded."[67] The corner of State Street and Madison Street gained notoriety for its daily crowds, and tourists commented upon the jams of vehicles and pedestrians they discovered there. Standing at that corner in 1876, Ephraim Turland expressed anxiety with "all the hurry and rushing" as well as "all the noise and din" created by "all the business energy and excitement"—a substantial transformation for what was once a "silent" landscape.[68] Henry Lucy did not notice unusually large crowds at State and Madison; for him, the city was crowded everywhere. "In whatever part of the city one walks," he wrote, "he is sure to be jostled by a crowd moving at high pressure."[69] These crowds were problematic for tourists on any number of levels. For English writer Morley Roberts, searching for work and shelter when he arrived alone in Chicago in the late 1880s, the "great city" even made him feel lonely and desolate. "I walked the crowded streets for hours," he wrote, "hardly knowing in what direction I was going nor in what direction I should go."[70]

The visual noise of the city provided little consolation—or direction—in Chicago or elsewhere in the urban West. Signs and advertising on buildings, awnings, storefronts, leaflets, and billboards confronted tourists at nearly every turn—even, at times, along the pavement. Henry Lucy could not avert his eyes from the sidewalk advertisements when he visited Chicago in the 1880s, although he found them feeble attempts to conceal the poor condition of the city's infrastructure. He noted the "ditches" that masked themselves as streets and "along which the vehicles flounder, and through which men and women pick their perilous way." Many sidewalks remained well above street level, for the city, even by the 1880s, had not yet raised all the streets to meet those buildings that were hoisted to accommodate a new gravity-fed wastewater system intended to reduce water-borne diseases. Thus, at intersections, Lucy noted that many pedestrians must awkwardly "leap off the pavement into the road" but acknowledged that "the advertiser sees his opportunity, and all along the edge of the pavement advertisements are pasted, and are very conveniently seen from the roadway."[71] The safety and well-being of the pedestrian did not consume planners' attention in nineteenth-century Chicago, and unimproved streets below the sidewalk grade with advertisements plastered everywhere complicated Chicago's characterization as a "garden city." Yet negotiating urban infrastructure comprised a substantial part of the city's late nineteenth-century everyday life. Visitors could not be entirely shielded from the messiness of this process.

San Francisco demonstrated a similar emphasis on large-scale advertising, without the additional hassle of variances in the street grade. John W. Boddam-Whetham, visiting in the early 1870s, explained that if "advertising is necessary to success in trade, San Francisco ought to be a most flourishing city. Houses, windows, and dead walls teem with advertisements, and even the pavements are made use of as places of puffing."[72] Tourist Mary Blake noticed this too in the early 1880s, remarking on the "enormous size of everything," which included the "sidewalk advertisements."[73] And no amount of advertising could conceal the condition of San Francisco's infrastructure, either; when John Leng visited in 1876, he claimed—"without exception"—that the city's streets were the worst paved in the country. He implored the city supervisors to start a "revolution" to improve them.[74]

Advertising dominated urban America in the nineteenth century, and the West was not unlike elsewhere in the country in this respect.[75] No urban visitor could have been oblivious to advertising, no matter how often cities promoted themselves as refined environments countering the crass commercialism of the marketplace. Indeed, so prevalent was advertising in San Francisco that W. G. Marshall found it necessary to alert readers to specific marketing slogans he remembered from his journey. San Francisco, for Marshall, was simply one of the worst offenders for what he considered to be a "nuisance" of which the entire country was "simply white-washed."[76] While booster material happily announced western cities' commercial prowess, they quite naturally steered away from its less aesthetically pleasing effects. This made their appearance as such all the more striking to visitors—even if it meant they bore much in common with their urban brethren in the older and more established eastern seaboard.

Following the completion of the transcontinental railroad and the surge in western settlement that followed in the 1870s, cities of the American West regularly necessitated infrastructural changes, from streets, sidewalks, and streetcar tracks to telegraph wires, electric lighting, and the reconfiguration of water systems to accommodate expanding populations. Most travelers understood these changes as necessary, but they nonetheless required physical upheaval that conflicted with the polished look of western cities discussed in the tourist literature or depicted in bird's-eye views. By the 1890s, western-bound tourists seemed to take many of these changes for granted, but in the 1870s and 1880s, a number of travelers devoted passages or entire sections of their memoirs to them. "In my progress through the streets," noted Samuel Smiles's son, when he walked Chicago's avenues in 1870, "I came upon two huge steam cranes at work, hoisting up stuff from a great depth below."[77] Smiles's son seemed less concerned with the "stuff" than with an everyday Chicago consistently building, rebuilding, and moving.

In some cases, western cities *did* move. In Chicago, the street-raising operation that followed the installation of the sewer system required private property owners to lift and, in some cases, transport preexisting houses to higher ground. Although most of the major changes to the city's infrastructure were completed by the 1860s, many visitors witnessed the transference of entire houses from one part of the city to the other, providing fodder for some colorful accounts. "Everything must keep moving in Chicago," wrote John W. Boddam-Whetham of his early 1870s visit. "The houses are continually shifting their position, and a moving building is no longer an uncommon sight. We were greatly amused one day by suddenly coming upon a good-sized three-storied house, standing dejectedly in the middle of the street, as if it did not know where to settle down. The next day, and for two or three following ones, we were continually meeting this same house, and always at different places." Daniel Pidgeon, in the early 1880s, remarked that one might discover houses moving through the streets "with chimneys smoking, and perhaps even the piano going." He claimed to have witnessed two such houses during his early 1880s visit, and considered nothing else he saw in Chicago to be so illustrative of the city's pulse.[78]

Travelers also reported on houses in transit elsewhere in the rapidly changing urban West. When visiting San Francisco in the late 1870s, Harry Jones explained that the city was "thriving" and spreading "like fire," noting that the "moving of whole houses down the streets from one part of the city to another" marked a "curious" feature of this "shifting" growth.[79] House moving seemed less curious to T. S. Hudson in the early 1880s, for the "calling of house-remover is a very general one in San Francisco."[80] For Hudson, the physical transformation of the urban environment signaled everyday life in the late nineteenth-century urban American West.

The ground moved, too—at least during earthquakes. While not a daily occurrence, natural disasters, including earthquakes and fires, shaped the late nineteenth-century western urban environment. Most tourists did not actually experience an earthquake (as Henry Lucy claimed to have done while asleep in the Palace Hotel in October in the mid-1880s), but tourists regularly experienced their aftermath. Major earthquakes or fires, after all, necessitated substantial alterations to the urban fabric, and the rebuilding process routinely turned streets

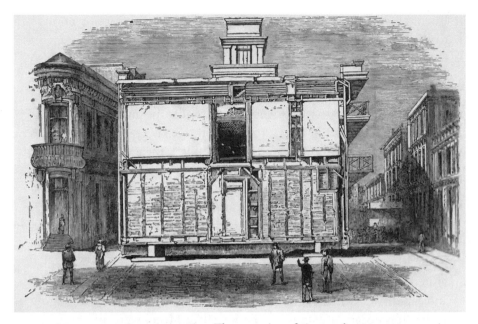

MOVING A HOUSE IN SAN FRANCISCO. The expansion of nineteenth-century western cities frequently necessitated the removal of structures in the path of development. Although
this disruptive process was not promoted in guidebooks, tourists never ceased to discuss
this phenomenon when they came across it. British tourist Harry Jones found it interesting enough during his San Francisco visit that he included this image of a moving
house—possibly cut apart to facilitate easier transport—in his traveler narrative. (Source:
Harry Jones, *To San Francisco and Back*, p. 87. Courtesy of Internet Archive, http://archive
.org/details/franciscotosanba00jonerich.)

into construction zones and disrupted the everyday life of the metropolis. They also affected traveler readings of the city; rarely did tourist
descriptions of urban reconstruction match the positive light in which
booster publications attempted to spin the recovery process.

In the wake of the 1871 Chicago fire, many tourists sought out the
path of destruction; a number of journalists, in particular, descended
upon the city specifically to gauge the city's recovery process and
evaluate its preparedness in the event of future disaster. In the early
1870s, tourists could visit the fire's lingering effects and the remains of
edifices, even if the buildings themselves had long ceased to smolder.

Encountering the ruins of the Chicago fire was important enough to the Russian Grand Duke of Alexis during his winter 1871–72 visit that he hired a city official to fend off large crowds of well-wishers so he could tour the burned area without distraction.[81] Tourists visiting anytime after 1873 arrived too late to see anything more than vestiges of the fire's destruction, but even this proved to be an attraction.

Unfortunately for boosters, tourists did not always read those ruins in relative comparison to a quickly rebuilt Chicago.[82] Hotels were among the building types to receive prompt attention after the fire, and much of the attention focused upon the major hotels, such as the Grand Pacific Hotel, the Palmer House, and the Tremont House, each of which attempted to rebuild more substantially than before.[83] Not all travelers could afford to stay in the larger hotels, however, and not all hotels were immediately ready for occupation anyway. George Medley visited Chicago in the fall of 1873 and noted the "marvelous energy and rapidity" with which the city was being rebuilt, but his lodging at the "temporary premises" of the Sherman Hotel were anything but. There, guests were required to sleep four to a room—and apparently sometimes two to a bed. Concerned about having to share a bed, Medley left rather earlier than he intended.[84]

J. F. Campbell traveled to Chicago from England in the summer of 1874 and set out immediately to "see the ruins" upon arrival in the city. He did write of "grand" shops and wide streets and expressed satisfaction with his lodging at the Tremont House. But to Campbell the city, for the most part, seemed a "careless" and disorganized place with "Germans selling lager beer from sheds" and a landscape "strewed with glass and a tangle of pipes, of all kinds, sorts, and sizes, and yet fresh fires."[85] To Charles E. Lewis, another British traveler, who visited Chicago in 1875 following a trip to New York, Philadelphia, and Washington, D.C., the city bore traces both of the fire and the subsequent financial panic of 1873, which hampered the recovery efforts. Lewis's account, however, revealed nothing remarkable about Chicago's appearance, despite booster claims about its rapid and stunning recovery. He noted that city officials had enacted more stringent municipal codes intended to prevent further conflagrations but stated that "in all its rugged deformity" the city still featured reminders of the fire in "the ruins of some house or building not yet re-erected" along some of the main thoroughfares.[86] Chicago—especially after the fire—was a disconcerting, haphazard place.

Despite an increased number of fire stations and the general claims of firefighting effectiveness in promotional sources, visitors to western cities remained wary of disaster. As far as Martindale C. Ward was concerned, Chicago's firefighters did an admirable job, but they had no choice. The city, he wrote, "provides about three large fires every night." He claimed to have witnessed two of them.[87] In certain instances, a heavy firefighting presence and the alleged promise of security had the reverse effect. To Robert Louis Stevenson, visiting San Francisco in the 1870s before settling further to the north on a more permanent basis, the city's geological makeup and the ubiquity of its fire-signal boxes suggested the terrifying potential and reality of earthquakes and fires. To Stevenson, San Francisco seemed "beleaguered with alarms" and the sound of the bell "is soon familiar to the ear." He explained that landfill characterized much of the city near the bay and that an earthquake "might drown the business quarters in an hour." He imagined the fear of earthquakes beginning to wear on any San Francisco resident.[88] The fear was real: when *New York Tribune* journalist Albert D. Richardson visited San Francisco shortly after the completion of the transcontinental railroad in 1869, discussion in the Lick House lobby, where he stayed, focused upon the "frightfulness and havoc" caused by an earthquake some eight months earlier. As he surveyed the city, Richardson noted the "wrecks of buildings not yet cleared away." The worst of the destruction occurred on landfill.[89]

Booster materials shied from discussing the threat of disaster or encouraging tourists to visit sites of catastrophe—unless the reconstruction process was such that they could point to significant progress. Promotional sources were far more likely to focus on newly completed buildings and working factories as indicative of any city's determination to move beyond the scars of its troubled past, not to dwell on those characteristics that made western cities notorious in the public imagination. This was especially the case for Salt Lake City, where city leaders eagerly wished to deflect long-standing public criticism regarding Mormons' purportedly blasphemous religious practices by demonstrating that the city was every bit as progressive as cities elsewhere.

To encourage investment, stimulate the local economy, provide convenient shipments of agricultural and mining products, and attract tourists who would—he hoped—report favorably on the city, by 1870 Mormon president Brigham Young had convinced the Utah Central Railroad to build a branch line to Salt Lake City from the new transcontinental depot in Ogden. The city's burgeoning mining industry, which had emerged in 1863 with the extraction of gold, silver, copper, lead, and zinc from nearby Bingham Canyon, did receive a boost. First, there was the extension of a rail line from the city to the canyon in 1873, and soon ore was being shipped directly from the mine to smelters for refinement. This spurred the construction of smelters in and around Salt Lake City itself—one of which, the Germania Smelting and Refining Works in Sandy, just eight miles south of the city, became a part of a tourist circuit promoted by Brigham Young himself.[90] These smelters were soon accompanied by woolen factories, sawmills, grist mills, tanneries, breweries, and foundries.

By the mid-1870s, one local magazine editor confidently characterized Salt Lake City primarily as "a manufacturing community"; and by 1889, a souvenir book noted merchants handling the "great cereal and mineral products of the Territory." Manufacturing and commerce had apparently become so central to everyday life in Salt Lake City that in 1890, a guidebook, distributed by the Denver and Rio Grande and Rio Grande Western Railroads, claimed that Salt Lake City was "destined to be the next great commercial center in the westward march of empire."[91] To provide evidence of this production, promotional materials encouraged tourists to visit breweries, factories, and the Deseret Woolen Mills.[92] Yet the development of industries in Salt Lake City had only a minimal effect on tourism. What mattered most was the building of the rail link bringing tourists to the city. Tourist encounters with industry only marred the overall vision that Salt Lake City marketed to the wider world. It became much less of a beautiful, organized place in a spectacular natural setting.

Of course, cities promoted specific industries to demonstrate the kind of manufacturing precision that would cast the urban environment in a positive and progressive light. Those tourists who visited the industrial areas of the urban American West to inspect the engines driving the urbanization of the alleged frontier—docks, waterworks, grain elevators, lumber yards, stockyards, and mills—occasionally received personal escorts, permitting industry officials to ensure that visitors would encounter potentially messy sites as fine examples of efficiency. During the Russian Grand Duke of Alexis's 1871 trip to Denver following his visit to Chicago, city leaders accompanied the duke to the Holly Water Works to demonstrate "the powerful machinery employed to force water into the city" and to the Denver Ale Company on the city's western edge. "The whole operation of brewing was most minutely shown and described to the Grand Duke," stated the official report on his visit, "and before leaving he refreshed himself with a draught or two of some of the choicest productions of the establishment."[93] But few tourists experienced sites of urban production as completely smooth, mechanized operations; only a handful received the kind of grand treatment enjoyed by the grand duke.

Chicago's principal industrial operations were held up as exemplars of progress as well, but they often elicited puzzling responses from visitors. Chicago's grain elevators, in particular, had been long highlighted as attractions for their abilities to sort, weigh, measure, and store vast quantities of grain and corn without much human effort, as well as their capacities for receiving and unloading goods via railway or ship. Along with the lumber district and the meat-processing plants, many of the grain elevators located away from the business district escaped the 1871 Chicago fire largely unharmed, and their continuing operations helped fuel the city's economic recovery.[94] The grain elevators, together with the Chicago Water Tower, also permitted the best views of the city and lake before skyscraper construction began in the 1880s, and they continued to be promoted as tourist attractions until well into the 1890s.[95] As early as 1869, William Robertson and W. F. Robertson described the "interesting" method by which the grain was transferred from railcars to elevators, and Henry H. Vivian, visiting from Britain in 1877, noted that the mechanical precision of the "lofty warehouses" made the grain elevators among the "sights" of Chicago.[96]

The loftiness and efficiency of grain elevators often vanished upon closer inspection, however. Tourists frequently described plain, hulking structures lining the banks of the dirty Chicago River filled day and night with a staggering number of lake-bound vessels negotiating their way under and around a series of bridges. Daniel Pidgeon acknowledged that the facilities for handling grain may be "unequalled in the world" and that no tourist could claim to have "seen Chicago" without a grain elevator visit, but he characterized the one he visited as little more than "a very ugly wooden structure."[97] Some visitors interpreted the speed and noise of the elevator operation as indicative of the *inefficiency* of the process: with so much grain arriving in nineteenth-century Chicago from the hinterland, the supply of existing grain elevators struggled to keep up with demand. One 1880s visitor learned that a few weeks before his arrival, all twenty-five elevators had quickly filled with corn and "another was built in a hurry, being completed within two weeks, and big enough to hold 400,000 bushels."[98]

The operations of Chicago's revamped system of freshwater distribution also drew tourist attention when it was still a novelty in the late 1860s and 1870s. Ellis Sylvester Chesbrough's system, which began construction in 1865, was unquestionably a complex feat of engineering. It included an intake crib in Lake Michigan that captured fresh water two miles offshore, tunnels some sixty feet below the lake surface bringing water into the city, and a new pumping station and water tower standpipe on flat ground. Although no boats regularly brought visitors to the water crib, to underscore the city's sophistication as it adjusted to its rising nineteenth-century population, guidebooks flooded readers with statistics regarding the length, pumping capacity, and power of the system and invited tourists to visit the pumping station and standpipe.[99] Willard Glazier acknowledged that the waterworks ranked among the city's "titanic achievements" and stood awed before the "immense" city standpipe that regulated water pressure. Across the street, in 1876 Charles E. Lewis noted the "great water works," which were "striking" and which "form one

CHICAGO RIVER, LOOKING WEST FROM THE WELLS STREET BRIDGE. To most tourists, the grain elevators lining the banks of the Chicago River appeared as hulking monoliths regardless of their usually efficient operations. A tourist standing at the Wells Street Bridge in the late nineteenth century would have found it difficult to ignore their context: a confusing morass of boats, smoke, and buildings, all seemingly resistant to order. The "Air Line" grain elevator (far right) stands approximately where the Merchandise Mart is today. (Source: Louis Schick, *Chicago and Its Environs*.)

of the principal sights of the city," while Ephraim Turland felt "awe-struck" by the "mighty" and "enormous" engines and wheels of the water works. "What power is there!," he exclaimed.[100] James Aitken, as late as 1881, was fascinated enough with the system that his published account included a five-page pullout supplement with a woodcut depicting sectional views of the crib, tunnels, pumping station, shafts, machine shops, and water tower—along with the LaSalle Street passenger tunnel with carriages moving north and south against a skyline backdrop mixed with churches, trees, factories, smokestacks, grain elevators, bridges, and ships. Although Aitken described the workings of the "gigantic and marvelous" system, the illustrations spoke as much to his interest in the system as his words.[101]

Yet English traveler J. F. Campbell felt less awed when he toured Chicago as part of an around-the-world journey in 1876. He visited the water tower, climbed the stairs, and noted only a "curious and strange view" from a tower that "rocked in the strong westerly breeze."[102] Oscar Wilde, the Irish playwright and poet, interpreted the waterworks as suggestive of America's obsession with immensity and technological prowess during his 1882 visit. Wilde remarked that "the symmetrical motion of the great wheels is the most beautifully rhythmic thing I have ever seen" but found overbearing "the inordinate size of everything. The country," he added, "seems to bully one into a belief in its power by its impressive bigness."[103]

OPPRESSION AND SLAUGHTER

For tourists, Chicago was the biggest bully of them all—if not in the entire country, then certainly in the American West. Its size, crowds, noise, smells, grime, and smoke proved overwhelming for many visitors, who often found themselves teetering on the precipice of Hell. Ostensibly in town for the fair, during a one-week visit in 1893 Giuseppe Giacosa claimed never to have seen anything but "darkness" in Chicago, while recalling "smoke, clouds, dirt and an extraordinary number of sad and grieved persons." He found Chicago oppressive rather than impressive; a city where the "senses of the visitor" are barraged with "all the customs and all the laws of life." Whatever those "laws of life" might have been, Giacosa wanted nothing to do with them. French visitor L. de Cotton was equally disgusted when he visited in 1886, likening the city to a huge factory where the red brick of the buildings "blackens rapidly under the effect of the smoke," and Parisian Mme Léon Grandin complained bitterly of the scorching heat in August 1892 and, while staying at the Everett Hotel, of the constant noise of trains that disturbed her sleep.[104]

While European tourists with a critical eye toward upstart, profit-driven America quickly found fault with Chicago, visitors of all backgrounds also found the city rather foreboding—no matter the efforts at refinement in the city center. "The business part of the city is very handsome," proclaimed Anne Mathilda Bright in a letter she wrote from Chicago in 1869, "but still it lacks that [smart] clean look that

Philadelphia has. I can hardly get used to [the] sooty appearance of every thing."[105] By the late 1880s, the factories and mechanical processes that made western cities tick—no longer a novelty—generated fewer responses from tourists, as tourists sharpened their critique upon the detrimental effects of industry. *Harper's Magazine* editor Charles Dudley Warner, visiting Chicago in 1889, recoiled at the factories that "vomit dense clouds of bituminous coal smoke, which settle in a black mass . . . so that one can scarcely see across the streets in a damp day, and the huge buildings loom up in the black sky in ghostly dimness."[106] For Viennese-born traveler Ernst von Hesse-Wartegg, Chicago emerged as "a true Hell" when he visited during an early 1890s winter and the city's prevailing winds failed to blow the smells and smoke away.[107]

Wintertime typically presented Chicago at its worst. Any semblance of the "Garden City" disappeared altogether under a cloud of smoke and a perennially bitter cold, the weather exacerbating an already intolerable situation of crowds and racket in Chicago's streets. Determined to reach the "semi-tropics" of the Far West during a late 1880s winter, East Coast–based American Henry Brainard Kent received a blast of the city's reality when he stepped onto an open streetcar, "called by citizens 'the refrigerator,'" that carried him a half mile and made "life no longer worth living."[108] Thomson P. McElrath arrived with a traveling party of journalists in January 1893 but could make out almost nothing in the city. He complained of the wind and a storm that kept the town in a "nebulous condition that effectually concealed it from view."[109] Winter conditions in Chicago often continued into the spring, compelling Morris Phillips, visiting in 1891, to provide an honest account of the view from atop the Auditorium Building in his *Abroad and at Home: Practical Hints for Tourists*. He claimed that one could obtain an "extended view" of the city from the top floors of the tower but only "when the fog from the lake is not dense, and when the chimneys of the town are not emitting black smoke." He advised travelers to visit the tower on a clear Sunday, "when many of the factory fires are extinguished."[110] Smoke, darkness, oppression, brutal heat, a deep freeze, and Hell—many late nineteenth-century Chicago visitors reacted to the city with repulsion or disgust.

Tourists expressed their distaste with several aspects of Chicago. The pollution and smoke proved most distasteful, but the city could—and did—intimidate visitors with its overwhelming scale, extent, and repetition.[111] For many, Chicago seemed infinite, endless, relentless. British journalist and novelist Rudyard Kipling wrote that Chicago's streets seemed "long and flat and without end." He expressed horror while peering "down interminable vistas flanked with nine, ten, and fifteen-storied houses, and crowded with men and women."[112] An anonymous foreign visitor in 1887 chose to explore the residential districts further from the city center, hinting at the repressive monotony of everyday life by noting that "long rows of dwelling houses are running out for miles over the prairie."[113]

While repetition, smoke, and climatic extremes troubled many Chicago tourists, few traveler experiences in the late nineteenth-century American West contrasted so markedly with their promotion than visits to the Union Stock Yards. About five miles southwest of downtown, the enormous 355-acre stockyards opened in late 1865 and, by the late nineteenth century, had become instrumental to Chicago's economic stability and prowess. Already by 1871, the yards received nearly three million hogs and cattle—a figure that more than doubled by 1892 as the emergence of ice-cooled packing plants, the refrigerated railroad car, the canning process, and assembly-line machinery allowed workers to process meat year-round.[114] The stockyards soon employed tens of thousands of workers, and its volume of animals and the mechanization of its slaughtering process stretched its fame well beyond American shores. Sir Henry Lepel Griffin, a British traveler visiting America in the 1880s, claimed that only Niagara Falls surpassed the "Chicago slaughter-yards" in preeminence, while Henry Lucy acknowledged that "nine out of any ten visitors who pass through Chicago" find imperative a visit to the stockyards.[115] "To see Chicago and not see the Union Stock Yards," declared a guidebook to the fair produced by the Pennsylvania Railroad, "is to see the play of 'Hamlet' with *Hamlet* left out."[116] Personal tour guides were regularly available to let tourists witness the ham-manufacturing process—as well as that of sausage, bacon, pork, and beef.

Promotional materials enticed tourists to the stockyards by high-lighting the mechanistic efficiency of the assembly-line process. A. N. Marquis and Company's 1893 *Ready Reference Guide to Chicago and the World's Columbian Exposition* promised that tourists "will see animals slaughtered by means of labor-saving appliances." Those "appliances," the reference guide declared, offered "rapidity, dexterity and the least suffering to the animal, each detail being attended to by an expert having a single duty to perform." Readers were assured that "all is done in the most systematic and cleanly manner."[117] Quick to emphasize the productivity of the slaughterhouse operations, promotional sources transformed the flesh and blood of animals into statistics by listing the numbers of sheep, hogs, and cattle received and slaughtered per year. Meanwhile, they boasted of the large number of employees, the enormity of the grounds, and the stockyards' ability to generate revenue, thus transforming the killing of animals into a rational and calculated operation feeding the economic engine of the city and indicative of Chicago's overall efficiency, organization, and progress.[118]

Based upon their recollections of the stockyards, however, several tourists might have preferred to avoid a visit altogether. Visitors often described what promotional sources would not: the brutality of animal slaughter, the squeals of the animals, and the smells of blood and death. Although some tourist accounts glossed over the killing process and echoed the impersonal booster rhetoric about assembly line efficiency, others offered vivid accounts of animal butchery and cruelty. Their accounts demonstrated that the process was neither efficient nor impersonal.

English tourist Harry Scott Barton spent two full pages detailing his 1881 visit to the Union Stock Yards, which included a graphic description of the pig slaughter at the Armour Packing Plant. Barton recoiled at the odor, claiming never to have seen "such a ghastly sight as those wretched brutes hanging by their legs squealing and wriggling, with the blood pouring out of their throats." Later, he observed the slaughter of cattle, watching as officials led pairs of "poor beasts" up an inclined plane into narrow stalls. When about fifteen of these stalls had filled, he explained, "a man comes with a rifle which he holds a few inches off the beast's head and then fires, death is generally instantaneous, though sometimes he doesn't take a good shot and while the poor beast is kicking he polishes it off with another."[119]

Reactions were similar no matter the national origin of the visitor. French journalist Léon Paul Blouet chose only to note, in 1881, that the "process is somewhat sickening, and I will not enter into any more details."[120] Five years later, French traveler Georges J. Joyaux offered more details, describing a less-than-orderly killing process and adding that when one leaves the place, "he feels like being a vegetarian for the rest of his life." Regarding the slaughter of pigs, Joyaux recalled how the pig "convulses" after being stabbed in the throat while another worker unhooked the "agonizing animal" and dropped it into a pool of boiling water. He also explained that workers fired "carelessly" at the cattle, often necessitating the use of a mallet to break open the heads of those that were still alive. "I was spared nothing," Joyaux wrote, "though I would have liked to leave the place."[121] Many tourists did.

Although journalist George Augustus Sala originally sent dispatches of his mid-1880s American tour to the newspapers, when he compiled those accounts for his massive, two-volume *America Revisited*, he concluded the entire two-volume set with a particularly chilling account of the stockyards—a set of experiences that left him "uncomfortable for full eighteen months." Sala refused to watch the killing of the animals, but he heard their cries and could not easily forget the "spectacle of long trains of freight cars receiving their bellowing and squealing freight."[122] Three illustrations depicting the plight of the animals commissioned for *America Revisited* accompanied his text. Although Sala's book was intended for mass readership, he did not describe the stockyards in a fashion that highlighted their productivity or illuminated their supposed tourist appeal. His compassion for the animals superseded any impulse he might have had to underscore the efficiency of the operations. To a large degree, they characterized his impression of the city.

Few late nineteenth-century cities, in the American West or elsewhere, elicited such visceral reactions as did Chicago. But tourists hardly remained neutral about Denver, Salt Lake City, or San Francisco, and their remarks often stood in an uneasy relationship with those cities' presentation as idyllic blends of nature and culture. Did tourists perceive late nineteenth-century western cities as pastoral, orderly environments, where vibrant urban activity moved in tune with the rhythms of nature? Or as dusty, smoky, noisy, immoral, seething, terrifying, competitive places, wrestling with the challenges of explosive urban growth? Or, perhaps, as some combination of the two, where expectations of orderly grandeur met with the unexpected, sometimes sublime, realities of late nineteenth-century city life? There is no easy answer to these questions. Taken as a whole, the conflicting tourist accounts reveal the contradictions and confusion of modern, western cities.

CHAPTER 4

Civilization

Architectural Art, Pretense, and Process

"To see the city at its best," announced the 1889 edition of *The "Mormon" Metropolis: An Illustrated Guide to Salt Lake City and Its Environs*, "one must climb to the rock-crowned summit of Ensign Peak." From that elevated vantage point just north of Salt Lake City, the guidebook promised, visitors would be awarded with a spectacular panoramic view, from which they could peer down upon "houses, streets, trees, and green squares."[1] An illustration in that guidebook depicted a traveling party slightly below the peak, gazing upon a verdant urban landscape while majestic snow-capped mountains marked the horizon. Visible in the near distance stood the Mormon Temple and the Mormon Tabernacle—the city's principal markers of urban civilization. This was the "best" of Salt Lake City: lush, tranquil, established, and distinguished. Civilized.

The most prominent physical indicators of civilization in nineteenth-century Salt Lake City were the buildings set within the Temple Square, which included the Assembly Hall along with the temple and tabernacle. The buildings also comprised the principal setting of religious assembly for the Latter-Day Saints and, as such, made the square "the chief attraction to strangers from abroad."[2] No guidebook to the city or region failed to discuss them. Promotional materials regularly championed the temple for its length and height, its six ornamental spires,

VIEW OF SALT LAKE CITY. Promotional materials routinely encouraged Salt Lake City visitors to ascend to elevated vantage points for views of the city and surroundings. In this 1889 engraving, an individual in the foreground points south toward the city's principal markers of civilization—the Mormon Temple and Mormon Tabernacle (upper right). Yet the temple remained three years from completion in 1889, and the spires were not yet in place. Tourists who investigated Salt Lake City's architecture more closely often did not find it as civilized as urban boosters hoped they would. (Source: *The "Mormon" Metropolis*, 1889, p. 13. Courtesy of Internet Archive, http://archive.org/details/mormonmetropolis00rey.)

and its granite construction; the Assembly Hall for its Gothic exterior, twenty-two spires, spacious assembly room, and interior frescoes; and the massive, oval-shaped tabernacle for its grand organ, splendid acoustics, and America's largest self-supporting roof.[3] For prospective tourists leafing through guidebooks, in word and image the buildings in Salt Lake City's Temple Square emerged as civilized, stately works of art.

Civilization faded upon closer inspection. Approaching the city by train in the early 1880s, British visitor Daniel Pidgeon marveled at the detached white houses and individual gardens and found the tabernacle and rising temple "enveloped in an atmosphere of indescribable purity." But as he moved closer to the buildings, Pidgeon's initial impression shifted. The canopy of trees and orchards that, from afar, obscured the built environment now revealed ordinary houses made of adobe, while the city's more monumental edifices suggested to Pidgeon that in Salt Lake City, "architectural taste is conspicuously absent." He considered the temple's design "hardly worthy of a carpenter" and thought the tabernacle "a hideous oval building, crowned with a kind of shingle dish-cover." It was a "fact," Pidgeon declared, "that cultured taste, whether in architecture or decoration, does not exist among the Mormons."

What had happened? As with so many Salt Lake City visitors in the late nineteenth century, Pidgeon's architectural analysis did not rely exclusively on structure, materials, or aesthetics. He also attended a religious service and his opinions of the built environment ultimately became intertwined with his cultural encounters—in this case, with a percentage of Salt Lake City's Mormon population that attended the service. He found the faces of the Mormons even more "commonplace" than he anticipated, while noting that the "American type was not to be seen anywhere, but the people looked like, what they indeed are, the dregs of Britain and Scandinavia."[4] Pidgeon's negative assessment of Salt Lake City's built environment may have been shaped by his opinion of the Mormon belief system or practices and formulated long before his arrival. Even so, factors extending beyond the buildings themselves generated his opinion of the built environment. For visitors to the late nineteenth-century American West, civilization would not be measured by bricks and mortar alone.

Urban boosters had a different vision: for them, civilization meant architectural order, efficiency, and grandeur, and, from their perspective, buildings could—and should—convey these principles without human presence or interference. Promotional materials regularly described building dimensions, materials, and ornament (the proverbial bricks and mortar) but rarely encouraged tourists to penetrate beyond the walls or to visit buildings in active use. This way, there would be less of a chance for unexpected encounters with the urban population—encounters that might otherwise negatively color tourist assessments of the built environment (and thus tourist assessments of the city). They did not wish for late nineteenth-century visitors to come away with a sense of western cities as complicated or fragmented places. To the arbiters of urban taste (businessmen, land owners, rail-road magnates, publishers, and religious leaders) architecture in the American West had to appear organized, tasteful, and traditional; it needed to suggest an inexorable march towards civilization. Or it had to establish that civilization outright.

Religious edifices were but one building type boosters championed as notable examples of civilization. Office buildings, hotels, banks, governmental buildings, and private residences of urban elites also could represent it, and guidebooks depicted many of them in ways suggesting their contribution to urban order and refinement. They paid little attention to the ordinary and less-permanent landscape of the late nineteenth-century city. Boosters, elites, and publishers of tourist literature in the West understood that any sense of a disorderly urban environment could be tempered in the tourist imagination by accentuating those buildings whose designs recalled an architectural past— or at least by featuring those that superficially resembled buildings and styles of Europe and the East Coast through permanent materials, ornament, and imposing scale.[5] For the rapidly growing cities of the late nineteenth-century American West, highlighting such buildings announced, indirectly, that the cities had come of age.[6] At the same time, cities wished to appear progressive and up-to-date, and the tourist literature boasted of buildings with "modern" conveniences (such as elevators, lighting, and intercom systems) as well as "modern" construction (such as iron or steel)—but never to the degree that modernity offered the dominant architectural impression, and so long as such conveniences and construction were ultimately cloaked in traditional materials or shrouded in ornamental detail.[7]

The appearance of the western city mattered both to boosters and tourists, although boosters commonly focused on the exterior appearance of prominent building types, while tourists considered the whole of the built environment—interiors, exteriors, and context as well as commercial, civic, or residential functions. For tourists, this meant that the ordinary vernacular built environment (including mass-produced

row houses and small, seemingly insubstantial, wooden commercial storefronts) mattered as much to their encounters as did high-
style, monumental architecture. Tourists typically subsumed the built
environment within the urban cultural landscape, as well. Buildings
remained active participants in active cities: they stood cheek by jowl
with other buildings and, at street level, joined a motley population of
tenants, politicians, workers, traders, visitors, vagrants, or casual passersby. Whether or not the everyday urban West appealed to visitors,
tourist accounts nonetheless complicated elite attempts to attain civilization solely through the design of grandeur and monumentality.

Standards of evaluation differed, as well. Boosters and elites boasted
of architectural façades that featured traditional materials or designs
that recalled European buildings, but visitors occasionally interpreted
exterior detail as mere appliqué—or did not find the attempts to recall
European examples particularly intriguing. English tourist Julius Medley, who traveled in the United States in 1873 but only got as far as
Chicago, found little of architectural interest in America; the "cities
and public buildings being mere copies of those in Europe."[8] George
Augustus Sala, visiting San Francisco from London in 1885, mocked
the city's efforts to recall historical styles; instead, he invented new stylistic categories to describe the built environment: "ultra-Byzantine,"
"exaggerated Italian-Gothic," and "turgid Renaissance." In Sala's opinion, San Francisco's efforts to achieve civilization through design suggested an American tendency to strive for refinement by any means
necessary—even if this meant proclaiming that materials were brought
in from elsewhere. There was "no country," Sala wrote, where architecture and taste were at "so low an ebb" as in America.[9]

A handful of perceptive tourists also understood the promotion of
architecture as mere pretense; a number of buildings, they thought,
hid their insubstantiality through particular materials or paint. In 1869
British traveler M. Philips Price noted, "All the Western cities . . . are
built to a great extent of wood. The large stores and public buildings,
of course, are of stone, but most of the private residences are wooden,
and are sometimes faced with stone."[10] When New Yorker Edward
Pierrepont visited San Francisco in 1883, he called it the "mushroom

city" because buildings that seemed to be constructed of white marble, sandstone, or granite upon first glance were, in reality, painted wood. Phil Robinson was less kind. Visiting San Francisco around the same time as Pierrepont, he explained not only that the buildings were wooden, but that they were "sham." Robinson was offended by façades attached to frames that made the buildings look "finer" than they were. To Robinson, such façades also seemed suggestive of San Francisco's transitory character—these were not homes to *live* in but houses in which to briefly pass the time.[11] Throughout the late nineteenth century, tourists frequently considered the built environment of the urban American West to be temporary, poorly constructed, imitative, or downright crude, suggesting little about civilization beyond its impossibility.

Tourists also penetrated beyond the façades to discover urban life inside—and found it much as it occurred on the streets. In the interiors of well-promoted western buildings (such as hotels, railroad depots, theaters, skyscrapers, and merchants' exchanges) tourists encountered rowdy, loud, and seemingly unrefined human behavior that clashed with the impressive exteriors featuring traditional materials and decorative elements that drew upon the western architectural tradition. Such activity belied what often were stately interiors, as well: for major private buildings, developers often hired architects to provide expansive atria with elaborate detail, thereby shielding building occupants from the uncertainties of the streets. But visitor descriptions revealed that urban life flowed unimpeded from outside to inside. This chapter makes evident that tourists rarely interpreted urban buildings as isolated retreats from the city. Instead, they *were* the city. If civilization did exist in the urban West, tourist encounters demonstrated that this civilization—at least where architecture was concerned—would not necessarily cohere with booster concerns about style, décor, or decorum.

REFINEMENT BY DESIGN

At its most inclusive, the notion of civilization—derived from the Latin *civitas*, which means "citizenship"—suggests the "art of living in towns."[12] Throughout nineteenth-century America, civilization held a distinct meaning for urban elites, who had the means and wherewithal to shape urban society. For elites (and urban boosters), civilization meant high culture; to be civilized was to conduct oneself with refinement and gentility. This was the "art" of living in towns. Elites hoped that the towns they crafted, both rhetorically and physically, would bestow particular codes of moral order and behavior upon the residents. In effect, they hoped to inspire lower and middling classes to act in ways befitting a higher class.

Civilization was not so inclusive in the late nineteenth-century American West, however. Not everyone lived in towns, and not all members of the town-dwelling population could be extended the kind of citizenship deemed crucial for the civilization thought appropriate by elite standards. As had been the case throughout the nineteenth century, some urbanites surrendered their chances at citizenship by conducting themselves in ways that ran counter to nineteenth-century notions of urban propriety.[13] Others had little chance of achieving citizenship based upon nationality, ethnicity, race, or class. In these cases, it made no difference whether upstanding behavior could be learned through exposure to unwritten codes of moral refinement and gentility. From an elitist perspective, people of lower classes or non–European American ethnicities could never be true citizens; a collection of them could never constitute urban civilization. It is perhaps for these reasons that promotional materials chose to set aside or minimize discussions of the urban population and presented western cities instead as a collection of architectural objects and high-end institutions.

Civilization also was a distinctively urban notion, for elites did not consider any civilization possible beyond the metropolis. Given these standards, urban civilization could not exist in the countryside or in small towns without cultural institutions or amenities such as parks, museums, or religious buildings, and it could not exist in towns lacking architecture that featured historical styles. Such institutions or amenities existed in European capitals and the large cities of the eastern American seaboard, and elites believed that replicating or transplanting them across oceans or continents could, at least, provide the veneer of civilization for the new western cities—never mind whether the veneer was "sham" or not.[14] Elites concerned themselves less with trying to make civilization "interesting" (as British poet and critic Matthew Arnold considered vital in order for Americans to create a society of beauty, elevation, and distinction) than in boasting of cultural institutions housed in buildings suggesting a civilized existence.[15]

Promotional materials also typically highlighted the city's "leading citizens" and their abodes. These citizens typically were entrepreneurs, who had risen to elite status, and were partly responsible for the establishment of urban institutions—individuals to whom the sponsors of promotional literature thought middle-class tourists might aspire.[16] While a handful of visitors and journalists secured "letters of introduction" permitting them to meet or interview civic leaders and industrialists in their homes or inside otherwise difficult-to-access settings, direct access to the "leading citizens" remained essentially out of reach for most tourists. In this case, architecture served as a noteworthy substitute: guidebooks still could convey elite civilization through engraved illustrations or lofty descriptions of extravagant dwellings, whose architectural detail borrowed from all manner of Victorian styles. Such characterizations implied that visitors, merely by glancing at fanciful residential exteriors in person or in print, might understand how closely western cities approached civilization.[17] Denver tourists inspecting W. A. Barbot's *Souvenir Album of 1891: City of Denver Colo.*, for example, would not discover any written descriptions of the city's residences. Yet illustrations of some of the grander homes, together with owners' names, were sprinkled on pages featuring Denver's monumental public and private buildings.[18] Architecture was one principal method elites wielded to accentuate the civility of western cities, regardless of the cultural and physical urban cacophony that surrounded individual buildings on the streets. As it was, many references to civilization in sources promoting the urban American West related either peripherally, or exclusively, to the built environment.

As a barometer of civilization, late nineteenth-century architecture in the urban West had to conform to particular norms understood not only by elites but also by those in the architectural profession. Similar to painting, sculpture, music, theater, poetry, and literature, architecture was a "fine" art, practiced by "gentlemen" whose classical education provided the requisite training and knowledge to produce appropriate designs. In the late nineteenth century, architects in western Europe and the United States still had to be *men* of ideas—not engineers or builders who worked with their hands. And not women, either: in the nineteenth century, the profession restricted credentials to men.

Architecture's position as a fine art and a civilized profession in America was established in the early nineteenth century, as architects attempted to set themselves apart from the more technical professions by convincing clients that they possessed specialized knowledge unattainable by ordinary builders. Architects claimed to possess "taste" and the unique ability to create works of "architecture" or "art," while builders, carpenters, or engineers only could produce functional, utilitarian structures.[19] Such professional distinctions came to be accepted over the course of the nineteenth century, and given that professionally trained architects more frequently designed buildings of high culture, while developers relegated builders and engineers to housing and industrial works, there also came to be little doubt as to what constituted "architecture" and what did not.

Although guidebooks and souvenir view books occasionally included descriptions and images of railroad sheds, bridges, factories, and other works of engineering and industry, they did so with an eye toward urban economic progress, not their role in the production of urban civilization. Works of engineering and industry were necessary components for the establishment and maintenance of the urban economy, yet to a nineteenth-century elite sensibility they were neither aesthetically pleasing—nor were they architecture. Unless builders or engineers designed industrial buildings with conscious references to the past, the functional landscape did not represent the type of urban civilization that elites wished to convey. There was little question, for example, that San Francisco's U.S. Mint and the Mormon Temple in Salt Lake City could be upheld as "architecture"; there was equally little question that Chicago's grain elevators and Denver's gold smelters could not.

The art and architecture of civilization arrived gradually in the nineteenth-century urban American West, in part because the initial rush to exploit natural resources and accumulate personal wealth placed economic priorities before cultural ones. Early civic leaders focused their initial efforts on improving transportation connections to the outside world, providing adequate internal infrastructure, and establishing local police and fire protection to maintain policy and order. They did not emphasize the bringing of high culture to cities through monumental architecture or the establishment of urban institutions such as art museums or symphony halls. During the rush to urbanization in the 1830s and 1840s in Chicago and in the 1850s in Salt Lake City, Denver, and San Francisco, most buildings lacked much attention to detail and suggested little about architectural tradition. In 1865, the engineer William le Baron Jenney, who later designed a handful of early skyscrapers and parks in Chicago, claimed that in "the West . . . there [is] little knowledge and little desire for Art."[20]

This would change. As western cities became more than temporary settlements, elites increasingly desired to temper the haphazard commercial life of the city with institutions and architecture that, to them, exemplified a more refined version of urban civilization. Architects—as gentlemen and members of elite classes (or striving to be so)—typically catered to elite tastes. They relied on the marketplace to fuel commissions but also desired to mitigate the visibility of the market by hiding the commercial or utilitarian functions of buildings through ornamentation or traditional materials such as stone or brick.[21] Shortly after Chicago's Great Fire of 1871, a number of new masonry buildings featuring cornices and engaged classical columns rose in the city's Loop—in part to signal Chicago's resilience but also to demonstrate refinement in the wake of catastrophe. Visiting Chicago in the late 1870s, Londoner Harry Jones found "a city with great stone and brick-built houses, six-storeys high." Architecture contributed to his feeling that Chicago contained "all the luxuries of civilisation."[22]

References to an architectural past proved an important component in the western drive to produce such luxuries. But this would be a particularly western European past that recalled long-standing traditions in the lineage of architectural history in the western *world*—not just in the history of the American West. The specific past being employed in the American West seemed to matter less than the fact that an identifiable architectural past was recalled; this alone could constitute civilization. Already by the early nineteenth century, the proliferation of architectural pattern books and a gradual tendency towards eclecticism permitted the extraction of historic styles from the political and cultural contexts in which they were originally produced. Any and all Western styles—from the classical to the medieval—could be liberally applied.

Thus, architectural elements, proportions, or decorative touches recalling medieval or classical styles appeared on all manner of building types in the American West. By the late nineteenth century, the Gothic appeared frequently as a specific revival style—though stripped both of its spiritual origins in twelfth-century France and the moral and anticapitalist rhetoric that enveloped its proliferation in early nineteenth-century England. In the late nineteenth-century urban American West, the Greek idiom—which had frequently appeared for buildings of civic and democratic import in early nineteenth-century cities along the eastern seaboard—now graced the façades of churches, banks, and mass-produced housing. References to the architecture of pharaonic Egypt, with the exception of funerary monuments, had lost their strict connection to a culture of death and also could be—and were—employed to suggest connections to architectural tradition, monumentality, and longevity. In the rapidly urbanizing West, architecture needed to convey permanence and stability, even if the consistently volatile economy rendered rather flimsy the apparent monumentality of the city.

THE URBAN LIFE OF BUILDINGS

If civic leaders or architects chose specific styles to convey particular messages about stability for buildings or building types, however, tourists generally were less discriminating. They seemed little concerned with the underlying reasons behind building styles or elements and—if they were even aware that western cities wished to attain higher standards of refinement through architecture—usually left such a discussion off the pages of their narratives. Many tourists simply reacted. For Parisian Mme Léon Grandin, visiting Chicago in 1893, the extent to which developers and architects ornamented the exterior of the city's skyscrapers made little difference. For Grandin, her first look at the gigantic "houses" lining State Street offered no comfort: these were products of a "whimsical architecture" bordering on "frenzy." Perhaps enamored of the stylistic regularity of the Paris cityscape facilitated by Georges-Eugène Haussmann's reconstruction of the French capital in the mid-nineteenth century, Grandin found Chicago's buildings rather distasteful by comparison. They were, she wrote, a "mélange of all styles and periods; some are like chateau-forts, with crenellated [sic] towers, others flanked with turrets like sentry boxes, some constructed as to defy, it seems, the laws of equilibrium, inclined to the right and left like the leaning tower of Pisa."[23] There was no civilization in Grandin's Chicago.

If elaborate building façades did not permit architects and other elites effectively to minimize the rough edges of early, often unstable, urban growth through design, they turned to the refinement of interior spaces—particularly those of large, "semipublic" buildings such as hotels, railroad depots, office buildings, and department stores.[24] Interior design frequently meant the use of particular architectural elements and materials that recalled more traditional forms, but building developers also included amenities, such as restaurants, barber shops, travel agencies, ticket booths, and bootblacks, to make the interiors practical—as well as comfortable—for the visiting public. Occasionally, too, this meant the inclusion of a domesticated natural landscape inside the buildings.

For some of these building types, such as hotels and high-rises, guidebooks promised tourists interior luxury and their florid descriptions seemed almost to implore guests to remain isolated from western cities—even while they lodged, arrived, or shopped in their heart. Tourist literature and advertising boasted of such interior comfort and décor at Chicago's Palmer House and Grand Pacific Hotel, Denver's

Windsor Hotel, and San Francisco's Palace Hotel that they seemed to beg visitors never to leave. Some Chicago buildings attempted to mask their commercial functions with extravagant lobby ornamentation, soaring atria, foliage, and—in the case of Chicago's Masonic Temple and the Grand Northern Hotel—rooftop conservatories doubling as observation platforms. John S. Hittell's 1888 *Guide Book to San Francisco* tried to entice visitors to the city's Lick House hotel, for example, by advertising its large California scenery paintings by Thomas Hill and G. J. Denny.[25] Overall, private developers hoped tourists and clients would escape the unpredictable, everyday world of the western city streets and retreat, if only temporarily, into the domesticated urban wilderness by lingering in the sumptuous interiors of downtown buildings. As privately created venues, developers hoped these lavish interiors would generate profits by encouraging visitors to linger and to partake in the services offered therein.

Urban parks and boulevards offered visitors a similar set of conditions, yet because many of these were publicly funded venues, the desire for profit was less direct. Their manicured grounds, patterns, and trees provided the kind of ordered, refined landscape not immediately apparent elsewhere in the city; they were intended to immerse tourists in the tranquil and civilizing pleasures of the natural environment and provide them with antidotes to urbanity. Yet neither guidebooks nor the desires of powerful elites to shape society through genteel landscapes designed for passive contemplation could convince tourists that the urban West had achieved the levels of refinement that suggested civilization. Within the parks or along boulevards of late nineteenth-century western cities, visitors experienced the more haphazard, and supposedly uncivilized, aspects of the urban built environment as well as unrefined behavior from some of the city inhabitants. Tourists gazed simultaneously upon the natural scenery intended to cultivate refinement and participated in the attractions that more closely resembled the commercial marketplace of everyday urban life.

Although many urban parks existed closer to unsettled areas of western cities or beyond the nineteenth-century municipal boundaries altogether, they also remained connected to the city in important ways that guidebooks did not promote. In addition to remaining conveniently accessible to a diverse population via public transportation, parks also benefited from city services and their presence raised property values for nearby landholders. Furthermore, despite the intention to encourage passivity, contemplation, and refined behavior through picturesque landscape designs, western city parks also featured structures and spaces with entertainment functions, such as conservatories, band shells, and playing fields. Such entertainment venues had a broadly urban character: they permitted large gatherings of people to participate in events that might otherwise take place within the dense urban environment. Those venues infrequently graced the pages of promotional materials, for the motley population attracted to them rarely met the elite standards of civilization.

Tourists neither mistook the manicured city park or landscaped boulevard for the natural environment nor a thoroughly refined urban civilization, for locals regularly used them for recreation and entertainment—and classes intermingled freely. In Chicago, for example, municipal laws may have disallowed advertisements, commercial vehicles, and boisterous conduct in its parks to provide the proper respite from urban life, yet they permitted rapid vehicular movement and class mixing. This allowed certain aspects of everyday metropolitan life to persist.[26] Tourists who desired to "escape" to urban parks frequently discovered that urbanity extended into the manicured natural environment. The visit of Mary Rhodes Carbutt, passing through San Francisco in the late 1880s, offers one example. Hoping to relax in Golden Gate Park, she reported that her traveling party "reached the band stand one Sunday afternoon, and found hundreds of carriages and a number of pedestrians listening to the music." This was distressing enough for Carbutt, but she added in her ironically titled travel narrative, *Five Months Fine Weather in Canada, Western U.S., and Mexico*, that the "fog came pouring up from the ocean before we had been there ten minutes, so we fled."[27]

Even the original Cliff House, perched above the Pacific Ocean on San Francisco's dramatic western edge, never elicited much response as a work of architecture—if it could be seen at all on account of the frequent fog. Even on clear days, tourists typically reserved comment instead for the ocean and what they interpreted as the competitive, near-human behavior of the sea lions who gathered on the rocks just offshore. Tourists visiting in the late 1880s would have encountered the Cliff House being rebuilt anyway, as the powder-laden schooner *Parallel* had smashed and exploded against the coastline in January 1887 and had partially destroyed the building. While noting that the building was in "repairs," John H. C. Church, visiting San Francisco four months after the *Parallel* explosion, considered the explosion and its effect on the seals more worth his attention than anything else he encountered during his Cliff House visit.[28] Civilization was difficult to find in San Francisco.

If civilization *did* exist in western cities, tourists more likely would find it downtown. Examples of monumental architecture stood downtown and—although trolley lines stretched to new subdivisions in the late nineteenth century—most of the nineteenth-century urban population still lived closer to the center. Tourists wishing to be transported via carriage from their plush downtown hotel rooms to parks, gardens, suburbs, or bodies of water on the edges still had to negotiate life in the streets that spilled out from the center. And encountering that life, even from the perspective of a carriage ride, meant that most tourists could not help but understand the buildings lining the streets as something more than passive, isolated objects to be appreciated for their architectural merit.

Chicago, Denver, Salt Lake City, and San Francisco each provided different architectural experiences to the visitor due to the uniqueness of particular buildings, building types, or—in the case of Chicago's skyscrapers—methods of construction, but tourists' impressions of the built environment typically intermingled with the cultural life of the city. Tourists did not often interpret that life as genteel, and it contrasted with the civilized impression that civic leaders hoped monumental architecture and refined landscapes alone would convey. Contrasts themselves characterized many tourist impressions in the urban American West, and the built environment was but one area where those contrasts were illuminated. Tourists noted the vivid differences among building types and functions even within the same geography: between the glitzy monumental buildings and hastily erected structures in the downtown; between the commercial center and the domestic edges; between the world of work and the spaces of leisure.

DIGNITY AND DANGER: CHICAGO AND ITS SKYSCRAPERS

In Chicago, aside from those tourists who visited in 1893 and focused their accounts almost entirely on the World's Columbian Exposition, most visitors gauged civilization from their encounters with the city itself. The exposition, after all, took place eight miles from the downtown Loop and the vast majority of 1893 visitors still arrived in Chicago at rail depots close to downtown and lodged in downtown hotels. Tourists, who might have hoped to be enchanted by the Beaux-Arts architecture and impressed by the baroque splendor of the exposition, found that merely getting there brought them into contact with Chicago's skyscrapers, industries, interstitial spaces, and everyday life. New York visitor and journalist Julian Ralph, similar to millions of tourists in 1893, visited Chicago to see the exposition. But he thought tourists would discover that the "the city itself will make the most surprising presentation," for there was "no other result of human force so wonderful, extravagant, or peculiar."[29] Architecture played an especially forceful role in Ralph's account; like the city itself, the built environment could not be ignored, but it was difficult to interpret as civilized. The city may have appeared to him as a "force," but he could not determine whether that force was wonderful and extravagant—or peculiar.

For more than twenty years, tourists offered similarly equivocating assessments of Chicago's architectural attempts at civilization. The rapidity with which the city rebuilt after the 1871 fire inspired much comment as visitors noted the contrasts between new buildings rising amid piles of rubble and ruins. Not all of their comments were positive. Within a decade after the fire, however, many of these newer buildings were forgotten; they became victims of a booming economy, frenzied speculation, and the rise of much larger, metal-framed towers that brought Chicago international notoriety as the world's first skyscraper city. And notorious it was: the city's skyscrapers evoked awe, wonder, fear, and disgust among the traveling clientele, which disagreed about the appropriateness of their aesthetics and the rapidity of their construction process. Visitors could not agree on a name for the new building type, either, referring to them interchangeably as "houses," "sky-scrapers," "skyscrapers," or "sky-piercers."[30] But there was no debate that by the 1880s, the new high-rise office buildings had become one of Chicago's principal tourist attractions.

Chicago provides something of an unusual case. European city centers typically featured building types of "high" culture, such as theaters and museums, made of traditional materials such as brick, stone, or wood. Monumental buildings of commerce—especially those with metal frames—were largely absent from nineteenth-century European cities. Yet Chicago's promotional literature did not wish to convey the impression of a brawny city displaying its commercial might and engineering acuity. At least not strictly. Instead, it shaped an orderly Chicago of stately and historically referential buildings intended to elevate or defuse the evils of the commercial marketplace. John J. Flinn's 1892 guidebook entitled *Chicago: The Marvelous City of the West* contended that all tourists coming to the metropolis "must acknowledge that this is the best built city in the universe to-day ... [with some of the] grandest achievements of the art to be found on the face of the earth."[31]

To demonstrate these grand achievements, promotional materials highlighted luxury hotels, religious structures, civic buildings, parks, and high-rise office buildings. For the latter, they emphasized façade decoration and sumptuous lobbies rather than steel frames, rapid construction, or commercial functions. They did occasionally celebrate "modern" technological innovations that permitted convenience and comfort for tourists—telephones, elevators, and electric lighting, for example—without allowing those technologies to overwhelm the overall dignified effect. In pictorial guides, captions told of architectural grandeur and, with a few exceptions, concerned themselves with the look, not the function, of buildings.[32] Flinn's guidebook, for example, presented tourists with a sample thirty-day itinerary. On the very first day in the city, he recommended that tourists visit the city hall and courthouse building not only for its central location but also because it was "stately," "striking," and "altogether, the handsomest structure in the city."[33]

Noted architects and engineers also shaped Chicago as a civilized document. Their designs, and occasionally their rhetoric, attempted to elevate the architecture of commerce to high-end art. Louis Sullivan regularly provided his commercial buildings with profuse street-level ornament and wrote of the ability for design to tame commerce and inspire higher values in its viewers, occupants, and visitors. William le Baron Jenney offered enough architectural detail to ensure passers-by that office buildings did not forgo art in favor of commerce. John Wellborn Root—despite being associated with a severe, stripped-down aesthetic—provided ornament desired by clients and wrote that architecture must contain the "conditions of civilization." Daniel Burnham spent much of his career attempting to dignify commerce through design, whether in single buildings or the scale of the city as a whole. Henry Ives Cobb's eclectic, arguably retrogressive, designs for civic and institutional buildings also assisted in providing the city's cultural elite—of which he was one—with the proper buildings and styles thought vital to counteract Chicago's increasing obsession with commerce.[34] Even the engineer Dankmar Adler, who worked with Sullivan on the Auditorium Building, felt strongly that the "Western American" was able to "combine sentiment with thrift" and thus maintain a focus on profit while simultaneously summoning "his higher artistic ideals."[35] Boston-based architect Charles Blackall, visiting Chicago in 1887, understood the representational power of skyscraper design and construction, adding that "if Chicago does not win an equal position in the lines of artistic design, it will not be for lack of hard, persistent effort."[36]

If late nineteenth-century guidebooks and architects considered significant the aesthetics of Chicago skyscrapers, the legacy of the tall office building in the history of architecture and art has revolved around its supposedly frank expression of engineering and technology. Historians have championed Chicago's early skyscrapers and a select group of architects—the so-called Chicago School of Architecture—for their role in determining the course of an American modernism based upon technologically determinant principles. This view, generated by critics such as Montgomery Schuyler in the nineteenth century and codified by scholars such as Lewis Mumford, Henry Russell Hitchcock, Siegfried Giedeon, and Carl Condit in the twentieth, has understood skyscrapers as isolated developments set apart from their social and cultural contexts. By isolating particular examples or focusing on certain characteristics of buildings to fit their narratives, these critics and historians created an evolutionary story that demonstrated gradual moves towards a stripped-down aesthetic that became identifiable with modern architecture.[37]

But their analyses largely ignored the dynamics of urban culture. In more recent years, architectural and urban historians have instead highlighted skyscrapers' contemporary role in the everyday commercial life of late nineteenth-century Chicago.[38] To understand the skyscraper aesthetic, this position pays closer attention to Chicago's economic conditions and architect-client relationships, where façade decoration and interior details become relevant for appeasing tenants and attracting clients or customers, not as fanciful ornament detracting from the structural function of the steel frame. Skyscraper design in Chicago, therefore, can be understood as part of a commercial vernacular emerging from a unique economic, cultural, and geographical situation where demand for office space spurred a frenzy of construction in a concentrated area.[39] Everyone wanted to be downtown, and there was nowhere to go but up.

Architects and developers were not as concerned with structural innovations as they were with meeting demands for quality office space and for providing design effects befitting an established institution. For those clients required to spend the majority of their days inside high-rise offices, architects and developers considered it crucial that they provide building occupants with a comfortable, inviting work environment that counteracted the uncertain life of the streets. If commercial services were to be included, developers requested that architects provide details such as ironwork, atria with glass skylights, and rooftop observatories. Some developers even chose names for their buildings recalling natural features (such as the Monadnock and the Tacoma) to help establish the solidity and security of their enterprise.[40] In these ways, developers and the architects they hired attempted to elevate commerce to a high art form, gracing the cityscape with dignified skyscrapers befitting a civilized society.[41]

A number of elaborate Chicago skyscrapers emerged from this developer-architect relationship, and guidebooks sold the most exquisite of these as items of touristic interest—not only the Auditorium Building and the Masonic Temple, but also the Chamber of Commerce Building and the Rookery. Flinn's comprehensive guidebook to Chicago also highlighted the Home Insurance Building, the Tacoma Building, the Ashland Block, the Monadnock Building, the Manhattan Building, the Leiter Building, the Unity Building, the Columbus Memorial Building, the Board of Trade, the Women's Temple, the Phoenix Building, and the Pullman Building, among others. Promotional materials typically featured skyscrapers as elaborate objects to be celebrated for their size, technological innovations, luxury, and ability to shield the visitor from everyday street life, but the guidebooks were thoroughly unconcerned with whether they suggested moves towards a new design aesthetic.

The Auditorium Building provides an appropriate example, for it probably received more press attention than any single building in nineteenth-century Chicago.[42] The enormous, multipurpose building, completed in 1889 and designed by Adler and Sullivan, included an office building, hotel, observatory, a theater featuring the world's largest stage, seating for four thousand, and gold leaf lobby decoration. Flinn's guidebook proclaimed that the Auditorium Building was the "most famous building on the American continent" and, because of its multipurpose function, mass, and combination of "art, beauty, and utility," represented the "modern" idea of architecture and thus symbolized the city as a whole.[43] Other late nineteenth-century guidebooks offered similar praise. *King's Handbook of the United States* declared the

building among the "high culminating points of American civilization" because of its mix of traditional and modern materials and its
"impressive and commanding facades of Romanesque architecture,"
while the *World's Fair Chicago 1893 Souvenir Illustrated* refused to stop
at the continental borders, proclaiming the building greater "than all
other buildings ever erected by man."[44]

Burnham and Root's Masonic Temple also received its fair share of
acclaim. The temple was intended to function as a high-rise advertisement for the strength, philanthropy, equality, and brotherhood of the
Freemasonry Order of Illinois. The order, which funded the building,
incorporated four floors of exclusive, well-appointed halls and suites
for its members and apparently saw no conflict between its traditional
support for the premodern craftsman (the mason) and a high-tech,
steel-framed building, whose standardized construction signaled the
decline of craft production. Yet the building included numerous spaces
and functions for the public, and upon its 1892 completion, the twenty-
two-story and 302-foot tall skyscraper immediately became the world's
tallest commercial building and a source of considerable civic pride.[45]
Tourist literature described the enormous structure as "stupendous,"
"sumptuous," and one of the finest buildings in the world.[46]

There was more to the Masonic Temple than its height, however.
Its exterior included granite, terra cotta, and gray brick, and an enormous forty-two-foot high Romanesque entrance arch framing the
entrance—its materials and historic forms lending the gravitas of
architectural tradition and helping to establish civilization on a busy
corner of this rapidly expanding modern metropolis. Civilization continued inside, where British interior designers William Henry Burke
and William Pretyman provided some tantalizing ornamental effects.
Whether building-goers descended to a basement-level restaurant or
rose upward to fashionable shops, offices, Masonic halls, or the roof
garden, they did so amid multicolored mosaic floors, alabaster-encased
columns, oak woodwork, a staircase with bronze railings, and walls of
Italian marble stretching to a domed glass canopy. To reach the top
floor, where the conservatory and observation deck were located, tenants or visitors could choose between fourteen different hydraulic pas-

THE AUDITORIUM BUILDING, CHICAGO. Designed by Louis Sullivan and engineered by Dankmar Adler, the Auditorium Building marked the epitome of nineteenth-century architectural civilization. A steel-framed, multipurpose skyscraper featuring a performance space and observation tower (left) and a hotel and offices (right), the building was noted for its dazzling interior decorations, its technological advancements, and its traditional exterior in the Romanesque style. One of John J. Flinn's guidebooks to Chicago declared the Auditorium Building to be the "most famous building on the American continent." (Source: John J. Flinn, *The Standard Guide to Chicago*, p. 50. Courtesy of Internet Archive, http://archive.org/details/standardguidetoc00flin.)

senger elevators, each featuring grilles of decorative iron. Once there, tourists could stroll among floral displays, enjoy the various theatrical or music performances, visit the exhibitions, or enjoy the city and lake views for which the two-thousand-person capacity roof garden became notable. If the weather cooperated, operable windows permitted tourists to experience a fresh-air setting, with steam heat available during the winter.[47] With its array of functions, the temple's interior offered visitors an ideal environment. Lit with some seven thousand electric bulbs to supplement the natural light streaming in from the glass roof, the Masonic Temple protected visitors from the climate, excessive noise, and potential danger of the streets outside.

Guidebooks also featured the thirteen-story Chamber of Commerce Building, designed by Edward Baumann and Harris W. Huehl and completed between 1888 and 1890. Despite the rustication and classical features of the façade, the tourist literature typically focused upon its exquisite interior, which featured a light court with an iron and glass skylight. This was architecture that could inspire civilized behavior: the *World's Fair Chicago 1893 Souvenir Illustrated* explained that visitors would discover "fully three thousand inhabitants—and all of them bright, money-making people, but never too busy to stop and pleasantly answer any inquiry that is properly made."[48] The guidebook acknowledged that the building's twelve interior balconies could contain "enough mortals to make a good sized little city" and subsumed the likely helter-skelter of business competition within the refinement and gentility of the visit: the purported willingness for tenants to stop and provide pleasant answers to the "properly made" questions. Despite "fully three thousand inhabitants" inside the Chamber of Commerce Building, the guidebooks organized and sorted those inhabitants within an overall vision of urban tranquility.

Not all visitors to Chicago found the competitive culture of commerce so tranquil or dignified. Julian Ralph appreciated the skyscrapers' aspirations to architectural art and their technological advances but wrote less graciously about the hour between five thirty and six thirty in the evening, when "the famous tall buildings of the city vomit their inhabitants upon the pavement."[49] With their observatories, shops, and cafeterias serving both locals and visitors, Chicago's privately owned and operated skyscrapers also served a public purpose, for they displayed Chicago's external appearance to the world. But tourists did not necessarily separate them from everyday urban life, even if they enjoyed the interiors and found impressive the technological advancements. For Mable Treseder, visiting Chicago in 1893, William le Baron Jenney's Siegel, Cooper and Company Building sparked interest only because of its array of goods on different levels; she empathized with the elevators, for they had to endure human "confusion" bringing weary shoppers from floor to floor.[50] The human activity in and around

STATE STREET, LOOKING NORTH FROM MADISON AVENUE, CHICAGO. The twenty-two story Masonic Temple, designed by Daniel Burnham and John Wellborn Root and noted for its richly appointed interior, soaring atrium, and top-floor conservatory and observation deck, looms above Chicago's State Street in this 1890s photograph. Tourists focused less on the civilizing details of individual buildings, however, than on the role of architecture within the modern city of the American West, where the fluctuations of commerce and cacophony of modern life were everywhere apparent. With smoke from nearby buildings clouding this view of the Masonic Temple, it appears mysterious—almost menacing. (Source: Louis Schick, *Chicago and Its Environs*, between p. 26 and p. 27. Courtesy of Internet Archive, https://archive.org/details/chicagoitsenviro01schi.)

Chicago's buildings often muddied the pristine architectural view as conveyed by guidebooks—and desired by developers and architects.

What was stately, exquisite, and tranquil in text and image—or in the minds of developers or architects—was not always reflected in tourist experiences. Except as emblematic of progress, rarely did promotional materials discuss the process of construction, and, not surprisingly, no guidebook explained that tourists might come across several buildings in an unfinished state. And yet tourists visiting Chicago's Loop in the late nineteenth century would have encountered the city in a constant state of physical change. This was patently evident in the 1870s, with the feverish pace of rebuilding downtown after the fire of 1871. When Polish traveler Henry Sienkiewicz arrived one evening in 1876, he immediately noticed some streets where newly completed buildings suddenly gave way to "crumbled brick and debris" and others where "scaffolding after scaffolding" stretched as "far as the eye could see." Impressed as Sienkiewicz was with the pace of rebuilding, the telegraph wires stretching every which way, the crowds, and the noise, civilization was difficult for him to behold. With a focus on the "new and contemporary" and a lack of museums and churches, he felt Chicago failed to exhibit that which could "conjure up memories of a historic past."[51] Never mind that many of the new buildings Sienkiewicz likely witnessed that evening were those whose façades harkened back to specific periods of architectural history.

With the introduction of metal frames into Chicago construction by the 1880s, however, tall buildings shot skyward in dramatic profusion and quickly began to displace or overwhelm many of the five or six story buildings that had risen in the wake of the fire. The quick assemblage of steel frames symbolized the active pace of everyday life in America's fastest-growing metropolis, and the frames themselves jostled for attention alongside completed buildings.[52] Tourists had little choice but to encounter skyscraper construction by the 1880s; in the case of British writer William P. Stead the "building of one of these sky-scrapers from the top downwards" was among his first sights in the city.[53] The city as process combined with the sense of elegance to characterize architectural civilization in the tourist imagination.

The construction of tall buildings presented a dangerous prospect, too. Skyscrapers not only rose to dizzying heights (which concerned Thomas Dewar in the early 1890s, when he asked a bystander if it was not dangerous to build so high for fear of collapse and loss of life), but they also rose as sheer vertical masses of steel and masonry against sidewalks and streets in the midst of an already busy nineteenth-century city.[54] City officials hoped to minimize the danger by requiring contractors to provide pedestrians with temporary, wooden planks should skyscraper construction and the storage of materials necessitate the temporary closure of existing sidewalks. Building contractors, however, did not always provide sufficient protection along their edges closest to the street, thus bringing pedestrians—including tourists—within arm's length of streetcars, carriages, and horses. This could make for a harrowing experience.[55]

Encountering construction was one thing; approving of it was another. For those tourists with some understanding of architectural traditions in the Western world, the use of the metal frame conveyed instability, for it defied age-old building practices, where tall buildings featured load-bearing masonry walls. European architects visiting Chicago, in particular, found it difficult to accept the use of the metal frame for facilitating the application of a decorative stone or brick façade; such façades, they contended, were "dishonest" because they concealed the building's structural support system. Employed in such a way, iron or steel threatened the "enduring majesty" of the art of architecture. Although some European tourists acknowledged the obvious time-saving advantages of metal construction and appreciated the attempt by Chicago architects to break away from academic tradition, they still thought Chicago architects sacrificed artistic and architectural taste for speed and efficiency. Debates over metal-framed construction raged in the pages of the contemporary European architectural press.[56] Even *Harper's Weekly*, a New York–based publication, thought that London architects would find Chicago's towers notable only for their "barbarity," for London designers more typically were concerned with comfort, light, and air.[57]

Most tourists, however, were not keen to the concerns of professional designers, and it was a rare tourist who ever mentioned the name of an architect. No matter how much architects attempted to soften the effect of the frame through traditional materials or historic references, some tourists simply found the buildings offensive—or frightening. Morris Phillips, editor of the *New York Home Journal*, recalled an 1891 interaction in the Chicago streets with a noted British actor, who refused to stay in the Auditorium Building's hotel because it appeared "too large, and such a stronghold that it almost reminded me of a prison."[58] Parts of the heavily promoted interior of the Auditorium

Building did not meet with widespread approval, either. Paul de Rousiers, visiting Chicago from France in the early 1890s, considered
"perfect" the elevator hoisting hotel visitors to the dining room but
found the adjoining theater to be "in poor taste" with an "excess of
decoration" and a "strangeness and lack of repose of the architectural
features."[59] And Martindale C. Ward, visiting the city at the time of
the fair, exclaimed that the "very tall houses are anything but pleasing
to look at, making one's neck show symptoms of cracking."[60] For the
most part, tourists reacted viscerally to skyscrapers' appearance, size,
construction process, and human activity and concerned themselves
more with their personal safety than with the building type's place
within architectural history.

Tourists also encountered hotels differently from how they were promoted. In Chicago, Flinn's guidebook championed the Palmer House
in particular as the most exquisite of all places of lodging. Completed
in 1875 and designed by John van Osdel, the Palmer House featured a
gray granite exterior with pediments, a rounded corner, and a Renaissance dome, while the elaborate interior boasted a large dining room
and fittings of the "first order."[61] None of this mattered in the late
1880s to British author Rudyard Kipling, whose opinion of the architecture could not be separated from what he observed within, where
"barbarians" raced frantically about in a space entirely too "gilded and
mirrored," spitting and conversing incessantly about money.[62] Traveler
Cornelia Adair, originally from western New York state, discovered
"gorgeous" rooms and "beautiful" carpets at the Palmer House but
noted that "Western men had an odious habit of spitting on them."[63]
New Yorker Edward Pierrepont, on a trip westward in the early 1880s,
had nothing to say about his lodging at the Palmer House beyond a
description of his room key—to which was attached a six-inch piece
of lead, twisted at right angles. When he entered the billiard room of
the hotel, he reported that his key was mistaken for a six-shooter.[64] For
many tourists, the rough urban life they discovered inside such semi-
public places seemed to replicate the conditions outside—probably
more often than developers, architects, and boosters hoped.

Tourists discovered more "barbarians" inside the Chicago Board of Trade—another of the city's oft-promoted tall buildings. Guidebooks praised the Board of Trade for its granite façade and 322-foot-tall clock tower from which a "grand" view of the city might be obtained, as well as its expansive trading floor with frescoes and a skylight.[65] But to Scottish visitor John Leng, the Board of Trade was of no architectural value whatsoever; instead, he described it as nothing more than "a large room," albeit one "in which great and sometimes enormous transactions are carried on daily in a manner quite unintelligible to the uninitiated."[66] Visitor attention at the Board of Trade focused upon the trading-floor activity; there, tourists watched traders "run and jostle" in what one British visitor in 1887 described as a "typical American life scene of concentrated and boiling energy."[67] Accurate or not, this seemingly chaotic "life scene" spurred some tourists into broad generalizations about the character of Chicago and America, which they read as competitive and shallow. In the elite mind, this was not civilization.

Aside from a smattering of large homes belonging to Chicago's wealthy and powerful, the city's residential districts mostly escaped the attention of boosters. Perhaps this was intentional: much residential construction in late nineteenth-century Chicago proceeded at a rapid pace to keep up with demand, as developers encouraged the speed of construction over architectural ornament and detail. Yet visitors who ventured beyond downtown expressed interest in the city's housing, particularly if they encountered the "balloon frame" process of construction, where workers rapidly nailed together light, standardized wooden studs and joists to create a basic framework. Those tourists who encountered this process interpreted its rapidity as a mirror to the pace of urban life but thought that speed left refinement behind.

Visiting Chicago in the early 1890s, German traveler Julius Lessing wrote that there was "hardly anything more remarkable for us than to see an American house being built."[68] He noted the precision, speed, and standardization of the process: carts laden with wooden boards and nails arriving at the site, the sorting of boards, and the cutting of boards to their proper sizes. Then he observed workers erecting the frame in a couple of hours. But visitors did not describe the aesthetic beauty of this system. Although wooden post-and-beam construction and various methods of reducing labor and hastening the building process had been introduced to American architecture over the centuries, to those visitors more familiar with the use of load-bearing masonry or heavy timbers with mortise-and-tenon joint connections, balloon-frame residential construction did not convey craftsmanship, permanence, or civilization.[69] Daniel Pidgeon found "wretched little wooden houses" and "detached shanties" all over nineteenth-century Chicago—even in "the best parts of town."[70]

THE SHADOW OF SCENERY AND RELIGION: ARCHITECTURAL ENCOUNTERS IN DENVER AND SALT LAKE CITY

Visitors often interpreted architecture in the late nineteenth-century urban American West as insubstantial—or, in the case of Denver, as insignificant. Stories about the rapid growth of western cities received national attention in the press, as did their periodic fires and rebuilding processes. Tourists hardly could have expected the urban West to be characterized solely by permanent buildings. Unsurprisingly, promotional materials ignored the insubstantiality that typically resulted from rapid reconstruction. Denver, which suffered a major fire in 1863, featured far fewer architectural highlights than Chicago, even after the burned area was mostly rebuilt. However, guidebook writers and editors still attempted to accentuate the city's effort to convey refinement and civilization through its built environment. "The buildings which grace the principal streets are principally made of brick," noted Henry T. Williams's *Pacific Tourist* in 1884, "and in general appearance are superior to those of any city west of the Missouri River."[71] It was evidently important to have such a superior appearance.

The 1863 fire, interestingly, proved fortuitous for Denver's desired architectural image: it spurred the adoption of a city ordinance banning the erection of wooden buildings in the business district. In 1876, municipal authorities extended this ordinance to cover the entire city, which, together with the earlier ordinance and the subsequent construction of stone or brick buildings throughout the city, gave Denver a more substantial appearance.[72] Still, boosters only promoted a handful of buildings regularly in the 1870s and 1880s. Among the hotels, these included the stone and cast-iron Windsor Hotel, completed in 1879, and the St. James Hotel, completed in 1881—hotels, according to Colorado promoter Ernest Ingersoll, worthy of gracing the grandest streets in New York or Philadelphia.[73] Another attraction was the Tabor Grand Opera House, also completed in 1881, which Frank S. Woodbury's 1882 *Tourist's Guide Book to Denver* proclaimed as the "pride of Denver" and a Denver and Rio Grande Railroad handbook declared was rivaled only by Garnier's Opera in Paris.[74] By the early 1880s, the University of Denver and the court house had begun construction, and the new Union Depot, an elaborate Gothic Revival structure, neared completion. In 1890, *Colorado Cities and Places* argued that Denver's architecture underscored the city's "wealth, refinement, intelligence, good taste, and good government," and *King's Handbook of the United States*, in 1891–92, thought early Denver settlers would be amazed at the transformation of the city should they return to it—with nothing so surprising as the new fireproof Broadway Theater, with its "stage of steel and terra cotta, the most comfortable and luxurious of furnishings, and an asbestos curtain."[75] It might be more surprising to find reports of the Broadway Theater in late nineteenth-century traveler accounts.

Nonetheless, a handful of tourists echoed the general sentiment of promotional materials: Solomon Mead, during a mid-1880s visit, for example, thought Denver had "fine and substantial" public buildings as well as the "finest residences."[76] But most visitors paid little mind to Denver's architecture; they instead discussed the city's climate and setting. The city, according to J. H. Bates in 1887, "presents few objects to specially interest the visitor."[77] Even when the State Capitol Building and the Brown Palace Hotel were complete by the 1890s, tourists still found little of architectural merit in Denver. James Fullarton Muirhead visited in the 1890s and noted new construction since his previous 1880s visit. But he claimed that the capitol, the Hotel Metropole (where he stayed), and the smelting works did not compare to the view of the Rocky Mountains from within the city.[78] Mary Rhodes Carbutt offered a similar assessment, finding herself relegated to exploring Denver because poor weather hampered her intended sojourn into the Rockies. She could not determine whether the city's built environment made it a "fine" place or whether its architectural appeal arose because of its nearby scenery. "In Denver itself there is little of interest," Carbutt wrote, but the "long range of snow mountains in the distance is very fine."[79] S. M. Lee, visiting in 1885, thought the court house was the "finest" in the country because of its "soft, reddish-brown stone," but she was far more enamored with the site for the future capitol building, the "view from which is unsurpassed."[80] It would seem that if architectural civilization existed in Denver, it was because the natural environment deemed it to be so.

Tourists found more of architectural interest in Salt Lake City; indeed, no visit to the city was complete without a trip to Temple Square to inspect the tabernacle and temple. But curious visitors also explored the streets, blocks, residences, parks, and industrial areas of this western metropolis to better understand Mormon life and customs. With some exceptions, however, it seemed that no matter how impressed tourists might have been with the organization and clarity of the city's built environment, and no matter how close many of the building styles resembled those with which they were familiar in Europe or the eastern seaboard, they could not bring themselves to understand Salt Lake City's architecture as representative of civilization. Most tourists seemed incapable of, or unwilling to, separate the physical environment from their preconceived, steadfast notions of Mormons and Mormonism and looked to confirm their negative preconceptions at nearly every turn.

Tourist literature tried valiantly to deflect attention away from Mormon beliefs, deportment, or appearance. It offered instead what New York journalist Henry Brainard Kent referred to as an "outdoor" Mormonism: an emphasis on "mammoth buildings," "flowing streams," and "floral gardens" but not the "forbidding labyrinths" of the Mormon city.[81] Whether produced by Mormon or non-Mormon companies, guidebooks and souvenir view books sought to promote the city for visitation, settlement, and investment and focused on Salt Lake City's remarkable rise, dramatic setting, planning, and monumental architecture in historical styles—including its local governmental buildings, schools, businesses, industries, hotels, parks, pleasure resorts, and, on some occasions, churches. In this respect, there was little fundamentally different from the presentation of Salt Lake City in text and image than with any other major city in the late nineteenth-century American West.

Yet Salt Lake City *was* fundamentally different. No large city in nineteenth-century America, let alone the American West, projected so dominant an image of any single religion or denomination. The physical manifestation of that image was Temple Square, where the major buildings of Mormon worship and assembly rose amid walled and landscaped surroundings. The tabernacle captured the majority of the tourist attention within the square, for its elongated roof had risen by 1867 and the Mormon hierarchy welcomed the general public inside for speeches, assemblies, and concerts. The temple, however, remained under construction for much of the late nineteenth century, and non-Mormons were not permitted entry upon its completion. Still, several nineteenth-century visitors commented on the lengthy construction process; the temple's unfinished state indicating something to them about Mormon aspirations—as well as failures.

Promotional materials denied that which may have appeared unsettling or less than ideal to the long-distance traveler, however. The new, elongated tabernacle may have been necessary, for the earlier 1850s combination of an adobe building with an adjacent open-sided log structure had neither the capacity to house a growing Mormon population for large assemblies nor could it provide a permanent all-weather setting for those gatherings.[82] The new structure, finished in 1867, alleviated those functional concerns. Architect William Folsom, who designed the building, apparently followed Mormon president Brigham Young's original sketches, which offered a vast space with seating on two levels for approximately ten thousand people. Engineer

Henry Grow, meanwhile, designed an enormous lattice-truss system that could support a roof to cover the gaping interior—an achievement in itself. The shingled roof atop the truss provided the necessary protection from the elements, but its ungainly appearance ensured that guidebooks would not spend much time promoting the building's exterior. Appleton's 1882 guidebook to the United States and Canada explained that the tabernacle was the first object tourists would see upon approaching the city but that it was "destitute of any architectural beauty."[83]

Instead, guidebooks directed tourists' attention towards the tabernacle's interior, which better represented Salt Lake City's aspirations to civilization. They highlighted the more traditional aspects of the building—including the pine columns (painted to resemble marble) supporting the galleries—while stressing the grandiosity of the "immense" organ; the "perfect" acoustics, where "the dropping of pin can be heard from any part"; and the twenty double doors that opened to the outside to allow for convenient ingress and egress. Promotional materials occasionally highlighted the enormous wooden trusses supporting the roof, as well, which permitted the lower seats to remain mostly free from view-obstructing columns.[84] But the tourist literature did not encourage tourists to spend much time contemplating the tabernacle from the outside. The 1887 edition of The "Mormon" Metropolis put it bluntly: "There is nothing very attractive about the outside appearance of the building. . . . To be appreciated it must be viewed from the inside."[85]

The temple, however, had to be appreciated from the outside—if it was to be appreciated by tourists at all. Although Brigham Young laid the cornerstone of the Truman Angell Sr. design in 1853, the temple remained in an unfinished state until 1893, and the vast majority of late nineteenth-century tourists encountered the temple with the walls only partly erected. A brief glance at promotional imagery published during this forty-year period would seem to suggest otherwise, however. Most illustrations depicted the temple as a completed object. Written descriptions highlighted the temple's substantial cost and dimensions; its thick, six-to-eight-foot white granite walls; and its six spires—even if those spires had not yet emerged at the time of publication.[86] To help counter stereotypes about the Mormons, local bookseller James Dwyer printed cards with a picture of the temple on one side and the Mormon articles of faith listed on the other—and handed them to Temple Square visitors on a daily basis.[87] Such portrayals suggested the civility and sophistication of a city that was only decades removed from initial settlement.

Guidebooks occasionally promoted the Assembly Hall (also designed by Angell) within Temple Square as well, but rarely did they mention the Endowment House, which was disassembled in 1889 and had been off-limits to non-Mormons prior to that point. Just beyond Temple Square, guidebooks promoted the built environment of the Mormon leadership, although less for its architecture than for its notable residents. This included the Beehive House (Brigham Young's residence), the Lion House (where ten of Brigham Young's wives reportedly lived), the Gardo House (the official residence of the Mormon president), and the original Eagle Gate, which spanned a street leading to these buildings.

Beyond Mormon religious and domestic architecture, only a handful of buildings received much attention. Among these were the Salt Lake Theater, promoted for its "imposing" and "handsome" exterior "in the Doric style" and an interior "decorated with taste" by the "best artists." A few hotels were promoted as well, including the Walker House, which James Dwyer's 1888 *Album of Salt Lake City, Utah* proudly described as a building with four stories featuring a portico supported by four Corinthian columns.[88] But given the international curiosity about the Mormons, any building types that lacked obvious ties to Mormonism had little chance of becoming prominent Salt Lake City tourist attractions.

Because of tourist fascination with the manners and customs of the Mormons, building types that may have merited little more than a passing glance in other western cities received sustained attention in Salt Lake City. Per usual, however, guidebooks tried to divert attention away from anything that might cast Mormons in a negative light. The Zion's Co-operative Mercantile Institution (ZCMI) provides one prominent example. The building was incorporated in 1868, but its massive headquarters, designed by William Folsom and Obid Taylor, was not constructed until 1876. The ZCMI represented the heart of the nineteenth-century Mormon economic engine, as it encouraged trade and exchange within the greater Mormon domain. Already by the late nineteenth century this included nearly the whole of Utah, much of southern Idaho, and portions of Wyoming, Nevada, and California. While ZCMI buildings existed in other Mormon cities, when Folsom and Taylor's three-story, 318-foot-long building was completed in Salt Lake City in 1876, it was by far the largest ZCMI in the world and featured one of the first cast-iron façades in the American West.[89] A handful of sources tried to raise the ZCMI to the level of architectural civilization, focusing less on the building's function or its materials than on its elegantly composed façade. With its Corinthian colonnades, Doric pilasters, large pediment, and tripartite façade division, the building's design lodged it firmly within a long-standing classical architectural tradition and helped temper its commercial function and modern materials.

Some tourists remained content with gazing at the exterior of the Mormon domain as the tourist literature hoped: marveling at the hotels as well as the orderly houses with their manicured gardens, the regularity and width of the streets, and the clear streams of water running alongside those streets. But they did not penetrate much further to gain a sense of Mormon practices and traditions. Kansas-based visitor A. H. McClintock, in 1875, thought tourists would be surprised to discover that—from a bird's-eye view, anyway—Salt Lake City did not match the negative portrayal of Mormons in the popular press; it was not a "flat, dull, filthy, broken-down, monotonous, poverty stricken, accursed, alkali-looking place, the fitting, forlorn abode of a hopeless Providence punished people." At the Walker House, McClintock found close ties to a more familiar civilization: the hotel's "Philadelphia" brick front, its "Brussels" carpeted halls, and its mahogany furniture and finishings reminded him of the Lindell Hotel in St. Louis.[90] British writer and tourist Iza Duffus Hardy stayed at the Walker, too, in the early 1880s and reported that the city's high-quality built environment was matched by the refined manners of the hotel attendants. "Is this Paris or New York we wonder? Have we taken the wrong train," she asked, "or is this really Salt Lake City?"[91]

Most tourists knew exactly where they were. Visiting the Mormon Tabernacle, in particular, suggested to them that there was something distinctly odd about Salt Lake City. Tourists almost universally ridiculed the building—an impression often accentuated by the content of the sermon or event taking place inside, no matter how civil the behavior of the audience. The jokes about the exterior, meanwhile, were legion: "sea turtle," "fish-kettle," "soup kettle," and a "large, oblong bag pudding" were some of the many likenesses to which visitors compared it.[92] The tabernacle's interior received its fair share of abuse, as well. Many visitors cared not a whit about the engineering skill required to carry the enormous roof on timber trusses and refused to accept its much-ballyhooed acoustics at their proverbial word. Harvey Rice, visiting Salt Lake City in 1870, implicitly questioned their quality by noting that Brigham Young did not enjoy preaching in the tabernacle for he had worn his lungs "threadbare" over the past twenty-five years. Susie Clark was more direct when she visited twenty years later. While she detected whispers and heard a brass pin drop from more than two hundred feet away, she "strongly" suspected this was because of her particular positioning for she "noticed a disturbing echo when sitting on the side of the sanctuary."[93]

Nor were visitors entirely swayed by the promotion of the Mormon Temple as a finished object. Tourists reported on their encounters, not what they thought they might experience upon the temple's completion. Similar to the built environment of many western cities, the temple was a work in progress, and tourists encountered it as such. They found fascinating the construction process from the ox teams, hauling granite blocks from Little Cottonwood Canyon at the foot of the Wasatch range more than twenty miles away, to the sheer size of the massive blocks themselves at the temple site, waiting for erection.[94] With construction ongoing during the late 1870s, W. G. Marshall explained that the temple had risen "no more than thirty feet above its foundations, although it was begun twenty-seven years ago," and

Solomon Mead remarked on the workers busily erecting the structure.[95] Samuel Manning, who also visited in the late 1870s with little of the building completed, had no delusions about its final appearance—never mind that its design was purportedly "given by revelation." As far as Manning was concerned, the temple for these "strange people" was "never likely to be carried forward to completion."[96]

The Mormon Temple was far from complete in the early 1880s, as well, when Glaswegian James Aitken visited and viewed the city from Ensign Peak. The view, he thought, was glorious—save for the "ponderous Tabernacle and the half-built temple forming prominent features in the foreground."[97] As the nine-foot-thick temple walls began to rise in the late 1880s, Brooklyn-based traveler J. H. Bates described its style as "nondescript" and thought its impressiveness would be manifest only in its bulk, while Edward Pierrepont found the rising walls suitable only should one desire a view of the surroundings.[98]

And if the ZCMI building earned some attention in the tourist literature for its elegant façade, visitors instead fixated on the extraordinary volume of commercial activity they encountered around and inside it—a system, according to one English visitor, designed to "crush the trade of Anti-Mormons."[99] Milwaukee traveler and merchant E. D. Holton visited Salt Lake City in January 1880 and paid respects to the store manager and noted the value of the goods he sold per year, while A. H. McClintock visited the ZCMI first, before Temple Square, expressing astonishment as tradesmen and farmers "filled their great covered wagons with goods of every description from reaping machines to baby wagons, from side-saddles to side meat."[100] Tourists did not seem concerned with whether the ZCMI met any standards for architectural civilization, and they did not remark on the architectural attempts to elevate the façade to high art. Instead, the building interested them for what it said about Mormon everyday life. Observing the bustling activity at the ZCMI, visitors did not find much—if anything—different from the active marketplaces in any city, and in this sense, they were tempted to see Mormons as little different from themselves.

But a more intimate encounter with the Salt Lake City built environment told them something else. From an elevated or distant perspective, tourists frequently remarked on the orderliness of the houses and their tidy gardens, tucked beneath ample shade trees and watered by the clear streams they knew flowed alongside the streets. In those instances, Salt Lake City emerged as picturesque, too far away for visitors to notice anything beyond a seemingly perfect urban arrangement with an extraordinary mountain backdrop. From up close, visitors often noted the adobe or "unburned brick" of many one- or two-story houses, as if to set apart the built environment as a foreign presence and to highlight a lack of architectural sophistication.[101] Such opinions may have been colored by the travelers' opinions of the Mormons more generally, as could be surmised by James Bonwick's comment regarding Salt Lake City's "sombre-looking" adobe houses of "unattractive stupidity" when he visited in the early 1870s.[102] "Unattractive" could be interpreted as reasonable aesthetic criticism. But *stupid*?

The particular materials did not always matter. Illinois resident Sue Sanders focused upon those houses made of wood during her 1886 visit, which to her presented a "careless and dilapidated appearance."[103] And W. G. Marshall could not help but notice how "strangely" the houses appeared—not because of the materials but because some of the houses were grouped in clumps of threes or fours, with several street-fronting doors. Marshall explained that each group represented a single Mormon family, with one house for the "gentleman" and then individual houses, or doors, for each of his wives.[104]

The hotels did not always measure up to their promotion either. New Zealander W. T. Locke Travers complained of a paltry few lodging choices in Salt Lake City, and chose the Continental Hotel over the Walker House only because the former featured a large verandah affording a "pleasant retreat" from the sun. But he added that the Continental was "not particularly nice or well managed." The Walker, meanwhile, was "pretentious and noisy."[105] If civilization was marked by pretention, Travers wanted nothing to do with it.

There were certainly visitors who marveled at the buildings in Temple Square and found exquisite the intersection of the built and natural environments in the Salt Lake Valley, but this did not deter tourists from reading the "outside" Mormonism as a type of façade draped over the entire city and left some with the idea, perhaps, that they were not quite getting the full picture. Samuel Manning declared in 1878 that buildings in Salt Lake City did not even have any "pretentions" to architectural merit, and most, he wrote, were "absolutely ugly."[106] During an 1890 visit, William Preston explained that Salt Lake City, despite a "fair exterior," was filled with "misery and poverty also, although the tourist sees nothing of it." Preston noted the beautiful surroundings but contended that the city "owes little of its beauty to its architectural attractions."[107] Matthew Johnson, visiting around the same time, agreed: "Salt Lake City," he wrote, "is not remarkable for architectural beauty."[108]

AN IMPOSING AND RAMSHACKLE ORDER: THE BUILT ENVIRONMENT OF SAN FRANCISCO

For many tourists, late nineteenth-century San Francisco—a city that "sprang up by magic" following the Gold Rush of 1849—did not appear particularly remarkable for its architectural beauty either.[109] But this hardly deterred promotional materials from presenting the city as a refined metropolis on the edge of the frontier, punctuated with a series of exquisite edifices. The 1882 *San Francisco Call* publication entitled *California As It Is*, in fact, explicitly attempted to counter any preconceived notions that visitors may have had about the city's rapid growth. By way of conclusion, in terms of "wealth and commercial importance," the booster publication contended that San Francisco "may well surprise strangers who come to the rapidly-built town expecting to see the roughest evidences of its recent birth, and find, on the contrary, that it is one of the foremost cities in the world in civilization."[110] Architecture would be an effective way to demonstrate the city's wealth and commercial success—and its civilization.

Late nineteenth-century San Francisco resembled other western cities in that promotional materials presented a grand urban built environment to stave off notions of incivility that lingered from the city's earlier periods of settlement. In the popular imagination, the city remained an unruly and poorly built place mired in its early years of gold rush volatility and vigilante justice.[111] There was some truth to this: due to the yields of nearby mines, San Francisco's built environment developed quickly, marked by wooden residential and commercial buildings. Although Jasper O'Farrell's survey of 1847 created a grid plan to provide a logical framework for future settlement, many wooden dwellings quickly crowded the barren hillsides fronting the bay, with no apparent regard for order.[112] For arriving tourists, the dominant first impression remained one of potential chaos. Along with the ferry building, the jumbled array of housing greeted many travelers as they arrived in the city. For the son of Samuel Smiles, visiting San Francisco in 1871, the architecture of the city hardly suggested the substantial qualities necessary for architectural civilization. "I was told that some of the finest buildings were of the Italian order," he wrote, "but I should say that by far the greater number were of the Ramshackle order."[113]

The susceptibility of San Francisco's built environment to natural disaster compounded the sense of disorder, largely because of the threat—and the reality—of earthquakes and fires. For many travelers, the notion of a flimsy, ramshackle wooden city in imminent danger of natural disaster remained a constant throughout the late nineteenth century. Noting the abundance of wooden buildings and wooden planks for streets, one 1877 British visitor feared that just one wayward match "would only take a little while for the wooden houses to catch & then whole streets would be destroyed, the sun dries the timber so thoroughly that there would be little chance of extinguishing the flames." This tourist was "struck with the particularly inflamable [sic] state of the place" and considered the potential for fires to be a more prevailing characteristic of San Francisco than "all the western places I had seen."[114]

The possibility of earthquakes exacerbated the potential for fires, although wooden construction was thought more resistant to earthquakes than masonry. Most housing in San Francisco thus continued to be built of wood, but for those intent upon providing a civilized appearance downtown, San Francisco's seismicity presented a challenge. Constructing with masonry (such as brick or stone, with individual pieces connected by mortar) could lend the city a more substantial appearance than building in wood, but masonry walls tended to break apart during strong seismic activity. Temblors in 1857, 1865, and 1868 did enough damage to San Francisco's built environment, however, to inspire architects, engineers, and builders to search for methods of iron reinforcement so that masonry buildings could more effectively move as entire units, thus resisting the lateral forces of earthquakes. Entrepreneurs patented various systems for bond iron construction in the late 1860s and early 1870s, and some new masonry buildings—including the new City Hall and the U.S. Mint—featured iron reinforcement.[115] A few tourists noted these changes.

Armed with some knowledge of—and trepidation for—earthquakes, tourists cast their gazes more attentively toward concerns of structural stability in San Francisco than they did when visiting other western cities. Visiting San Francisco in 1870, Harvey Rice explained that the new buildings in the business district rose in a "magnificent style, in blocks of stone, brick, or iron" and that they were "anchored or braced with iron bolts, so as to secure them against the action of earthquakes."[116] Later in the 1870s, City Hall captured Miriam Leslie's attention for the brick and iron columns, lintels, and cross ties used in its construction—an early attempt, as she noted, to fireproof and seismically reinforce a building.[117] Attention to such methods was one thing; confidence in them was another. Henry Alworth Merewether noted in the early 1870s that some wooden houses were being replaced by those of "red rock," but whether such houses were an improvement, he thought, "depends on the earthquakes."[118]

But the establishment of fire departments, suitable infrastructure, and the erection of grandiose buildings downtown could not soften the rather jarring prospect that San Francisco presented to the visitor. Much of this came from the juxtaposition of the traditional, imposing, and occasionally decorative architecture downtown with the ordinary commercial buildings of Chinatown, to which the Chinese adapted their own cultural traditions. All of this existed within a dramatic, but frequently inhospitable, terrain that had been dramatically transformed to provide for urban development. Tourist literature, per usual, wished to defuse anything potentially jarring. They instead limited their notions of civilization—architecturally, anyway—to those monumental buildings whose grandiosity and décor suggested something of an established tradition, with its roots allegedly in Europe or the American eastern seaboard. Despite—or perhaps because of—its sudden growth, shaky ground, and "Wild West" reputation, urban elites wished nineteenth-century San Francisco to appear established and permanent. The urban juxtapositions provided intrigue for the traveler, but civilization they were not.

Many of the usual architectural suspects emerge as exemplary of civilization in San Francisco, as they did elsewhere in the urban West: private office buildings, government edifices, hotels, and parks. Among the more regularly promoted buildings or collections of buildings included, in the 1870s, the U.S. Mint, the Palace Hotel, and the mansions of the city's millionaire railroad magnates perched atop Nob Hill; and by the late 1880s and early 1890s, the new City Hall (although it remained under construction) and the Mills Building designed by Burnham and Root of Chicago.[119] But there were some relatively unique aspects as well. San Francisco's boosters emphasized the city's many hotels over other building types, proclaiming San Francisco as the nineteenth-century American hotel city par excellence.[120] They regularly encouraged visitors to tour hotels for their architectural splendor—not just to seek them out for lodging. William Doxey's 1881 *Guide to San Francisco and Vicinity* upheld San Francisco's hotels as "unsurpassed" worldwide, and more than ten years later in 1892, F. K. Warren's *California Illustrated: Including a Trip through Yellowstone Park* still considered the city's hotels "first and foremost among the attractions" and argued that there "are none in any part of the globe" to compete with them.[121]

To better attract tourists, developers and their architects provided hotel designs in familiar, reassuring styles, while incorporating the latest features and technological innovations. To make them comforting to the elite tourists that hotel proprietors most desired to attract, architects modeled some of these hotels after notable buildings in Europe and the eastern seaboard of the United States. Guidebooks promoted the Lick House for its comfort, marble floors, and enormous dining room modeled after that of Versailles, the Occidental Hotel for its enormous dining room and its theater, the Cosmopolitan Hotel for its elevators (the city's first), and the Baldwin Hotel for its modern conveniences, elegant interior, and theater.[122]

William Ralston and William Sharon's Palace Hotel rose above this crowd. Upon its 1875 completion, at seven stories, 755 rooms, and $3.25 million dollars, the Palace Hotel was the city's tallest, most capacious, most expensive, and most exclusive hotel. Because of its dominance and far-flung fame, local businesses frequently advertised themselves by noting their proximity to it. By the early 1890s, the Palace Hotel had garnered enough attention nationwide that James Hutchings used it as a benchmark upon which to indicate the height of Yosemite's El Capitan. "Within and without," Doxey's *Guide to San Francisco and Vicinity* boasted, "the kingly structure . . . far surpasses not only in size but in grandeur all the hotels of Europe and America."[123] To attain some of this grandeur, a brochure advertising the Palace Hotel prior to its opening boasted that the hotel's architect, John P. Gaynor, had examined hotels in the "principal cities" of America and Europe before executing the design.[124] Perhaps more than any other building in the city, the Palace Hotel served as an architectural representative of the elites' attempt to civilize the city.[125]

But the Palace Hotel was not a direct copy of European architectural sophistication. Some of its unique features included three courtyards (the central one of which included circular carriage entry area with a glass roof), a marble-tiled and colonnaded promenade, and a tropical garden with exotic plants, statuary, and fountains. Guidebooks emphasized the retreat-like aspects of this atrium, or courtyard, far more than its massive exterior. In the manufactured environment of the garden courtyard, around which the rooms were arrayed, the hotel provided travelers with luxurious and comforting shelter from the uncertainties of the city streets.

Not all tourists felt so comforted. British tourist Thomas Dewar's impression of the Palace Hotel—and the atrium in particular—was characterized by his overnight stay during a presidential election. Although Dewar seemed moderately impressed with the hotel's size, he fixated on the band of musicians that attempted to entertain hotel guests with the "terrible row" they created in the courtyard."[126] E. R. Hendrix also visited from Britain as part of a worldwide trip, but he did so back in the 1870s, only a couple of years after it opened. He called the interior "elegant" but the exterior "unsightly" and "lacking in architectural beauty." The hotel's enormity did not appeal to Hendrix, and it typified San Francisco boosters' tendencies to promote the city's "big things."[127]

No matter what luxuries they offered, urban hotels could not permanently shelter tourists from the city. In some cases, the city itself seemed to penetrate into the hotel. Illinois tourist W. S. Walker offered a glowing account of the Palace Hotel's interior with its "superb marble floors," "beautiful fountains," and "tropical plants" when he visited in 1879 or 1880, but he appeared distracted, if not annoyed, by the "brilliant lights" and "the tramp of a thousand feet" parading across the floors.[128] Rudyard Kipling, meanwhile, wrote only of the poor service and the omnipresent and well-used spittoons, which he discovered in the hotel bar, along the staircases, and in the bedrooms.[129] City hotels provided only fleeting moments of respite, and tourists could not hide altogether from the urban environment. Tourists read urban architecture as part of the larger context of the city; instead of isolated buildings, tourists confronted densities, juxtapositions, neighborhoods, and the general collision of culture and commerce in a spectacular natural landscape. This collision did not always reveal much clarity, however. For visitors to late nineteenth-century San Francisco, the city's architecture provided a backdrop, or a container, for the natural, cultural, and occasional technological drama appearing at the continent's edge.

The U.S. Mint, completed in 1873, provides another relevant example. John Hittell's 1888 *Guide Book to San Francisco* advertised the building by noting its "Doric style" and "massive fluted columns," and C. P. Heininger's *Historical Souvenir of San Francisco, Cal.* noted its "elegant and imposing" appearance because of its use of granite and sandstone.[130] Tourists were not terribly concerned. John Leng mentioned that the mint was "one of the most substantial examples of architecture in San

PALACE HOTEL AND MARKET STREET, SAN FRANCISCO. Tourist literature promoted San Francisco's Palace Hotel for its garden court, enormous size, and ultimate luxury. But its design did not generate universal praise. Many tourists thought the hotel too large, and when British visitor E. R. Hendrix visited in the early 1870s, he considered the exterior thoroughly "lacking in architectural beauty." Outside the doors, the everyday life of late nineteenth-century San Francisco proceeded apace. (Source: *Guide Book and Street Manual of California*, p. 177. Courtesy of Internet Archive, http://archive.org/details/guidebookstreetm00warn.)

Francisco," but his interest was clearly focused upon the aesthetics of the machinery for milling and stamping—no doubt assisted by the "well-dressed" and "sprightly young ladies" who were employed there.[131] Solomon Mead visited the mint in 1883, but he had nothing to say about the architecture. As with Leng, far more interesting to Mead were the technologies in place that allowed for coinage and the printing of money, which he described in his diary.[132]

Just as intriguing to tourists were those buildings that seemed to capture the energy and pulse of San Francisco. Architecture, however, could not create that alone. The buildings needed to be active—whether with machinery or the intensity of urban life. The city's stock exchanges offered tourists one such glimpse into this life. In writing about one of the exchanges in 1875, London visitor Arthur Guillemard discussed only the cultural life of the interior, where the "crowding, pushing, and heat are almost unbearable, but the scene is sufficiently lively to induce one to become a spectator for a few minutes." He noted the "frantic" gestures and shouting of the traders and wondered whether the London Stock Exchange could furnish a scene quite as exciting.[133] A number of tourists offered similar accounts of the exchange, at times embellishing their descriptions for literary effect, but unconcerned about whether that activity contributed to urban civilization.[134]

For those tourists who did direct attention towards San Francisco's architecture, they occasionally read the attempt to design buildings after more established styles as mere pretensions to grandeur—not as exemplary of civilization. Guidebooks regularly championed the splendor of the Nob Hill mansions, boasting of their size and architectural detail and celebrating the achievements of the entrepreneurial railroad tycoons, such as Charles Crocker, Mark Hopkins, Collis P. Huntington, and Leland Stanford, who lived in them. S. M. Lee was clearly struck by the presence of these stately mansions when she visited in 1886 but could not figure out exactly how they struck her. "These great mansions . . . do not strike me as being very handsome," she wrote, "but they are immense and gorgeous."[135] Could buildings be "gorgeous" but not "handsome"? What, then, were the criteria?

James Fullarton Muirhead was less equivocal when he visited San Francisco in the 1890s. Noting the timber construction of the Nob Hill mansions, Muirhead bemoaned the "misdirected efforts of the architects," who shaped that wood in such a way to "slavishly imitate the incongruous features of stone houses in the style of the Renaissance." He thought the architects missed an excellent opportunity for architectural innovation by failing to take advantage of the flexibility of wood, and he was not fooled into thinking the buildings were actually made of stone. "Indeed," Muirhead wrote, "we shall feel that San Francisco is badly off for fine buildings of all and every kind.[136]

Not everyone felt this way. Some visitors found the city's most compelling architecture to be that which characterized the ordinary residential environment, although few tourists sought out the city's neighborhoods and their impressions typically revolved around the juxtaposition of housing with topography. As with much else in San Francisco, those impressions were mixed. Aside from Chinatown, most tourists encountered neighborhoods unintentionally—they may have passed through them on a carriage ride to Golden Gate Park or to the Cliff House or on their way up to Nob Hill. Many of the residential areas were marked by two-story detached houses built of wood and typically painted white or gray for working- and middle-class residents. Their details loosely recalled medieval architecture, but their "bay" or "bow" windows provided local distinctiveness in developers' efforts to add space and light. Highly recognized today as integral to San Francisco's iconic image, nineteenth-century guidebooks almost entirely ignored these "Victorians" or "Painted Ladies" as potential tourist attractions. In the late nineteenth century, they were vernacular residential building types erected quickly and mass-produced for rapid sale.[137]

But that did not mean they lacked ornament or detail. Even as speculative ventures with designs that adhered to standardized plans derived from architectural pattern books, developers hired carpenters to carve decorative features into the façades to lend them individual dignity and to defuse their otherwise mass-produced character. With a steady supply of redwood shipped from northern California and the Pacific Northwest, as well as available machinery for detailing, San Francisco carpenters had little difficulty ornamenting house façades.[138] When British traveler T. S. Hudson visited San Francisco in the early 1880s, he took note of the "handsome cornerings, facings, and carving above and around the windows." Unlike Muirhead, who recoiled at San Francisco's tendency to shape wood as if it were stone, Hudson applauded the decorative efforts that made it possible to mistake the façades of San Francisco's houses for finely wrought stone. James Bonwick, in the early 1870s, found the entire city to be delightful, in part because of the many wooden houses in "every possible fanciful style of architecture, set off by painters and sculptors."[139]

Travelers predominantly focused on the larger topographical context of San Francisco's neighborhoods, rather than singling out architectural features or commenting on individual buildings. Novelist Helen Hunt Jackson visited the city in the early 1890s, stepped out of the

Occidental Hotel, boarded a carriage, turned a corner, and moved up "extraordinarily" steep streets with "small, wooden, light-colored, and picturesque" houses lining them. The density and the juxtapositions in the city surprised her, but the housing itself was not offensive.[140] Emily Pfeiffer, writing of her mid-1880s San Francisco visit from the perspective of her East Coast home, recalled an absence of trees in the landscape but explained that the city's hilly topography with its "suburban blocks and villas" lent the built environment "a picturesqueness not common on this side of the Atlantic."[141]

On the other hand, the lack of trees struck Harriet Harper to such an extent that she could not focus on whatever aesthetic merits the residential environment might have had. Gazing down upon the residences of the city from Nob Hill in the late 1880s, Harper saw an "interminable mass of wooden buildings, not drowned in green or softened by clambering vines, but standing out, every point and pinnacle bare, in the brazen sunshine. There is scarce a tree to be seen in any direction you may choose to look," she wrote. "The general impression is barrenness."[142] Benjamin Parke Avery, visiting in the 1870s, noted how the city's grid seemed to cut "arbitrarily" through this landscape. To Avery, such actions suggested the "tasteless energy" of the early settlers and contributed to the "mean architecture," which he found "cold," "monotonous," and "gray."[143] And Australian Alfred Falk, who toured the city in the mid-1870s, noted the contrast between a solidly built downtown core with buildings of stone and the "straggling" outskirts, with houses of wood.[144] Robert Louis Stevenson offered a more puzzling, almost melancholy account. Visiting in the late 1880s, the monumental houses on Nob Hill impressed him but not the more ordinary examples on Telegraph and Rincon Hills. There, Stevenson discovered "a world of old wooden houses snoozing together all forgotten." On Telegraph Hill in particular, he explained that one could traverse "doubtful paths from one quaint corner to another. Everywhere the same tumble-down decay and sloppy progress, new things yet unmade, old things tottering to their fall."[145]

The process of decay could be made alluring: at least with San Francisco's oldest surviving building complex. The Mission San Francisco de Asis (Mission Dolores), since its establishment in 1776, had existed on the edge of downtown near a carriage drive leading to the city's southern suburbs. Erected under the supervision of Spanish colonists in the eighteenth century, the mission church—not completed until 1791—demonstrated immediate ties to the Old World by virtue of its construction when California existed under Spanish jurisdiction. Guidebooks to late nineteenth-century San Francisco struggled to promote the mission complex as worthy of tourist attention, however. Nearly a century after its construction, the mission was in a state of considerable disrepair and, according to contemporary accounts, sat within a dilapidated, impoverished, and run-down part of the city. The tourist literature ignored the mission's contemporary condition and— when they included it at all—focused instead on its European heritage. The mission church, according to Appleton's 1882 guide, was designed in the "old Spanish style." Should tourists venture inside, they would see what Doxey's 1881 *Guide to San Francisco and Vicinity* described as well-preserved interior decorations that were "sufficient to recall the times of the early Fathers."[146] To a large degree, the tourist literature romanticized Mission Dolores by implying that it conveyed a distant past uncorrupted by the modernizing city all around it.[147]

Doxey's guidebook, similar to many others that included the mission, ignored the idea that Mission Dolores only partly resembled European prototypes, employed local adobe rather than stone, and featured little ornamentation linking it to the western architectural tradition. Promotional materials also ignored the involvement of native Ohlone Indians, who built the mission under duress, and disregarded their role with the chapel's interior design. They overlooked the mission as a place of toil, enslavement, and ultimate transformation of Native American lifeways in the American West. In essence, such publications rhetorically discredited Native American contributions, while erasing a violent and troubling past. They sanitized the mission in an attempt to make it appear more civilized—and thus more palatable for the curious visitor.[148]

Many tourists who visited Mission Dolores, however, were either oblivious to these earlier histories or unmoved by guidebooks' attempts to romanticize the current conditions of the building or site. William and W. F. Robertson, when they visited in 1869, thought the mission was set up for "Mexicans" and explained that the site was "a village now deserted." David L. Phillips, in 1876, had nothing positive to say about the mission, although he had hardly anything to say at all, noting only that the "old adobe buildings of the Mission lend a dismal hue to a rather repulsive portion of the city."[149] Although the mission church was the oldest surviving building in the city, tourists would not easily find civilization amid the ruins of Mission Dolores.

A far greater challenge for the maintenance of San Francisco's civility, at least from a booster perspective, arose from the existence of the Chinese Quarter—or Chinatown—whose dense nineteenth-century built environment was clustered within nine square blocks just north and slightly west of the nineteenth-century downtown. Early arriving European American settlers who came to San Francisco in the wake of the gold rush constructed many of the district's buildings initially as two-story commercial and residential structures of brick and wood. The Chinese, who also emigrated to San Francisco during the gold rush, settled in this area of the city and began to adapt the existing built environment to their own cultural and spiritual traditions. They hung signs promoting their places of business, converted basements into stores and residences, and added balconies, canopies, lanterns, and verandahs. In many cases, they lacquered building elements with particular colors of spiritual significance, and erected picket fences on rooftops to serve as protection against police or local rivals.[150]

But such alterations did not shift the overall image of Chinatown's built environment in the estimation of the city's elites, for they perceived the neighborhood as an urban slum with no monumental buildings that met the alleged standards of civilization. They never even attempted to uphold Chinatown as a civilized environment. Rather, to separate it entirely from the rest of San Francisco, they characterized it as entirely foreign—either as an exotic destination, where tourists could find a primitive society, or as a dangerous environment, where visitors should proceed with caution. That many tourists did explore Chinatown and found the built environment to be far more safe and ordinary than it was described is one more testament to the idea that tourist encounters often revealed a far more complex picture of urban civilization than might otherwise be assumed from rhetorical and illustrative construction.

San Francisco's Chinatown presented a distinctive situation in the urban American West because issues of race and discrimination were deeply intertwined into descriptions and perceptions. Yet in Chinatown, as in the rest of San Francisco and in other western cities, tourists uncovered a rather different picture from the one presented to them in promotional materials. Where the publications and their illustrations highlighted the civility of western cities through fine examples of architectural art, tourists understood urban architecture as far more than single buildings to be appreciated for their designs. Tourists did not always judge the architecture of the West upon how closely it approximated European architectural traditions, either. If the architecture exemplified civilization, that civilization had to be immersed in the whole of the urban cultural environment. For late nineteenth-century visitors to the urban American West, civilization proved elusive.

CHAPTER 5

Cosmopolitanism

Editing and Revising Culture

The grand opening for San Francisco's Cosmopolitan Hotel was not exactly cosmopolitan. Inspired by a newspaper announcement that the front doors would be thrown open to the general public on August 31, 1864, a swarming, motley collection of people descended upon the hotel—from "refined gentlemen, elegant ladies, and tender children" to "thieves, ruffians, and vandals." The spacious halls and staircases filled quickly with visitors, and more lined up outside the doors, awaiting entrance. The crowd soon became unmanageable. A report in the next day's *San Francisco Daily Morning Call* recounted incidents of pilfered silverware, sheets, shirts, pillowcases and the destruction of parlor ornaments and curtains. One police officer, attempting to maintain order, found himself hoisted aloft by the crowd and carried through the lobby.[1]

The Cosmopolitan Hotel's developers did not forecast the opening night melee when they financed the project. They had hoped the hotel would establish itself as one of the city's choice lodgings and convey a worldliness they considered lacking in early 1860s San Francisco.[2] To establish that worldliness, they hired renowned architect David Farquharson to provide a dignified Renaissance classicism with arches, keystones, pediments, engaged Doric columns, and rustication; to emphasize technological prowess, they outfitted the hotel with the city's first elevators. They considered San Francisco's "cosmopolitan character" worth celebrating, and chose the hotel's name, "Cosmopolitan," to commemorate it. If New York City had its "Metropolitan" Hotel, *New York Tribune* correspondent Albert D. Richardson quipped, then San Francisco—boasting an international population from every continent—must have its "Cosmopolitan."[3]

The design and promotion of San Francisco's Cosmopolitan Hotel represented a specific cosmopolitanism favored by urban elites in the late nineteenth-century: one that conveyed refinement, sophistication, and taste. To demonstrate such characteristics through architectural design was not the same, however, as attracting a refined late nineteenth-century urban population working together for the greater good of the metropolis—regardless of race, ethnicity, gender, age, or class. The hotel's proprietors celebrated the city's cosmopolitan character in name, but they also wished to separate the hotel from certain aspects of the urban population, such as the "thieves, ruffians, and vandals" who wreaked havoc on opening night. Any such clientele disturbing the Cosmopolitan's guests on a regular basis would be disastrous for the hotel's—and the city's—reputation. It was one thing to name the hotel the "Cosmopolitan"; it was entirely another to welcome the city's cosmopolitan makeup into the doors. With the transcontinental railroad on track for completion five years after the opening, tourists from everywhere would soon be visiting the city. Could San Francisco afford to showcase such a rowdy image to the world? Cosmopolitanism had to be shaped, controlled, and contained.

The rowdy segment of the opening-night crowd at the Cosmopolitan Hotel reportedly emerged from San Francisco's infamous Barbary Coast, a district with a reputation for vice and crime and an area where elite claims to urban cosmopolitanism were put to the test. In the nineteenth century, the Barbary Coast stood between Chinatown and the wharves: characterized physically by rooming houses, boardinghouses, saloons, and small factories and culturally by newcomers from places such as Ireland, Australia, Central America, and South America. Many of these newcomers sought employment in the city's various industries.[4] Sensationalist accounts, such as Benjamin Lloyd's

1876 *Lights and Shades in San Francisco,* depicted the Barbary Coast as
San Francisco's roughest area: a den of iniquity filled with hoodlums,
rascals, and drunks.[5] Although the danger may have been exaggerated and the Barbary Coast offered plenty of salacious entertainment
options for the city's general population, those few guidebooks that
mentioned the neighborhood also suggested that tourists exercise caution or, according to George A. Crofutt's *Trans-continental Tourist,* "keep
away" altogether; that is, if "you value your life."[6] The Barbary Coast
did not showcase the refined trappings of civil society with urban
institutions, grand hotels, fashionable promenades, and architectural
splendor; its reputation did not lend it to fluid acculturation into elite
nineteenth-century European American society. The racially and ethnically diverse Barbary Coast did not represent the kind of cosmopolitanism desired by the arbiters of cultural taste.

These arbiters—the urban West's leading politicians, businesspeople,
corporate barons, publishers, and journalists—considered racial, spiritual, and class diversity acceptable so long as they conformed to particular standards regarding urban gentility and refinement. The Barbary
Coast did not meet these standards, nor did San Francisco's adjacent
Chinatown, Chicago's Levee, Denver's bordello district, or, for that
matter, nearly all of Salt Lake City. The diversity that characterized
these areas, as well as their lingering reputations of vice, illustrated
the elite cosmopolitan model only insofar as they remained curiosities lending flavor to the urban West but did not threaten the region's
perceived European American superiority. Otherwise, they had to be
set aside as deviant—*in* the city, perhaps, but not *of* it.

Diversity alone did not equal cosmopolitanism in the nineteenth-
century elite vision of the city. To be cosmopolitan, ethnically, racially,
spiritually, or economically diverse peoples either had to contribute
to the city's overall prosperity, or they had to be set aside—at least
rhetorically. In some cases, this meant rendering the urban population
invisible or powerless and boasting instead of the city's cultural institutions (such as museums, libraries, benevolent societies, and religious
structures) or claiming industrial and technological advancements
that suggested a global reach. These versions of cosmopolitanism were

not always presented in mutually exclusive ways; a harmonious mix of races and a collection of high cultural institutions together could announce a progressive, cosmopolitan city.[7] Employing various written and illustrative tactics that denied the often unequal social and economic circumstances of western cities, different late nineteenth-century publications could thus champion Chicago, Denver, and San Francisco each as America's "most cosmopolitan city."[8] Indeed, the word "cosmopolitan" appears frequently in late nineteenth-century promotional materials and traveler accounts alike. But there was no consistently shared understanding of the term.

Tourists paid little mind to whether the mix of people they encountered collectively advanced the economic interests of the city, which was how cosmopolitanism was championed by elites. Perhaps uncritically, tourists neither dissected the notion of cosmopolitanism to reveal its elitist or bourgeois overtones nor did they consider how increased flows of capital and commodities were controlled principally for the benefit of the few rather than the many. They also did not ponder whether the increased numbers of immigrants in the same urban space signaled the emergence of a new transnational, pluralistic world peopled with "global citizens" who recognized that the traditional walls between cultures, ethnicities, races, classes, and nations were dissolving. Although these popular, yet fiercely debated, ideas have gained considerable academic currency in the late twentieth and early twenty-first centuries, such matters did not concern nineteenth-century tourists.[9]

This chapter asserts that tourists read cosmopolitanism as ethnic, racial, class, and spiritual diversity in the city. With some exceptions, tourists did not suggest that this diverse population had to forgo cultural or ethnic differences in favor of a larger community spirit in order to be cosmopolitan. In the tourist imagination, the urban West's cosmopolitanism was not due to civic institutions, which elites considered part of the cosmopolitan recipe, or to its featured residents, who merely added ethnic or spiritual color to an otherwise monochrome cultural palette. For tourists, the existence of diversity *did* signal cosmopolitanism in the urban West, but the power or meaning of this diversity was not always evident. Tourist readings of cosmopolitanism were as diverse as the people they encountered.

SORTING THE POLYGLOT CITY

That the nineteenth-century urban West was an ethnically, spiritually, and racially diverse place would have been apparent to any visitor well before the completion of the transcontinental railroad, regardless of how this diversity was sold in text and image.[10] The diversity of the West, in addition to extremes of topography and climate, has always been a major part of its distinctiveness—even if underrepresented peoples have been overlooked regarding their contributions to western urban development or ignored for resistance to hegemonic forces threatening their cultural traditions.[11] Depending upon the city to which they migrated (or, in the case of Native Americans and Mexican Americans, the land that they had been compelled to relinquish or surrender), the West included a mix of western Europeans (particularly English, Irish, Germans, and Scandinavians), eastern Europeans, South Americans, Mexicans, African Americans, and Chinese. Mormons, though racially white and predominantly European in ethnicity, added spiritual diversity to a predominantly Protestant Christian region. Many of these ethnic or religious groups ventured into western cities in search of economic opportunity or freedom from persecution in an increasingly mobile nineteenth-century world. And while European and American tourists were familiar with diversity, the West provided an ethnic and spiritual array—including the largest number of Asians, Mormons, and South Americans in the United States. Western-bound tourists had not encountered many of these people before.[12]

Demographics bear out the diversity of the urban West. By the 1890s, Chicago featured the greatest percentage of foreign-born residents in America (71 percent to New York's 45 percent), while earlier, in the 1880s, that distinction belonged to San Francisco, with 44.6 percent of the population born abroad.[13] Foreign-born residents also comprised at least a third of the 1880 Salt Lake City population. Yet promotional material did not typically champion these statistics unless they could be categorized for tourists in ways that allowed a particular elite cosmopolitanism to persist. Some material sorted the city into specific ethnic districts with their own subheadings, and certain areas, such as San Francisco's Chinatown, merited their very own guidebooks. The more that guidebooks could edit the polyglot city into particular districts for tourist consumption, the easier they could proclaim for it an overall urban cosmopolitanism.

Perhaps the most common method of cultural presentation put a positive spin on ethnic neighborhoods and heterogeneity in the growing metropolis. While not unique to the late nineteenth-century urban American West, this method (popular in guidebooks, newspapers, and magazines) rendered the ethnic Irish "hoodlum" of San Francisco's Barbary Coast relatively harmless, transformed new European immigrants into welcome additions to already vibrant cities, and celebrated the Chinese and Mormons for their "odd" practices and "unusual" built environments. Often sponsored by urban elites or written by those connected politically or financially to them, such publications promoted ethnic neighborhoods as colorful urban attractions.

By presenting neighborhoods as such, elites manufactured culture in ways that disregarded or stereotyped ethnic and cultural traditions. In guidebooks and illustrations, they depicted ethnic districts and inhabitants as picturesque and quaint, thereby taming the potentially rowdy edges of urban ethnicity by casting people and their environments as objects for visual consumption.[14] The ethnic "other" thus could be made to seem less menacing and their environments less foreboding, and cultural peculiarities and ethnic differences could be read as suggestive of urban richness and variety. This rendered the city more cosmopolitan in precisely the fashion boosters and elites hoped it would. With their ostensibly dangerous aspects removed, elites could point to the polyglot of nationalities and claim it as crucial to urban cosmopolitan makeup.

Another frequent method of presentation depicted the West's diversity as so outlandish that it could be set apart from the city—a common portrayal in dime novels and illustrations in the nineteenth-century popular press. Perhaps no genre was more explicit in this vein than the urban sensationalist literature that had earlier proliferated in America and Europe and appealed to a wide public intrigued by the illicit aspects of the metropolis.[15] This genre of literature commonly divided the city into "lights" and "darks" to illuminate a double-sided nature of urban life. Benjamin Lloyd's *Lights and Shades in San Francisco* was but one example of this type: it contrasted the supposed "daylight" city of parks, drives, stately buildings, prominent civic institutions, tranquility, and genteel European Americans with its supposed "nighttime" counterpart of alleys, dilapidated buildings, prostitution, confidence men, gambling, theft, murder, and nonwhite peoples.

Urban sensationalist literature included the cheerful daylight city seemingly as a foil, for most tourists and strangers unacquainted with the city could obtain information about its daytime attractions from a variety of published matter. Instead, the authors, many of whom were journalists already familiar with the intricacies of the urban environment, concentrated their efforts on the nighttime world of the hoodlum, thief, gambler, and prostitute. This was a dark world of alleys, street corners, dance halls, gambling "hells," saloons, brothels, oyster cellars, and opium dens, and it was a world that threatened the urban—and urbane—cosmopolitanism of the late nineteenth-century city. Most urban sensationalist writing was just that—sensationalist—and did not accurately depict urban conditions. But accuracy was not necessarily the purpose. Some writers had political or evangelical aims and wished to expose the dangers of particular urban districts to raise awareness and encourage reform.[16] Those who came West may have been doubly motivated to spread Protestantism to a remote region they perceived more generally as boorish and sacrilegious.

Overall, the urban sensationalist literature helped readers navigate imaginatively through the cities' mean streets populated by allegedly immoral and spiritually degenerate people, but they neither delineated clear paths through those streets nor directed visitors to particular locales.[17] In many cases, they did not even encourage anyone to visit— not alone, anyway. By depicting such areas as dens of iniquity and hotbeds of moral depravity, this literature served to keep the lower classes and ethnically othered—already separated physically from the rest of the city by economic circumstances or, in the case of the Chinese, by law—separate in thought and mind as well. The cosmopolitan city would have to reside elsewhere.

In some cases, booster publications located cosmopolitanism abstractly in objects, processes, and institutions, such as the arts, newspapers, architecture, and hotels. But not just anything would do. The arts constituted museums, concert halls, and theaters but they did not account for street performers. Newspapers meant big dailies, not the cheap penny press. Architecture meant important, centrally located, and large public or private buildings, not ordinary commercial buildings, industrial districts, or housing. Hotels meant first-class establishments with chandeliers and bell captains, not transient lodging with long-term living options. Even a working port with ships or a railroad depot with trains laden with goods could indicate progress and suggest cosmopolitanism.[18] Promoting these aspects of the urban environment was strategic: if tourists envisioned a neat, orderly city with established institutions and grand architecture, then they might report favorably on that city, patronize local businesses, and extend their visits.

A RIVER OF HUMANITY

Yet the attempts to discursively sort the urban environment by race or class or to render diversity invisible by focusing upon urban institutions and high cultural offerings did not always mesh with tourist experiences. Literature aimed at potential travelers to Chicago, nonetheless, tried to organize city residents for visitor understanding—and exploration. With its substantial number of foreign-born residents in the late nineteenth century, Chicago featured an ethnically diverse population as fractured and initially unassimilated into American culture as that of New York City. Immigrants to Chicago came from an array of European countries, including Germany, England, Scotland, Ireland, Sweden, Norway, Denmark, Holland, Italy, Poland, Russia, and Hungary, and they settled first near the downtown. The English, Germans, Scandinavians, and more prosperous Irish gradually abandoned the center for better housing in areas served by streetcar lines or in the newly expanding suburbs, while those immigrants who arrived later—particularly eastern Europeans and Irish escaping the potato famine—took up spaces vacated by earlier settlers.[19]

As early as the late 1840s, the Underground Railroad also had propelled many African Americans, fleeing slavery in the South, toward what had become for them the relatively safe haven of Chicago.[20] Although racial tensions, segregation, and other forms of discrimination—including labor riots—proliferated in the nineteenth century, by the early 1860s nearly one thousand African Americans had settled in the city, four thousand by 1870, and by 1893, about fifteen thousand. Most African Americans were, however, concentrated in a long sliver of land south of downtown, tucked between a stately white neighborhood to the east and a working-class, predominantly Irish, community to the west.

Instead of embracing Chicago's diversity as characteristic of a cosmopolitan city, promotional sources relegated ethnicities instead to statistics, charts, and abstractions. Louis Schick's *Chicago and Its Environs*, published in 1891, claimed that Chicago featured a "decidedly cosmopolitan character" but implied that its cosmopolitanism was apparent because the "various nationalities are grouped in different sections."[21] John J. Flinn's massive tome *Chicago: The Marvelous City of the West*, published the following year, claimed that Chicago was a "thoroughly cosmopolitan city." But Flinn reduced discussion of the city's demographics into part of just one page, with a statistical breakdown of the city's nationalities—including its "Mongolians," whose population outpaced that of several groups but were nonetheless buried at the bottom of the chart.[22] Such classification sorted the population by type, thereby emphasizing the dominance of the European or American born and thus characterizing the kind of cosmopolitanism desired by urban elites.[23]

Yet tourists were just as likely to understand Chicago's cosmopolitanism through its diverse, albeit cacophonous, population. Chicago's diversity caught the attention of travelers, who frequently remarked on the multitude of different languages spoken in the Chicago streets.[24]

of the 292,463 native-born citizens are of immediate foreign extraction. The following is a careful estimate of the nationalities represented.

American	292,463	Hollanders	4,912
German	384,958	Hungarians	4,827
Irish	215,534	Swiss	2,735
Bohemian	54,209	Roumanians	4,350
Polish	52,756	Canadians	6,989
Swedish	45,877	Belgians	682
Norwegian	44,615	Greeks	698
English	33,785	Spanish	297
French	12,963	Portuguese	34
Scotch	11,927	East Indians	28
Welsh	2,966	West Indians	37
Russian	9,977	Sandwich Islanders	31
Danes	9,891	Mongolians	1,217
Italians	9,921		1,208,669

Population by Divisions.—According to the census of 1880 the South Division had a population of 127,266, the West Division 276,321, and the North Division 99,717. Between 1880 and 1889 the West gained rapidly on the other sides, until, before the annexation of adjoining towns, it was estimated to contain two-thirds of all the inhabitants in the city. The acquisition of the populous towns of Hyde Park and Lake, on the South, and Lake View and Jefferson, on the North, by the vote of 1889, however, swelled the population of these divisions to a point which considerably weakened the ascendency of the West Division.

Following is the population by Divisions, according to the school census of 1890:

Total population of South Division, comprising the South Town wards and those of Lake and Hyde Park, male, 222,077; female, 191,845; total, 413,922.

Total population West Division, comprising the West Town wards and Twenty-eighth ward (annexed portion of Cicero), male, 297,722; female, 258,261; total, 555,983.

Total population North Division, comprising the North Side wards and those of Lake View and Jefferson, male, 126,091; female, 112,673; total 238,764.

Population Summary.—Of the 1,208,669 inhabitants in Chicago in 1890, 645,890 were males and 562,779 were females. There were 735,435 persons over 21 years of age, of whom 409,676 were males and 325,759 were females. The total number of persons under 21, 473,234; 236,214 being males and 237,020 being females. The number of school children between 6 and 14 was males, 84,272; females, 81,344; total 165,621. The total number of children under 6 was 183,801. The blind numbered 183; deaf and dumb, 427—males, 203; females, 224. The total number of pupils in private schools was 39,906; total number of pupils in public schools 135,551. The total number of children under 21 who had finished their studies was 35,246, while there were 35,246 who had to work but would have attended school had they an opportunity. The total number between 12 and 21 who could not read or write English was but 2,599, of whom 1,200 were males. The total number between 6 and 14 who did not attend school was 6,216. The colored people of all ages in the city were 14,490—7,932 males, 6,558 females. The Mongolians numbered 1,217, of whom only 10 were females. The population of the annexed districts was 262,640, as against 216,213 in 1889, and within the old city boundaries 946,029, as against 802,651 in 1889.

BREAKDOWN OF NATIONALITIES IN CHICAGO. John. J. Flinn's guide to the World's Columbian Exposition in 1893 claimed Chicago as a "thoroughly cosmopolitan city" and employed this chart from the 1880 census as evidence. Yet by sorting the population into nationalities based upon place of birth, boosters and elites kept people separate in thought and mind—even if they wished to understand all nationalities working together toward the greater good of the metropolis. The Chinese, here listed as "Mongolians," are placed at the end of the chart despite a larger population than many groups listed above them. (Source: John J. Flinn, *Chicago: The Marvelous City of the West*, p. 82. Courtesy of Internet Archive, http://archive.org/details/chicagomarvel000inflin.)

Some of these languages could be heard in the Levee: an area of run-down, two- and three-story brick and wooden residential buildings, subdivided into multiple units, on the southern edge of downtown bordered by Harrison Street, Dearborn Street, Twelfth Street, and Fifth Avenue.[25] The Levee filled with many new arrivals seeking—and finding—work in Chicago's expanding industries, but it nonetheless garnered a reputation as the city's preeminent nineteenth-century vice district for its history of violence, saloons, and "houses of ill-repute."[26]

Not surprisingly, urban sensationalist writers targeted the Levee (which included Italians and Jews as well as African Americans) as Chicago's most dangerous, dirty, and immoral neighborhood—not a cosmopolitan place at all.[27] Regarding a section of the Levee referred to as "Cheyenne," journalist Harold Vynne, in the 1892 sensationalist tract *Chicago by Day and Night: The Pleasure Seekers Guide to the Paris of America*, warned explorers that its "negro colony" and "large numbers of foreigners" contained "more dangerous characters" than elsewhere in the city. Vynne explained that it is "just as well" the Cheyenne area is clustered in one location within the Levee, for the "authorities know exactly where to look for it."[28] Tourists did discover the Levee and often partook in its salacious entertainments but also found themselves the objects of derision by unappreciative residents.[29]

Tourists also encountered a multicultural river of humanity in Chicago's streets and establishments, but hardly characterized the city as dangerous. Anne Mathilda Bright described Chicago as such in 1869, when she noted "people of all descriptions," some of whom looked as if "they had first crawled out of the Ark." French educator Marie Dugard noted the "cosmopolitan whirlwind" of the city when she visited some twenty-four years later during the exposition, and Parisian Mme Léon Grandin explained that Chicago was filled with people from "every country on the globe," including "Negroes in great number, along with Chinese who struck a gay and bright note with their oriental dress."[30] In fact, several French women travelers to late nineteenth-century Chicago noted the ethnic mix that characterized the city. As Mary Beth Raycraft explains in her introduction to a translation of Grandin's diary, these visitors stuffed the pages of their accounts with descriptions illustrating the diverse life of the metropolis, including "African-American shoe-shine boys, German immigrants, and various types of American women."[31]

The interest in everyday diversity was restricted neither by gender nor country of origin. British visitor Phil Robinson, in the early 1880s, did not attempt to make any grand proclamations about ethnic or racial diversity per se but did enjoy watching two African American boys attempting to pin an "April Fool" sign on the coattails of a presumably white hansom cab driver.[32] French tourist L. de Cotton, visiting Chicago in 1886, observed that on "a normal street, you can generally see at the same time, Negroes, Indians, yellows, and several shades of white." He added that if one was to "artistically" arrange the people, "they could form *parterres*."[33] Tourists may have desired such an aesthetic arrangement, but while the reality of their encounters was not especially chaotic, it was still far less orderly than a formal French garden.

When Charles Lewis visited Chicago in 1876, he noted the approximately 150 African American servants at the Palmer House of "almost every shade of colour" but was clearly aware that there still existed a "line of demarcation" that stood as "an impassable barrier to the full emancipation of the colored man."[34] Some tourist accounts, in Chicago and elsewhere, did stereotype cultural practices and occasionally reinforced the compartmentalization of ethnic groups found in promotional materials, but this may have been a product of short visits or an inability for visitors to process multiple stimuli when faced with complex and sometimes contradictory information.[35] As it was, accounts such as that of Lewis demonstrated that enough tourists would discover for themselves whether reports of an ethnically or racially integrated city—or country—were mostly fact or fiction.

If tourist literature attempted to make Chicago cosmopolitan by sorting its ethnic groups, they hardly made an effort with Denver. The people of Denver appear infrequently in nineteenth-century booster publications, in part because of the overwhelming promotional emphasis on the natural environment. "Denver society is cosmopolitan," declared Ernest Ingersoll in his 1883 book *The Crest of the Continent: A Record of a Summer's Railroad Ramble through the Rocky Mountains* (a work that straddled the lines between a personal travel narrative and a marketing ploy encouraging the settlement and development of the Rocky Mountain region). But for Ingersoll, Denver's cosmopolitanism resulted from the "surprise" that comes upon visitors "at the totally unexpected degree of intelligence, appreciation of the more refined methods of thought and handiwork, and the knowledge of science, that greet them here."[36]

To illustrate Denver's cosmopolitanism, promotional sources heralded the entrepreneurial energy of its citizens and the physical manifestations of economic progress—especially its industry, technology, and civic buildings. What people *produced* in the form of architecture and institutions could thus be rendered cosmopolitan but not the people themselves. The geography was treated in this fashion, as well. Explorer and one-time Colorado governor William Gilpin, among Denver's greatest nineteenth-century boosters, nicknamed the city "Cosmopolis" and upheld its geographical location as an obvious reason for settlement and investment. "Here the geography and drainage of the Atlantic comes to an end; that of the Pacific is reached," he proclaimed. "Here is the propitious point to receive the column from Asia, debouching from the ocean and the mountains to radiate and expand itself *eastward* over the unobstructed area of the Mississippi Basin!"[37]

Claims to cosmopolitanism in Denver thus focused upon its economic potential, the promise of high culture signaled by a handful of sophisticated buildings, the supposed intelligence of its population, and its geography—not its ethnic diversity. An 1891 souvenir album of Denver, for example, announced that visitors will find "40,000 buildings of brick and stone, owned and occupied by 100,000 cosmopolitan people, who brought with them to Denver the most advanced thoughts of the countries, states or towns from whence they came."[38] For most boosters, those "advanced thoughts" were not indigenous to the region but had to be brought from the East Coast. Bostonian William Thayer, promoting the American West in his massive 1887 tome entitled *Marvels of the New West*, argued that Denver's seventy-five thousand people comprised as "intelligent, enterprising, and generous a population as can be found in New England."[39]

New England's intelligence notwithstanding, Denver's nineteenth-century population hardly could be said to carry with it a generosity permitting it to be so easily classified. Denver's reputation suffered from its Wild West origins following the 1859 discovery of gold in the Rockies, and pigs, pistols, prostitutes, drunks, and vigilantes were apparently regular features in the 1860s urban streetscape.[40] A series of railroad lines converged in Denver in the 1870s, followed by smelters, railroad shops, and other industries—including a rise in prostitution, gambling, and drugs.[41] Along with them came settlers from China, Ireland, Sweden, Italy, and eastern Europe to join those from Germany, England, Scotland, and Wales, nearly all of whom moved into urban neighborhoods based upon religion, regional origin, or dialect. The newcomers, in particular, could not easily be subsumed under Denver's elite cosmopolitan rubric.

Denver's Chinese population grew from 250 in the 1870s to more than 1,000 by 1890, but it faced constant discrimination. Most Chinese worked in laundries, restaurants, or as house servants and were crowded along "Hop Alley," bounded by Market, Blake, Nineteenth, and Twenty-second Streets and adjacent to the brothel district that stretched along Market Street. In 1880, a saloon argument erupted into a race riot, resulting in the destruction of many Chinese businesses and the death of at least one Chinese resident.[42] Denver's African American population was four times that of the Chinese in the nineteenth century but fared no better. African Americans were funneled into the poorest schools, denied access to many hospitals, and consistently harassed by police. Three hangings took place in the city after 1870, and the victims were African American, Chinese, and Italian. Denver remained segregated throughout the nineteenth century, and while urban elites invested heavily in office buildings, churches, and their own residences, they provided little for the city's growing poor.[43] To whom was Denver's supposed generosity extended?

Booster claims to Denver's enterprise, generosity, and intelligence did not convince visitors, who encountered a decidedly uncosmopolitan set on the Denver streets. Isabella Lucy Bird, passing through the city in 1873 during her remarkable eight-hundred-mile solitary journey through the Rocky Mountains, encountered nothing of the "advanced thoughts" of the population. In letters to her sister, she reserved her colorful descriptions instead for a population as diverse in clothing and accoutrements as it was in ethnicity: one with "hunters and trappers in buckskin clothing" along with "Broadway dandies in light kid gloves; rich English sporting tourists, clean, comely, and supercilious-looking; and hundreds of Indians on their small ponies."[44] Recollections of frontier conditions were not as apparent when British engineer and tourist Daniel Pidgeon passed through Denver in the early 1880s, but he still thought that the men—who seemed to vastly outnumber the women—formed a "fugitive" population. The only exception were the city's Chinese, who Pidgeon regarded as exemplary and industrious—a view shared by compatriot Henry Lucy in the mid-1880s, when he noted the "fair sprinkling" of Chinese in the laundry business.[45]

Yet neither Pidgeon nor Lucy considered the Chinese integrated with the city's overall population; indeed, Dayton, Ohio, editor and traveler William Denison Bickham, who visited Denver and the Rockies in 1879, accused the "oriental 'John'" from glancing "indifferently" with "almond eyes at every corner."[46] For nineteenth-century visitors, Denver featured people from different walks of life, but the notion of "intelligence" did not characterize their cultural encounters. The residents appeared not as a like-thinking mass of entrepreneurs but as ordinary folks trying to make ends meet in a western city better known for its proximity to a spectacular natural environment. Tourist encounters with Denver's people seemed almost incidental.

SALT LAKE CITY: THE "MORMON METROPOLIS"

In Salt Lake City, however, tourists did wish to encounter the local population. Mary Wills, recalling a one-way transcontinental railroad trip from San Francisco back to her suburban Philadelphia home in 1889, suggested that future travelers should stop on the return journey only for the "objects of the greatest interest." For Wills, those "objects" included the entire city of Salt Lake, which, she wrote, "more than any other town, seems to demand a visit."[47] Indeed it did. By the end of the nineteenth century, approximately 150,000 to 200,000 people were visiting the city every year.[48]

Tourists' demand stemmed from their desire to encounter those residents who were members of the Church of Jesus Christ of Latter-day Saints (the Mormon Church). The presence of Mormons—the population majority of late nineteenth-century Salt Lake City—provided tourists the opportunity to experience what they perceived as a deviant population on native soil. Mormons held much in common with travelers: European American origins, a steadfast work ethic, and a shared history of overcoming difficult geographical and environmental conditions. Yet the Mormons practiced and condoned polygamy for most of the nineteenth century. This alone set them apart from most tourists, and as historian Patricia Limerick has argued, cast them as exotic and "other" in the popular imagination—although their nineteenth-century racial makeup was almost exclusively white.[49] Tourists, nonetheless, remained fascinated: the prospect of encountering polygamists held extraordinary intrigue. Phil Robinson, during his early 1880s visit, noted that visitors traversed the city while "staring at the houses that they pass as if some monsters lived in them."[50] Salt Lake City met the tourist demand.

The demand had risen long before the transcontinental railroad began depositing tourists in Utah, however, spurred by international attention depicting the Latter-day Saints in a less-than-flattering light. Beginning as early as 1834, a series of anti-Mormon tracts exposed Mormonism as a fanatical cult based largely on a disreputable treasure hunter named Joseph Smith who reshaped a preexisting text as *The Book of Mormon*.[51] Those who practiced the religion, meanwhile, emerged in the anti-Mormon literature as immoral and reprehensible. Yet the phenomenal nineteenth-century growth of the church and its acceptance of polygamy never ceased to entice journalists—and even some opportunist Mormons—who reveled in the lurid characterization of the saints favored by publishing houses of the day. Despite the existence of more even-handed accounts, such portrayals only gathered steam with the 1870 arrival of the railroad to Salt Lake City.[52]

John W. Buel's 1882 *Metropolitan Life Unveiled; or, The Mysteries and Miseries of America's Great Cities* offers a glaring example of the sensationalism that characterized nineteenth-century anti-Mormon literature. In a chapter entitled "Salt Lake City—Polygamy," Buel detailed the spiritual beliefs of the Mormons and attempted to explain how polygamy did not cohere with those beliefs. He included passages on Mormon incest and on the practice of blood atonement, where Mormon officials apparently executed accused sinners through a process of torturous blood-letting.[53] John Beadle, a Cincinnati journalist who spent two years in Salt Lake City to report on its conditions, featured a number of illustrations of grieving Mormon women in his 1882 book *Polygamy; or, The Mysteries and Crimes of Mormonism.*[54] But such disparaging accounts, regardless of accuracy, served only to pique tourist interest, even after polygamy was abolished by federal legislation in 1882 when Utah was still a U.S. territory. The tourist demand did not relent even after Mormon president Wilson Woodruff, supporting Utah's desire to achieve statehood, issued an 1890 manifesto discouraging polygamy.

The challenge for tourist-related businesses and city elites was to divert tourist attention away from polygamy and toward cosmopolitanism of a more refined sort. The 1886 version of the *"Mormon" Metropolis* warned, "Visitors are cautioned against giving credence to the stories told by unprincipled liverymen and hack drivers [for] . . . many of them take a special pride in imposing upon the credulity of strangers by relating the most outrageous fables regarding prominent citizens and their families."[55] Salt Lake City officials had a vested interest in promoting the city to visitors. They knew that positive reports from travelers would speak volumes about the city's reputation, improve the local economy, and contribute to national support for the recognition of Utah as a state.[56]

To help fight a lingering reputation of Mormon immorality, tourist literature, produced by Mormon and non-Mormon companies alike, located cosmopolitanism in the idea of a calmly productive and efficient city—one where brave American pioneers overcame enormous hardship, persecution, drought, and privation to transform a near-inhospitable desert landscape into a great metropolis. The Mormons emerge as enterprising visionaries, engineers, builders, and agriculturalists who, in the late 1840s, established a clean, organized, cosmopolitan settlement, where none should have existed. But this cosmopolitanism regarded the fruits of Mormon labor, not Mormon spiritual practices or places of origin. Printed matter advertising Salt Lake City ossified the Mormons as relics of the mid-nineteenth-century past; it relegated the contemporary situation and the everyday environment to the background—if it included those circumstances at all.[57] Should travelers arrive seeking close encounters with polygamy, boosters hoped to direct them instead to the city's architecture, religious services, musical venues, and theatrical performances.[58]

Brigham Young adopted this general philosophy as well. Mormon president from 1847 to 1877, Young not only encouraged tourism when he sponsored the construction of the Utah Central Railroad link from Ogden to Salt Lake City in 1871, but he met regularly with visiting tourists who called upon him. Young was confident that tourist visits would reverse any negative preconceived notions about the Mormons, and that they would leave the city "with feelings greatly modified and often afterwards have a kind word for the people of Utah when they hear them assailed."[59] George Q. Cannon, a political strategist who served under four different Mormon presidents, also favored tourism as a potential benefit to the city's reputation. Cannon thought that if tourists visited the beautiful and well-organized city, they would connect Mormon ambitions to those of the eastern U.S. population. Such parallels, he hoped, would contribute to the recognition and respect of Mormonism at the national level.[60]

Visitors—the vast majority of whom were non-Mormons (and who Mormons considered "Gentiles")—were not so easily convinced. Nearly all nineteenth-century tourist accounts focused upon contemporary Mormon life, and many of them discussed the evils of polygamy, even if their Salt Lake City experiences exposed them to nothing of the kind. Tourists looked for signs of abnormal or immoral activity, attempting to glean information to confirm their assumptions about Mormon religious and cultural practices. They did not necessarily know what abnormality or immorality might look like, but they searched for signs of it in clothing, movement, expressions, and the physiognomy of those they encountered. An "agreeable youth who looked like a gentleman" accompanied German tourist Alexandra Gripenberg around Salt Lake City in 1888, but she could not help but wonder "how many wives he was blessed with." "That dreadful thought," she added, "inevitably slips into the visitor's mind in seeing a masculine resident of Utah."[61]

Few travelers, however, likely encountered the Mormons as abnormal or immoral, for the privacy of family life and spiritual practices made it improbable that tourists were privy to witnessing the immorality they so desperately wished to see. Danish visitor Vilhelm Topsöe, in the early 1870s, had no such luck. He described Mormon houses that stood in the middle of blocks but surrounded by trees and shrubbery, permitting tourists to "see less of Mormon domestic life than you would like."[62] Henry Brainard Kent fared no better when he visited in 1890, explaining that few tourists enter the "forbidding labyrinths" of Mormon private life. Tourists, he argued, must be content with understanding Mormons from the monumentality and beauty of the built environment.[63] Furthermore, whether accurate or not, many Mormon women justified the institution of polygamy as part of their spiritual obligation, although tourists half expected to see Mormon women rebelling against their husbands.[64]

What tourists did or did not observe did not prevent them from writing of Mormon degeneracy. The reverend E. R. Hendrix, in 1878, wrote that he had spoken to a range of people, Mormons and non-Mormons alike, all of whom agreed that Mormonism was a curse to an otherwise beautiful city and "an offense to Christianity and civilization throughout the world."[65] Caroline Churchill even claimed to have seen "great numbers of deformed people" in the streets, while Susie Clark not only noted the "strange history" and "strange land" of the Mormons but a general "lack of intelligence" in the urban population.[66] Harvey Rice referred to Salt Lake City more generally as the "holy land of many wives" and noted that intermarriage made polygamy even more "revolting" than it already was. "The time is rapidly approaching," Rice wrote, "when this corroding stain, this foul plague-spot on our national escutcheon, will be forever obliterated."[67]

The Mormons were neither oblivious to the attention foisted upon them by visitors nor unaware of the manner in which they were described and discussed. Needless to say, curious tourists irritated a Mormon population struggling to establish a place of spiritual freedom. One Mormon woman apparently told Rudyard Kipling that she "hated the idea of Salt Lake City being turned into a show-place for the amusement of the Gentile." There was no reason, she said, that tourists should come to Salt Lake City to "stare" at the Mormons.[68] Her sentiment was justified, of course. But in the nineteenth century, few tourists could resist. Massachusetts-based tourist John H. C. Church admitted as much when he attended a theatrical performance in 1887—"more for the curiosity of seeing the Mormons than seeing the play."[69]

Not all travelers treated Mormons as if they were mere fodder for reinforcing their negative preconceptions. As early as 1870, Fitz Hugh Ludlow, anticipating Mormon women "either shamefaced or brazen" and looking for "dejected "faces . . . or hard, defiant faces," discovered "nothing of the kind." William Preston, some twenty years later, wrote of seeing the occasional female face with signs of grief and anguish, but "there were not nearly so many of these as might be expected."[70] Similarly, Georgia-based traveler M. Dwinell, in 1878, claimed to have met a polygamous family but had nothing derogatory to say. "I have enjoyed my little trip down here very much," he wrote.[71] In 1882, traveler Mary Bradshaw Richards looked around and could tell no difference between "the forms and faces of old and young men and women around me" and those of "a civilized community."[72] Solomon Mead, who visited Salt Lake City a year later, noted that the Gentiles tended to provide "unfavorable reports" on the Mormons, but recommended that travelers should visit Salt Lake City and make up their own minds.[73]

Many did. Rather than accept the rhetoric of tourist literature or simply repeat previously published accounts, several tourists sought out everyday Mormon activities, made arrangements to stay with Mormon families, or attempted to visit with Mormon elders. They often discovered information that revised popular—and negative— impressions of Mormon life. Phil Robinson stayed with Mormons for three months in the early 1880s and declared that nearly all Gentile reports on the Mormons published up to that point were invariably unkind—and inaccurate.[74] Those who visited Salt Lake City during Brigham Young's lifetime often hoped to hear Young deliver a sermon; barring that, they attempted to secure invitations to meet him or other leading Mormon citizens privately. Visiting in 1890, Julia Thomas asked Emiline Wells—editor of the church-issued *Woman's Exponent* and the "fourth or fifth wife of a prominent Mormon elder"—about the Mormon practice of "blood atonement." Wells declared that such practices were pure myth: among the "many slanders, cruel and malicious, circulated by our enemies."[75]

Hoping for insight, E. D. Holton used various letters of introduction to his advantage in 1880. He first sought out "Mr. Eldridge," the manager of the Zion's Co-operative Mercantile Institution, noting that Eldridge struck him as a "sober, sensible, and candid man"—despite his four wives. Later, Holton presented a letter of introduction from Wisconsin governor William Smith to John Taylor, the third president of the Mormon church. Taylor immediately dismissed the gentlemen to whom he was speaking and, Holton wrote, "gave my wife and myself a most courteous and polite audience, continuing it as long as we chose to remain." Holton's impressions were positive overall, and he described Taylor as a "gentleman in manners" with a "strong, benevolent, and I may say handsome face."[76]

Taylor was a British-born member of the church. This was not uncommon: the Latter-day Saints recruited actively in Britain, although most Brits who made the trek to Salt Lake City in the nineteenth century did not rise to such elite status. There was diversity among the nineteenth-century Salt Lake City Mormon population, but it was a

class-based diversity more so than an ethnic or racial one. The promise
of community, unification, and salvation told in the *Book of Mormon*
held extraordinary appeal, particularly to that segment of the population whose lot in life had suffered an unfortunate blow. The spread
of church doctrine through missionary efforts in the decades after
the 1830 founding of the church attracted thousands of converts—not
only in America but also overseas, especially in economically depressed
British and Scandinavian countries. Facing discrimination at home,
many British and Scandinavian converts—together with a rising number from continental Europe—embarked on the lengthy journey to
Utah once pioneers settled the Salt Lake Valley in the late 1840s and
early 1850s. By the 1860s, Utah's foreign born made up 35 percent
of the territory's population, and, by 1870, British-born immigrants
comprised a quarter of that population. Scandinavian immigrants were
not far behind.[77]

A diverse people drawn principally from conditions of economic
hardship—coupled with the international attention given to Mormon polygamy—did not always equate to a cosmopolitan Salt Lake
City in the tourist imagination. Some visitors were decidedly negative;
Rev. John Todd, for example, explained in 1870 that Mormons were
mostly "foreigners" hailing from the "lowest, most illiterate strata of
society in Europe." English visitor Henry Alworth Merewether was
more specific in 1874, when he claimed that the Latter-day Saints from
Wales and Scandinavia were people of "low intellect." This sentiment
was echoed by Brooklyn tourist J. H. Bates in 1887, when a tabernacle visit revealed a congregation of Norwegians, English, Welsh, and
Dutch—the "plainest and humblest folk" from the "many lands out of
the lower, if not lowest, walks of life."[78] Others offered less judgmen-
tal assessments. Walter P. Ryland, visiting Salt Lake City as part of an
around-the-world trip from England in 1880–81, noted the "mixed
features" of the Mormons and concluded that such features were only
"natural," given their origins in "all the different nations in Europe,
and other parts of the world." In 1890, Matthew Johnson outlined
the "very mixed character" of the population, represented by almost
"every nationality."[79]

Yet some tourists considered diversity in class—even religion—beneficial to the city's fortunes. At times, they read it as cosmopolitan, too. Travelers visiting Salt Lake City following the completion of the Utah Central Railroad link from Ogden remarked on the emerging non-Mormon, business-oriented influence they encountered in the city streets, which gave the city a spiritual and economic diversity that was less apparent in earlier years. This diversity lent Salt Lake City a vibrant air that some tourists may have ignored because of their desire to seek out polygamy—but other tourists did not. New Yorker John Codman, visiting in 1874, noted that Gentile-owned millineries and dressmaking shops selling "jaunty hats, ribbons, and expensive silks," much to Brigham Young's chagrin, increasingly appealed to Mormon women—including his wives and daughters. British journalist and tourist George Augustus Sala, visiting in early 1886, stayed at the city's Walker House hotel and discovered cosmopolitanism in every detail, from the hotel workers to the food. "I have rarely seen a more cosmo-politan *carte*," he wrote, "nor, from the matter of that, a more cosmo-politan hotel. The baker in the basement was German; the bar-keeper was a Scandinavian—whether a Swede, a Norwegian, a Dane, or an Icelander, I could not well make out. The head waiter was a Dutch-man, and the 'baggage-smasher,' or luggage porter, an Italian." Refer-ring to class-based Mormon diversity, Sala added that it "was the poor and ignorant Cosmopolitans who have converted the valley of the Great Salt Lake into a land of milk and honey."[80] And tourists certainly did not consider all foreign-born Latter-day Saints to be immoral and drawn from the "lowest" walks of life. English tourist W. G. Marshall, visiting the tabernacle in 1878, explained that his personal guide was also an Englishman—yet a distinguished one who once performed in London orchestras and had only one wife.[81]

Times changed as well—although not always, in some tourists' esti-mation, for the better. While the tourist literature attempted to locate Salt Lake City in the past when its meticulous planning, orderly houses, and crystal-clear streams of water running alongside the streets were more evident, visitors encountered the city in the present. Despite the contributions of commerce and industry to the city's economic growth, tourists generally found unappealing that emerging world in late nineteenth-century Salt Lake City, which they attributed—not always accurately—to a non-Mormon presence.

Non-Mormons had begun settling in Salt Lake City as early as the 1870s to work the nearby mines, and a number of businesses—including saloons—catered to them.[82] A bustling urban center would have been less visible to visitors in the 1850s, when Salt Lake City was a small and exclusive Mormon settlement, but it was apparent by the 1870s. In 1871, British traveler Charles Marshall reported on the "shaggy-looking, roughly-dressed, dare-devil miners," who hung about hotel doors and street corners and "spit, and chew, and smoke," while James Bonwick, from England, noted the loud talking, swearing, and drinking in the city's main street and money "flying about freely"—particularly "at the bars of the newly opened Gentile *palaces*."[83] The Latter-day Saints comprised a majority in Salt Lake City, but the smaller Gentile population made its presence felt.

The Gentile effect became a bit more pronounced as the decades progressed. When Mary Bradshaw Richards first visited Salt Lake City in 1870 she made no mention of the non-Mormon population and considered the city a pastoral place in tune with the rhythms of nature. But when she returned in 1882 she was dismayed to find that Gentiles had made the city far more businesslike and competitive. Richards noted that her party rushed "amid street cars, saloons, clouds of dust, a diminished supply of water, and warring of religious and social beliefs and the increasing contentions of business competition."[84] Gentiles struck Italian correspondent Giovanni Vigna dal Ferro similarly in 1881: he complained that they had begun to "invade" the city with their "Yankee institutions"—saloons most notable among them.[85] Bostonian Susie Clark found little redeeming about the Salt Lake City population as a whole in 1890 but suggested that recent non-Mormon immigration marked a "boom." She entered city streets "thronged" with people—a vivid contrast from the calm, wide avenues and sense of propriety that dominated descriptions and illustrations of Salt Lake City from the 1870s.[86]

SECOND SOUTH STREET, LOOKING EAST FROM MAIN STREET, SALT LAKE CITY. Telegraph
wires and façade signage in this 1887 image reveal the commercial growth of Salt Lake
City. By the 1880s, tourists noticed an increasing non-Mormon (or Gentile) presence
in the streets, marked by saloon-goers who disrupted the orderly cosmopolitan city
that boosters wished to uphold. For tourists, cosmopolitanism in Salt Lake City was
beginning to resemble that of modernizing cities elsewhere: economically and spiritually diverse but not necessarily fostering the common good. (Source: Sidney W. Darke,
Salt Lake City Illustrated, p.17. Courtesy of Internet Archive, http://archive.org/details/
saltlakecityillu00dark.)

For late nincteenth-century Salt Lake City visitors, encounters
with a range of people did not go missing from their diaries, letters,
and travelers' accounts. These encounters revealed an economically
and spiritually diverse city that was neither immoral nor progressing
smoothly toward an efficient future with a cohesive population that
had relegated all potential troubles to the past. When W. Henry Barneby
encountered two groups of card-playing Native American families on
a hill behind the city, he commented on their lack of beauty but noted
their peacefulness and that they did not mind being observed as they
played. He made no attempt to subsume them within some larger
cosmopolitan rubric; to Barneby, nothing about the Native Americans

seemed immoral—or progressive.[87] Cosmopolitanism existed in Salt Lake City, but tourists could not easily characterize the city as such. It may have appeared unusual because the majority of its residents held fast to religious beliefs at odds with those of the traveling population. But the on-the-ground tourist experiences suggest a late nineteenth-century Salt Lake City population far more akin to that of other western cities than tourists either expected or desired: diverse, businesslike, ordinary, complex, and refined—as well as uncouth.

SAN FRANCISCO AND THE "CELESTIAL KINGDOM"

For the complexities of cosmopolitanism, however, no western city compared to nineteenth-century San Francisco. Well known is the story of the city's emergence as a vital conduit for goods and people following the 1849 gold rush. Less well known is that San Francisco's growth in the last decades of the nineteenth century depended heavily on its foreign-born immigrants—especially the polyglot group of settlers from England, Scotland, Australia, Germany, Italy, Ireland, and China who arrived in the wake of the gold discovery. These settlers were later joined by other immigrants hailing from Japan, Korea, Mexico, Peru, Chile, and the Philippines. Together, they coexisted in what may have been the most ethnically diverse city in nineteenth-century North America.[88] But it was not always a peaceful coexistence, and not all ethnic groups received equal treatment.

Only a handful of immigrants found immediate work or lucrative pay, thus creating an economically—as well as ethnically—diverse population that compelled thousands of men to find lodging in San Francisco's many long-term residential hotels. As a result, late nineteenth-century San Francisco may have featured a higher percentage of hotel dwellers relative to its overall population than any large city in America. This density was apparent to tourist Harriet Harper, who wrote, during an 1888 visit, that the "great mass of people have no home life" and "live the lives of transient tourists."[89] The residential situation contributed to a kaleidoscopic urban street scene on any given day: even along the fashionable thoroughfares of Market Street and Montgomery Street, one could discover new, usually poor, immigrants occupying the same spaces as upper-class European Americans.

Yet San Francisco's ethnic and economic diversity did not, in itself, amount to an elite cosmopolitan city. To fit the cosmopolitan vision— as with elsewhere in the urban West—that diverse population had to be understood as prosperous and working toward a common goal. John Hittell's 1888 *Guide Book to San Francisco* was one of many publications that attempted to ignore ethnic, economic, and cultural differences and subsume the population under a single umbrella. Acknowledging that no cities in Europe featured as many nationalities as did San Francisco, Hittell stressed that the "enterprise and intelligence of many races are blended among her population, and the dull, the slothful, and the faint-hearted seldom find here an abiding-place."[90] Guidebooks such as Hittell's cast San Francisco as a place where a diverse population upheld diversity as color-blind and where the city's peoples strove to guarantee its economic well-being.

To showcase the city's cosmopolitanism, promotional materials occasionally disregarded San Francisco's citizens altogether. E. M. Jenkins' 1883 guidebook *An Excursion to Colorado, California, and the Yosemite Valley* presented San Francisco's cosmopolitanism as driven by money and transportation—not people. "San Francisco is the most cosmopolitan city in the world," Jenkins declared, pointing to the city's ability to "float vessels from all parts of the world," which led to the "fabulous fortunes of some of her citizens."[91] Similarly, N. W. Griswold's 1883 *Beauties of California* argued that San Francisco was "thoroughly cosmopolitan," citing as evidence an accompanying bird's-eye view depicting "the forest of masts of vessels lying at the wharves receiving and discharging cargoes from every nation of the globe."[92] According to Marcus Boruck's 1877 *California Illustrated*, San Francisco was "as cosmopolitan as Cairo and as lively as Paris," in part because of the rapidity of its growth, its prodigious wealth, the "riches and sin" that "jostle each other on the streets" and its "crowded" harbor with "shipping from all parts of the world."[93] The "riches" and "sin" were not, in this vision, at odds. Painting the San Francisco population with a broad brushstroke, Boruck managed to ensure that everybody somehow contributed to San Francisco's progress.

Yet the discrepancies between rich and poor and the constant influx of immigrants from the eastern United States, Europe, South America, and parts of Asia could not be so easily edited into a like-thinking and enterprising mass. Visitors frequently offered revisions to this reading of the urban population, rendering more complex the notion of cosmopolitanism in San Francisco. At times, these revisions were descriptive rather than analytical. There was, for example, French engineer Georges Duloup, who visited San Francisco in the late 1870s to report on its conditions for the French government. He noted the diversity: "La population de San Francisco est très mélangee: elle se compose d'Allemands, d'Irlandais, d'Anglo-Saxons, de Français, d'Italiens, de Mexicains et de Chinois." There was also British visitor Daniel Pidgeon, who stated that the city's population is "extremely cosmopolitan and contains only a small proportion of native Americans," and British author Morley Roberts—despite his near-fruitless search for employment and food during a difficult visit—still noticed the "cosmopolitan character of the place" because of the "numerous races to be seen." And there was New York–based editor and reporter Julian Ralph who, in 1893, proclaimed a "decidedly cosmopolitan community" along San Francisco's Market Street—mostly because it was "stamped as foreign in a great degree."[94]

Many other visitors, however, offered more analytical assessments of urban diversity, although they rarely mirrored the elite cosmopolitan vision of a cohesive population effectively working to achieve prosperity. Rather than boasting of the international origins of ships docked in the city wharves, New Yorker Banyer Clarkson, visiting San Francisco in 1874, explained that the Brannan Street Wharf was "always the scene of confusion and also a Babel of Languages on the arrival of a steamer from Yokohama or Australia." And while Scottish journalist John Leng, in 1876, stated that San Francisco was "one of the most cosmopolitan places in the world," his description was inclusive, featuring those groups "low down" on the social ladder (the "Chinese, the negroes, and occasionally the Indians") as well as wealthier folks relaxing in the lobbies or dining room of the Palace Hotel.[95] To British traveler Harry Jones, in 1878, every "nation and tongue" seemed be represented in San Francisco. "The way in which society, as seen in the streets and inns, is jumbled up here," he wrote, "is very striking."[96] That "society" struck tourist Harvey Rice as troubling when he visited in the early 1870s: he attributed the city's lingering reputation for vice and crime—which it had established during the 1850s—to the large numbers of "idlers" at every street corner and to the transient hotels "with strangers coming and going, all on the rush."[97] Those strangers also came from all over the nation and world, and their presence hardly fulfilled the vision of an elite cosmopolitan city.

Yet nothing threatened the elite notion of cosmopolitanism in San Francisco so much as the presence of the Chinese Quarter, or "Chinatown." Laws virtually quarantined Chinatown from the rest of the city and forbade the Chinese from owning property outside the seven, eight, or nine blocks bounded variously in the nineteenth century by Stockton and Kearney Streets on the west and east, respectively, and Pacific Avenue and initially California Street then Sacramento Street on the north and south.[98] Few Chinese settlers ventured beyond the quarter anyway, for they feared persecution and physical harm from inhabitants of nearby non-Chinese neighborhoods, such as the Barbary Coast, and generally were not welcome elsewhere in the city. But Chinatown remained within a stone's throw of the city's more fashionable areas—where a proper cosmopolitanism was thought to reside. From an elite perspective, this was problematic.

Chinatown grew rapidly following the gold rush. By the 1880s, due in part to the completion of the Central Pacific Railroad (for which many Chinese worked) and laws that forbade the Chinese from living anywhere in San Francisco *but* Chinatown, the neighborhood reached a startling density with a population of 21,745—more than 20 percent of the entire Chinese population in the United States. Chinese employment in a variety of industries crucial to the national and local economy—including railroads, agriculture, mining, laundries, and cigar factories—was not, however, wholly appreciated. The Chinese

accepted lower pay than whites, and many jobs normally employing whites were filled instead by Chinese. This was desirable for the
industrial tycoons, who could reduce the cost of labor while demand-
ing the same level of production, but it infuriated white-run labor
organizations and raised the "Chinese Question" about whether Chinese immigration was beneficial to the United States if it eliminated
white labor—even if the Chinese clearly contributed to the American economic engine. These circumstances also spurred the rise of the
predominantly Irish-American Workingmen's Party of California in
the late 1870s in San Francisco—a party organized to restrict, if not
eliminate, Chinese labor. With their rallying cry, "The Chinese Must
Go!," the San Francisco–based party drew upon long-standing preju-
dices and targeted the Chinese (rather than the tycoons) as part of their
antimonopolist campaign. They succeeded in fomenting popular—and
legislative—opinion against the Chinese, and their persistence eventually persuaded the U.S. Congress to pass the 1882 Chinese Exclusion
Act, which suspended all immigrant labor from China for ten years.[99]

Despite occasional rioting by anti-Chinese mobs and a decrease in
new Chinese immigrants, the Chinese were not excluded from San
Francisco's Chinatown. Somewhat inexplicably, the population of San
Francisco's Chinatown *increased*—by 1890, in fact, some thirty thousand Chinese residents crowded into its houses, streets, and alleys.[100]
The presence of tens of thousands of Chinese packed into a tight
urban environment, hard up against San Francisco's business district,
created problems for any version of cosmopolitanism the city's elites
wished to uphold. Yet the neighborhood's density also made it easier
for boosters to set aside Chinatown (and the Chinese) as tourist attractions, distinct from the cosmopolitan city they hoped to maintain—or
create.

Tourists would have sought out Chinatown regardless. The presence
of a large Chinese community in the United States had attracted visitors at least since the early 1860s—even before the completion of the
transcontinental railroad.[101] Already by the 1870s Chinatown may have
been the most-anticipated and most-visited attraction in all of the late
nineteenth-century urban American West. Mary Wills, during a late

1880s visit, remarked that you "do not see your friends at the hotel, but you are sure to meet them in Chinatown."[102] Indeed, you did.

San Francisco's Chinatown attracted tourists for reasons similar to those luring them to Salt Lake City. As with Salt Lake City's Mormons, the Chinese suffered religious or ethnic persecution and, for these reasons and others, garnered considerable attention in the press—much of it unsympathetic to their plight. Similar to the Mormons and the vices associated with polygamy, the reputation for prostitution among the Chinese linked San Francisco's Chinatown with Salt Lake City as harbors for illicit sexual promiscuity and overall impropriety. The Chinese, like the Mormons, represented a deviant presence in America.

Yet there were differences, too, and those differences may have made the Chinese even *more* alluring to tourists. Published descriptions and imagery cast the Mormons as spiritually and sexually deviant; the Chinese as spiritually, sexually, *and* ethnically deviant. And where the Mormons built Salt Lake City's most substantial buildings and held considerable political power within the city, the Chinese held almost no power within city government and struggled to eke out an existence in the only San Francisco district in which they were permitted to live. But this was enticing, too—at least for tourists. The poverty-stricken district attracted visitors for purposes of reform, curiosity, or perhaps something more sinister: the act of "slumming" through poor areas had long been popular among visitors in modernizing European and eastern U.S. cities—trips undertaken occasionally to reinforce tourists' moral superiority over those they visited.[103] In San Francisco, many tourists believed they could go slumming in what was sold to them as China itself. Tourists were encouraged to imagine that Chinatown offered a brief foray into the exotic Orient—a transplanted slice of Asia on American soil.

For civic boosters interested in maintaining San Francisco as a properly cosmopolitan place for visitors, the challenge was rhetorically to shape Chinatown and the Chinese so they could be kept separate from the rest of San Francisco. This would legitimize white superiority and, among other things, prevent the Chinese from citizenship and assimilation into San Francisco's—and America's—culture. To manage this separation, writers and publishers of promotional materials typically segregated information on the Chinese and Chinatown from the bulk of their San Francisco description. While the level of detail varied among sources, several guidebooks featured an overview of the Chinese labor question, along with a discussion of Chinese manners and customs: their language, holidays, burial practices, food, and community organization. Invariably, a list of sites worthy of visitation accompanied this cultural summary—most notably theaters, joss houses, and opium dens. Restaurants were less frequently promoted as tourist attractions because of public health fears, but tourists sought them anyway.[104] The more sordid, risqué, and seemingly different from European American spaces and practices, the easier it was to separate them from the rest of San Francisco. And the better to pique tourist interest.

The tourist literature tended to approach Chinatown in two principal ways, both of which maintained the neighborhood as a separate, exotic entity apart from the rest of the city, but neither attempted to understand Chinatown on its own terms or those of its residents. These approaches were not always mutually exclusive. One method was to sell Chinatown as a tight-knit community frozen in an imaginary past, where "primitive" peoples carried on daily activities in a dilapidated environment, just as they purportedly had done for millennia in China itself. In this vein, Chinatown was linked to "old China" and the Chinese to an unchanging culture oblivious to, and unaffected by, the rush to modernization in San Francisco. One often discovers the Chinese referred to interchangeably as "Celestials" or "Mongolians" and their neighborhood as the "Flowery Kingdom" or the "Celestial Kingdom"—patronizing terms intended to make the Chinese appear alien to a supposedly more pure American population but, in their supposed otherworldliness, not threatening to it.[105] To mitigate their presence in contemporary urban culture, to construct them for tourist consumption, and to maintain an elite cosmopolitanism for the city, many sources banished the Chinese to the distant past.

To further a sense of exoticism, tourist literature also characterized San Francisco's Chinatown as a miniature version of mainland Chinese cities: guidebooks compared Chinatown to the city of Canton

(Guangzhou) as often as they likened it to Peking (Beijing), Hankow (Wuhan), or Shanghai, although it was never clear that the writers knew or understood anything about the circumstances of Chinese cities, past or present. The nineteenth-century San Francisco Chinese, however, came predominantly from the rural areas of southern China's Guangdong Province and most had never experienced urban life prior to their emigration from China.[106] Yet such geographical or historical details did not concern the writers or producers of San Francisco's nineteenth-century promotional material. For them, Chinatown had to appeal to tourists and claiming that San Francisco's Chinatown was essentially a Chinese city located in America was good enough. After all, most European and American tourists had never traveled to China, and they might not know the difference. There was little risk.

Another common literary and illustrative tactic manufactured Chinatown as dangerous and decrepit—yet still enticing. This mode of urban description shaped Chinatown as a filthy, illicit, disease-ridden neighborhood that should be eliminated from the landscape for the sake of the health and morality of San Francisco's population. The genre of literary urban sensationalism was particularly effective in depicting Chinatown in this fashion, with authors consistently describing Chinatown as a district of "vice" and "filth," where cramped conditions bred physical, moral, and spiritual degeneracy. If they recommended tourist visits at all, writers urged those visits only in the daytime. At night, they warned, only men should venture forth, and only with the accompaniment of a police officer.[107] Tourists only occasionally heeded such warnings.

Benjamin E. Lloyd's *Lights and Shades in San Francisco*, published in 1876, and Walter J. Raymond's *Horrors of the Mongolian Settlement*, published in 1886, are representative of the genre: they included appalling descriptions of the Chinese and uncomplimentary illustrations of the neighborhood and Chinese life. Focusing on opium consumption, gambling, and prostitution, works such as these were quick to depict Chinatown as an alien, decrepit place in which no "civilized" human could ever dwell. Highlighting Chinatown's oppressive population density (without noting the laws that restricted its geographical spread), such literature also commonly referred to the neighborhood as a breeding place for sickness and disease.[108] Lloyd's text did not focus wholly on Chinatown, but to accentuate its differences he celebrated the "merry" voices and "happy hearts" of nearby European American–dominated Kearney Street, which he upheld as a model of "refinement, comfort, happiness, and prosperity." Chinatown, he noted, featured streets and narrow lanes, "mantled in dismal gloom" with "listless idlers lolling upon the curb or against the walls, perhaps dreaming of crime and heathen debauchery." Raymond's *Horrors of the Mongolian Settlement* went further. "It is a well-known and authenticated fact," Raymond wrote, "that, in Sullivan's alley, the home of the scavenger element of Chinatown, the miserable wretches, who wholly subsist upon the refuse picked from the gutters and ash barrels of the city, live forty feet underground in mud holes, whose filth and horrors are forever shut out from the light of day." Such descriptions were common.[109]

Chinatown was neither disease ridden, filthy, or horrific, but its widespread depiction in this fashion created an indelible perception of the place that proved difficult for visitors to shake. A budding tourist industry in late nineteenth-century San Francisco, replete with guides who occasionally hired local Chinese for assistance, reinforced this perception—especially at a few opium dens that were apparently staged to cater to tourists. According to one account, tour guides led visitors through subterranean passages to specific dens with "hidden" entrances. As part of the tour, Chinese men were employed to lurk around in these passages, carry unconcealed weapons, and appear "evil."[110] Such performances served to reinforce the separation between Chinatown and the rest of what elites upheld as cosmopolitan San Francisco. But they seemed only to encourage tourist visitation.

Promotional sources also cast Chinatown's built environment, specifically, both ways: as an exotic and quaint collection of buildings and alleys that conjured up notions of "old China" and as thoroughly dilapidated, dirty, and potentially dangerous structures and passageways. As opposed to the presentation of downtown buildings, tourists were not encouraged to understand the built environment of Chinatown as an excellent specimen of architectural art but rather to understand its general differences from "American" architecture and to experience the interior decorations and the activities held inside. To best illustrate these differences, tourists were directed, in particular, to attend the performances in the Chinese theaters and to inspect the displays inside the joss houses.

Guidebooks mainly promoted two Chinese theaters for tourist visitation: the Jackson Street Theater and the Washington Street Theater, although they did not recommend tourists sit through one of the full seven- to eight-hour Chinese operas regularly performed at either of them. At a loss to describe the meanings behind the performances or to understand their cultural specificity, literature aimed for the tourist market described the stage, the visitor standing areas, the performers' costumes, the props, and the musicians, while adding that visitors would find the entire experience rather unusual. Some sources were more emphatically critical: John Hittell's *Guide Book to San Francisco* explained that tourists would detect the "barbaric" sounds performed by the musicians, which he likened to "squeaks" and "rattles" that sounded "ludicrous" or "violent."[111]

Promotional sources also encouraged tourists to visit Chinatown's joss houses—local temples where worshippers paid respects to a variety of indigenous Chinese deities. Such unfamiliar spaces and practices clashed significantly with church design and the monotheistic Christian belief system to which many visitors subscribed, making comprehension difficult but still heightening tourist intrigue. To accentuate their difference from churches, tourist literature provided outlandish descriptions of the interior design of these local Chinese folk temples, mocked the spiritual significance of images and idols, and caricatured the spiritual practices of the Chinese who worshipped there. No essential difference existed in the manner of description throughout the late nineteenth century. Charles Nordhoff's 1873 *California: For Health, Pleasure, and Residence* stated that tourists would find the joss houses "decorated with cheap tinsel" and designed in the "shabby style" of the theater, while a guidebook dedicated solely to Chinatown published some twenty years later noted the "bizarre surroundings" of the joss house, which included a "garish and inharmonious mingling of color" that simply did not "consort with the Caucasian idea of the worship of a Supreme Being."[112] Unable or unwilling to respect or understand eastern religions or symbols, guidebook authors proceeded instead to critique joss houses as unworthy, further separating them from western spaces of worship and ensuring that the cosmopolitan city would be a monotheistic one. Some tourists made no attempt to learn about cultural or religious differences; J. J. Upchurch, visiting with a company of four in 1885, claimed that the Chinese worshipped "the devil as well as other gods."[113]

Writers and editors of late nineteenth-century guidebooks tapped into long-standing derogatory perceptions toward the Chinese in America—they did not create them.[114] Such perceptions had been established with the earliest accounts of Chinese, who arrived during the gold rush, and were accentuated by noted writers in national publications. California poet Bret Harte was one of those; his widely publicized piece for the *Overland Monthly* in 1870 entitled "Plain Language from Truthful James" characterized the Chinese as scheming and mischievous. Harte claimed innocence from the poem's anti-Chinese undertones, but it would be republished nationwide shortly thereafter as "The Heathen Chinee," and its vast readership contributed to a national distaste for the Chinese. In a journal entry of that same year, George Templeton Strong, writing from New York, wrote that the "Ballad of the Heathen Chinee, by some Californian is in everybody's mouth, and very funny."[115] Given the aristocratic circles in which Strong traveled, it is likely "everybody" referred to those with the financial wherewithal to make a transcontinental railroad journey. No doubt many of these potential tourists sought to familiarize themselves with the "heathen Chinee" in San Francisco, and plenty of tourist material was available to assist them.

Many visitors claimed to have discovered such "heathens" upon arrival in Chinatown, often intertwining their disgust for the Chinese with a refusal to accept religions beyond their own. Most were unlikely aware of the discrimination that led to the density and conditions in Chinatown's built environment, and perhaps such awareness may not have made a substantial difference. Indeed, in the early 1870s, Rose Georgina Kingsley ventured into an opium den and described a "horrid" scene filled with "a dozen or more opium-eaters" lying on beds and "covered with sheets like corpses."[116] Frank Green, a British traveler also visiting Chinatown in the 1870s, recalled its "abominable stenches . . . to which hog slaughtering in Chicago," by comparison, was but "a trifle."[117] Thomas Chard, writing more than fifteen years later in 1888, characterized Chinatown as an "inferno" and recalled stenches that could "turn the stomach of an ostrich," while Thomas Dewar, in 1893, warned the Chinatown visitor to "prepare his nerves" because "he will be surrounded by dirt, stench, and immorality."[118] Several traveler accounts echoed guidebook and sensationalist characterizations, reinforcing existing stereotypes and keeping Chinatown separate from cosmopolitan San Francisco.

But not all. Englishwoman Mary Rhodes Carbutt, visiting Chinatown in the mid-1880s, discovered that the warnings she had read and heard were exaggerated. "Travellers are told that Chinatown is full of bad characters and that it is not safe to go there after dark without police escort," she wrote, "but this seems to be only a means of extorting money. Nothing does ever happen to the inquisitive tourist."[119] Phil Robinson heeded no such warning and explored Chinatown alone at night. There, he met a resident who explained that the cramped conditions into which the Chinese were placed resulted from contemporary municipal laws. Robinson found the San Francisco Chinese to be "quiet-mannered," clean, and hard working.[120] In fact, numerous accounts reveal a discrepancy between how Chinatown was sold and how tourists experienced it. While acknowledging Chinatown's differences, many visitors commented on its everyday character and likened it to other working-class or urban residential areas with which they were familiar. They also noted Chinatown's efficiency and organization, describing its industrious, well-dressed, well-behaved, clean, and rarely intoxicated residents—attributes to which they hoped all American workers could aspire. The past remained elusive for tourists even if they searched for it; many tourists, instead, read the neighborhood as a particularly Chinese *American* environment that was shaped by particulars of the modernizing, nineteenth-century world. China-town was not a museum.

Along these lines, some tourists understood that the Chinese simply desired to make ends meet in economically volatile nineteenth-century San Francisco. A number of full-length traveler narratives devoted sections or entire chapters to the so-called Chinese Question; their authors were often sympathetic to the Chinese and unsupportive of the nativist workingman's crusade to blame the Chinese for their willingness to accept low-paying jobs. These narratives expressed concern for the difficult physical and social conditions faced by the Chinese, including the constant harassment from local "hoodlums." An 1874 San Francisco visit suggested to British traveler John W. Boddam-Whetham that the Chinese defied the subservient and helpless portrayal they received in the press. "I have been gratified on three or four occasions by seeing a very complete thrashing administered to some great hulking hoodlum by an inoffensive-looking John Chinaman," he wrote, "whose patience had been exhausted by the attacks of his cowardly and astonished enemy."[121]

Many tourists avoided or ignored the political issues, however, offering general impressions of the neighborhood or the Chinese based upon firsthand encounters—impressions that revised their oft-denigrating portrayal. One British traveler in 1872, for example, considered Chinatown a "great sight" and wrote in his diary that the Chinese comprised "the best cooks, washmen, nurses, domestic servants, gardeners, workmen, labourers & artisans in California." He considered the Chinese "marvelously clean & they have a patience which is wonderful."[122] Six years later, in 1878, British tourist Henry Hussey Vivian noted the diligent work habits and "impeccable hygiene" of the Chinese. He explained that in Chinatown "there is but little disease and little to offend the senses" and that the neighborhood was a "garden of roses compared to many Continental towns, Berlin among the number, not to mention Cologne, Italian towns par excellence, and some French."[123] M. Philips Price, visiting from Britain in 1869, remarked in his diary that he and his party visited Chinatown one evening, for most of the group had never seen "a Chinaman at home." But he noted only that they "went to the theatre, and a gambling-house, took tea with a China merchant, Sing Man." Price, who had previously visited China, added that the Chinese were "peaceful, contented, and highly civilized. I have always had a very high opinion of the Chinese people. I liked what I saw of them in their own country, and I like even more what I have seen of them in America."[124]

Visitors rarely considered the Chinese a monolithic entity that could be conveniently edited from cosmopolitan San Francisco; in many cases they operated under the same profit-based model, and economic competition materialized in Chinatown just as it did in downtown. These similarities struck some tourists as indications that the Chinese ought to be considered in the same light as merchants elsewhere. London-based tourist Harry Jones noted the mercantile progress of the Chinese when he arrived in the late 1870s, for example, explaining that visitors not only see the "humble laundry" of Ho Ki, but also the more stately offices of "Ho Sing, Wo Ching & Co," while E. R. Hendrix thought that some of the Chinese were "very wealthy" and engaged in "every profession and business—physician, ministers, brokers, cigar manufacturers, chair-makers, etc." In 1887, New Yorker James Hale Bates praised the array of goods sold in Chinatown's stores, acknowledging the "bright, smart-looking, pleasant salesmen," who surprised him with their business acumen and honesty.[125] W. G. Marshall, in 1878, acknowledged the skills of a Chinese opium den proprietor, who demonstrated the use of an abacus to solve an accounting problem—far more quickly than Marshall and his party were able to devise a solution.[126] Many tourists recognized that the Chinese adapted quite well to their conditions and often succeeded within the system.

Tourists rarely encountered Chinatown's built environment as dirty, dilapidated, and dangerous. A number of visitors remarked instead on the alterations or additions that local merchants and residents made to existing buildings to reveal their cultural distinction, and a few were able to appreciate the intricacy of the joss houses—even if they did not fully understand their meanings. Mrs. J. Gregory Smith, touring San Francisco in the 1880s, pointed out the restaurant façades and their "balconies, verandahs, lanterns, and streamers—all painted in bright

TOURISTS IN CHINATOWN, SAN FRANCISCO. Tourists (lower left and far right) stroll through San Francisco's Chinatown in this engraving drawn by Paul Frenzeny for *Harper's Weekly* in 1880. To accentuate its differences from the rest of the nineteenth-century city, promotional materials frequently cast Chinatown as an exotic labyrinth of filth and immorality. Yet tourists often found the neighborhood more ordinary than they expected, recognizing that its density resulted from legal restrictions over which the Chinese had no control. (Source: *Harper's Weekly*, March 20, 1880, p. 188. Reproduced in Lucius Beebe and Charles Clegg, *San Francisco's Golden Era*.)

colors, vermillion and green, with a profusion of gilt," while Daniel Pidgeon marveled at the manner in which the Chinese demonstrated their "national character" by adding balconies and colored signs to advertise the businesses within.[127] The alleged dangers of the nocturnal environment ran counter to many tourists' experiences, as well. Harriet Harper, visiting one evening in 1888, considered the district almost magical, with its small alleys accentuated by "fanciful illuminations, which give to them a fantastic gala appearance."[128] And S. M. Lee wrote in an 1886 letter that her visit to the joss house revealed a "work of art, the gods beautifully carved, the screens and panels of the most costly description, many lanterns and inscriptions inlaid with ivory—and altogether as interesting as any museum."[129]

Where they could, tourists entered Chinatown's shops and restaurants and directed their attention to the items sold or served within. Some of these establishments catered to tourists; others were directed toward locals. Harriet Harper, who traveled with a friend, recalled having "looked a great deal, and we have bought very little." And yet she and her friend "admired everything, even the Chinese babies."[130] Mary Wills also visited in the late 1880s and found much to her distaste in Chinatown but nevertheless explained that the neighborhood is "dear to the heart of every woman" in part because of its "neat" stores with their "tastefully arranged" goods. She described the variety of products sold, from "bric-a-brac" to basic staples such as food and clothing—and the conscientiousness with which the salespeople carried on their various trades.[131] Harper's and Wills's impressions of everyday Chinatown resembled the tenor of Oscar Wilde's account when, in 1882, he found Chinatown to be the "most artistic town" he had ever encountered. In the Chinese restaurants, Wilde observed the Chinese "drinking tea out of China cups as delicate as the petals of a rose-leaf" and marveled at a rice paper bill printed with "Indian ink as fantastically as if an artist had been etching little birds on a fan."[132]

Promotional materials arranged Chinatown as a tourist playground, with the Chinese little more than objects for visual inspection. But some tourists found this arrangement rather uncomfortable as they walked through the neighborhood, gradually becoming aware of themselves as intrusions upon a living community. The Chinese themselves were hardly oblivious to the presence of outsiders, either, and many resented Chinatown being transformed into an attraction for the white, tourist population. Miriam Leslie's 1877 visit demonstrated this very process, as did novelist Helen Hunt Jackson's visit one year later. As Leslie wandered down crowded Chinatown alleys, she noticed groups of Chinese "gathering in knots to gaze at and discuss the strangers." She further explained that as whites "arrogantly try and civilize and Christianize [the Chinese] by our own standard, [the Chinese] complacently seat themselves upon the heights of their own civilization, their own religion, and consider us as outside barbarians whom it is not worth their while to convince of error or ignorance."[133] Jackson, meanwhile, also encountered resistance to her own penetrating gaze as she admired the shops and restaurants of Chinatown in the early 1880s. She noted the occasional Chinese woman who would pass by and return the gaze— one of "such contempt that I winced a little. Judged by her standard, I must sink very low, indeed."[134]

Perhaps due to the frequent portrayal of Chinatown as a mysterious and illicit community lodged in an earlier time—or perhaps to justify their community's existence in an area so close to downtown—some Chinese entrepreneurs chose instead to capitalize on the neighborhood's economic viability as a tourist environment. Increasingly by the 1890s Chinese entrepreneurs chose to accentuate the image of deviance and mystery and charged tourists for special attractions or goods, including sexual favors, opium-smoking demonstrations, and opium itself. It is possible, too, that local Chinese worked with white police officers to permit tourists special entry into Chinatown's otherwise private spaces.[135]

That Chinatown might have been arranged in such a fashion lends credence to the possibility that the Chinese were aware of the civic desire to keep the neighborhood separate from cosmopolitan San Francisco. Local Chinese thus catered to tourists rather than incur the wrath of civic officials or residents. In this respect, Chinatown can be read as a product of a late nineteenth-century time when the Central and Union Pacific Railroad now comfortably brought curious *tourists* to the American West, to San Francisco, and to Chinatown—not an earlier time that required Chinese to spend difficult and often dangerous hours laying tracks, bridges, and tunnels across mountains, deserts, and plains. If tourists claimed to have encountered a distant past in Chinatown, what they often received was such a world staged to their satisfaction. The Chinese themselves simply participated.

As it was, some visitors did provide accounts of Chinatown and the Chinese that suggested their awareness of the neighborhood as a condition of late nineteenth-century social, cultural, and economic circumstances in the American West—not a historical relic, transplanted from Asia. Although promotional materials typically cast Chinatown both as a squalid, dangerous place to be avoided and a picturesque environment comprised of peaceful residents ossified in a world before modernity, tourist experiences countered such portrayals as often as they accommodated them. In the tourist imagination, the neighborhood could not be conveniently tossed aside as an alien, foreign environment. Was San Francisco cosmopolitan *because* of Chinatown and the Chinese population—rather than despite them? The variety of tourist encounters lends no obvious answer. Civic elites may have desired a particular cosmopolitanism in San Francisco and elsewhere in the American West—one where urban culture behaved in specific ways—but tourist experiences did not always comply with their prescribed vision.

Solomon Mead visited many western cities in 1883 on a Cook's tour, including San Francisco. Reflecting upon that tour, he wrote that he "saw representatives of many nationalities that I had not met before." These urban cultural encounters seemed to him as significant in characterizing the western United States as did traveling over and across the dramatic western landscape, which, he acknowledged, included the "grandest and most lofty mountains of the globe."[136] Mead's assessment of these "representatives" does not appear in the pages of his diary. The many "nationalities" he encountered simply *were*; their variety and number struck Mead as remarkable but not necessarily efficient, cohesive, picturesque, industrious, dangerous, exotic, dirty, spiritually deviant, degenerate, or morally corrupt.

Like Mead, numerous visitors remarked on the cultural diversity and the everyday character of western cities without contemplating the urban population's alleged contribution to a bright economic future. Not all was positive, either: Wisconsin visitor Mable Treseder's 1893 visit to Chicago revealed to her the "contrasting sights of the great city," including parts of the metropolis, where "want, misery, and crime hold sway and where poverty deals out a full measure to all."[137] A cosmopolitan city—as conveyed in promotional materials—would be conferred upon the urban environment so long as the ethnic, racial, and economic diversity of the population could be edited, sorted, and segregated and ideally if it could be seen as contributing to progress— even if this meant casting some people outside of the imaginative sphere of the city altogether. Yet tourists proved that western cities could not be so easily delineated; tourist encounters often uncovered a less efficient, less refined, and less progressive urban cultural landscape than the cities' promoters might have preferred. Cosmopolitanism—as with much else in the late nineteenth-century urban American West— remained a complicated, complex, and contested terrain.

Epilogue

Return to an Unknown

The forecast called for intermittent afternoon rain showers when I began my hike to Salt Lake City's Ensign Peak. Only a baseball cap offered me protection from the inclement weather, but it was clear and sunny when I set out from downtown. In no particular hurry and with plenty of daylight to spare, I stopped for nearly thirty minutes at the Utah State Capitol Building, admiring the results of a recent renovation and watching in amusement as a frustrated wedding party attempted photographs while dodging busloads of tourists.

Dark clouds had gathered upon departure, but I paid them little mind—until I began my final ascent to the summit of Ensign Peak. Then they unleashed their fury. I sought shelter, briefly, under one of the few trees marking the mostly barren trail, but it was futile. Still, I was determined to proceed to the top along the now drenched and muddy trail on my final day in Salt Lake City. The peak was notable for its spectacular views and legendary as the site where a party of Mormon elders determined the original town plat days after their 1847 arrival in the valley. My interest in visiting it, however, was because it was among the more heavily promoted late nineteenth-century destinations in the urban American West. Reaching the summit, I thought, would permit me an intimate connection with a tourist past I had been tracing in this book.

I connected intimately instead with the eighteen-foot obelisk-shaped column marking the summit. The rains lightened when I arrived at the peak, but gale-force winds picked up and threatened to hurtle me into the Great Salt Lake, so the column's cobbled bulk provided a much needed barrier. I emerged from behind the column periodically to manage a few wobbly photographs and remained long enough to note the expanse of the Salt Lake Valley and watch as a rainbow bent magnificently into the University of Utah. But my soaked shirt and socks reminded me that the view would be a small part of my experience. The vision of a bucolic Salt Lake City—so common in illustrations in nineteenth-century publications—largely eluded me. Little turned out the way I had imagined.

For several years, I had planned a transcontinental journey of my own. I wished to revisit the cities and many of the sites that lured tourists in the late nineteenth century and to gather material for a conclusion to *Manifest Destinations*. I had long felt destined to bring full circle a set of experiences that manifested themselves for tourists beginning in 1869, and I thought by revisiting the cities of Chicago, Denver, Salt Lake City, and San Francisco, I would be able to understand something important about tourist encounters—and perhaps about the urban West in the early twenty-first century. To best approximate those experiences, I chose to arrive in the cities the way of the late nineteenth-century tourist: by train. So in July 2013, I did exactly that.

But the trip was never so exact. It couldn't be, anyway: I had either toured or lived in all of the cities before (Chicago and San Francisco on multiple occasions), but the late nineteenth-century tourists I traced in *Manifest Destinations* were first-time visitors to western cities. Furthermore, a central theme of the book regarded the late nineteenth-century negotiation between promotion and encounter, but I could not determine a logical way to bring this theme into the present. Too much had changed about the urban West, and the main attractions today—with a few exceptions—differed radically from those of the past. I could ill-afford the expense or the time of a planned three-week journey with multiple stops and hotel stays, and I wondered what more I would learn about the cities, the West, or tourism by following a nineteenth-century itinerary. I assumed I was heading into a world of cities, sites, and experiences that I knew rather well.

I was wrong. Orienting visits around late nineteenth-century points of interest introduced me to places and experiences ordinary and extraordinary, leading to disappointment and hassle as often as discovery and serendipity. This, in turn, immersed me in the everyday pulse of the urban West, yet brought me no closer to understanding it. When Mable Treseder descended by elevator in 1893 from the seventeenth floor of Chicago's Masonic Temple—that elevator operated by a mechanism she could not see and did not understand—she feared she was heading "to an unknown by an unknown route." Regardless of my basic familiarity with the actual transcontinental route, I too headed to an unknown.

In keeping with the past, I chose to begin my journey just outside of Chicago. This way, I could determine if the approach was as jarring to me as it was to countless late nineteenth-century tourists. I chose Pullman, Illinois, some fourteen miles south of the downtown Loop as my specific starting point; most tourists, after all, approached Chicago from the south along train routes beginning in the East. The original railroad right-of-way did not pass directly through Pullman, but I knew that the Chicago area Metra commuter trains stopped there today. I also thought Pullman a particularly fitting choice for the start of the journey. Not only was it a popular nineteenth-century tourist attraction, but the Pullman Palace Car Company manufactured, outfitted, and operated the vast majority of the sleeper rail cars tourists rode across the continent. At the time, I was also on the graduate committee of a Chicago-area student, who had chosen to reimagine the ruins of the former market hall in Pullman for her design thesis. To be a more informed committee member, I planned to visit the site in the morning and then catch the Metra heading northward to the Loop. Besides, I had never been to Pullman, Illinois, and for the past ten years, I had been living in Pullman, Washington. Yet several unexpected factors conspired to derail my plans.

I did, however, manage to visit Pullman. The compact town seemed rather incongruous, if simultaneously extraordinary and haunting: rows upon rows of diverse, tidy, architecturally detailed brick row houses along tree-lined streets extending along the cardinal points from the market site, while a diverse smattering of residents relaxed on their steps on a pleasant early summer evening. Just north, factory ruins and the recently rebuilt Clock Tower stood forlorn behind a long fence topped with three rows of menacing barbed wire. There was a hint of restoration plans and a sign announcing the occasional factory tour, but "no trespassing" warnings provided the dominant effect.

The market itself stood roofless and melancholy, embraced on the street corners by Solon Beman's stately loggias that, at a more prosperous time, might have suggested the sophistication of the Florentine Renaissance. A group of friends, probably in their forties, huddled around their cars on the southeast edge, one of them openly drinking from a bottle of beer. I briefly pondered what George Pullman himself might have thought about such transgressions; he envisioned the town as a social experiment, banning alcohol but trusting that a steady factory job, dignified residential architecture, and services of a high order—including an arcade containing a well-appointed theater and library—would transform the working class into a refined citizenry.[1] But my project mostly concerned the heart of the larger cities, even if Pullman was once a regular stop along the late nineteenth-century tourist circuit of greater Chicago. The sun had dipped below the horizon, and fireflies were crackling in the early evening air. I still had not checked into my hotel, and I was getting hungry. Was the train still running?

I opted for an automobile ride to the Loop. Speeding northwards, I detected no pollution, no confusion, no "host of factories, workshops, and smoke" that greeted Martindale C. Ward when he approached downtown Chicago in 1893.[2] The spectacular, illuminated downtown skyline captured my attention—even the otherwise less striking Blue Cross/Blue Shield Tower, whose window display was configured to celebrate the Chicago Blackhawks' recent Stanley Cup hockey championship. I managed to snap a few quick photos as the car maneuvered through Grant Park and entered the Loop. I appreciated the ride, but I already had veered from my route.

And so began my personal quest to retrace the first major stage of tourist travel to the American West—the stage between 1869 and 1893 that established cities as crucial to tourist encounters. By no means did tourism to the West cease after 1893, however. After a brief economic downturn in the mid-1890s, the urban tourist industry became more regularized. By the 1910s and 1920s, automobiles provided tourists with more convenience, and in the years following World War II, one finds the proliferation of hotel chains, air conditioning, and package tours attempting to rationalize visitor experiences at an unprecedented scale. By the turn of the millennium, cities everywhere had erected entertainment and shopping areas offering tourists safe, clean, nostalgic, and predictable environments, and in the twenty-first century, the Internet, real-time cameras, street views, social media, smart phones, "QR" codes, and downloadable "apps" of every imaginable type seem to leave almost nothing to chance.[3] Along with the convenience of twenty-four-hour food, retail chain stores, and malls, such technologies threaten to flatten tourist encounters into a deadening global sameness.

Yet guidebooks, websites, and television shows continue to flaunt the unique attributes of cities, only some attributes of which were promoted in the nineteenth century: Chicago for its architecture, music, and food; Denver for its open spaces and views to the mountains; Salt Lake City for its recreational opportunities and Temple Square; and San Francisco for its geography, icons, cultural diversity, and eccentricity. Yet the prevalence of tourists at well-promoted monuments, streets, parks, and restaurants also has contributed to a widespread backlash, with some materials directing visitors and locals to sites and activities "off the beaten track" and titles of city guides such as *Not for Tourists* implying that tourism—today among the world's leading industries—has decimated local flavor. My journey in 2013 taught me something rather different. No matter the prepackaging of cities and the attempts to standardize tourist experiences, the unexpected—even if it led me to the ordinary and mundane—still dominated my encounters and transformed the urban West from a known to an unknown.

I did try to visit as many attractions as I could, however, briefly entertaining the possibility that a comparative study between the past and present might lead to some intriguing revelations. But to examine the potential discrepancy between promotion and encounter for today's most popular urban attractions, such as Chicago's Millennium Park or the former federal penitentiary on San Francisco's Alcatraz Island (neither of which existed when nineteenth-century tourists were visiting these cities), would have brought my project too far afield. Moreover, many sites no longer exist today—including Chicago's Union Stock Yards, Salt Lake City's Zion's Cooperative Mercantile Institution (ZCMI), or San Francisco's Palace Hotel—and for the handful of once major attractions that are still extant—Salt Lake City's Temple Square and San Francisco's Chinatown, for example—the differences between then and now are too vast.

For a potentially tighter study, I could have restricted my investigation to physical changes. I could have reported that parts of San Francisco's Chinatown had been remade as a purpose-built, Orientalist fantasy for tourists not long after the 1906 earthquake and fire.[4] Perhaps it was worth mentioning that the façade of the ZCMI in Salt Lake City remained but that the Macy's inside of it (as of 2013, part of the city's retractable roof, climate-controlled downtown City Creek Center development) seemed to belie its earlier cooperative function. Maybe readers would be interested to know that the Union Stock Yards in Chicago ceased operation in 1971 and, save for the original stone gateway and an interpretive display, was now a vast industrial park characterized by mostly low-rise buildings and parking lots. But much of this was either old news or information that easily could be discovered online. After all, French economist Paul de Rousiers, traveling West in 1892, wrote that everything had changed in Denver since the mining rush of just thirty years earlier.[5] I was traveling some 121 years later—and not only to Denver.

Moreover, I had neither the time, patience, nor discipline to conduct a rigorous, scientific study, and I was highly skeptical such rigor would reveal much more than would a casual investigation. It took neither a seasoned scholar of tourist studies nor a historian of cities or of the American West to recognize that there have been changes over time, many of which were dramatic and sweeping. I did not, for example, find it particularly compelling to note that the railway journey annihilated time and space and permitted me the comfort of viewing potentially forbidding landscapes from the comfort of an observation car: high-speed modern travel had long been castigated for eliminating the ability to engage the landscape in a more intimate, supposedly authentic manner.[6] I also was well aware that western cities were larger in size and population than in the late nineteenth century (if not also in density). I knew that, geographically anyway, Chicago had not been considered a city of the American West for more than a century; that San Francisco, with its cafés and social consciousness, was perhaps better characterized as America's most European city; and that largely reconstructed "historic" districts vaguely suggesting the nineteenth-century urban frontier—such as Denver's Larimer Square or Salt Lake City's Heritage Village—provided architectural fodder for those critics who contend that the West was immersed in the global economy of gentrification, consumption, or invented tradition.[7] Did a distinctive urban West exist at all anymore? I was curious about this, but it was not my only motive for travel.

With the possible exception of traveling journalists on a mandated assignment, I did not imagine most late nineteenth-century western-bound tourists had a single objective for travel, either—although the relative smoothness of a published traveler narrative often made it seem so. I had no such mandate. I had no desire to bend my experiences, or my recollection of those experiences, to support the arguments of the book. I also did not claim a "post-tourist" attitude in an age of hyper-capitalism—where cities and tourist-oriented environments (such as Chicago's Navy Pier, Denver's Sixteenth Street Mall, or San Francisco's Pier 39) had become so inauthentic that to fully understand them, or to draw conclusions about the culture of tourism, I needed to remove my critical lens and plunge headlong into the sheer spectacle of the contemporary city.[8] I did not set out to determine if there was authenticity left in the American West; indeed, my motives and questions were less theoretical, less scientific, and less cohesive. Beyond hoping that my trip might yield material for an epilogue, I wished to know whether my findings about nineteenth-century tourists and their attention to the everyday were commensurate with my own. Did my experiences parallel or diverge from those of late nineteenth-century tourists, and if so, in what ways? Did cities still matter in the tourist encounter of the American West—regardless of whether they were identifiably western?

I discovered that cities mattered (after all, the right-of-way of the "California Zephyr"—as close to the original route of the transcontinental railroad that one can travel today—stops near the downtowns of Denver and Salt Lake City rather than requiring a transfer to a branch line), and, following my experience in Pullman, Illinois, I learned that my plans and expectations would exist in a constantly shifting state. I learned that no matter what guidebook, website, or Internet street view I examined, nothing could predict the weather, noise, light, people, traffic, buildings under construction or undergoing restoration—let alone my thoughts, perceptions, or feelings. Importantly, too, I learned that no matter how I mapped my route, things could go awry—especially when I did not account for meals. And I discovered that my experiences, in their haphazard way, paralleled those of nineteenth-century tourists more closely than I imagined.

Quite often, too, it was that which surrounded the visits to specific sites of late nineteenth-century interest that loomed most prominently in my encounters—not the sites themselves. When I sought Chicago's Levee District along Clark Street, for example, I turned a corner and immediately found myself in the imposing shadow of the heavily policed, high-rise Metropolitan Correctional Center—the much-publicized site of a December 2012 incident, where two prisoners, via a rope of bed sheets, rappelled fifteen floors to temporary freedom. In Denver, my Saturday lunchtime exploration of the former bordello district brought me face-to-face with a lawn bowling setup attached to a sports bar and entirely too close to staff members clad in shorts, T-shirts, and tennis shoes who implored me to come inside for a "good time." In Salt Lake City, my visit to Fort Douglas—once a U.S. military garrison and a tourist attraction—seemed only to provide the setting for the thousands of coordinated yells emanating from a high school cheer camp. Or at least that is how I will always remember Fort Douglas.

On the other hand, frequently I found myself reverting to everyday habits that resembled patterns at home. I imagined this, too, paralleled the experiences of nineteenth-century tourists more often than they cared to admit, although my experiences featured an early twentieth-century twist: buying food at late-night convenience stores; obsessively checking my phone for calls, emails, and text messages; and snapping digital photos of everything—despite knowing that I would never find much time to examine or sort those images. My habits occasionally came in handy, however: in Denver, for example, when I needed to return my rental bike and a handy phone app I had recently down-loaded indicated the location of the nearest racks; or in Salt Lake City, when my ability to access the Internet while riding the TRAX street-car revealed the restaurants still open near my hotel. But frequent use rapidly depleted my phone's battery and sent me on a constant search for electrical outlets. Incidentally, this drove me more often than not into public and semipublic spaces, such as public libraries, cafés, and hotel lobbies, where I had not initially planned to spend time—from the Salt Lake City Public Library to the San Francisco Hyatt Regency. Experiences there remain memorable, although they have far less to do with their striking (if occasionally maligned) design or designers than with the random occurrences that happened while I waited for my phone to charge.

Even my visits to popular late nineteenth-century attractions (some of which are still popular) immersed me as much in the ordinary and unplanned as often as the celebrated or monumental. Neither the design nor its much-ballyhooed ability to withstand the fire of 1871 mattered much to me when I visited the Chicago Water Tower. What I remember is the security guard who acknowledged the existence of the once-functional observation area at the top but, despite our friendly conversation, would not permit me to climb the stairs to see what he described as a "really hot" and cramped space "filled with old, rusting pipes." My short ride on a San Francisco cable car, meanwhile, did not reveal the picture-perfect views of city and landscape that I sought but reminded me instead that there are still modes of modern transportation where the enforcement of safety regulations—as well as the prevention of serious injury—is nearly impossible, and the collection of fares even more so. I am not likely to forget a man wearing a suit, presumably returning home from work, calmly sitting inside the cable car but hemmed in by several camera-toting tourists, me included, consistently repositioning themselves for the best views. Perhaps this is what it means to live and work in San Francisco in the twenty-first century, although I was not entirely sure.

At Salt Lake City's Temple Square, I was only one of nine total people in the cavernous tabernacle, listening to two missionaries offering historical and architectural background, one of whom translated into Mandarin. But next door there were easily one hundred people enjoying the displays at the North Visitors' Center, at least twenty of whom sat on plush seats gazing upon an eleven-foot-tall replica of Bertel Thorvaldsen's *Christos* sculpture—the oft-reproduced image of the risen Christ adopted by the Latter-day Saints. Visiting Salt Lake City to see the Mormons may once have been the top attraction in the Rocky Mountain West—at least among non-Mormons—but I could not tell if I was observing non-Mormon tourists or out-of-state Latter-day Saints on a pilgrimage to an ancestral or spiritual homeland.

During a nighttime walk in San Francisco's Chinatown, I cannot deny that tourists who shopped or dined there may have treated or imagined the locals and their establishments as curiosities for their personal entertainment. But I encountered nothing particularly unusual beyond the familiar array of souvenir shops and restaurants with upturned eaves, imitation duo-gong brackets, guardian lion sculptures, and colors of red, green, and yellow that one finds in Chinatowns all over the world—which today is not unusual at all. Similarly, I cannot deny that the handful of locals I saw may have considered me a voyeur interested in the ways of the "Orient" (issues of race are far too ingrained in contemporary society to discount this). But only in writing this epilogue and relating my experiences to the nineteenth-century past did I find myself thinking consciously about ethnicity. My

SPOFFORD STREET, SAN FRANCISCO, IN 2013. What were described as filthy, mysterious, dangerous, and occasionally picturesque alleyways in late nineteenth-century tourist material appeared as nothing of the sort to the author on a nighttime stroll through Chinatown in 2013. The mostly tidy, quiet streets were punctuated with roll-cart garbage receptacles and the clicking sounds of mahjong tiles audible behind gated entryways. (Photo courtesy of the author.)

Chinatown visit instead was characterized by mostly empty streets, the sound of mahjong and Cantonese rising from below-ground spaces, and what looked distinctly like the bright light of a smart phone penetrating the walls of a cardboard dwelling on Hang Ah alley.

Not everything made sense. How would I characterize these cities, this trip? What to mention and what to leave out? Were there selected encounters that were more illustrative of my travels, and of the urban West, than others? Having discovered, during my research, so many late nineteenth-century tourists whose narratives resembled the rhetoric of promotion, I briefly empathized with those who may have chosen to highlight specific monuments or focused upon single issues. A multiple-day trip anywhere offers too many experiences that one has the time to describe, and it was certainly possible that some travelers operated under deadlines or failed to keep a proper diary. Perhaps they required assistance from other sources to jog their memories when they returned home to write. Perhaps some travelers assumed that readers were not interested in the everyday. Or, perhaps, visits to monumental, well-promoted attractions simply stood out in greater relief, and tourists either suppressed or ignored the other moments that made up so much of their traveling time.[9]

But there was Walter P. Ryland, whose brief visit to a busy Salt Lake City in the early 1880s necessitated a stay at the "very small insignificant looking" White Hart Hotel and, frustratingly, did not coincide with the regular service in the tabernacle. But he visited Temple Square anyway, attended a concert in the tabernacle, peered into a small Mormon chapel "filled with Swedes or Scandinavians," and noted the "great excitement" of the "Base Ball" game between Salt Lake and Idaho. Was Ryland's visit unusual, or did he just choose to mention what were more common experiences for late nineteenth-century tourists? There was Louise Bourbonnaud, who visited Chicago during a rainstorm in 1888 and complained about the poor food and service in the train station but nonetheless praised the beer and the skyscrapers. And there was Ellen Walworth, touring San Francisco in 1877, who nearly aborted her trip to Seal Rocks when her party missed the last omnibus departing from Lone Mountain. But her earlier conversation with a local male resident on the Lone Mountain–bound streetcar resulted in the offer of a personal lift to Seal Rocks. For Walworth, importantly, it became "a pleasant remembrance of the genial kindness we met with in this part of the country."[10] This was at least as significant as the rocks themselves.

Recollections of unexpected—even rather ordinary—encounters appear in late nineteenth-century tourist memoirs enough to suggest that they were significant. They were significant for me, as well, although they did not necessarily bring me any closer to understanding the cities I visited—in Chicago, an otherwise leisurely morning coffee repeatedly interrupted by the thunderous clamor of discarded material hurtling down a chute during a renovation of a Michigan Avenue skyscraper; in Denver, the refreshing taste of a strawberry milkshake on an outdoor patio in the Highland neighborhood; in Salt Lake City, the comfortable feel of the handlebar grips as I biked next to the railroad tracks along South Sixth West; and in San Francisco, the pungent smell of marijuana and urine in several nooks, crannies, semi-public spaces, and public parks. Each of these nonvisual experiences was unplanned, unexpected, and memorable, but they neither characterized the entirety of the urban environment nor gave me definitive insight into the urban West.

Prior to completing my trip, I recognized the futility of drawing conclusions about the urban West. But my personal commitment to follow the general transcontinental route to its *actual* late nineteenth-century end led to a rather interesting, if by now predictable, finish. I knew it had been more than a half century since the railroad reached its terminus at the Oakland Mole (from which tourists caught ferries to San Francisco), and I had never been able to track its former site within a dizzying industrial array of roads, freeway overpasses, parking lots, warehouses, container cranes, and port facilities that had characterized the area for as long as I could remember.[11] But still I wished to approximate transcontinental travel by catching the current-day ferry from Oakland's Jack London Square to San Francisco's Ferry Building and then trace something of a common late nineteenth-century tourist excursion to the edge of the continent, viewing Seal Rocks and the Pacific Ocean from the Cliff House. Nineteenth-century tourists often remarked upon the chaotic scene of touters attempting to lure passengers to city hotels at the ferry terminal and rarely missed an opportunity to describe the barking sea lions, struggling for position on the rocks. Though San Francisco was hardly a new experience for me, I had never boarded the ferry in Oakland and it had been at least ten years since I had been anywhere near the Cliff House. What would my trip disclose?

As with the beginning of my journey in Pullman, Illinois, however, several circumstances arose to complicate this plan. I did catch the ferry, but my Monday afternoon arrival at the San Francisco Ferry

Building presented a mostly quiet scene with somebody reading a book, a private security guard, a beer delivery truck, and a handful of seagulls. I had intended to ride a streetcar towards the eastern boundary of Golden Gate Park and walk its length to the ocean, pausing at some of the late nineteenth-century park attractions along the way. But I became distracted by the gourmet market in the ferry building and then, in turn, by Market Street, the Embarcadero Center, and the old Barbary Coast—transformed into today's Jackson Square. By the time I arrived in Golden Gate Park, it was late—too late, in fact, to explore more than one or two park sites if I were to reach the Cliff House before nightfall. I hailed a cab to the park and walked quickly to the Conservatory of Flowers and Stow Lake before an unmarked trail deposited me into a harrowing, high-speed intersection—a situation I frustratingly negotiated for nearly twenty minutes until I reached the other side.

But the sun had now dipped below the trees and hunger was taking over. I had little choice to accept a nighttime view of the old tourist attractions by the ocean—if they were visible at all. So I slowed my pace and settled down for two mediocre slices of pizza in the Outer Richmond District while my phone once again ran out of power. But the pizza joint had no available outlets. Annoyed but determined, I left and made my way toward the shadowy darkness of Sutro Heights Park, feeling around the ruins of a nineteenth-century tourist parapet until I sensed two figures walking behind me. I proceeded briskly to the Cliff House, relieved to discover that it was still open at ten fifteen at night, that there was a staircase leading to the balcony overlooking the ocean, and that I could surreptitiously charge my phone outside the restrooms as I waited at the entrance—which I did for nearly thirty minutes. No matter the quality of the photos, I was committed to documenting the final stage of my journey: what a 2011 guidebook promised would be a "spectacular ocean view" with vistas "30 mi or more on a clear day."[12] There was surprisingly little fog, but spotlights protruding from Sutro's restaurant allowed me to decipher the outlines of Seal Rocks and watch the waves crashing against the shore. Whether there were living creatures on those rocks I will never know, although I later discovered that warmer ocean temperatures had returned sea lions to the San Francisco area beginning in 2009.[13] I wanted to imagine their presence, of course, thus reassuring myself that my transcontinental journey had reached a planned and fitting end.

I received no such reassurance. It was more fitting that my desire to charge my phone shortened considerably my time on the Cliff House balcony. Once there, I snapped a few grainy and mostly indecipherable photos but spent the rest of the time nervously checking my watch to ensure that I would catch the various transportation connections returning me across the bay. The bus ride back downtown at that late hour was more interesting than the Cliff House: near the Tenderloin, a woman boarded with a Rottweiler and then stepped off a few blocks later at Union Square. Nobody batted an eye—not even the bus driver. In its inexplicability, that moment provided a far more fitting conclusion to my transcontinental journey.

So the end of the trip, much like the beginning—and everything in between—differed from my expectations, forced the abandonment of several plans, and taught me probably as much, if not more, about the urban West than had I followed a more prescriptive agenda or focused *only* on my visits to late nineteenth-century tourist attractions. But my unexpected, yet revealing, experiences seemed in keeping with late nineteenth-century tourist encounters; urban everyday encounters remained central to the broad picture of western cities. Certainly they did for me.

What these everyday encounters meant about these cities was no easier for me to determine than it had been for late nineteenth-century tourists. I did not feel prepared to offer a comprehensive assessment, and—even without the frequent derailments—I had never intended my trip to be comprehensive. But the trip was far from insignificant; its significance manifest most commonly in the everyday, ordinary, and unexpected, which returned me to an unknown. The destinations themselves—whatever they may have been—became subsumed in the swirl of life that is the twenty-first-century urban American West.

Notes

1. In the 1990s, a large sign behind the end zone at Candlestick Park, at the time the home of the San Francisco 49ers football team, read "San Franciscans Welcome You to the World's Most Popular City." This sign appeared regularly on television broadcasts.

2. Seminal texts on tourism and issues of authenticity include MacCannell, *The Tourist;* Smith, ed., *Hosts and Guests;* and Urry, *The Tourist Gaze.*

3. Notable exceptions in the late 1990s included Harris, "Urban Tourism and the Commercial City," 66–82, and Sears, *Sacred Places,* 87–121. Cocks's *Doing the Town,* the most comprehensive book regarding nineteenth-century urban tourism in the United States, had yet to be published.

4. For the pitfalls of traveler accounts as clues to tourist experiences, see Cronon, *Changes in the Land,* 6; Gilbert and Hancock, "New York City and the Transatlantic Imagination," 84; Herlihy, "Visitors' Perceptions of Urbanization," 125; or Towner, "Approaches to Tourism History," 47–62. For the challenges of uncovering tourist encounters more generally, see Stanonis, *Creating the Big Easy,* 23.

5. On the role of various media in shaping tourist experiences, see Limerick, "Seeing and Being Seen," 45; or Urry, *The Tourist Gaze,* 13. That traveler narratives may have been shaped by the reading public is discussed in Liebersohn, *The Travelers' World,* 8.

6. Hudson, in *A Scamper through America,* 183, identifies George Crofutt's guidebook; Sala, *America Revisited,* cites Charles Nordhoff on p. 134 and Henry Williams on p. 175. Crofutt's work was so popular that even Nordhoff himself recommended it for those travelers heading to Yosemite (Nordhoff, *California,* 37). Meanwhile, Nordhoff was popular enough that he was referred to as "Mr. Nordhoff" and quoted directly in Thomas Cook and Son's *California Excursions,* 34–35. Dwinell cites Crofutt in *Common Sense Views of Foreign Lands.* Specific city guidebooks also borrowed information from one another.

Compare, for example, the description of the Chamber of Commerce Building in Flinn's *Chicago,* 570–71, with that of *World's Fair Chicago 1893 Souvenir Illustrated,* 223; or that of San Francisco's Palace Hotel in Doxey, *Guide to San Francisco and Vicinity,* 15–16, with Heininger, *Historical Souvenir of San Francisco, Cal.,* 19–20.

7. Merewether, *By Sea and by Land,* preface; Kent, *Graphic Sketches of the West,* 13. For similar disclaimers, see the opening passages in Church, *Diary of a Trip through Mexico and California;* Coop and Exley, *A Trip around the World;* Bickham, *From Ohio to the Rocky Mountains;* or Hendrix, *Around the World.*

8. On the notion of cultural boundedness, see Billington, *Land of Savagery, Land of Promise,* 74–76; Levenstein, *Seductive Journeys,* x; Lewis, *An Early Encounter with Tomorrow,* 4; or Olsen, *The City As a Work of Art,* 6. For the range of factors that could affect tourist impressions of a city, see Duis, *Challenging Chicago,* foreword, xi–xiii, xv.

9. Walworth, *An Old World,* 312–33.

10. Savage, *Salt Lake City,* 14.

11. Woodbury, *Tourists' Guide Book to Denver,* 15.

12. Crofutt, *Grip-Sack Guide to Colorado,* 32.

13. Lucy, *East by West,* 67, 69.

14. Naylor, *Across the Atlantic,* 82.

15. For the various ways historians use storytelling to craft a narrative—regardless of claims to objectivity and science—see Cronon, "A Place for Stories"; Klein, *Frontiers of Historical Imagination,* 1–12; or White, *Tropics of Discourse,* 81–100. For storytelling as a tactic for histories of the built environment, see Smith, "Viewpoint," 1–14.

16. For studies employing this method, see, for example, Burchell, "Accretion, Syncretion and Repetition," Raycraft, "Introduction," or Snow, "British Travelers View the Saints."

17. de Certeau, *The Practice of Everyday Life,* 91–97. For an account of how working-class residents linguistically reconfigured the modernizing city of late nineteenth-century Stockholm, see Pred and Watts, *Reworking Modernity,* 118–54.

18. On the bodily inconveniences of rail travel, see Cocks, *Doing the Town,* 41–69, or Dunlop, *Sixty Miles from Contentment,* 197–228. For an account of the smells and sounds of antebellum Philadelphia, New Orleans, and New York—and how residents negotiated elite attempts to curb and order them—see Upton, *Another City,* 41–83, 306–33.

19. See, for example, Veijola and Jokinen, "The Body in Tourism," 125–51; Pritchard et al., "Editors' Introduction," 6–7. The use of the term "corporeal" travel taken from Urry, "Regazing on the Tourist Gaze," 25. The dominance of vision in the sensory history of western culture is highlighted in Urry, "Sensing the City," 72–80.

20. On broader, more interdisciplinary methods for architectural history, see, for example, Upton, "Architectural History or Landscape History?," 195, or Stieber, "Architecture between Disciplines," 176–77.

21. For the methods of cultural landscape studies, see, for example, Groth, "Frameworks for Cultural Landscape Study," 1–21; Meinig, introduction, 1–7; Davis and Nelson, "Editors' Introduction," iv–vi.

22. For the many interpretations of "manifest destiny," see Merk, *Manifest Destiny and Mission in American History,* 24–60.

INTRODUCTION

1. Treseder, "A Visitor's Trip to Chicago in 1893," 30–31.

2. Accounts vary slightly on the exact height, number of stories, and functions on each floor of the Masonic Temple. See, for example, "A City under One Roof," 81–82; A. N. Marquis and Company, *Ready Reference Guide*, 218; Flinn, *Chicago*, 584–85; or Rand, McNally & Company, *A Week in Chicago*, 70.

3. Flinn, *Chicago*, 584.

4. Treseder, "A Visitor's Trip to Chicago in 1893," 30.

5. Tourism was one of the few arenas of late nineteenth-century urban life affording women nearly equal participation as men, although guidebooks promoting the West did caution women against venturing into San Francisco's Chinatown at night and occasionally suggested they might bypass Chicago's Union Stock Yards. For the frequency of women travelers in the West, see Fifer, *American Progress*, 9–10; Löfgren, *On Holiday*, 100; and Pomeroy, *In Search of the Golden West*, 6.

6. Most books regarding travel in the American West focus upon the natural environment. See, for example, Pomeroy, *In Search of the Golden West;* Hyde, *An American Vision;* or Wrobel and Long, eds., *Seeing and Being Seen.*

7. Cincinnati and St. Louis received their share of nineteenth-century visitors but predominantly in the antebellum period. Once the first transcontinental railroad was complete, those cities became less accessible via the principal routes of travel.

8. The cost of cross-country railroad travel in the 1870s remained prohibitive to those without much expendable income. Round-trip train travel from New York to San Francisco in the 1870s and early 1880s averaged $300—a fare that did not include meals or side trips to places such as Denver or Salt Lake City, which could escalate costs considerably. In 1884, one of Thomas Cook's "personally-conducted" excursions cost $500, a fare that included first-class traveling accommodations, hotels, meals, a trip to Yosemite, and special carriage drives in Manitou Springs, Los Angeles, and San Francisco. See Thomas Cook and Son, *California Excursions*, 5, or Pomeroy, *In Search of the Golden West*, 7.

9. References to Chicago as either part of, or as a gateway to, the West are common in nineteenth-century sources. See, for example, Blackall, "Notes of Travel—I," 299, and "Notes of Travel—II," 303; Butterworth, *Zig-zag Journeys in the White City*, 98; *Chicago Daily Tribune*, July 12, 1892, 1; Dean, *The World's Fair City and Her Enterprising Sons*, 17; Jones, *To San Francisco and Back*, 24; Lucy, *East by West*, 35; Mushet, *Chicago, Yesterday and To-day*, 8; Rousiers, *American Life*, 172; Sala, *America Revisited*, 124; Sears and Webster, *The Guide from the Pacific to the Atlantic*, 4; Vivian, *Notes of a Tour in America*, 86; or *World's Fair Chicago 1893 Souvenir Illustrated*, 184.

10. Pomeroy, *In Search of the Golden West*, 14–15.

11. Fifer, *American Progress*, 7–9; Gilbert, *Perfect Cities*, 61.

12. Gibson, "Population of the 100 Largest Cities."

13. For a passage that refers to tourists as "travelers," "health seekers," and "pleasure seekers" as well as "tourists," see Denver and Rio Grande and Rio Grande Western Railroads, *Valleys of the Great Salt Lake*, 11. Similarly, in a three-paragraph stretch in Stone, *The Colorado Hand-Book*, 37–38, the tourist is referred to as a "stranger," a "traveler," and a

"visitor" as well as a "tourist." The debates regarding allegedly elite and active "travelers" seeking knowledge and more frivolous and passive "tourists" seeking distraction is mostly of late twentieth-century scholarly concern. Tourists to the late nineteenth-century American West cared little about such distinctions, and promotional material rarely discussed them.

14. The notion of "elites" refers to a class of individuals whose nineteenth-century economic rise allowed it to set standards for taste. Many middle-class Americans sought to emulate this class. See Gilbert, *Perfect Cities*, 11.

15. Clifford, "Of Other Peoples," 121–30.

16. Oversubsidization was a major factor leading to the Panic of 1873. On the declining public fascination with the railroads, see Nye, *American Technological Sublime*, 77–78.

17. On the rise of a tourist industry by the end of the nineteenth century, see Cocks, *Doing the Town*, 107–108, 125–73; Fifer, *American Progress*, 7–8; Rothman, *Devil's Bargains*, 49; and Shaffer, *See America First*, 17–26.

18. Nye, *American Technological Sublime*, 127–34, 173–98.

CHAPTER 1

1. Ralph, *Our Great West*, v.

2. For the number of nineteenth-century published travel narratives dedicated either in whole or part to the American West, see Wrobel, "The World in the West," 26, 97n1.

3. Ralph, *Our Great West*, v.

4. Ibid., vi.

5. Rousiers, *American Life*, 15–16.

6. Perhaps the best example of a traveler who attempted to gauge America through its institutions is Alexis de Tocqueville, whose early nineteenth-century trip to examine the American prison system provided the basis for his book *Democracy in America*.

7. See, for example, Rousiers, *American Life*, 72–79.

8. Martineau cited in Jakle, *Images of the Ohio Valley*, 152.

9. Marx and Engels, *The Communist Manifesto*, 13. For a summary of modernization and its effects in the nineteenth century, see Berman, *All That Is Solid*, 18–19.

10. For modernity's paradoxes and Marx's discussion of it, see Berman, *All That Is Solid*, 90–97, and Harvey, *The Condition of Postmodernity*, 99–112.

11. Some of these themes as characteristic of the West, at least from a European perspective, are summarized in Billington, *Land of Savagery, Land of Promise*, 195–218. Even if western cities remained small relative to eastern cities (Denver in 1890, for example, had fewer people than Detroit and Rochester), to travelers western cities seemed larger due to the lack of physical development in the surrounding area. See Athearn, *Westward the Briton*, 9, 47.

12. The geographical boundaries of the nineteenth-century American West have been exacerbated by a constantly shifting border. For the problems of definition, see Cronon, Miles, and Gitlin, "Becoming West," 24, or Nash, *Creating the West*, 101–58.

13. Weber, *The Growth of Cities in the Nineteenth Century*, 30–33; Hine and Faragher, *The American West*, 401.

14. For the dynamic nineteenth-century environment that appealed to visitors to Chicago, see Burg, *Chicago's White City of 1893,* 44–74, 333–34; or Spears, *Chicago Dreaming,* 3–23.

15. Cronon, *Nature's Metropolis,* 60–74.

16. Rousiers, *American Life,* 171, 172.

17. Rothman, *Devil's Bargains,* 38.

18. Robertson and Robertson, *Our American Tour,* 71.

19. Codman, *The Mormon Country,* 211.

20. Marshall, *Through America,* 86–103.

21. For discussions of personal guides in nineteenth-century Salt Lake City, see Goddard, "Temple Square's Early Warm Welcome," 30, or Hafen, "City of Saints, City of Sinners," 357–62; for San Francisco, see Rast, "The Cultural Politics of San Francisco's Chinatown," 44–45.

22. The "instant" appearance of the urban West is examined in Barth, *Instant Cities.*

23. Tourists were so pervasive in nineteenth-century Europe that they became subjects of ridicule in the press. See Withey, *Grand Tours and Cook's Tours,* 162; Buzard, *The Beaten Track,* 80–97.

24. F. A. F. de La Rochefoucauld-Liancourt, cited in Barth, "Demopiety," 254.

25. O'Rell, *Jonathan and His Continent,* 42.

26. Simmel, "The Metropolis and Mental Life," 409–24.

27. Glazier, *Peculiarities of American Cities,* 169; Hittell, *Guide Book to San Francisco,* 26, 28; Lloyd, *Lights and Shades in San Francisco,* 29; Manning, *American Pictures,* 97; Phillips, *Letters from California,* 13; Rice, *Letters from the Pacific Slope,* 81; Thayer, *Marvels of the New West,* 355, 357; and Vynne, *Chicago by Day and Night.* Flinn, *Chicago,* 583, also compares Chicago's State Street to Freidrichstrasse in Berlin, Regent Street in London, and the Ringstrasse in Vienna.

28. *Guide Book and Street Manual of San Francisco, California,* 38.

29. As cited in Anon., *Denver: By Pen and Picture,* 4. It is unclear exactly when, or to whom, Orton delivered his address. The source, published in 1898, does note that Orton was a member of the governing committee of the New York Stock Exchange and that he had visited Denver "years ago."

30. Regarding the myth of the West, see Billington, *Land of Savagery, Land of Promise;* Cronon, Miles, and Gitlin, "Becoming West," 3–27; Fabian, "History for the Masses," 223–38; Groseclose, *Nineteenth-Century American Art,* 145–71; Hine and Faragher, *The American West,* 472–511; Johnson, *Hunger for the Wild,* 111–86; and White, *It's Your Misfortune and None of My Own,* 613–32. On Buffalo Bill's role in creating tourist expectations, see Sears, *Sacred Places,* 180.

31. Nordhoff, *California,* 18.

32. Bird, *A Lady's Life in the Rocky Mountains,* 138.

33. Pfeiffer, *Flying Leaves,* 100–101.

34. Thomas Cook & Son, *Cook's California Excursions,* 21.

35. Trachtenberg, *The Incorporation of America,* 25–37; Hine and Faragher, *The American West,* 482.

36. Turner, "The Significance of the Frontier in American History," 22–23.

37. For the discomforts of rail travel on the Pullman cars, see Cocks, *Doing the Town,* 62–66.

38. See, for example, Baker, Journal, July 8, 1871; Hendrix, *Around the World,* 41; Merewether, *By Sea and by Land,* 250; Walworth, *An Old World,* 311.

39. Beadle, *A Trip to the United States in 1887,* 90.

40. For the difficulties en route to Yosemite, see Pomeroy, *In Search of the Golden West,* 8. On pages 56–57, Pomeroy notes that after completing the transcontinental journey, travelers would remain in San Francisco to visit the Cliff House and the opium dens in Chinatown before departing to the Geysers, the petrified trees, Yosemite, or the Hotel del Monte in Monterey.

41. Rothman, *Devil's Bargains,* 45, 54; Shaffer, *See America First,* 45.

42. Gladden, "Sunday in Chicago," 151.

43. Ingersoll, *Crest of the Continent,* 22. Tourists also reached Denver via the Kansas Pacific Railroad in the late nineteenth century. The Kansas Pacific, completed in 1870, stretched westward from Kansas City.

44. Jenkins, *An Excursion to Colorado, California and the Yosemite Valley,* 20.

45. Whitman is cited in Spence, ed., *The American West,* 379.

46. Stevenson is cited in Allen, ed., *Transatlantic Crossing,* 307.

47. Handlin, *The Uprooted.*

48. Pfeiffer, *Flying Leaves,* 188.

49. For literary impressions of modern urban life in America, see the summaries in Kolodny, *The Land before Her,* 161–63; Lees, *Cities Perceived,* 91–96; or White and White, *The Intellectual Versus the City.*

50. Jones, *To San Francisco and Back,* 25; Adams, *To and Fro,* 278.

51. Milner, O'Connor, and Sandweiss, *The Oxford History of the American West,* 538.

52. Zehme, *The Diary of Friedrich Wilhelm Heinrich Zehme,* 48.

53. Kingsley, *South by West,* 44, 45. For similar impressions of Denver, see Muirhead, *Land of Contrasts,* 214, or Pfeiffer, *Flying Leaves,* 120–21.

CHAPTER 2

1. Sanders, *A Journey to, on and from the "Golden Shore,"* 13.

2. Boosters were often those working for railroad companies or for local organizations looking to profit from increased development or settlement. See Wrobel, *Promised Lands,* 6.

3. For more comprehensive studies on the connection between hot springs and health in nineteenth-century America, see Aron, *Working at Play,* 16–23; Chambers, *Drinking the Waters;* or Wrobel, *Promised Lands,* 38–45.

4. A. N. Marquis and Company, *Ready Reference Guide,* 2. John J. Flinn's Chicago guidebooks also downplayed the temperature extremes of the city, promoting its weather instead as "healthful" and "stimulating." See Flinn, *Chicago,* 39; and Flinn, *Official Guide to the World's Columbian Exposition,* 173.

5. Williams, ed., *The Pacific Tourist,* 5. On the popularity of Williams's guidebook, see Shearer, ed., *The Pacific Tourist,* 5. For the emergence of the philosophical idea of the

sublime in popular discourse, see Nye, *American Technological Sublime,* 17–43, especially pp. 8–9.

6. In the late nineteenth century, "America's Switzerland" most commonly referred to the Rocky Mountains and Sierra Nevadas but occasionally to the Cascade Range of the Pacific Northwest. For references to Colorado or the Rocky Mountains as "America's Switzerland" see, for example, *Colorado Cities and Places,* or Thomas Cook and Son, *Cook's California Excursions,* 23. For a chapter that refers to the Cascades as "America's Switzerland," see Adams, *To and Fro.* For "America's Switzerland" applied to the White Mountains and the Catskills, see Brown, *Inventing New England,* 66, or Löfgren, *On Holiday,* 34.

7. Hyde, *An American Vision,* 19–20; Löfgren, *On Holiday,* 38–40; Nye, *American Technological Sublime,* 24–25; Sears, *Sacred Places,* 4–5.

8. Addison cited in Andrews, *Search for the Picturesque,* vii, 3. For more on the importance of the picturesque to tourism, see ibid., Adler, "Origins of Sightseeing," 7–29; Löfgren, *On Holiday,* 16–21.

9. Crafting cities in this fashion was not necessarily new, nor was it restricted to the American West. D. Appleton and Company's two-volume set entitled *Picturesque America,* first published in 1872–73, included hundreds of plates featuring western cities but nearly always featured their "natural" environments. Illustrations either highlighted the trees, hills, mountains, oceans, lakes, rivers, sky, or bays from ground level, or they depicted the urban environment from distant perspectives in order to demonstrate efficiency and progress. See Rainey, *Creating Picturesque America,* 195–205. The construction of a readable nineteenth-century city through literature and imagery is argued by Kasson, *Rudeness and Civility,* 70–111. For a discussion about how guidebooks produced for the World's Columbian Exposition characterized Chicago as bucolic, see Gilbert, *Perfect Cities,* 48, 52, 55.

10. For a discussion of strangers' guides in nineteenth-century San Francisco, see Michalski, "Portals to Metropolis," 193–95, 199–202.

11. Sweetser, *King's Handbook of the United States,* 212.

12. See advertisement for Watkins in *Disturnell's Strangers' Guide to San Francisco and Vicinity,* 131, or Taber in *Guide Book and Street Manual of San Francisco, California,* 11.

13. Faithfull, *Three Visits to America,* 223.

14. Harris, *Eadweard Muybridge and the Photographic Panorama of San Francisco, 1850–1880,* 37.

15. Hales, *Silver Cities,* 78–82. Muybridge and Watkins were not the first photographers to portray San Francisco this way. On pp. 47–57 of ibid., Hales explains that George Fardon, in his 1856 *San Francisco Album,* established the city view book genre by photographing buildings and streets but eliminating or minimizing people. As with Muybridge, city boosters supported and financed Fardon's work. For an account reading Muybridge's idealized panoramas as defying the turbulent social and economic conditions of late 1870s San Francisco, see Solnit, *River of Shadows,* 153–76.

16. Reps, *Views and Viewmakers of Urban America,* 22.

17. When viewed through a stereoscope, stereographs—two identical photographic images placed side by side on stiff-backed cardboard—produced a three-dimensional effect that single photographs could not match.

18. For the "civilizing mission" of nineteenth-century landscapes, see Miller, *Empire of the Eye,* 11.

19. For a detailed discussion about how lithographic viewmakers constructed their nineteenth-century pictures, see Reps, *Views and Viewmakers of Urban America,* 3–23; on exaggeration, see ibid., pp. 20–21. For bird's-eye views as both promotional and fanciful, see Reps, *Cities on Stone,* 31–35.

20. Bluestone, *Constructing Chicago,* 42.

21. Hittell, *Guide Book to San Francisco,* 39.

22. Schneyer, *Illustrated Hand Book and Guide,* 3.

23. A. N. Marquis and Company, *Ready Reference Guide,* 243.

24. Schneyer, *Illustrated Hand Book and Guide,* 3; Bluestone, *Constructing Chicago,* 39.

25. For references to Chicago as the "Garden City," see *Chicago and the World's Columbian Exposition Illustrated,* 12; *Godey's Illustrated Souvenir Guide to Chicago World's Fair and New York,* 15; Mushet, *Chicago, Yesterday and To-day,* 20; and Rae, *Westward by Rail,* 58.

26. *World's Fair Souvenir Illustrated,* n.p.

27. *Season of 1888,* 8–9.

28. Schneyer, *Illustrated Hand Book and Guide,* 5–8, 11–12.

29. On Graceland, see Flinn, *Chicago,* 159. For more promotion of Chicago cemeteries, see A. N. Marquis and Company, *Ready Reference Guide,* 201–204, or *Godey's Illustrated Souvenir Guide to Chicago,* 66–67. On the tourist appeal of Pullman, see Gilbert, *Perfect Cities,* 131–68.

30. See, for example, *Colorado and Its Capital* or *A Report on the Resources, Wealth, and Industrial Development of Colorado.*

31. *Facts about Colorado and Denver,* 8–9.

32. Baedeker, ed., *The United States,* 407. For the mineral baths, see Denison, *Rocky Mountain Health Resorts,* 51.

33. Stone, *The Colorado Hand-Book,* 38.

34. For examples where Denver is treated as a way station to other sites, see *Appleton's Hand Book of Winter Resorts,* 75; Denver and Rio Grande Railroad, *Tourists' Hand-Book Descriptive of Colorado, New Mexico and Utah,* introduction; or Shearer, *Pacific Tourist,* 75. For references to Denver's "healthful" climate, see *Colorado Cities and Places,* 6; *Report on the Resources, Wealth, and Industrial Development of Colorado,* 82; *Facts about Colorado and Denver,* 8; or Denison, *Rocky Mountain Health Resorts,* 48–51. Of the views to the Rocky Mountains, see Thomas Cook and Son, *California Excursions,* 24.

35. *Appleton's Hand Book of Winter Resorts,* 75.

36. Sweetser, *King's Handbook of the United States,* 113.

37. Chamberlain's panorama is briefly discussed in Hales, *Silver Cities,* 76.

38. For slightly different versions of this same story, see Bickham, *From Ohio to the Rocky Mountains,* 73–74; English Tourist, "Land of the Mormons," 589; or Manning, *American Pictures,* 43.

39. Denver and Rio Grande and Rio Grande Western Railroads, *Valleys of the Great Salt Lake,* 11.

40. For examples of official publications presenting Salt Lake City in this fashion, see

Culmer, *Tourists' Guide Book to Salt Lake City,* 3–5; *Historical and Descriptive Sketches of Salt Lake City;* or Thayer, *Marvels of the New West,* 404.

41. Shearer, *The Pacific Tourist,* 132, 133.

42. A number of official publications stressed these aspects of Salt Lake City in the nineteenth century. For two examples, see *A Souvenir of Salt Lake City and Utah,* descriptive section, or Donan, *Utah,* 87.

43. *The "Mormon" Metropolis* (1891), 44–45, 47–48; Denver and Rio Grande and Rio Grande Western Railroads, *Valleys of the Great Salt Lake,* 12–14.

44. See, for example, Jones, *Resources and Attractions of Salt Lake City;* Jackson, "Great Salt Lake and Great Salt Lake City," 147.

45. Heininger, *Album of San Francisco, Cal.,* "retrospective" section.; Hittell, comp., *Bancroft's Pacific Guide Book,* 66.

46. Cone, *Two Years in California,* 144.

47. Cited in Lotchin, *San Francisco, 1846–1856,* 285.

48. For San Francisco's Golden Gate Park as a "pleasure ground," see *Midwinter Scenes in Golden Gate Park,* 1. For a discussion of Golden Gate Park's construction within the social, political, and environmental context of nineteenth-century San Francisco, see Dreyfus, *Our Better Nature,* 67–90.

49. Muirhead, *Land of Contrasts,* 209.

50. The assertion that San Francisco featured the most parks in America is from Reps, *The Forgotten Frontier,* 156. According to Heininger's *Album of San Francisco, Cal.,* the city featured twenty-one "public parks and squares, varying in size from 200 feet square to 1,013 acres." San Francisco boosters inflated the number of San Francisco parks by including public squares and plazas in that tally. With the exception of Golden Gate Park, Mountain Lake Park, Washington Square Park, Buena Vista Park, and a tiny park known as Pioneer Park on Telegraph Hill, nineteenth-century San Francisco had very few parks.

51. For Sutro Heights as an attraction, see Heininger, *Album of San Francisco, Cal.,* 24–26.

52. Crofutt, comp., *Trans-continental Tourist,* 148. For Oakland as a city of "homes," see Warren, ed., *California Illustrated,* 26.

53. Barthes, "The Tour Eiffel," 3–18; de Certeau, *The Practice of Everyday Life,* 91–93; Harvey, *The Urban Experience,* 1.

54. Greenwood, *A Tour in the United States and Canada,* 84.

55. Bluestone, *Constructing Chicago,* 115.

56. Sanders, *A Journey to, on and from the "Golden Shore,"* 15; Upchurch, *The Life, Labors and Travels of Father J. J. Upchurch,* 78. On the view of the Rocky Mountains from Denver in general, see Shearer, *The Pacific Tourist,* 75. For a 150-mile-long view of mountain scenery from Denver, see *Facts about Colorado and Denver,* 8; for a 170-mile-view, see Baedeker, *The United States,* 406; and for a 300-mile view, see *Colorado and its Capital,* 35. The view from the Equitable Building is mentioned in Baedeker, *The United States,* 406.

57. Salt Lake City's "tourist's tower" is mentioned in Savage, *Views of Utah,* 4–5, and *The "Mormon" Metropolis* (1891), 46–47.

58. Shearer, *The Pacific Tourist,* 269.

59. Flinn, *Chicago,* 21.

60. Regarding a search for the past at times of dramatic change, see, for example, Lears, *No Place of Grace,* xiv–xv, 4–5; Lowenthal, *The Heritage Crusade and the Spoils of History,* 5–6, 10–11, 14–15.

61. On the search for the past in nineteenth-century England, see Mulvey, *Anglo-American Landscapes,* 19, or Lockwood, *Passionate Pilgrims,* 331–49.

62. *Chicago Illustrated,* n.p., *Chicago Checker-Board Guide,* 7.

63. *San Francisco,* 4.

64. For the characterization of New York this way in the eighteenth and nineteenth centuries, see Harris, "Urban Tourism," 70; Upton, "Inventing the Metropolis," 35, and Hood, "Journeying to 'Old New York,'" 699–719. On the importance of the past for the purposes of national identity in nineteenth-century America, see Boyer, *City of Collective Memory,* 309–10.

65. Harris, *Eadweard Muybridge,* 42.

66. Cited in Barth, *Instant Cities,* 205.

67. On the creation of traditions as a way to suppress or slow the effects of change in the modern world, see Hobsbawm, "Introduction: Inventing Traditions," 1–2. On photography as an agent for creating nostalgia in the throes of change, see Harris, *Eadweard Muybridge,* 4; or Harris, "Urban Tourism," 70–74.

68. Harris, *Eadweard Muybridge,* 42.

69. Merewether, *By Sea and by Land,* 278.

70. On panoramas, see Boyer, *City of Collective Memory,* 252–57.

71. For the promotion of Chicago panoramas, see Flinn, *Chicago,* 601; Lewis, *An Early Encounter with Tomorrow,* 84; or Mushet, *Chicago Yesterday and To-day,* 2. On Chicago panoramas in general, see Duis, *Challenging Chicago,* 207–208.

72. On the panorama inside San Francisco's "polygonal" building, see Heininger, *Historical Souvenir of San Francisco, Cal.,* 22.

73. Advertisement in Reynolds, *The Mormon Metropolis,* 1893, n.p.

74. Joseph C. Kingsbury, trade card, n.d.

CHAPTER 3

1. Leng, *America in 1876,* 73–74.

2. Ibid., 78.

3. For more on agency in the city, see de Certeau, *The Practice of Everyday Life,* 24–28. The notion of "constructed visibility" here is borrowed from Gregory, "Colonial Nostalgia and Cultures of Travel," 112.

4. On multisensory encounters in the city, see Upton, "The City As Material Culture," 53, or Urry, "Sensing the City," 71–86.

5. Holand, *My First Eighty Years,* 27–28.

6. Rae, *Westward by Rail,* 225–25, 233.

7. Robinson, *Sinners and Saints,* 290.

8. Bridges, *A Tour around the World,* 238.

9. Clark, *The Round Trip,* 85.

10. Thomas Cook and Son, *California Excursions,* 24–25, 41, 45–46. On San Francisco, see Jenkins, *An Excursion to Colorado, California and the Yosemite Valley,* 19.

11. Journalist Frank Harrison Gassaway, whose articles appeared in the *San Francisco Post* under the pseudonym "Derrick Dodd," expressed disappointment in 1882 when he first glimpsed Yosemite Valley, in large part because it could not meet the "exaggerated conception of the general proportions of the valley, resultant upon the descriptions of the 'gush writers.'" Dodd, *Summer Saunterings,* 109, 112. Similarly, one British visitor told diarist Cornelia Adair in 1874 that California was the only "mistake" of his American tour, for the "Yosemite did not pay." Adair, *My Diary,* 105. For more disappointment with Yosemite, see Wills, *A Winter in California,* 134.

12. References to the "urban sublime" regarding the late nineteenth-century urban American West are uncommon in secondary material, but they appear in a few sources describing cities in Europe and the American East. For some examples, see Barth, "Demopiety," 258; den Tandt, *The Urban Sublime in American Literary Naturalism;* and Taylor, "The Awful Sublimity of the Victorian City," 431–47. David Nye makes an indirect reference to the urban sublime by noting that the "classic" location for the technological sublime was the "urban metropolis." See Nye, *American Technological Sublime,* 286.

13. Taylor, *Between the Gates,* 54.

14. Thomas Cook and Son, *California Excursions,* 26–27; Johns, "Settlement and Development," 222; Manning, *American Pictures,* 87; and Pine, *Beyond the West,* 424–35.

15. Whitman, "Denver Impressions," in *Specimen Days & Collect,* 1882, in Spence, *The American West,* 378. Some twenty-three years later, the smelting process in Denver remained of interest, as Thomson McElrath's tour group made an excursion to visit the "enormous smelting works on the outskirts of the city." McElrath, *A Press Club Outing,* 29.

16. McElrath, *A Press Club Outing,* 41.

17. See, for example, Anderson, "'The Kiss of Enterprise,'" 239–40; Hales, *William Henry Jackson,* 43–48; Kasson, *Civilizing the Machine,* 167–68, 174–75; Marx, *Machine in the Garden,* 190–209; Nye, *American Technological Sublime,* 35–36, 59; and Sears, *Sacred Places,* 189.

18. On the contradictory effects of the machine in late nineteenth-century America, see Trachtenberg, *The Incorporation of America,* 38–69.

19. This theme is explored in Smith, *Chicago and the American Literary Imagination,* 2–3.

20. Robinson, *Sinners and Saints,* 12.

21. Ward, *A Trip to Chicago,* 45; Naylor, *Across the Atlantic,* 81–82.

22. Joyaux, trans., "A Frenchman's Visit to Chicago in 1886," 48.

23. Smith, *Chicago and the American Literary Imagination,* 104.

24. Duis, *Challenging Chicago,* 18–27, 32.

25. Ibid., 16.

26. Travelers heading to San Francisco on the transcontinental railroad were required to exit the Central Pacific in Sacramento and transfer to a different line. The most common route headed southwest, where in the 1870s and 1880s the enormous ferryboat *Solano* waited in Benicia to transport passengers—and the train—across the Carquinez

Strait to Port Costa. For a traveler's description of the *Solano,* see Hudson, *Scamper through America,* 124–25.

27. Clarkson, "Overland Journey to California and the Western Territories."

28. Travers, *From New Zealand to Lake Michigan,* 1889.

29. The ferry building was completed in 1875, and known officially as the Oakland, Alameda, and Berkeley Ferry Building. It stood until 1896, when it was replaced by a larger structure.

30. Emmons, ed., *Around California in 1891,* 21–22.

31. Carbutt, *Five Months Fine Weather,* 79.

32. Robertson and Robertson, *Our American Tour,* 83.

33. Barneby, *Life and Labour in the Far, Far West,* 89.

34. Carbutt, *Five Months Fine Weather,* 81.

35. Marshall, *Through America,* 262.

36. Reynolds, letter, September 21, 1875.

37. Clark, *The Round Trip,* 73.

38. Rice, *Letters from the Pacific Slope,* 69.

39. Falk, *Trans-Pacific Sketches,* 24.

40. Wills, *Winter in California,* 103; Lucy. *East by West,* 128–29.

41. Aitken, *From the Clyde to California,* 84.

42. Dewar, *A Ramble Round the Globe,* 67.

43. Smiles, ed., *A Boy's Voyage Round the World,* 246.

44. Emmons, *Around California in 1891,* 13.

45. Johnson, *America Pictorially Described,* 89.

46. English Tourist, "The Land of the Mormons," 587.

47. On the problems with water supply and distribution in late nineteenth-century Salt Lake City, see Alexander and Allen, *Mormons and Gentiles,* 107–109.

48. Merewether, *By Sea and by Land,* 265.

49. Hardy, *Between Two Oceans,* 122–23. It is worth noting that Hardy had previously published a slightly different account of her same travels, discussing "streams of water with their pleasant gurgling music." See Hardy, *Through Cities and Prairie Lands,* 105. For more positive accounts of the streams, see, for example, Ludlow, *Heart of the Continent,* 328–32; Rice, *Letters from the Pacific Slope,* 31; or Todd, *The Sunset Land,* 174.

50. Pierrepont, *Fifth Avenue to Alaska,* 39.

51. Phillips, *Abroad and at Home,* 240, 241.

52. See, for example, Baker, Journal, June 7, 1871; Barneby, *Life and Labour in the Far, Far West,* 32; Bonwick, *The Mormons and the Silver Mines,* 21; Campbell, *My Circular Notes,* 48, 61; Falk, *Trans-Pacific Sketches,* 43; or Travers, *From New Zealand to Lake Michigan,* 145.

53. Pidgeon, *An Engineer's Holiday,* 191.

54. Lucy, *East by West.* 66.

55. Ralph, *Our Great West,* 321–22.

56. Bickham, *From Ohio to the Rocky Mountains,* 70.

57. Marshall, *Through America,* 403.

58. Johnson, *Journey around the World,* 38.

59. Mohr, *Excursion through America,* 56.

60. On negative impressions of Chicago vis-à-vis the World's Columbian Exposition from tourists and boosters alike, see Marcus, "Up from the Prairie," 150–85.

61. Jones, *To San Francisco and Back,* 24–25.

62. Pierce, comp. and ed., *As Others See Chicago,* 210. On the numerous cable car system malfunctions in Chicago, see Duis, *Challenging Chicago,* 26.

63. Ralph, *Our Great West,* 4–5.

64. Lewis, *An Early Encounter with Tomorrow,* 38.

65. Naylor, *Across the Atlantic,* 105–106; Grandin, *Impressions d'une Parisienne à Chicago,* 58.

66. Giacosa, "Chicago and Her Italian Colony," in Pierce, *As Others See Chicago,* 280.

67. Anonymous, "A Visit to the States," *(London) Times* (1887), in Pierce, *As Others See Chicago,* 233.

68. Turland, *Notes of a Visit to America,* 71.

69. Lucy, *East by West,* 39–40.

70. Roberts, *The Western Avernus,* 26.

71. Lucy, *East by West,* 37. On the sewage system and the raising of city streets, see Miller, *City of the Century,* 122–26.

72. Boddam-Whetham, *Western Wanderings,* 184.

73. Blake, *On the Wing,* 135–36.

74. Leng, *America in 1876,* 155.

75. Boyer, *City of Collective Memory,* 298. For the prevalence of signage in antebellum New York, see Henkin, *City Reading,* and for Philadelphia, see Upton, "The City As Material Culture," 56.

76. Marshall, *Through America,* 284–85.

77. Smiles, *A Boy's Voyage Round the World,* 285.

78. Boddam-Whetham, *Western Wanderings,* 33; Pidgeon, *An Engineer's Holiday,* 149. A related account can be found in Robertson and Robertson, *Our American Tour,* 54–55.

79. Jones, *To San Francisco and Back,* 80.

80. Hudson, *Scamper through America,* 134.

81. *The Imperial Highness the Grand Duke of Alexis,* 129. The grand duke was the fourth son of Czar Alexander II.

82. For the touristic interest in Chicago's postfire landscape and the perseverance of its residents, see Lewis, *An Early Encounter with Tomorrow,* 11–13, or Nye, *American Technological Sublime,* 23–24.

83. Duis, *Challenging Chicago,* 36.

84. Medley, *An Autumn Tour in the United States and Canada,* 90.

85. Campbell, *My Circular Notes,* 35, 36.

86. Lewis, *Two Lectures on a Short Visit to America,* 52.

87. Ward, *A Trip to Chicago,* 52

88. Stevenson, cited in Allen, ed., *Transatlantic Crossing,* 305–306.

89. Richardson, *Garnered Sheaves.*

90. See Codman, *The Mormon Country,* 176–79; Kane, *Twelve Mormon Homes,* 2–3. For Brigham Young's efforts to attract a railroad, see Cannon, *The City of the Saints,* 42.

91. Pomeroy, *Pacific Slope,* 134; *A Souvenir of Salt Lake City and Utah,* n.p.; Denver and Rio Grande and Rio Grande Western Railroads, *Valleys of the Great Salt Lake,* 17.

92. For the promotion of manufacturing or industrial attractions in Salt Lake City, see Culmer, *Tourists' Guide Book to Salt Lake City,* 20; Denver and Rio Grande and Rio Grande Western Railroads, *Valleys of the Great Salt Lake,* 16–17; *The "Mormon" Metropolis* (1891), 59; Salt Lake Chamber of Commerce, *Salt Lake City,* 21–23; or Savage, *Views of Utah,* 20. The growth of manufacturing more generally in nineteenth-century Salt Lake City is discussed in Alexander and Allen, *Mormons and Gentiles,* 87–91.

93. *The Imperial Highness the Grand Duke of Alexis,* 181–82. The Denver Ale Company, however, was not commonly listed among the industrial attractions of Denver. Instead, guidebooks promoted the city's smelters involved in the reduction of gold and silver, including the Boston and Colorado Smelting Company, the Omaha and Grant Smelter and, on Denver's outskirts at Globesville, the Globe Smelting and Refining Company. See Thomas Cook and Son, *California Excursions,* 25–26.

94. Cronon, *Nature's Metropolis,* 345.

95. For grain elevators as tourist attractions, see Flinn, *Official Guide to the World's Columbian Exposition,* 179, or Schick, *Chicago and Its Environs,* 118–19.

96. Robertson and Robertson, *Our American Tour,* 55; Vivian, *Notes of a Tour in America,* 87–88.

97. Pidgeon, *An Engineer's Holiday,* 135–36, 142.

98. Anon., "A Visit to the States," in Pierce, *As Others See Chicago,* 233.

99. For a discussion of Chesbrough's waterworks, see Miller, *City of the Century,* 127–29. For the water crib as a tourist attraction, see Hill, *Souvenir Guide to Chicago and the World's Fair,* 192; Schneyer, *Illustrated Hand Book and Guide,* 3; Thomas Cook and Son, *California Excursions,* 51; and Wilkie, *Walks about Chicago.*

100. Glazier, *Peculiarities of American Cities,* 271; Robertson and Robertson, *Our American Tour,* 56; Lewis, *Two Lectures on a Short Visit to America,* 53, and Turland, *Notes of a Visit to America,* 73. For more impressions of Chicago's water system, see Medley, *An Autumn Tour in the United States and Canada,* 90.

101. Aitken, *From the Clyde to California,* 120–22. The illustrations appear between pages 120 and 121.

102. Campbell, *My Circular Notes,* 39.

103. Wilde, *Impressions of America,* 25.

104. Giacosa, "Chicago and Her Italian Colony," in Pierce, *As Others See Chicago,* 276, 277, 285; Joyaux, "A Frenchman's Visit to Chicago in 1886," 48; Grandin, *Impressions d'une Parisienne à Chicago,* 224–25.

105. Bright, letter, June 30, 1869.

106. Warner, *Studies in the South and West,* 185.

107. Hesse-Wartegg cited in Lewis, *Early Encounter with Tomorrow,* 30.

108. Kent, *Graphic Sketches of the West,* 19.

109. McElrath, *A Press Club Outing,* 22.

110. Phillips, *Abroad and at Home,* 244.

111. Burke, *A Philosophical Enquiry,* 131.

112. Kipling, *American Notes,* 216.

113. Anon., "A Visit to the States," in Pierce, *As Others See Chicago,* 231.

114. Mayer and Wade, *Chicago,* 48–52.

115. Griffin, cited in Allen, *Transatlantic Crossing,* 324; Lucy, *East by West,* 38. Despite Lucy's proclamation about the stockyards' popularity, however, he considered a visit rather pointless given that one could see a pig killed in London-based slaughterhouses.

116. *Pennsylvania Railroad to the Columbian Exposition,* 76. Also see A. N. Marquis and Company, *Ready Reference Guide,* 228–29.

117. A. N. Marquis and Company, *Ready Reference Guide,* 221. For a similar description, see Hill, *Souvenir Guide to Chicago,* 192.

118. A typical description of the Union Stock Yards in this fashion is found in Rand, McNally and Company, *A Week in Chicago,* 33. The process of transforming animals into commodities in Chicago is discussed in Cronon, *Nature's Metropolis,* 207–59.

119. Barton, *What I Did in "The Long,"* 71–74.

120. O'Rell, *Jonathan and His Continent,* 46.

121. Joyaux, "A Frenchman's Visit to Chicago in 1886," 52–54.

122. Sala, *America Revisited,* 320, 321.

CHAPTER 4

1. *The "Mormon" Metropolis* (1889), 48, 50.

2. *Historical and Descriptive Sketches of Salt Lake City,* n.p.

3. See, for example, Culmer, *Tourists' Guide Book to Salt Lake City,* 5–9; *The "Mormon" Metropolis* (1887), 18–28; Roberts, *Salt Lake City and Utah By-Ways,* 22–25.

4. Pidgeon, *An Engineer's Holiday,* 241–42, 248.

5. Barth, *Instant Cities,* 187–88, contends that early settlers in the cities of San Francisco and Denver imitated the architecture, customs, and manners of eastern metropolitan centers. For the argument that nineteenth-century architects in California imitated eastern styles, see Kirker, *California's Architectural Frontier,* or Gebhard et al., *A Guide to Architecture in San Francisco & Northern California,* 14–15.

6. Hales, *Silver Cities,* 48–57, notes how George Fardon's *San Francisco Album* had this effect for San Francisco in the 1850s.

7. The notion of what constituted modern architecture at this stage is a matter of debate. Barr Ferree, a professor at the University of Pennsylvania in the late nineteenth century, argued that modern architecture was, simply, commercial architecture—although a "commercial" style was popularly identified with Chicago high-rises in the late nineteenth century. See Ferree, "The High Building and Its Art," 307. Most tourist literature, meanwhile, considered modern buildings to be those that featured the latest in technological advancements. Tourists, however, were less discriminating. They seemed to classify most new buildings as modern—even if their façades were clad in traditional materials such as brick or stone. See, for example, Bridges, *A Tour around the World,* 259; or Dwinell, *Common Sense Views of Foreign Lands,* 334.

8. Medley, *An Autumn Tour in the United States and Canada,* 1.

9. Sala, *America Revisited,* 445–46.

10. Price, *America after Sixty Years,* 24.

11. Pierrepont, *Fifth Avenue to Alaska,* 44–45; Robinson, *Sinners and Saints,* 290. Pierrepont nonetheless acknowledged that the San Francisco buildings were wooden, rather than masonry, to better withstand earthquakes.

12. Kostof, *A History of Architecture,* 43.

13. See, for example, the passage in "Great Cities," *Putnam's Magazine* 5 (March 1855): 256–57, cited in Upton, "Inventing the Metropolis," 4.

14. Barth, *Instant Cities,* 183.

15. Arnold, "Civilization in the United States," in Allen, *Transatlantic Crossing,* 316–17.

16. Hales, *Silver Cities,* 70, makes this argument regarding late nineteenth-century city view books and photographs of the cities' entrepreneurial class.

17. See, for example, Hittell, *Guide Book to San Francisco,* 31.

18. Barbot, *Souvenir Album of 1891.*

19. Upton, "Pattern Books and Professionalism," 107–50. See especially Upton's description of Benjamin Henry Latrobe on pp. 112–14 and 118–20.

20. In Bluestone, *Constructing Chicago,* 49.

21. Bluestone, in *Constructing Chicago,* 123, argues that architects did precisely this in late nineteenth-century Chicago.

22. Jones, *To San Francisco and Back,* 25.

23. Grandin, *Impressions d'une Parisienne à Chicago,* 60–61. On Grandin's tendency to use Paris as a frame of reference during her Chicago visit, see Raycraft, "Introduction: A Parisienne's Adventures in Chicago," xix.

24. Duis, *Challenging Chicago,* 35–39.

25. Hittell, *Guide Book to San Francisco,* 35.

26. Bluestone, *Constructing Chicago,* 57.

27. Carbutt, *Five Months Fine Weather,* 84–85.

28. Church, *Diary of a Trip through Mexico and California,* 55. On the fog at the Cliff House, see Pidgeon, *An Engineer's Holiday,* 292, and Walworth, *An Old World,* 311. On the schooner explosion and the damage to the Cliff House, see Smith, *San Francisco's Lost Landmarks,* 62–63.

29. Ralph, "Chicago," 425.

30. Promotional materials were equally indecisive. For "sky-scrapers," see Flinn, comp., *Official Guide to the World's Columbian Exposition,* 175; for "sky-piercers," see Schneyer, *Illustrated Hand Book and Guide,* 4.

31. Flinn, *Chicago,* 128.

32. See, for example, Dean, *The World's Fair City and Her Enterprising Sons,* or *Chicago Album,* souvenir view book.

33. Flinn, *Chicago,* 562–66.

34. Bluestone, *Constructing Chicago,* 144; Siry, *Carson Pirie Scott;* Smith, *Chicago and the American Literary Imagination,* 127; Monroe, *John Wellborn Root,* 72–108; Wolner, *Henry Ives Cobb's Chicago,* 1–7.

35. Adler, "The Chicago Auditorium," 415.

36. Blackall, "Notes of Travel, Chicago—I," 299.

37. Summaries of versions of this historiography can be found in Bruegmann, "Myth

of the Chicago School"; van Leeuwen, *The Skyward Trend of Thought,* 2n7; Merwood, "Western Architecture," 361n1; and Willis, *Form Follows Finance,* 10–11.

38. Bluestone, *Constructing Chicago;* Bruegmann, *The Architects and the City;* Siry, *Carson Pirie Scott;* van Leeuwen, *The Skyward Trend of Thought.* Also see Banham, "An Introduction," xiii.

39. Willis, *Form Follows Finance,* 49–65. Also see Jordy, *American Buildings and Their Architects,* 73–75.

40. Bruegmann, *The Architects and the City,* 80. The Monadnock Building was named for Mount Monadnock in New Hampshire, while the Tacoma Building presumably referred to Mount Tahoma, or Mount Rainier, in Washington.

41. Ferree, "The High Building and Its Art," 303–304; Bluestone, *Constructing Chicago,* 115.

42. Siry, *The Chicago Auditorium Building,* 1, 405n1.

43. Flinn, *Chicago,* 138–42.

44. Sweetser, *King's Handbook of the United States,* 215; *World's Fair Chicago 1893 Souvenir Illustrated,* 195.

45. Merwood-Salisbury, *Chicago 1890,* 79–84; Wolner, "Chicago's Fraternity Temples," 101–103.

46. See, for example, *World's Fair Chicago 1893 Souvenir Illustrated,* 199; Flinn, *Chicago,* 583–84; Schick, *Chicago and Its Environs,* 214–15.

47. Wolner, "Chicago's Fraternity Temples," 107–108, 111

48. *World's Fair Chicago 1893 Souvenir Illustrated,* 223.

49. Ralph, "Chicago," 425.

50. Treseder, "A Visitor's Trip to Chicago in 1893," 30. The building is today known as the Second Leiter Building.

51. Sienkiewicz, *Portrait of America,* 48–50.

52. On the prevalence of skyscraper construction in the city, see Lewis, *Early Encounter with Tomorrow,* 61–66; Miller, *City of the Century,* 308; Muirhead, *Land of Contrasts,* 206–207; Ralph, "Chicago," 425–28.

53. Stead, "My First Visit to America," in Pierce, *As Others See Chicago,* 363–65.

54. Dewar, *A Ramble Round the Globe,* 66.

55. Lewis, *Early Encounter with Tomorrow,* 38–40.

56. Lewis, *Early Encounter with Tomorrow,* 66, 109–10. For more on the concerns with the steel-frame, skeletal system of construction, see Bruegmann, *The Architects and the City,* 81–82; 104–106. Not all European architects found the skyscrapers distasteful. For some favorable impressions, see Cohen, *Scenes of the World to Come,* 21–23.

57. Lane, "High Buildings in Chicago," 858.

58. Phillips, *Abroad and at Home,* 243.

59. Rousiers, *American Life,* 79.

60. Ward, *A Trip to Chicago,* 49.

61. Flinn, *Chicago,* 356.

62. Kipling, *American Notes,* 92.

63. Adair, *My Diary,* 22. According to Julian Ralph, *Our Great West,* 40, expectoration

was so common in nineteenth-century Chicago that signs were posted inside streetcars to discourage people from engaging in it.

64. Pierrepont, *Fifth Avenue to Alaska,* 5.

65. Schneyer, *Illustrated Hand Book and Guide,* 11; *World's Fair Chicago 1893 Souvenir Illustrated,* 183; Flinn, *Chicago,* 260.

66. Leng, *America in 1876,* 80.

67. Anon., "A Visit to the States," *(London) Times,* (1887), in Pierce, *As Others See Chicago,* 236.

68. Julius Lessing, cited in Lewis, *Early Encounter with Tomorrow,* 51.

69. Lewis, *Early Encounter with Tomorrow,* 53, 158. On timber framing, see Upton, *Architecture in the United States,* 149–53.

70. Pidgeon, *An Engineer's Holiday,* 135.

71. In Shearer, *The Pacific Tourist,* 75.

72. Barth, *Instant Cities,* 198.

73. Dallas, *Cherry Creek Gothic,* 96–99; Ingersoll, *Crest of the Continent,* 18.

74. Woodbury, *Tourist's Guide Book to Denver,* 3, 15; Denver and Rio Grande Railroad, *Tourists' Handbook,* 1.

75. *Colorado Cities and Places,* 6; Sweetser, *King's Handbook of the United States,* 113.

76. Mead, *Notes of Two Trips,* entry on Wednesday, May 16, 1883.

77. Bates, *Notes of a Tour,* 162.

78. Muirhead, *Land of Contrasts,* 213–15.

79. Carbutt, *Five Months Fine Weather,* 149–50.

80. Lee, *Glimpses of Mexico and California,* 121.

81. Kent, *Graphic Sketches of the West,* 186.

82. Hamilton, *Nineteenth-Century Mormon Architecture,* 57–59.

83. *Appleton's General Guide to the United States and Canada,* 358.

84. Views from those seats behind the gallery-supporting columns remained obstructed. Regarding the tabernacle's columns, see Hamilton, *Nineteenth-Century Mormon Architecture,* 59. For a sampling of guidebook descriptions of the tabernacle's interior, see Baedeker, *The United States,* 426; Savage, *Views of Utah,* 10; *The "Mormon" Metropolis* (1887), 23–26; or Denver and Rio Grande and Rio Grande Western Railroads, *Valleys of the Great Salt Lake,* 13.

85. *The "Mormon" Metropolis* (1887), 23.

86. For illustrations depicting the temple as complete before its actual completion, see, for example, Crofutt, *New Overland Tourist and Pacific Coast Guide,* 92; *The "Mormon" Metropolis* (1887), 11; Ingersoll, *Crest of the Continent,* 325; *Souvenir of Salt Lake City and Utah,* n.p.; Savage, *Views of Utah,* n.p.; or Shearer, *The Pacific Tourist,* 133, 135.

87. Goddard, "Temple Square's Early Warm Welcome," 30.

88. Culmer, *Tourists' Guide Book to Salt Lake City,* 9; *The "Mormon" Metropolis* (1891), 35–37, Savage, *Salt Lake City,* 18; Dwyer, *Album of Salt Lake City, Utah,* n.p.

89. Hitchcock, *Architecture,* 184, 351; Hamilton, *Nineteenth-Century Mormon Architecture & City Planning,* 134.

90. McClintock, *Illustrated School and Family,* 95.

91. Hardy, *Between Two Oceans,* 121.

92. See, for example, Kingsley, *Round the World*, 260; Manning, *American Pictures*, 70; Churchill, *Over the Purple Hills*, 246; and Wilde, *Impressions of America*, 29.

93. Rice, *Letters from the Pacific Slope*, 27; Clark, *The Round Trip*, 157.

94. *Notes of Journey from London to San Francisco and Back*. Rice, *Letters from the Pacific Slope*, 28.

95. Marshall, *Through America*, 173–74; Mead, *Notes of Two Trips* (June 21), 52; Sanders, *A Journey to, on and from the "Golden Shore,"* 36.

96. Manning, *American Pictures*, 70, 76.

97. Aitken, *From the Clyde to California*, 56.

98. Bates, *Notes of a Tour*, 147; Pierrepont, *Fifth Avenue to Alaska*, 21.

99. English Tourist, "The Land of the Mormons," 589.

100. Holton, *Travels with Jottings*, 23; McClintock, *Illustrated School and Family*, 96–97.

101. See, for example, Kingsley, *Round the World*, 258–59; Dwinell, *Common Sense Views of Foreign Lands*, 334.

102. Bonwick, *The Mormons and the Silver Mines*, 29.

103. Sanders, *A Journey to, on and from the "Golden Shore,"* 36.

104. Marshall, *Through America*, 181.

105. Travers, *From New Zealand to Lake Michigan*, 145.

106. Manning, *American Pictures*, 70.

107. Preston, "The Great Salt Lake City and Its People," 700.

108. Johnson, *America Pictorially Described*, 88.

109. *California As It Is*, 139.

110. *California As It Is*, 139–40.

111. For an in-depth glimpse into the turbulent 1850s in San Francisco, see Ethington, *The Public City*.

112. Reps, *Cities of the American West*, 157–79.

113. Smiles, *A Boy's Voyage Round the World*, 245.

114. *Notes of Journey from England to San Francisco and Back*, 56.

115. Corbett, *Building California*, 25–27.

116. Rice, *Letters from the Pacific Slope*, 68.

117. Leslie, *California*, 183.

118. Merewether, *By Sea and by Land*, 252.

119. City Hall, begun in 1872, was not complete until 1899. On the Mills Building, see Sweetser, *King's Handbook of the United States*, 96.

120. Accounts vary regarding San Francisco's total number of nineteenth-century hotels. *California As It Is*, 139, contended that San Francisco featured seventy-seven hotels in 1882, while Henry Brainard Kent, in *Graphic Sketches of the West*, 134, claimed one hundred hotels existed in 1890. Tourists did not make distinctions, however, between hotels for temporary lodging and those catering to permanent residents. The difficulties in providing accurate numbers of hotels in San Francisco is discussed in Groth, *Living Downtown*, 18–20.

121. On the promotion of San Francisco's hotels, see Crofutt, *Trans-continental Tourist*, 150; Doxey, *Guide to San Francisco and Vicinity*, 15, 16–17; and Warren, ed., *California Illustrated*, 25.

122. *Lick House Tourists' Guide,* 18; *California As It Is,* 139; Griswold, *Beauties of California,* advertisement, n.p.

123. *California Illustrated;* Doxey, *Guide to San Francisco and Vicinity,* 15–16; *California As It Is,* 139; Green, *Notes on New York, San Francisco, and Old Mexico,* 57; Taber, *Hints to Strangers;* Taylor, *Between the Gates,* 71–73. Doxey's statement about the Palace Hotel is remarkably similar to that put out by the lessees themselves. See, for example, the passage in Heininger, *Historical Souvenir of San Francisco,* 20.

124. *The Palace Hotel,* n.p.

125. Berglund, *Making San Francisco American,* 42.

126. Dewar, *A Ramble Round the Globe,* 103–104.

127. Hendrix, *Around the World,* 42–43.

128. Walker, *Glimpses of Hungryland,* 53.

129. Kipling, *American Notes,* 16.

130. Hittell, *Guide Book to San Francisco,* 28; Heininger, *Historical Souvenir of San Francisco,* 15.

131. Leng, *America in 1876,* 166.

132. Mead, *Notes of Two Trip,* Monday, June 4.

133. Guillemard, *Over Land and Sea,* 199–200.

134. See, for example, Leslie, *California,* 138–39; Vivian, *Notes of a Tour in America,* 148.

135. Lee, *Glimpses of Mexico and California,* 78.

136. Muirhead, *Land of Contrasts,* 210–11.

137. For the San Francisco Victorian houses as vernacular architecture, see Kirker, *California's Architectural Frontier,* 105–11.

138. Hittell, *Guide Book to San Francisco,* 25; Kirker, *California's Architectural Frontier,* 107–11; Bloomfield, "The Real Estate Associates," 15.

139. Hudson, *Scamper through America,* 133; Bonwick, *The Mormons and the Silver Mines,* 29.

140. Jackson, *Bits of Travel at Home,* 77.

141. Pfeiffer, *Flying Leaves from East and West,* 189.

142. Harper, *Letters from California,* 25–26.

143. Avery, *Californian Pictures in Prose and Verse,* 240, 243.

144. Falk, *Trans-Pacific Sketches,* 22.

145. Stevenson, cited in Allen, *Transatlantic Crossings,* 308.

146. *Appleton's General Guide to the United States and Canada,* 369; Doxey, *Guide to San Francisco and Vicinity,* 27.

147. For a contemporary account of Mission Dolores that interpreted its tranquility in contrast to the "great commercial mart" of San Francisco that enveloped it, see Powers, *The Story of the Old Missions of California,* v, 54.

148. Shaffer, *See America First,* 196.

149. Robertson and Robertson, *Our American Tour,* 84; Phillips, *Letters from California,* 14.

150. Tchen, *Genthe's Photographs of San Francisco's Old Chinatown,* 12, 21–23. Visitor

appreciation for Chinatown's built environment is discussed in Rast, "The Cultural Politics of Tourism in San Francisco's Chinatown," 38–39. Also see Pidgeon, *An Engineer's Holiday,* 300–301.

CHAPTER 5

1. "The Cosmopolitan Hotel Besieged," *San Francisco Daily Morning Call,* September 1, 1864. The accuracy of the account is questionable, in part because the *Call's* report, filed by Mark Twain, contended that thirty thousand people attended the opening— approximately one-third of the city's 1864 population. On the Cosmopolitan's opening, see www.twainquotes.com/18640901.html, or Van Orman, "San Francisco," 12.

2. According to nineteenth-century California historian Charles B. Turrill, by the 1870s, the Cosmopolitan had become a hotel of choice for business travelers. Turrill, *California Notes,* 62.

3. Boruck, comp. and ed., *California Illustrated,* 18; Richardson, *Garnered Sheaves,* 294.

4. Asbury, *The Barbary Coast,* 33–41. For a detailed discussion of the nineteenth-century Barbary Coast, see Berglund, *Making San Francisco American,* 60–69.

5. Lloyd, *Lights and Shades in San Francisco,* 78–87.

6. Crofutt, *Trans-continental Tourist,* 152.

7. On locating cosmopolitanism with nineteenth-century privilege and the elite, see, for example, Lee, "The Contradictions of Cosmopolitanism," 279, or Walkowitz, *City of Dreadful Delight,* 16. On the attempts to shape late nineteenth- and early twentieth-century New York City in this fashion, see Gilbert and Hancock, "New York City and the Transatlantic Imagination," 94–101.

8. For Chicago as the most cosmopolitan American city, see *The English-German Guide of the City of Chicago and the World's Columbian Exposition,* 20–21. For Denver, see Ingersoll, *Crest of the Continent,* 22. For San Francisco, see Raymond and Whitcomb, *Vacation Excursions;* Thomas Cook and Son, *California Excursions,* 41; or Jenkins, *An Excursion to Colorado, California and the Yosemite Valley,* 19.

9. On the rise of cosmopolitanism as characteristic of a new global citizen or culture, as well as the various debates about that idea, see, for example, Appiah, *Cosmopolitanism;* Harvey, *Cosmopolitanism and the Geographies of Freedom,* 77–97; Hollinger, "Not Universalists, Not Pluralists," 227–39; and Vertovec and Cohen, "Introduction," 1–22.

10. As early as 1859, Horace Greeley, editor of the *New York Tribune,* considered the diversity of the West's inhabitants among the region's most striking features. See Spence, *The American West,* 380–81. Regarding the diversity of the nineteenth-century urban West more generally, see Larsen, *The Urban West at the End of the Frontier,* 21.

11. White, "Race Relations in the American West," 396–97, 411.

12. Pomeroy, *In Search of the Golden West,* 47.

13. For figures on Chicago's nineteenth-century diversity, see Gilbert, *Perfect Cities,* 62. For San Francisco, see Matthews, "Forging a Cosmopolitan Civic Culture," 214–16. Figures for diversity in a variety of western cities are included in Hine and Faragher, *The American West,* 421–22.

14. Bramen, "The Urban Picturesque and the Spectacle of Americanization," 444–45. Earlier nineteenth-century examples of this method of cultural presentation can be found for cities along the eastern American seaboard, as well as for "exotic" non-Western cities that were subjects of colonial control by European powers. See, for example, Buzard, *The Beaten Track,* 323–24.

15. Stuart Blumin calls this genre "nonfictional urban sensationalism," although much of the literature was entirely fictional in its representation of urban peoples and their built environment. Contrary to the economic makeup of nineteenth-century American cities, this genre also typically divided urban culture into extremes of wealthy and poor—with nobody in between. See Blumin, "Introduction," 1, 20–27; or Hapke, "Down There on a Visit," 44–46.

16. Some tourists were religious leaders who considered it a moral imperative to visit the diverse, allegedly sacrilegious, western cities. To them, a western sojourn was more essential than visiting cities elsewhere in the United States. Regarding middle-class Protestant women extending this imperative by establishing rescue homes for women in the nineteenth-century urban West (including homes for polygamous wives in Salt Lake City and prostitutes in San Francisco's Chinatown), see Pascoe, *Relations of Rescue.* For an account of urban sensationalist literature in nineteenth-century London, see Walkowitz, *City of Dreadful Delight,* 15–39; for New York City, see Dowling, *Slumming in New York,* 4–5; 17–18.

17. Cocks, *Doing the Town,* 15–16.

18. This was also the case in the more distant past. See, for example, Schneider, "The Postmodern City from an Early Modern Perspective," 1671–72.

19. On Chicago's nineteenth-century demographics, see, for example, Burg, *Chicago's White City of 1893,* 65–67; or Mayer and Wade, *Chicago,* 150–54.

20. Drake and Cayton, *Black Metropolis,* 32, 39, 44, 47.

21. Schick, *Chicago and Its Environs,* 89.

22. Flinn, *Chicago,* 82. The same breakdown, with a few nationalities added—including "Negroes"—is found in *Godey's Illustrated Souvenir Guide to Chicago World's Fair and New York,* 22; *The English-German Guide,* 20–21; and Rand, McNally and Co., *Chicago and the World's Columbian Exposition,* 1.

23. For ethnic typing in antebellum New York, see Upton, "Inventing the Metropolis," 28.

24. Gilbert, *Perfect Cities,* 126.

25. There were several other vice districts in late nineteenth-century Chicago, but the Levee received the most publicity. See Heap, *Slumming,* 21, 38–39. According to Lindberg, *Chicago by Gaslight,* 111, the Levee's borders ran south from Adams Street to Twelfth Street and west from Wabash Avenue to the south bank of the Chicago River. For the nicknames of other vice districts, see Asbury, *Gem of the Prairie,* 100.

26. Lindberg, *To Serve and Collect,* 119. For the Levee as convenient housing for new immigrants, see Heap, *Slumming,* 22, 41.

27. See Flinn, *Chicago,* 577–79; Schick, *Chicago and Its Environs,* 104; or Vynne, *Chicago by Day and Night,* 200–205.

28. Vynne, *Chicago by Day and Night,* 157. The use of the term "Cheyenne" for the

rowdiest part of the Levee was apparently a reference to Cheyenne, Wyoming, which held a popular nineteenth-century reputation as the most lawless city in the American West.

29. Heap, *Slumming,* 102.

30. Bright, letter, June 30, 1869; Dugard cited in Raycraft, "Introduction," xxxi; Grandin, *Impressions d'une Parisienne à Chicago,* 206.

31. Raycraft, "Introduction," xxvii.

32. Robinson, *Sinners and Saints,* 13. Robinson did not identify the race of the cab driver but expressed some astonishment that African American children were permitted to engage in such shenanigans.

33. Joyaux, trans., "A Frenchman's Visit to Chicago in 1886," 51.

34. Lewis, *Two Lectures on a Short Visit to America,* 58.

35. Duis, "Foreword to the 2004 Edition," in Pierce, *As Others See Chicago,* xii; also see Raycraft, "Introduction," xxvii.

36. Ingersoll, *Crest of the Continent,* 22.

37. Gilpin cited in Larsen, *Urban West at the End of the Frontier,* 111–12.

38. Barbot, comp., *Souvenir Album of 1891.*

39. Thayer, *Marvels of the New West.*

40. Dorsett, *The Queen City,* 28–31.

41. On the rise of Denver's vice in the 1870s and 1880s, see Secrest, *Hell's Belles,* 101–28.

42. Leonard and Noel, *Denver,* 186. Hop Alley and the former red-light district of Market Street today have become largely incorporated within Denver's commercial "Lower Downtown" area.

43. Dorsett, *The Queen City,* 99, 105–106, 111–17.

44. Bird, *A Lady's Life in the Rocky Mountains,* 161.

45. Pidgeon, *An Engineer's Holiday,* 190. Lucy, *East by West,* 70.

46. Bickham, *From Ohio to the Rocky Mountains,* 71.

47. Wills, *A Winter in California,* 140.

48. Hafen, "City of Saints, City of Sinners," 355.

49. Limerick, *The Legacy of Conquest,* 286–87.

50. Robinson, *Sinners and Saints,* 130.

51. Walker, Whittaker, and Allen, *Mormon History,* 2–5.

52. Ibid., 12; Mulder and Mortensen, eds., *Among the Mormons,* vi. A number of fictional accounts appeared in the nineteenth century as well, characterizing Mormons in a similar light. See Homer, ed., *On the Way to Somewhere Else,* 187–90.

53. Buel, *Metropolitan Life Unveiled,* 447–58. Particularly graphic accounts of blood atonement can be found on pp. 448 and 455–56.

54. Beadle, *Polygamy.*

55. *The "Mormon" Metropolis* (1886), 47.

56. Hafen, "City of Saints, City of Sinners," 345–46.

57. See, for example, *A Souvenir of Salt Lake City and Utah; Salt Lake City Illustrated, Souvenir 1888–9;* or Darke, *Salt Lake City Illustrated.* Savage, *Views of Utah and Tourists' Guide,* includes a few tenets of the Mormon belief system but little about contemporary Mormon culture.

58. Hafen, "City of Saints, City of Sinners," 346.

59. Ibid., 370.

60. Ibid., 346, 369.

61. Gripenberg, *A Half-Year in the New World,* 175.

62. Topsöe cited in Homer, *On the Way to Somewhere Else,* 306.

63. Kent, *Graphic Sketches of the West,* 186.

64. Snow, "British Travelers View the Saints," 72; Limerick, *The Legacy of Conquest,* 285.

65. Hendrix, *Around the World,* 27.

66. Churchill, *Over the Purple Hills,* 246; Clark, *The Round Trip,* 155, 159, 160.

67. Rice, *Letters from the Pacific Slope,* 26.

68. Kipling, *American Notes,* 187.

69. Church, *Diary of a Trip through Mexico and California,* 60.

70. Ludlow, *The Heart of the Continent,* 333; Preston, "The Great Salt Lake City and its People," 701.

71. Dwinell, *Common Sense Views of Foreign Lands,* 339.

72. Slaughter, ed., *Camping Out in the Yellowstone 1882,* 10.

73. Mead, *Notes of Two Trips,* 55.

74. Robinson, *Sinners and Saints,* 245.

75. Thomas, *Miscellaneous Writings,* 34.

76. Holton, *Travels with Jottings,* 23–24.

77. Arrington and Bitton, *The Mormon Experience,* 128–29, 136, 139. On Scandinavian immigration, see Homer, *On the Way to Somewhere Else,* 303. There was a small Chinese community in nineteenth-century Salt Lake City primarily concentrated along "Plum Alley" just two blocks south and west of Temple Square. Yet the Chinese community—which grew following the completion of the transcontinental railroad and reached an 1890 population of 271—received no attention in promotional material and its presence is mostly absent from traveler accounts. On Salt Lake City's nineteenth-century Chinese, see Lansing, "Race, Space, and Chinese Life in Late Nineteenth-Century Salt Lake City," 219–38.

78. Todd, *The Sunset Land,* 181; Merewether, *By Sea and by Land,* 265; Bates, *Notes of a Tour,* 150–51.

79. W. P. R., *My Diary,* 240; Johnson, *America Pictorially Described,* 87.

80. Codman, *The Mormon Country,* 172; Sala, *America Revisited,* 520–21.

81. Marshall, *Through America,* 169.

82. Manning, *American Pictures,* 76–77.

83. Marshall quoted in Mulder and Mortensen, *Among the Mormons,* 378; Bonwick, *The Mormons and the Silver Mines,* 21, 169.

84. Slaughter, *Camping Out in the Yellowstone 1882,* 3–4.

85. Homer, *On the Way to Somewhere Else,* 329.

86. Clark, *The Round Trip,* 162.

87. Barneby, *Life and Labour in the Far, Far West,* 32.

88. Walker, "Another Round of Globalization in San Francisco," 65, 66.

89. Harper, *Letters from California,* 33, 34.

90. Hittell, *Guide Book to San Francisco,* 24.

91. Jenkins, *An Excursion to Colorado, California and the Yosemite Valley,* 19.

92. Griswold, *Beauties of California,* n.p.

93. Boruck, *California Illustrated,* 32.

94. Duloup, *San Francisco,* 12; Pidgeon, *An Engineer's Holiday,* 287; Roberts, *The Western Avernus,* 288; Ralph, *Our Great West,* 430.

95. Clarkson, "Overland Journey to California," 1874; Leng, *America in 1876,* 172.

96. Jones, *To San Francisco and Back,* 69.

97. Rice, *Letters from the Pacific Slope,* 80.

98. The boundaries of Chinatown were never fixed. In the 1850s and for much of the 1860s, the Chinese principally occupied a small, two-block area along Sacramento Street between Stockton and Dupont Streets. With increased immigration, the Chinese pushed further east to Kearney Street, and expanded north and south as well. For the shifting boundaries of nineteenth-century Chinatown, see Lee, *Picturing Chinatown,* 9–10, or Tchen, *Genthe's Photographs of San Francisco's Old Chinatown,* 19, 23.

99. The rising distaste for the Chinese in the nineteenth-century West is detailed in White, *Railroaded,* 290–305.

100. For the Chinese Exclusion Act, see www.ourdocuments.gov/doc.php?flash= true&doc=47. Given the reputation of San Francisco's Chinatown as the cultural and economic capital of Chinese America, it is possible that the increase in population during the 1880s can be attributed to Chinese from elsewhere in the United States settling in San Francisco. See Rast, "The Cultural Politics of Tourism in San Francisco's Chinatown," 34. Census figures from Sandmeyer, *The Anti-Chinese Movement in California,* 17.

101. See, for example, the comments by traveler William Brewster, who visited Chinatown in March 1862, in Farquha, ed., *Up and Down California in 1860–64,* 251, 366.

102. Wills, *A Winter in California,* 105.

103. For more on slumming and the touristic appeal of the poor, see Kasson, *Rudeness and Civility,* 78; Edwards, "Why Go Abroad?" 7; Dowling, *Slumming in New York;* Gilbert and Hancock, "New York City and the Transatlantic Imagination," 94–101; Heap, *Slumming,* 11; and Walkowitz, *City of Dreadful Delight,* 18–19.

104. On health fears and tourist fascination with Chinese cuisine, see Berglund, "Chinatown's Tourist Terrain," 18–21.

105. See, for example, *Album of San Francisco, Cal.,* 14–15; Boruck, *California Illustrated,* 9; or Buel, *Metropolitan Life Unveiled,* 269, 271, 272.

106. References to a transplanted "Canton" in San Francisco arrived along with the earliest Chinese settlement during the first years of the gold rush. See, for example, *San Francisco Evening Picayune,* "Young China," June 27, 1851, as reprinted in Johnson, ed., *San Francisco As It Is,* 170. Also see Boruck, *California Illustrated,* 33; and Taber, *Hints to Strangers,* 3. For references to Chinatown as "Peking," see Doxey, *Guide to San Francisco and Vicinity,* 58.

107. *Album of San Francisco, Cal.,* 15; Hittell, *Guide Book to San Francisco,* 44; Turrill, *California Notes,* 65; or Nordhoff, *California,* 63.

108. See, for example, Raymond, *Horrors of the Mongolian Settlement,* 12.

109. Lloyd, *Lights and Shades in San Francisco,* 254; Raymond, *Horrors of the Mongolian Settlement,* 9. For similar descriptions, see *Chinatown: San Francisco, Cal.,* 2–3; Raymond and Whitcomb, *Vacation Excursions,* 53.

110. Asbury, *Barbary Coast,* 166–67. For more on the tourism of opium dens, see Rast, "The Cultural Politics of Tourism in San Francisco's Chinatown," 46–47.

111. Hittell, *Guide Book to San Francisco,* 49.

112. Nordhoff, *California,* 63; Bancroft Co., *Chinatown,* 4.

113. Upchurch, *The Life, Labors and Travels of Father J. J. Upchurch,* 111.

114. Berglund, "Chinatown's Tourist Terrain," 17.

115. Strong is cited in Berger and Berger, eds., *Diary of America,* 506.

116. Kingsley, *South by West,* 168.

117. Green, *Notes on New York, San Francisco, and Old Mexico,* 65.

118. Chard, *California Sketches;* Dewar, *A Ramble Round the Globe,* 104–105.

119. Carbutt, *Five Months Fine Weather,* 82. Also see Pidgeon, *An Engineer's Holiday,* 300, and Pierrepont, *Fifth Avenue to Alaska,* 46.

120. Robinson, *Sinners and Saints,* 295–96.

121. Boddam-Whetham, *Western Wanderings,* 158–59.

122. Cumbrian, "Roving Cumbrian Journal," October 31, 1871–December 20, 1872.

123. Vivian, *Notes of a Tour in America,* 135–37.

124. Price, *America after Sixty Years,* 38, 40–41.

125. Jones, *To San Francisco and Back,* 73; Hendrix, *Around the World,* 45; Bates, *Notes of a Tour,* 119–20.

126. Marshall, *Through America,* 305.

127. Smith, *Notes of Travel in Mexico and California,* 100; Pidgeon, *An Engineer's Holiday,* 300–301.

128. Harper, *Letters from California,* 29.

129. Lee, *Glimpses of Mexico and California,* 101.

130. Harper, *Letters from California,* 28.

131. Wills, *A Winter in California,* 104–106.

132. Wilde, *Impressions of America,* 29.

133. Leslie, *California,* 217.

134. H. H., *Bits of Travel at Home,* 63.

135. Berglund, "Chinatown's Tourist Terrain," 9–10, 13, 29–30; Rast, "The Cultural Politics of Tourism in San Francisco's Chinatown," 47. For an account describing interactions with a Chinese policeman, see Marshall, *Through America,* 301.

136. Mead, *Notes of Two Trips* (Friday, June 29), 62.

137. Treseder, "A Visitor's Trip to Chicago in 1893," 32.

EPILOGUE

1. Gilbert, *Perfect Cites,* 152–55.

2. Ward, *A Trip to Chicago,* 45.

3. For the rise of automobile tourism in the United States, see Belasco, *Americans on the Road,* 19–39, and Jakle, *The Tourist,* 101–70. On the standardization accompanying

the rise of mass tourism in the post–World War II years, see Boorstin, *The Image,* 91–117; on predictable urban attractions at millennium's turn, see Judd, "Constructing the Tourist Bubble," 35–53; on the formulaic nature of the architectural tour, see Schwarzer, "Architecture and Mass Tourism," 12–33.

4. On Chinatown, see Eli, "Our New Oriental City."

5. Rousiers, *American Life,* 157.

6. Schivelbusch, *The Railway Journey;* 52–58; de Certeau, *The Practice of Everyday Life,* 111–14.

7. On San Francisco as America's most European city see, for example, Farr, "San Francisco's European Style." The transformation of Denver's Larimer Square is detailed in Morley, *Historic Preservation and the Imagined West,* 43–66; on the questionable notion of authenticity regarding re-creations of pioneer villages, of which Salt Lake City's Heritage Village is a part, see Fitch, *Historic Preservation,* 219–40; on invented tradition, see Hobsbawm, "Introduction," 1–14.

8. For the "post-tourist" and its various manifestations, see Ritzker and Liska, "'McDisneyization' and 'Post-Tourism,'" 101–109.

9. On the issue of selectivity and travel writing, see de Botton, *The Art of Travel,* 13–15.

10. Ryland, *My Diary during a Foreign Tour,* 239–40; Bourbonnaud in Raycraft, "Introduction," xxx; Walworth, *An Old World,* 309–11.

11. The Oakland Mole was demolished in the 1960s; its site is now part of the Port of Oakland.

12. Hart, ed. *Fodor's 2011 San Francisco,* 126.

13. Kay, "Sea Lions Swarm Long-Abandoned Seal Rocks."

Bibliography

PRIMARY SOURCES

Adair, Cornelia. *My Diary: August 30th to November 5th, 1874.* Austin: University of Texas Press, 1965.

Adams, Emma H. *To and Fro, Up and Down in Southern California, Oregon, and Washington Territory, with Sketches in Arizona, New Mexico, and British Columbia.* Cincinnati: Cranston & Stowe, 1888.

Adams, Henry. *The Education of Henry Adams.* Edited by Ernest Samuels. 1918. Reprint, Boston: Houghton Mifflin, 1973.

Adler, Dankmar. "The Chicago Auditorium." *Architectural Record* 1 (1892): 415.

Aitken, James. *From the Clyde to California: With Jottings by the Way.* Greenock, U.K.: William Johnston, 1882.

Appleton's General Guide to the United States and Canada. Edinburgh: Adam & Charles Black, 1882.

Appleton's Hand Book of Winter Resorts. New York: D. Appleton, 1888.

Appleton's Illustrated Hand-Book of American Travel. New York: D. Appleton, 1857.

Avery, Benjamin Parke. *Californian Pictures in Prose and Verse.* New York: Hurd & Houghton, 1878.

Baedeker, Karl, ed. *The United States, with an Excursion into Mexico.* 1893. Reprint, New York: Da Capo Press, 1971.

Baillie-Grohman, Wm. A. *Camps in the Rockies: Being a Narrative of Life on the Frontier, and Sport in the Rocky Mountains, with an Account of the Cattle Ranches in the West.* New York: Charles Scribner's Sons, 1882.

Baker, William Taylor. Journal. Typescript. Chicago Historical Museum.

Bancroft Company. *Chinatown: San Francisco, Cal.* San Francisco: Bancroft Company, 1893. California (geographical), box 4 of 4, folder #2, Souvenirs, Warshaw Collection of

Business Americana, Archives Center, National Museum of American History, Washington, D.C.

Barbot, W. A., comp. *Souvenir Album of 1891: City of Denver, Colo.* Denver: Collier and Cleveland Litho. Co., 1890. Colorado (geographical), box 1 of 2, folder #5, Warshaw Collection of Business Americana, Smithsonian Institution, Archives Center, National Museum of American History, Washington D.C.

Barneby, W. Henry. *Life and Labour in the Far, Far West: Being Notes of a Tour in the Western States, British Columbia, Manitoba, and the North-West Territory.* London: Cassell, 1884.

Barton, Harry Scott. *What I Did in "The Long."* Oxford: privately printed [1881?].

Bates, J. H. [James Hale]. *Notes of a Tour in Mexico and California.* New York: Burr Printing House, 1887.

Beadle, Charles. *A Trip to the United States in 1887.* London: Printed by J. S. Virtue, 1887.

Beadle, John H. *Polygamy; or, The Mysteries and Crimes of Mormonism.* Philadelphia: National Publishing, 1882.

———. *The Undeveloped West; or, Five Years in the Territories.* Philadelphia: National Publishing, 1873.

Bickham, William Denison. *From Ohio to the Rocky Mountains: Editorial Correspondence of the Dayton (Ohio) Journal.* Dayton: Journal Book & Job Printing House, 1879.

Bird, Isabella Lucy. *A Lady's Life in the Rocky Mountains.* 1879. Reprint, Norman: University of Oklahoma Press, 1960.

Black, William. *Green Pastures and Piccadilly.* London: Macmillan, 1877.

Blackall, C. H. "Notes of Travel: Chicago—I." *American Architect and Building News* 22 (December 24, 1887): 299–300.

———. "Notes of Travel: Chicago—II." *American Architect and Building News* 22 (December 31, 1887): 313–15.

Blake, Mary. *On the Wing: Rambling Notes of a Trip to the Pacific.* Boston: Lee & Shepard, 1883.

Boddam-Whetham, J. W. *Western Wanderings: A Record of Travel in the Evening Land.* London: Richard Bentley & Son, 1874.

Bode, Wm. *Lights and Shadows of Chinatown.* [San Francisco?]: Mrs. Kate Bode, 1896.

Bonwick, James. *The Mormons and the Silver Mines.* London: Hodder & Stoughton, 1872.

Boruck, Marcus D., comp. and ed. *California Illustrated: Spirit of the Times.* San Francisco: December 25, 1877. Bancroft Library, University of California, Berkeley.

Bowles, Samuel. *Across the Continent: A Summer's Journey to the Rocky Mountains, the Mormons, and the Pacific States.* Springfield, Mass.: Samuel Bowles, 1866.

Brace, Charles Loring. *The New West; or, California in 1867–1868.* New York: G. P. Putnam & Son, 1869.

Bridges, DeWitt C. *A Tour around the World.* Greencastle, Ind., 1882.

Bright, Anne Mathilda. Letter. June 30, 1869. Archives and Manuscripts Collection, Chicago Description, Folder 44: 33, Chicago History Museum.

Bryant, William Cullen, ed. *Picturesque America; or, The Land We Live In.* Vols. 1 and 2. 1874. Reprint, Secaucus, N.J.: Lyle Stuart, 1974.

Buel, John W. *Metropolitan Life Unveiled; or, The Mysteries and Miseries of America's Great Cities.* St. Louis: Historical Publishing, 1882.

Butterworth, Hezekiah. *Zigzag Journeys in the Occident: The Atlantic to the Pacific.* Boston: Estes & Lauriat, 1883.

———. *Zig-zag Journeys in the White City with Visits to the Neighboring Metropolis.* Boston: Estes & Lauriat, 1894.

California As It Is. San Francisco: San Francisco Call, 1882.

California Illustrated: A Guide for Tourists and Settlers. San Francisco: Carnall-Hopkins, 1891.

Campbell, J. F. *My Circular Notes: Extracts from Journals, Letters Sent Home, Geological and Other Notes, Written while Travelling Westwards round the World from July 6, 1874, to July 6, 1875.* London: Macmillan, 1876.

Cannon, George. *The City of the Saints, Containing Views and Descriptions of Principal Points of Interest in Salt Lake and Vicinity.* Salt Lake City: Geo. Q. Cannon & Sons, n.d.

Carbutt, Mrs. E. H. *Five Months Fine Weather in Canada, Western U.S., and Mexico.* London: Sampson Low, Marston, Searle, & Rivington, 1889.

Chard, Thomas S. *California Sketches.* Chicago, 1888.

Chicago Album. Souvenir view book. Warshaw Collection of Business Americana, Illinois (geographical), box 2 of 2, Archives Center, National Museum of American History, Washington, D.C.

Chicago and the World's Columbian Exposition Illustrated. Chicago: Rand McNally, 1893.

Chicago Checker-Board Guide, World's Fair Edition. Chicago: A. H. Pokorny [1893?].

Chicago Illustrated. Chicago: R. F. Griffis, 1982.

Chinatown, San Francisco. Souvenir view book. Warshaw Collection of Business Americana, California (geographical), box 4 of 4, folder #2: souvenirs, Archives Center, National Museum of American History, Washington, D.C.

Church, John H. C. *Diary of a Trip through Mexico and California.* Pittsfield, Mass.: Marcus H. Rogers, 1887.

Churchill, Caroline M. *"Little Sheaves" Gathered while Gleaning after Reapers: Being Letters of Travel Commencing in 1870, and Ending in 1873.* San Francisco, 1874.

———. *Over the Purple Hills; or, Sketches of Travel in California, Embracing All the Important Points Usually Visited by Tourists.* Denver: Mrs. C. M. Churchill, 1881.

"The City by the Golden Gate." *Scribner's Monthly* 10, no. 3 (July 1875): 266–85.

Clark, Susie C. *The Round Trip from the Hub to the Golden Gate.* Boston: Lee & Shepard, 1890.

Clarkson, Banyer. "Overland Journey to California and the Western Territories." Diary, 1874. Bancroft Library, University of California at Berkeley.

Cobden, Richard. *American Diaries.* Edited by Elizabeth Hoon Cawley. New York: Greenwood Press, 1952.

Codman, John. *The Mormon Country: A Summer with the "Latter-Day Saints."* New York: United States Publishing, 1874.

———. *The Round Trip: By Way of Panama through California, Oregon, Nevada, Utah, Idaho, and Colorado.* New York: G. P. Putnam's Sons, 1879.

Colorado and Its Capital. Denver: Chamberlain Investment Company, n.d. Warshaw Collection of Business Americana, Colorado (geographical), box 2 of 2, folder #3, Archives Center, National Museum of American History, Washington, D.C.

Colorado Cities and Places: Metropolitan Centres of Wealth, Luxury and Refinement. Chicago:

Passenger Department of the Chicago, Rock Island & Pacific Railway, 1890. Warshaw Collection of Business Americana, Colorado (geographical), box 1 of 2, folders #2 & #3, Archives Center, National Museum of American History, Washington, D.C.

Cone, Mary. *Two Years in California*. Chicago: S. C. Griggs, 1876.

Cook, Thomas, and Son. *Cook's California Excursions*. New York: David H. Gildersleeve, 1884.

Coop, Timothy, and Henry Exley. *A Trip around the World: A Series of Letters*. Cincinnati: H. C. Hall, 1882.

"The Cosmopolitan Hotel Besieged." *San Francisco Daily Morning Call,* September 1, 1864.

Crofutt, George. *Crofutt's Grip-Sack Guide of Colorado*. Vol. 2. Omaha: Overland Publishing Co, 1885.

————. *Crofutt's New Overland Tourist and Pacific Coast Guide*. Omaha: Overland Publishing, 1883.

————. *Crofutt's Trans-continental Tourist: From the Atlantic to the Pacific Ocean*. New York: Geo. A. Crofutt, 1874.

Culmer, H. L. A. *Tourists' Guide Book to Salt Lake City*. Salt Lake City: J. C. Graham, 1879.

Cumbrian, R. "Roving Cumbrian Journal." Diary, October 31, 1871–December 20, 1872. Bancroft Library, University of California, Berkeley.

Darke, S. W. *Salt Lake City Illustrated*. Salt Lake City: S. W. Darke, 1887.

Dean, C. *The World's Fair City and Her Enterprising Sons*. [Chicago?]: United Publishing, 1892.

Denison, Charles. *Rocky Mountain Health Resorts: An Analytical Study of High Altitudes in Relation to the Arrest of Chronic Pulmonary Disease*. Boston: Houghton, Mifflin, 1881. Warshaw Collection of Business Americana, Colorado (geographical), box 2 of 2, folder #8, Archives Center, National Museum of American History, Washington, D.C.

Denver and Rio Grande and Rio Grande Western Railroads. *Valleys of the Great Salt Lake, Describing the Garden of Utah and the Two Great Cities of Salt Lake and Ogden*. Chicago: R. R. Donnelley & Sons, 1890.

Denver and Rio Grande Railroad. *Tourists' Handbook, Descriptive of Colorado, New Mexico and Utah*. Denver: Denver & Rio Grande Railroad, 1890.

Denver: By Pen and Picture. Denver: Frank S. Thayer, 1898. Warshaw Collection of Business Americana, Colorado (geographical), box 1 of 2, folder #2, Archives Center, National Museum of American History, Washington, D.C.

Dewar, Thomas R. *A Ramble Round the Globe*. London: Chatto & Windus, 1894.

Dickens, Charles. *American Notes and Pictures from Italy*. 1842. Reprint, London: Oxford University Press, 1966.

Disturnell's Strangers' Guide to San Francisco and Vicinity. San Francisco: W. C. Disturnell, 1883.

Dodd, Derrick. *Summer Saunterings*. San Francisco: Francis, Valentine, 1882.

Donan, P. *Utah: A Peep into a Mountain Walled Treasury of the Gods*. Buffalo: Cassius C. Smith, 1891. Warshaw Collection of Business Americana, Utah (geographical), box 1 of 1, folder #2, Archives Center, National Museum of American History, Washington, D.C.

Doxey, William F. *Doxey's Guide to San Francisco and Vicinity: The Big Trees, Yo Semite Valley, the Geysers, China, Japan, and Sandwich Islands.* San Francisco: Doxey, 1881.

Duloup, Georges. *San Francisco: Souvenirs de Voyage.* Paris: Publications de la Revue Géographique Internationale, 1882.

Dwinell, M. *Common Sense Views of Foreign Lands: A Series of Letters from the East and the West.* Rome, Ga.: Office of the Courier, 1878.

Dwyer, James. *Album of Salt Lake City, Utah. Evening Standard* (Ogden, Utah), June 6, 1912.

Eli, Look Tin. "Our New Oriental City—Veritable Fairy Palaces Filled with the Choicest Treasures of the Orient." In *San Francisco: The Metropolis of the West.* San Francisco: Western Press Association, 1910.

Emmons, Terence, ed. *Around California in 1891.* Stanford: Stanford Alumni Association, 1991.

The English-German Guide of the City of Chicago and the World's Columbian Exposition. Chicago: Universe Publishing, 1892.

English Tourist. "The Land of the Mormons." *Kansas Magazine* 6, no. 10 (March 1887): 587–90.

Facts about Colorado and Denver, "The Queen City of the Plains." Denver: Chas. H. Sage, 1889. Warshaw Collection of Business Americana, Colorado (geographical), box 2 of 2, folder #3, Archives Center, National Museum of American History, Washington, D.C.

Faithfull, Emily. *Three Visits to America.* Edinburgh: David Douglas, 1884.

Falk, Alfred. *Trans-Pacific Sketches: A Tour through the United States and Canada.* Melbourne: George Robertson, 1877.

Ferree, Barr. "The High Building and Its Art." *Scribner's Magazine* 15, no. 3 (March 1894): 297–318.

Flinn, John J. *Chicago: The Marvelous City of the West, a History, an Encyclopedia, and a Guide.* Chicago: Flinn & Sheppard, 1891. https://archive.org/details/chicagomarvel000inflin.

———. *Official Guide to the World's Columbian Exposition.* Chicago: Columbian Guide, 1892.

———. *The Standard Guide to Chicago, Illustrated, World's Fair Edition 1893.* Chicago: Standard Guide, 1893. https://archive.org/details/standardguidetoc00flin.

Gilpin, William. *Three Essays: On Picturesque Beauty; on Picturesque Travel; and on Sketching Landscape: To Which Is Added a Poem, on Landscape Painting.* 1794. Reprint, Westmead, U.K.: Gregg International Publishers, 1972.

Gladden, Washington. "Sunday in Chicago." *Century Magazine,* November 1892, 151. www .unz.org/Pub/Century-1892nov-00151a02.

Glazier, Willard. *Peculiarities of American Cities.* Philadelphia: Hubbard Brothers, 1886.

Godey's Illustrated Souvenir Guide to Chicago World's Fair and New York. [Chicago?]: E. Lockwood, 1893.

Goodkind, Ben. *Roughing It from California through France.* Sacramento: A. J. Johnston, 1886.

Grandin, Mme Léon. *Impressions d'une Parisienne à Chicago.* Translated by Margaret Scriven. Paris: Librarie Ernst Flammarion, 1894.

Green, Frank W. *Notes on New York, San Francisco, and Old Mexico.* Wakefield, U.K.: E. Carr, 1886.

Greenwood, Thomas. *A Tour in the United States and Canada. Out and Home in Six Weeks.* London: L. Upcott Gill, 1883.

Gripenberg, Alexandra. *A Half-Year in the New World.* Translated and edited by Ernest J. Mayne. 1888. Reprint, Newark: University of Delaware Press, 1954.

Griswold, N. W. *Beauties of California: Including Big Trees, Yosemite Valley, Geysers, Lake Tahoe, Donner Lake, S.F. '49 & '83, Etc.* San Francisco: H. S. Crocker, 1883.

Guide Book and Street Manual of San Francisco, California. San Francisco: F. W. Warner, 1882.

Guillemard, Arthur C. *Over Land and Sea: A Log of Travel Round the World in 1873–74.* London: Tinsley Brothers, 1875.

Hardy, Iza Duffus. *Between Two Oceans; or, Sketches of American Travel.* London: Hurst & Blackett, 1884.

———. *Through Cities and Prairie Lands: Sketches of an American Tour.* New York: R. Worthington, 1881.

Harper, Harriet. *Letters from California.* Portland, Maine: B. Thurston, 1888.

Hart, Teresa Maria, ed. *Fodor's 2011 San Francisco.* New York: Fodor's Travel, 2011.

Heininger, C. P. *Album of San Francisco, Cal.* San Francisco: C. P. Heininger, n.d. Bancroft Library, University of California, Berkeley.

———. *Historical Souvenir of San Francisco, Cal.* San Francisco: C. P. Heininger [1886?].

Hendrix, E. R. *Around the World.* Nashville: A. H. Redford, 1878.

H. H. [Helen Hunt Jackson]. *Bits of Travel at Home.* Boston: Roberts Brothers, 1880.

Hill, Thomas E. *Hill's Souvenir Guide to Chicago and the World's Fair.* Chicago: Laird & Lee, 1892.

Historical and Descriptive Sketches of Salt Lake City. Portland, Maine: Chisolm Brothers, 1891.

Hittell, John S., comp. *Bancroft's Pacific Guide Book.* San Francisco: A. L. Bancroft, 1882.

———. *The Commerce and Industries of the Pacific Coast.* San Francisco, 1882.

———. *A Guide Book to San Francisco.* San Francisco: Bancroft Company, 1888.

Hoitt, Ira G., comp. *Pacific Coast Guide and Programme of the Knights Templar Triennial Conclave at San Francisco, August, 1883.* San Francisco: Ira G. Hoitt, 1883.

Holand, Hjalmar R. *My First Eighty Years.* New York: Twayne Publishers, 1957.

Holbrook, Rev. J. C. "Chinadom in California." *Hutchings' Illustrated California Magazine* 4, no. 3 (September 1859).

Holton, E. D. *Travels with Jottings. From Midland to the Pacific.* Milwaukee: Trayser Brothers, 1880.

Hotel Visitor and Stranger's Guide. No. 6, February 7, 1880. Bancroft Library, University of California, Berkeley.

Hudson, T. S. *A Scamper through America.* London: Griffith & Farran, 1882.

Hutchings, J. M. *Yo Semite and the Big Trees: What to See and How to See It.* San Francisco: J. M. Hutchings, 1894.

The Imperial Highness the Grand Duke Alexis in the United States of America during the Winter of 1871–72. Cambridge, Mass.: Riverside Press, 1872.

Ingersoll, Ernest. *The Crest of the Continent: A Record of a Summer's Railroad Ramble through the Rocky Mountains.* 1883. Reprint, Glorieta, N. Mex.: Rio Grande Press, 1969.

Jenkins, E. M. *An Excursion to Colorado, California and the Yosemite Valley.* New York: E. M. Jenkins, 1883.

Johnson, Angie. Letter to Abigail Bush. 1879. Bancroft Library, University of California at Berkeley.

Johnson, Kenneth, ed. *San Francisco As It Is: Gleanings from the Picayune.* Georgetown, Calif.: Talisman Press, 1964.

Johnson, Matthew. *America Pictorially Described.* London: James B. Knapp [1890?].

Johnson, Osmun. *Johnson's Journey around the World: Fifty Thousand Miles of Travel, from the Golden Gate to the Golden Gate.* Chicago: Rand, McNally, 1887.

Jones, Harry. *To San Francisco and Back.* London: Society for Promoting Christian Knowledge [1878?].

Jones, Marcus E. *Resources and Attractions of Salt Lake City.* Salt Lake City: Marcus E. Jones, 1889.

Joyaux, Georges J., trans. "A Frenchman's Visit to Chicago in 1886." *Journal of the Illinois State Historical Society* 47, no. 1 (Spring 1954): 45–56.

Kane, Elizabeth Wood. *Twelve Mormon Homes: Visited in Succession on a Journey through Utah and Arizona.* Philadelphia: privately printed, 1874.

Kent, Henry Brainard. *Graphic Sketches of the West.* Chicago: R. R. Donnelley & Sons, 1890.

Kingsbury, Joseph C. Trade card, n.d., Warshaw Collection of Business Americana, Utah (geographical), box 1 of 1, folder #10, Archives Center, National Museum of American History, Washington, D.C.

Kingsley, Calvin. *Round the World: A Series of Letters.* Cincinnati: Hitchcock & Walden, 1871.

Kingsley, Rose Georgina. *South by West; or, Winter in the Rocky Mountains and Spring in Mexico.* Edited by Charles Kingsley. London: W. Isbister, 1874.

Kipling, Rudyard. *American Notes.* Boston: Brown, 1899.

Lane, M. A. "High Buildings in Chicago." *Harper's Weekly* 35 (October 31, 1891).

Lee, S. M. *Glimpses of Mexico and California.* Boston: Geo. H. Ellis, 1887.

Leng, John. *America in 1876: Pencillings during a Tour in the Centennial Year: With a Chapter on the Aspects of American Life.* Dundee, Scot.: Dundee Advertising Office, 1876.

Leslie, Mrs. Frank. *California: A Pleasure Trip from Gotham to the Golden Gate.* New York: G. W. Carleton, 1877.

Lewis, Charles E. *Two Lectures on a Short Visit to America.* London: Blades, East & Blades, 1876.

Lick House Tourists' Guide: Giving Principal Routes from Chicago and Saint Louis to San Francisco. San Francisco: Lick House, 1871.

Lloyd, Benjamin E. *Lights and Shades in San Francisco.* San Francisco: A. L. Bancroft, 1876.

Lucy, Henry W. *East by West: A Journey in the Recess.* Vol. 1. London: Richard Bentley & Son, 1885.

Ludlow, Fitz Hugh. *The Heart of the Continent: A Record of Travel across the Plains and in Oregon.* New York: Hurd & Houghton, 1870.

Macgregor, W. L. *Hotels and Hotel Life in San Francisco.* San Francisco: S. F. News Company, 1877.

Manning, Samuel. *American Pictures: Drawn with Pen and Pencil*. London: Religious Tract Society, 1878.

Marquis, A. N., and Company. *A. N. Marquis & Co.'s Ready Reference Guide to Chicago and the World's Columbian Exposition*. Chicago: A. N. Marquis [1893?].

Marshall, W. G., *Through America; or, Nine Months in the United States*. London: Sampson Low, Marston, Searle, & Rivington, 1881.

Martineau, Harriet. *Retrospect of Western Travel*. 1838. Reprint, Armonk, New York: M. E. Sharpe, 2000.

McClintock, A. H. *Illustrated School and Family: History of Places and Objects of Great Historical Interest throughout the World*. Fort Scott, Kans.: Barter & Sargent, 1875.

McElrath, Thomson P. *A Press Club Outing: Across the Continent to Attend the First Convention of the International League of Press Clubs*. New York: International League of Press Clubs, 1983.

McKinsey, Elizabeth. *Niagara Falls: Icon of the American Sublime*. Cambridge: Cambridge University Press, 1985.

Mead, Solomon. *Notes of Two Trips to California and Return, Taken in 1883 and 1886–87*. Greenwich, Conn.: Library of Congress, American Memory Collection [1890?].

Medley, Julius George. *An Autumn Tour in the United States and Canada*. London: Harry S. King, 1873.

Merewether, Henry Alworth. *By Sea and by Land: Being a Trip through Egypt, India, Ceylon, Australia, New Zealand, and America*. London: Macmillan, 1874.

M. H., E. *Ranch Life in California*. London: W. H. Allen, 1886.

Midwinter Scenes in Golden Gate Park. San Francisco: A. J. McDonald & Son, 1893.

Mohr, Nicolaus. *Excursion through America*. Translated by Lavern J. Rippley. Edited by Ray Allen Billington. 1884. Reprint, Chicago: R. R. Donnelley & Sons, 1973.

The "Mormon" Metropolis: An Illustrated Guide to Salt Lake City and Its Environs. Salt Lake City: Jos. Hyrum Parry, 1886.

The "Mormon" Metropolis: An Illustrated Guide to Salt Lake City and Its Environs. Salt Lake City: Magazine Printing, 1887.

The "Mormon" Metropolis: An Illustrated Guide to Salt Lake City and Its Environs. Salt Lake City: J. H. Parry, 1889. http://archive.org/details/mormonmetropolis00rey.

The "Mormon" Metropolis: An Illustrated Guide to Salt Lake City and Its Environs. Salt Lake City: Magazine Printing, 1891.

The Mormon Metropolis: An Illustrated Guide to Salt Lake City. Salt Lake City: Magazine Printing, 1893.

Muirhead, James Fullarton. *The Land of Contrasts: A Briton's View of His American Kin*. Boston: Lamson, Wolffe, 1898.

Mushet, Robert. *Chicago, Yesterday and To-day: A Guide to the Garden City and the Columbian Exposition*. Chicago: Donohue & Henneberry, 1893.

Naylor, Robert Anderton. *Across the Atlantic*. London: Roxburghe Press, 1893.

Nordhoff, Charles. *California: For Health, Pleasure, and Residence*. 1873. Reprint, Berkeley: Ten Speed Press, 1974. http://cprr.org/Museum/Books/Calif_Nordhoff_1872.html.

———. *Northern California, Oregon, and the Sandwich Islands*. 1874. Reprint, Berkeley: Ten Speed Press, 1974.

Notes of Journey from London to San Francisco and Back. September 19 to November 7, 1877. Manuscript. Bancroft Library, University of California at Berkeley.

O'Rell, Max. *Jonathan and His Continent.* Translated by Mme Paul Blouet. New York: Cassell, 1889.

The Palace Hotel. Brochure. San Francisco: Palace Hotel, 1885.

Pennsylvania Railroad to the Columbian Exposition. Philadelphia: Pennsylvania Railroad Company, 1892. Warshaw Collection of Business Americana, World Expositions, box 5 of 18, Archives Center, National Museum of American History, Washington, D.C.

Pfeiffer, Emily. *Flying Leaves from East and West.* London: Field and Tuer, Leadenhall Press, 1885.

Phillips, David L. *Letters from California: Its Mountains, Valleys, Plains, Lakes, Rivers, Climate and Productions.* Springfield, Ill.: Illinois State Journal, 1877.

Phillips, Morris. *Abroad and at Home: Practical Hints for Tourists.* New York: Brentano's, 1891.

Pidgeon, Daniel. *An Engineer's Holiday; or, Notes of a Round Trip from Long. 0° to 0°.* London: Kegan Paul, Trench, 1882.

Pierce, Bessie Louise, comp. and ed. *As Others See Chicago: Impressions of Visitors, 1673–1933.* Chicago: University of Chicago Press, 1933.

Pierrepont, Edward. *Fifth Avenue to Alaska.* New York: G. P. Putnam's Sons, 1884.

Pine, George W. *Beyond the West.* Utica, N.Y.: T. J. Griffiths, 1871.

Player-Frowd, John G. *Six Months in California.* London: Longmans, Green, 1872.

Preston, William. "The Great Salt Lake City and Its People." *Sunday Magazine* 20 [1891?]: 700–703. Americana Rare, Tom L. Perry Special Collections, Brigham Young University, Provo, Utah.

Price, M. Philips. *America after Sixty Years: The Travel Diaries of Two Generations of Englishmen.* London: George Allen & Unwin, 1936.

Rae, W. F. *Westward by Rail: A Journey to San Francisco and Back and a Visit to the Mormons.* Leipzig: Bernhard Tauchnitz, 1874.

Ralph, Julian. "Chicago—The Main Exhibit." *Harper's Monthly Magazine* 84 (February 1892): 425–36.

————. *Our Great West: A Study of the Present Conditions and Future Possibilities of the New Commonwealths and Capitals of the United States.* New York: Harper Brothers, 1893.

Rand, McNally and Company. *Chicago and the World's Columbian Exposition.* Chicago: Midway Publishing, 1892.

————. *A Week in Chicago, Containing Descriptions of All Points of Interest.* Chicago: Rand, McNally, 1892.

Raymond, W., and I. A. Whitcomb. *Raymond's Vacation Excursions: Thirty Summer Tours!* Boston: Raymond & Whitcomb, 1890.

————. *Raymond's Vacation Excursions: A Winter in California.* Boston: Raymond & Whitcomb, 1886.

Raymond, Walter J. *Horrors of the Mongolian Settlement, San Francisco, Cal.: Enslaved and Degraded Race of Paupers, Opium-Eaters and Lepers.* Boston: Cashman, Keating, 1886.

A Report on the Resources, Wealth, and Industrial Development of Colorado. Chicago: Agricultural Department, Colorado Exhibit, at the World's Columbian Exposition, 1893.

Warshaw Collection of Business Americana, Colorado (geographical), box 2 of 2, folder #3, Archives Center, National Museum of American History, Washington, D.C.

Reynolds, J. W. Letter. September 21, 1875. Bancroft Library, University of California, Berkeley.

Rice, Harvey. *Letters from the Pacific Slope; or First Impressions.* New York: D. Appleton, 1870.

Richardson, Albert D. *Garnered Sheaves from the Writings of Albert D. Richardson, Collected and Arranged by His Wife; To Which Is Added a Biographical Sketch of the Author.* Hartford, Conn.: Columbian Book, 1871. http://cprr.org/Museum/Through_to_the_Pacific/Through_to_the_Pacific.html.

Roberts, Edwards. *Salt Lake City and Utah By-Ways.* Chicago: Lakeside Press [1883?].

Roberts, Morley. *The Western Avernus; or, Toil and Travel in Further North America.* London: Smith, Elder, 1887.

Robertson, William, and W. F. Robertson, *Our American Tour: Being a Run of Ten Thousand Miles from the Atlantic to the Golden Gate in the Autumn of 1869.* Edinburgh: W. Burness, 1871.

Robinson, Phil. *Sinners and Saints. A Tour across the States, and round Them; With Three Months among the Mormons.* London: Sampson Low, Marston, Searle, & Rivington, 1883.

Rousiers, Paul de. *American Life.* Translated by A. J. Herbertson. Paris: Firmin-Didot, 1892.

Sala, George Augustus. *America Revisited: From the Bay of New York to the Gulf of Mexico and from Lake Michigan to the Pacific.* Vol. 2. 3rd. ed. London: Vizetelly, 1886.

Salt Lake Chamber of Commerce. *Salt Lake City: A Sketch of Utah's Wonderful Resources.* Salt Lake City: Salt Lake Chamber of Commerce, 1888.

Salt Lake City Illustrated, Souvenir 1888–9. Omaha: D. C. Dunbar, 1888.

Salt Lake City, Utah. Salt Lake City: Pembroke, 1890.

Salt Lake City, Utah. Salt Lake City [S. P. Teasdel?], n.d. Warshaw Collection of Business Americana, Utah (geographical), box 1 of 1, folder #9, Archives Center, National Museum of American History, Washington, D.C.

Sanders, Sue A. Pike. *A Journey to, on and from the "Golden Shore."* Delavan, Ill.: Times Printing Office, 1887.

San Francisco. Philadelphia: J. B. Lippincott, 1892. Library of Congress.

Savage, C. R. *Salt Lake City, and the Way Thither.* London: T. Nelson & Sons, 1870.

———. *Views of Utah and Tourists' Guide.* Salt Lake City: Art Bazar [1887?].

Schick, Louis. *Chicago and Its Environs: A Complete Guide to the City and the World's Fair.* Chicago: F. P. Kenkel, 1893. https://archive.org/details/chicagoitsenvir001schi.

———. *Chicago and Its Environs: A Handbook for the Traveler.* Chicago: L. Schick, 1891.

Schneyer, Louis J. *Schneyer's Illustrated Hand Book and Guide to Chicago and the World's Columbian Exposition.* Chicago: Louis J. Schneyer, 1892. Warshaw Collection of Business Americana, World Expositions, box 4 of 18, folder: Chicago 1893, Archives Center, National Museum of American History, Washington, D.C.

Sears, A. T., and E. Webster. *The Guide from the Pacific to the Atlantic, 1878.* Chicago: Dunn & Heggie, 1878.

Season of 1888: Three Grand Trips to the Yellowstone National Park. Boston: American Printing & Engraving, 1888. Warshaw Collection of Business Americana, Tours, box 4 of 6, folder: tour guides, Archives Center, National Museum of American History, Washington, D.C.

Shearer, Frederick E. ed. *The Pacific Tourist: Adams & Bishop's Illustrated Trans-Continental Guide of Travel from the Atlantic to the Pacific Ocean.* New York: Adams & Bishop, 1884.

Sienkiewicz, Henry. *Portrait of America: Letters of Henry Sienkiewicz.* Translated and edited by Charles Morley. New York: Columbia University Press, 1959.

Slaughter, William W, ed. *Camping Out in the Yellowstone 1882.* Salt Lake City: University of Utah Press, 1994.

Smiles, Samuel, ed. *A Boy's Voyage Round the World, Including a Residence in Victoria, and a Journey by Rail across North America.* London: John Murray, 1871.

Smith, Mrs. J. Gregory. *Notes of Travel in Mexico and California.* St. Albans, Vt.: Messenger & Advertiser Office, 1886.

Solly, Samuel E. *Manitou, Colorado, U.S.A.: Its Mineral Waters and Climate.* St. Louis: J. McKittrick, 1875.

A Souvenir of Salt Lake City and Utah. New York: A. Wittemann, 1889.

Stone, W. G. M. *The Colorado Hand-Book: Denver and Its Outings.* Denver: Barkhausen & Lester, 1892.

The Strangers' Guide to San Francisco. San Francisco: Jas. B. Bradford, 1875.

Sweetser, M. F. *King's Handbook of the United States.* Buffalo: Moses King, 1891–92.

Taber, Isaiah West. *Hints to Strangers.* San Francisco: I. W. Taber, 1890.

Taylor, Benjamin F. *Between the Gates.* Chicago: S. C. Griggs, 1878.

Thayer, William M. *Marvels of the New West.* Norwich, Conn.: Henry Bill Publishing Company, 1887.

Thomas, Julia M. *Miscellaneous Writings.* New York: John W. Lovell, 1890.

Tiffany, O. F., and A. C. Macdonald. *Pocket Exchange Guide of San Francisco.* San Francisco: Tiffany and Macdonald and Central Pacific, 1875.

Todd, John. *The Sunset Land; or, The Great Pacific Slope.* Boston: Lee & Shepard, 1870.

Travers, W. T. Locke. *From New Zealand to Lake Michigan.* Wellington, N.Z.: Edwards, 1889.

Treseder, Mable L. "A Visitor's Trip to Chicago in 1893." Edited by Sheldon T. Gardner. Reprint, 1943. Typescript. Chicago History Museum.

Truman, Benjamin C. *Semi-Tropical California: Its Climate, Healthfulness, Productiveness, and Scenery.* San Francisco: A. L. Bancroft, 1874.

Turland, Ephraim. *Notes of a Visit to America: Eleven Lectures.* Manchester: Johnson & Rawson, 1877.

Turrill, Charles B. *California Notes.* San Francisco: E. Bosqui, 1876.

Twain, Mark. *Roughing It.* 1872. Reprint, Harmondsworth, U.K.: Penguin Books, 1981.

Upchurch, J. J. *The Life, Labors and Travels of Father J. J. Upchurch.* San Francisco: A. T. Dewey, 1887.

"Utah Exposition Car." Trade card. Salt Lake City: Salt Lake City Chamber of Commerce, n.d. Warshaw Collection of Business Americana, Utah (geographical), box 1 of 1, folder #3, Archives Center, National Museum of American History, Washington, D.C.

Vivian, Henry Hussey. *Notes of a Tour in America.* London: Edward Stanford, 1878.

Vynne, Harold. *Chicago by Day and Night: The Pleasure Seekers Guide to the Paris of America.* Chicago: Thomson & Zimmerman, 1892.

Walker, W. S. *Glimpses of Hungryland; or, California Sketches.* Cloverdale, Calif.: Reveille Publishing House, 1880.

Walworth, Ellen H. *An Old World, As Seen through Young Eyes; or, Travels around the World.* New York: D. Appleton, 1877.

Ward, Martindale C. *A Trip to Chicago: What I Saw, What I Heard, What I Thought.* Glasgow: Alex Malcolm, 1895.

Warner, Charles Dudley. *Studies in the South and West with Comments on Canada.* New York: Harper & Brothers, 1889.

Warren, F. K., ed. *California Illustrated: Including a Trip through Yellowstone Park.* Boston: De Wolfe, Fiske, 1892.

Wilde, Oscar. *Impressions of America.* Edited by Stuart Mason. Sunderland, U.K.: Keystone Press, 1906.

Wilkie, F. B. [Franc Bangs]. *Walks about Chicago.* Chicago: Belford, Clarke, 1882.

Williams, Henry T., ed. *The Pacific Tourist: Williams' Illustrated Trans-continental Guide of Travel, from the Atlantic to the Pacific Ocean.* New York: Adams & Bishop, 1881.

Wills, Mary H. *A Winter in California.* Norristown, Penn.: M. R. Wills, 1889.

Wood, Stanley. *Over the Range to the Golden Gate.* 1894. Reprint, Chicago: R. R. Donnelley & Sons, 1904. http://archive.org/details/overrangegoldeng00wood.

Woodbury, F. S. *Tourist's Guide Book to Denver.* Denver: Times Steam Printing House and Blank Book Manufactory, 1882.

World's Fair Chicago 1893 Souvenir Illustrated. Chicago: Anabogue Publishing, 1893.

W. P. R. [Walter P. Ryland]. *My Diary during a Foreign Tour in Egypt, India, Ceylon, Australia, New Zealand, Tasmania, Fiji, China, Japan, and North America, in 1881–2.* Birmingham: Chas. Cooper, 1886.

Wylie, A. H. *Chatty Letters from East and West.* London: Sampson Low, Marston, Searle, & Rivington, 1879.

Zehme, Friedrich Wilhelm Heinrich. *The Diary of Friedrich Wilhelm Heinrich Zehme, May–July 1882.* Eureka, Calif.: David Dustin Clement, 1976.

SECONDARY SOURCES

Adler, Judith. "Origins of Sightseeing." *Annals of Tourism Research* 16, no. 1 (1989): 7–29.

Alexander, Thomas G., and James B. Allen. *Mormons and Gentiles: A History of Salt Lake City.* Boulder, Colo.: Pruett Publishing, 1984.

Allen, Walter, ed. *Transatlantic Crossing: American Visitors to Britain and British Visitors to America in the Nineteenth Century.* New York: William Morrow, 1971.

Anderson, Nancy K. "The Kiss of Enterprise: The Western Landscape As Symbol and Resource." In *The West As America: Reinterpreting Images of the Frontier, 1820–1920,* edited by William Truettner, 237–83. Washington, D.C.: National Museum of American Art, 1991.

Andrews, Malcolm. *The Search for the Picturesque: Landscape Aesthetics and Tourism in Britain, 1760–1800.* Stanford: Stanford University Press, 1989.

Appiah, Kwame Anthony. *Cosmopolitanism: Ethics in a World of Strangers.* New York: W. W. Norton, 2006.

Aron, Cindy S. *Working at Play: A History of Vacations in the United States.* Oxford: Oxford University Press, 1999.

Arrington, Leonard J., and David Bitton. *The Mormon Experience: A History of the Latter-day Saints.* New York: Alfred A. Knopf, 1979.

Asbury, Herbert. *The Barbary Coast: An Informal History of the San Francisco Underworld.* New York: Alfred A. Knopf, 1933.

———. *Gem of the Prairie: An Informal History of the Chicago Underworld.* Garden City, N.Y.: Garden City Publishing, 1942.

Athearn, Robert G. *Westward the Briton.* New York: Charles Scribner's Sons, 1953.

Banham, Reyner. "An Introduction." In *John Wellborn Root: A Study of His Life and Work,* by Harriet Monroe, vii–xvi. 1896. Reprint, Park Forest, Ill.: Prairie School Press, 1966.

Barth, Gunther. *City People: The Rise of Modern City Culture in Nineteenth-Century America.* Oxford: Oxford University Press, 1980.

———. "Demopiety: Speculations on Urban Beauty, Western Scenery, and the Discovery of the American Cityscape." *Pacific Historical Review* 52 no. 3 (August 1983): 249–66.

———. "The Hypothesis of Middle Class Formation in Nineteenth-Century America: A Critique and Some Proposals." *American Historical Review* 90 (April 1985): 299–338.

———. *Instant Cities: Urbanization and the Rise of San Francisco and Denver.* Albuquerque: University of New Mexico Press, 1988.

Barthes, Roland. "The Tour Eiffel." In *The Eiffel Tower and Other Mythologies,* translated by Richard Howard, 3–18. Berkeley: University of California Press, 1997.

Beebe, Lucius, and Charles Clegg. *The American West: The Pictorial Epic of a Continent.* New York: E. P. Dutton, 1955.

———. *San Francisco's Golden Era: A Picture Story of San Francisco before the Fire.* Berkeley: Howell-North, 1960.

Belasco, Warren James. *Americans on the Road: From Autocamp to Motel, 1910–1945.* Cambridge, Mass.: MIT Press, 1979.

Berger, Josef, and Dorothy Berger, eds. *Diary of America.* New York: Simon & Schuster, 1957.

Berglund, Barbara. "Chinatown's Tourist Terrain: Representation and Racialization in Nineteenth-Century San Francisco." *American Studies* 46, no. 2 (Summer 2005): 5–36.

———. *Making San Francisco American: Cultural Frontiers in the Urban West, 1846–1906.* Lawrence: University Press of Kansas, 2007.

Berman, Marshall. *All That Is Solid Melts into Air: The Experience of Modernity.* New York: Penguin Books, 1982.

Billington, Ray Allen. *Land of Savagery, Land of Promise: The European Image of the American Frontier in the Nineteenth Century.* New York: W. W. Norton, 1981.

Bloomfield, Anne. "The Real Estate Associates: A Land and Housing Developer of the 1870s in San Francisco." *Journal of the Society of Architectural Historians* 37, no. 1 (March 1978): 13–33.

Bluestone, Daniel. *Constructing Chicago.* New Haven, Conn.: Yale University Press, 1991.

Blumin, Stuart. "Introduction: George G. Foster and the Emerging Metropolis," In *New*

York by Gas-Light and Other Urban Sketches, edited by Stuart Blumin, 1–61. Berkeley: University of California Press, 1990.

Boorstin, Daniel J. *The Image: A Guide to Pseudo-Events in America.* 1961. Reprint, New York: Vintage Books, 1992.

Boyer, M. Christine. *The City of Collective Memory: Its Historical Imagery and Architectural Entertainments.* Cambridge, Mass.: MIT Press, 1994.

Boyer, Paul. *Urban Masses and Moral Order in America, 1820–1920.* Cambridge, Mass.: Harvard University Press, 1978.

Bramen, Carrie T. "The Urban Picturesque and the Spectacle of Americanization." *American Quarterly* 52, no. 3 (September 2000): 444–77.

Brechin, Gray. "San Francisco: The City Beautiful." In *Visionary San Francisco,* edited by Paolo Polledri, 40–61. San Francisco: San Francisco Museum of Modern Art, 1990.

Brown, Dona. *Inventing New England: Regional Tourism in the Nineteenth Century.* Washington, D.C.: Smithsonian Institution Press, 1995.

Bruegmann, Robert. *The Architects and the City: Holabird & Roche of Chicago, 1880–1918.* Chicago: University of Chicago Press, 1997.

———. "Myth of the Chicago School." In *Chicago Architecture: Histories, Revisions, Alternatives,* edited by Charles Waldheim and Katerina Rüedi Ray, 15–29. Chicago: University of Chicago Press, 2005.

Burchell, R. "Accretion, Syncretion and Repetition: British Travel Writers Describe San Francisco 1858–83." In *The American West As Seen by Americans and Europeans,* edited by Rob Kroes, 397–407. Amsterdam: Free University Press, 1989.

Burg, David F. *Chicago's White City of 1893.* Lexington: University Press of Kentucky, 1976.

Burke, Edmund. *A Philosophical Enquiry into the Origin of Our Ideas of the Sublime and Beautiful.* 1812. Facsimile. Charlottesville, Va.: Ibis Publishing.

Buzard, James. *The Beaten Track: European Tourism, Literature, and the Ways to Culture, 1800–1918.* Oxford: Clarendon Press, 1993.

Chambers, Thomas. *Drinking the Waters: Creating an American Leisure Class at Nineteenth-Century Mineral Springs.* Washington, D.C.: Smithsonian Institution Press, 2002.

"A City under One Roof—the Masonic Temple." *Scientific American* 70, no. 6 (February 10, 1894): 81–82.

Clifford, James. "Of Other Peoples: Beyond the Salvage Paradigm." In *Discussions in Contemporary Culture,* edited by Hal Foster, 121–30. Seattle: Bay Press, 1987.

Cocks, Catherine C. *Doing the Town: The Rise of Urban Tourism in the United States 1850–1915.* Berkeley: University of California Press, 2001.

Cohen, Erik. "A Phenomenology of Tourist Experiences." *Sociology* 13, no. 2 (May 1979): 179–201.

Cohen, Jean-Louis. *Scenes of the World to Come: European Architecture and the American Challenge, 1893–1960.* Montreal: Canadian Centre for Architecture, 1995.

Condit, Carl. *The Chicago School of Architecture: A History of Commercial and Public Building in the City Area, 1875–1925.* Chicago: University of Chicago Press, 1964.

Corbett, Michael R. *Building California: Technology and the Landscape.* San Francisco: California Historical Society, 1998.

Cronon, William. *Changes in the Land: Indians, Colonists, and the Ecology of New England.* New York: Hill & Wang, 2003.

———. *Nature's Metropolis: Chicago and the Great West.* New York: W. W. Norton, 1991.

———. "A Place for Stories: Nature, History, and Narrative." *Journal of American History* 78, no. 4 (March 1992): 1347–76.

Cronon, William, George Miles, and Jay Gitlin, "Becoming West: Toward a New Meaning for Western History." In *Under an Open Sky: Rethinking America's Western Past,* edited by Cronon, Miles, and Gitlin, 3–27. New York: W. W. Norton, 1992.

Culver, Lawrence. "Review of *Seeing and Being Seen: Tourism in the American West,* by David Wrobel and Patrick T. Long, eds." *Western Historical Quarterly* 33, no. 2 (Summer 2002): 234–35.

Dallas, Sandra. *Cherry Creek Gothic: Victorian Architecture in Denver.* Norman, Okla.; University of Oklahoma Press, 1971.

Davis, Howard, and Louis P. Nelson. "Editors' Introduction." *Buildings & Landscapes* 14 (2007): iv–vi.

de Botton, Alain. *The Art of Travel.* New York: Pantheon Books, 2002.

de Certeau, Michel. *The Practice of Everyday Life.* Berkeley: University of California Press, 1984.

den Tandt, Christophe. *The Urban Sublime in American Literary Naturalism.* Urbana: University of Illinois Press, 1998.

Deverell, William. *Railroad Crossing: Californians and the Railroad 1850–1910.* Berkeley: University of California Press, 1994.

De Voto, Bernard. "The West: A Plundered Province." *Harper's Magazine* 160 (August 1934): 355–64.

Dorsett, Lyle W. *The Queen City: A History of Denver.* Boulder, Colo.: Pruett Publishing, 1977.

Dowling, Robert M. *Slumming in New York: From the Waterfront to Mythic Harlem.* Urbana: University of Illinois Press, 2007.

Downs, Robert B. *Images of America: Travelers from Abroad in the New World.* Urbana: University of Illinois Press, 1987.

Drake, St. Clair, and Horace R. Cayton. *Black Metropolis: A Study of Negro Life in a Northern City.* 1945. Reprint, Chicago: University of Chicago Press, 1993.

Dreyfus, Philip J. *Our Better Nature: Environment and the Making of San Francisco.* Norman: University of Oklahoma Press, 2008.

Duis, Perry R. *Challenging Chicago: Coping with Everyday Life, 1837–1920.* Urbana: University of Illinois Press, 1998.

———. Foreword. In *As Others See Chicago: Impressions of Visitors, 1673–1933,* edited by Bessie Louise Pierce, x–xxxi. Chicago: University of Chicago Press, 2004.

Dunlop, M. H. *Sixty Miles from Contentment: Traveling the Nineteenth-Century American Interior.* New York: BasicBooks, 1995.

Dyos, H. J. "A Guide to the Streets of Victorian London." In *Exploring the Urban Past: Essays in Urban History by H. J. Dyos,* edited by David Cannadine and David Reeder, 190–201. Cambridge: Cambridge University Press, 1982.

Edwards, Justin D. "'Why Go Abroad?' Djuana Barnes and the Urban Travel Narrative." *Journal of Urban History* 29, no. 1 (November 2002): 6–24.

Ethington, Philip J. *The Public City: The Political Construction of Urban Life in San Francisco, 1850–1900.* Cambridge: Cambridge University Press, 1994.

Fabian, Ann. "History for the Masses: Commercializing the Western Past." In *Under an Open Sky: Rethinking America's Western Past,* edited by William Cronon, George Miles, and Jay Gitlin, 223–38. New York: W. W. Norton, 1992.

Faragher, John Mack, ed. *Rereading Frederick Jackson Turner: "The Significance of the American Frontier in American History" and Other Essays.* New Haven, Conn.: Yale University Press, 1999.

Farquha, F. ed. *Up and Down California in 1860–64.* New Haven, Conn.: Yale University Press, 1930.

Farr, Laurie. "San Francisco's European Style." *San Francisco Examiner,* May 20, 2012. www .examiner.com/article/san-francisco-s-european-style-spots.

Fifer, J. Valerie. *American Progress: The Growth of the Transport, Tourist, and Information Industries in the Nineteenth-Century West.* Chester, Conn.: Globe Pequot Press, 1988.

Fitch, James Marston. *Historic Preservation: Curatorial Management of the Built World.* Charlottesville: University of Virginia Press, 1990.

Frascina, Francis, Nigel Blake, Briony Fer, Tamar Garb, and Charles Harrison. *Modernity and Modernism: French Painting in the Nineteenth Century.* New Haven, Conn.: Yale University Press, 1993.

Fussell, Paul, ed. *The Norton Book of Travel.* New York: Norton, 1987.

Gebhard, David, Roger Montgomery, Robert Winter, John Woodbridge, and Sally Woodbridge. *A Guide to Architecture in San Francisco & Northern California.* Rev. ed. Santa Barbara, Calif.: Peregrine Smith, 1973.

Gibson, Campbell. "Population of the 100 Largest Cities and Other Urban Places in the United States: 1790 to 1990." Washington, D.C.: Population Division, U.S. Bureau of the Census, June 1998. www.census.gov/population/www/documentation/twps0027 .html.

Giedeon, Sigfried. *Space, Time and Architecture: The Growth of a New Tradition.* Cambridge, Mass.: Harvard University Press, 1941.

Gilbert, David, and Claire Hancock. "New York City and the Transatlantic Imagination: French and English Tourism and the Spectacle of the Modern Metropolis, 1893–1939." *Journal of Urban History* 33, no. 1 (November 2006): 77–107.

Gilbert, James. *Perfect Cities: Chicago's Utopias of 1893.* Chicago: University of Chicago Press, 1991.

Goddard, H. Wallace. "Temple Square's Early Warm Welcome." *Ensign,* February 1996, 30.

Gottlieb, Alma. "Americans' Vacations." *Annals of Tourism Research* 9 (1982): 165–88.

Gregory, Derek. "Colonial Nostalgia and Cultures of Travel: Spaces of Constructed Visibility in Egypt." In *Consuming Tradition, Manufacturing Heritage: Global Norms and Urban Forms in the Age of Tourism,* edited by Nezar AlSayyad, 111–51. London: Routledge, 2001.

Groseclose, Barbara. *Nineteenth-Century American Art.* Oxford: Oxford University Press, 2000.

Groth, Paul. "Frameworks for Cultural Landscape Study." In *Understanding Ordinary Landscapes,* edited by Paul Groth and Todd W. Bressi, 1–21. New Haven, Conn.: Yale University Press, 1997.

————. *Living Downtown: The History of Residential Hotels in the United States.* Berkeley: University of California Press, 1994.

Gruen, J. Philip. "Everyday Attractions: Generating Instant Heritage in Nineteenth-Century San Francisco." In *Consuming Tradition, Manufacturing Heritage: Global Norms and Urban Forms in the Age of Tourism,* edited by Nezar AlSayyad, 152–90. London: Routledge, 2001.

————. "The Urban Wonders: City Tourism in the Late-19th-Century American West." *Journal of the West* 41, no. 2 (Spring 2002): 10–19.

Hafen, Thomas K. "City of Saints, City of Sinners: The Development of Salt Lake City As a Tourist Attraction 1869–1900." *Western Historical Quarterly* 28 (Autumn 1997): 343–77.

Hales, Peter B. "Meditation I: The Museum of the City." In *The Perfect City,* by Bob Thall, 3–14. Baltimore: Johns Hopkins University Press, 1994.

————. *Silver Cities: The Photography of American Urbanization, 1839–1915.* Philadelphia: Temple University Press, 1984.

————. *William Henry Jackson and the Transformation of the American Landscape.* Philadelphia: Temple University Press, 1988.

Halttunen, Karen. *Confidence Men and Painted Women: A Study of Middle-class Culture in America, 1830–1870.* New Haven, Conn.: Yale University Press, 1982.

Hamer, David. *New Towns in the New World: Images and Perceptions of the Nineteenth-Century Urban Frontier.* New York: Columbia University Press, 1990.

Hamilton, C. Mark. *Nineteenth-Century Mormon Architecture and City Planning.* New York: Oxford University Press, 1995.

Handlin, Oscar. *The Uprooted: The Epic Story of the Great Migrations That Made the American People.* 1951. Reprint, Boston: Little, Brown, 1979.

Hapke, Laura. "Down There on a Visit: Late-Nineteenth-Century Guidebooks to the City." *Journal of Popular Culture* 20, no. 2 (Fall 1996): 41–55.

Harris, David. *Eadweard Muybridge and the Photographic Panorama of San Francisco, 1850–1880.* Montreal: Canadian Centre for Architecture, 1993.

Harris, Neil. "Expository Expositions: Preparing for the Theme Parks." In *Designing Disney's Theme Parks: The Architecture of Reassurance,* edited by Karal Ann Marling, 19–27. Montreal: Canadian Centre for Architecture, 1997.

————. "Urban Tourism and the Commercial City." In *Inventing Times Square: Commerce and Culture at the Crossroads of the World,* edited by W. R. Taylor, 66–82. Baltimore: Johns Hopkins University Press, 1991.

Harvey, David. *The Condition of Postmodernity: An Enquiry into the Origins of Cultural Change.* 1990. Reprint, Cambridge, Mass.: Blackwell Publishers, 1997.

————. *Cosmopolitanism and the Geographies of Freedom.* New York: Columbia University Press, 2009.

————. *The Urban Experience.* Baltimore: Johns Hopkins University Press, 1989.

Heap, Chad. *Slumming: Sexual and Racial Encounters in American Nightlife, 1885–1940.* Chicago: University of Chicago Press, 2008.

Henkin, David. *City Reading: Written Words and Public Spaces in Antebellum New York.* New York: Columbia University Press, 1998.

Herlihy, Patricia. "Visitors' Perceptions of Urbanization: Travel Literature in Tsarist Russia." In *The Pursuit of Urban History,* edited by Derek Fraser and Anthony Sutcliffe, 125–37. London: Edward Arnold, 1983.

Hine, Robert V., and John Mack Faragher. *The American West: A New Interpretive History.* New Haven, Conn.: Yale University Press, 2000.

Hines, Thomas. *Burnham of Chicago: Architect and Planner.* New York: Oxford University Press, 1974.

Hitchcock, Henry-Russell. *Architecture: Nineteenth and Twentieth Centuries.* Harmondsworth, U.K.: Penguin Books, 1983.

Hobsbawm, Eric. "Introduction: Inventing Traditions." In *The Invention of Tradition,* edited by Eric Hobsbawm and Terence Ranger, 1–14. Cambridge: Cambridge University Press, 1995.

Hollinger, David. "Not Universalists, Not Pluralists: The New Cosmopolitans Find Their Own Way." In *Conceiving Cosmopolitanism: Theory, Context, and Practice,* edited by Steven Vertrovec and Robin Cohen, 227–39. Oxford: Oxford University Press, 2002.

Hood, Clifton. "Journeying to 'Old New York.'" *Journal of Urban History* 28, no. 6 (September 2002): 699–719.

Homer, Michael W. "The Church's Image in Italy from the 1840s to 1946: A Bibliographic Essay." *BYU Studies* 31, no. 2 (Spring 1991): 83–114.

———, ed. *On the Way to Somewhere Else: European Sojourners in the Mormon West, 1834–1930.* Spokane, Wash.: Arthur H. Clark, 2006.

Horan, James D. Foreword to *The Pacific Tourist,* edited by Frederick Shearer, 2–4. New York: Bounty Books, 1970.

Hyde, Anne Farrar. *An American Vision: Far Western Landscape and National Culture, 1820–1920.* New York: New York University Press, 1990.

Jackson, John Brinkerhoff. *American Space, the Centennial Years: 1865–1876.* New York: W. W. Norton, 1972.

Jackson, Richard H. "Great Salt Lake and Great Salt Lake City: American Curiosities." *Utah Historical Quarterly* 56, no. 2 (Spring 1988): 128–47.

Jakle, John A. *Images of the Ohio Valley: A Historical Geography of Travel, 1740 to 1860.* New York: Oxford University Press, 1977.

———. *The Tourist: Travel in Twentieth-Century North America.* Lincoln: University of Nebraska Press, 1985.

Johns, Elizabeth. "Settlement and Development: Claiming the West." In *The West As America: Reinterpreting Images of the Frontier, 1820–1920,* edited by William Truettner, 141–235. Washington, D.C.: National Museum of American Art, 1991.

Johnson, Michael L. *Hunger for the Wild: America's Obsession with the Untamed West.* Lawrence: University Press of Kansas, 2007.

Jordy, William H. *American Buildings and Their Architects: Progressive and Academic Ideals at the Turn of the Twentieth Century.* Garden City, N.Y.: Anchor Books, 1976.

Judd, Dennis R. "Constructing the Tourist Bubble." In *The Tourist City,* edited by Dennis R. Judd and Susan S. Fainstein, 35–53. New Haven, Conn.: Yale University Press, 1999.

Kant, Immanuel. *Critique of Judgment.* Translated by J. H. Bernard. 1790. Reprint, New York: Hafner Press, 1950.

Kaplan, Caren. *Questions of Travel: Postmodern Discourses of Displacement*. Durham, N.C.: Duke University Press, 1996.

Kasson, John. *Amusing the Million: Coney Island at the Turn of the Century*. New York: Hill & Wang, 1978.

———. *Civilizing the Machine: Technology and Republican Values in America, 1776–1900*. New York: Grossman Publishers, 1976.

———. *Rudeness and Civility: Manners in Nineteenth-Century Urban America*. New York: Hill & Wang, 1990.

Kay, Jane. "Sea Lions Swarm Long-Abandoned Seal Rocks." *San Francisco Chronicle*, August 4, 2009. www.sfgate.com/green/article/Sea-lions-swarm-long-abandoned -Seal-Rocks-3223067.php.

Kirker, Harold. *California's Architectural Frontier: Style and Tradition in the Nineteenth Century*. 1960. Reprint, Salt Lake City: Peregrine Smith, 1986.

Klein, Kerwin. *Frontiers of Historical Imagination: Narrating the European Conquest of Native America, 1890–1990*. Berkeley: University of California Press, 1997.

Kolodny, Annette. *The Land before Her: Fantasy and Experience of the American Frontiers, 1630–1860*. Chapel Hill: University of North Carolina Press, 1970.

Kostof, Spiro. *A History of Architecture: Settings and Rituals*. New York: Oxford University Press, 1995.

Kwolek-Folland, Angel. *Engendering Business: Men and Women in the Corporate Office, 1870–1930*. Baltimore: Johns Hopkins University Press, 1994.

Lansing, Michael. "Race, Space, and Chinese Life in Late-Nineteenth-Century Salt Lake City." *Utah Historical Quarterly* 72, no. 3 (Summer 2004): 219–38.

Larsen, Lawrence H. *The Urban West at the End of the Frontier*. Lawrence: Regents Press of Kansas, 1978.

Lears, T. J. Jackson. *No Place of Grace: Antimodernism and the Transformation of American Culture 1880–1920*. New York: Pantheon Books, 1981.

Lee, Anthony W. *Picturing Chinatown: Art and Orientalism in San Francisco*. Berkeley: University of California Press, 2001.

Lee, Shelley S. "The Contradictions of Cosmopolitanism: Consuming the Orient at the Alaska-Yukon-Pacific Exposition and the International Potlatch Festival, 1909–1934. *Western Historical Quarterly* 38 (Autumn 2007): 277–302.

Lees, Andrew. *Cities Perceived: Urban Society in European and American Thought, 1820–1940*. Manchester, U.K.: Manchester University Press, 1985.

Lefebvre, Henri. *Critique of Everyday Life*. Vol. I. Translated by John Moore. 1947. Reprint, London: Verso, 1991.

———. *The Production of Space*. Translated by Donald Nicholson-Smith. 1974. Reprint, London: Blackwell, 1991.

Leonard, Stephen J., and Thomas J. Noel. *Denver: Mining Camp to Metropolis*. Niwot: University Press of Colorado, 1990.

Levenstein, Harvey. *Seductive Journeys: American Tourists in France from Jefferson to the Jazz Age*. Chicago: University of Chicago Press, 1998.

Lewis, Arnold. *An Early Encounter with Tomorrow: Europeans, Chicago's Loop, and the World's Columbian Exposition*. Urbana: University of Illinois Press, 1997.

Liebersohn, Harry. *The Travelers' World: Europe to the Pacific.* Cambridge, Mass.: Harvard University Press, 2006.

Limerick, Patricia Nelson. *The Legacy of Conquest: The Unbroken Past of the American West.* New York: W. W. Norton, 1987.

———. "Seeing and Being Seen: Tourism in the American West." In *Seeing and Being Seen: Tourism in the American West,* edited by David M. Wrobel and Patrick T. Long, 39–58. Lawrence: University Press of Kansas, 2001.

Lindberg, Richard. *Chicago by Gaslight: A History of Chicago's Netherworld, 1880–1920.* Chicago: Academy Chicago Publishers, 1996.

———. *To Serve and Collect: Chicago Politics and Police Corruption from the Lager Beer Riot to the Summerdale Scandal.* New York: Praeger Publishers, 1991.

Lockwood, Allison. *Passionate Pilgrims: The American Traveler in Great Britain, 1800–1914.* New York: Cornwall Books, 1981.

Löfgren, Orvar. *On Holiday: A History of Vacationing.* Berkeley: University of California Press, 1999.

Lotchin, Roger W. *San Francisco, 1846–1856: From Hamlet to City.* Urbana: University of Illinois Press, 1974.

Lowenthal, David. *The Heritage Crusade and the Spoils of History.* Cambridge, U.K.: Cambridge University Press, 1998.

MacCannell, Dean. *The Tourist: A New Theory of the Leisure Class.* 1976. Reprint, Berkeley: University of California Press, 1999.

Marcus, Sarah Susan. "Up from the Prairie: Depictions of Chicago and the Middle West in Popular Culture, 1865–1983." Ph.D. dissertation, University of Wisconsin–Milwaukee, 2001.

Marx, Karl, and Friedrich Engels. *The Communist Manifesto.* Northbrook, Ill.: AHM Publishing, 1955.

Marx, Leo. *The Machine in the Garden: Technology and the Pastoral Ideal in America.* London: Oxford University Press, 1964.

Matthews, Glenna. "Forging a Cosmopolitan Civic Culture: The Regional Identity of San Francisco and Northern California." In *Many Wests: Place, Culture & Regional Identity,* edited by David M. Wrobel and Michael C. Steiner, 211–34. Lawrence: University Press of Kansas, 1997.

Mayer, Harold M., and Richard C. Wade, *Chicago: Growth of a Metropolis.* Chicago: University of Chicago Press, 1969.

McKinsey, Elizabeth. *Niagara Falls: Icon of the American Sublime.* Cambridge: Cambridge University Press, 1985.

Meinig, D. W. Introduction to *The Interpretation of Ordinary Landscapes: Geographical Essays,* edited by D. W. Meinig, 1–7. New York: Oxford University Press, 1979.

Merk, Frederick. *Manifest Destiny and Mission in American History, a Reinterpretation.* New York: Alfred A. Knopf, 1963.

Merwood, Joanna. "Western Architecture: Regionalism and Race in the *Inland Architect.*" In *Chicago Architecture: Histories, Revisions, Alternatives,* edited by Charles Waldheim and Katerina Rüedi Ray, 3–14. Chicago: University of Chicago Press, 2005.

Merwood-Salisbury, Joanna. *Chicago 1890: The Skyscraper and the Modern City.* Chicago: University of Chicago Press, 2009.

Michalski, David. "Portals to Metropolis: 19th-Century Guidebooks and the Assemblage of Urban Experience." *Tourist Studies* 4, no. 3 (2004): 187–215.

Miller, Angela. *The Empire of the Eye: Landscape Representation and American Cultural Politics, 1825–1875.* Ithaca, N.Y.: Cornell University Press, 1993.

Miller, Donald L. *City of the Century: The Epic of Chicago and the Making of America.* New York: Simon & Schuster, 1996.

Milner, Clyde A., II, Carol A. O'Connor, and Martha A. Sandweiss. *The Oxford History of the American West.* New York: Oxford University Press, 1994.

Monroe, Harriet. *John Wellborn Root: A Study of His Life and Work.* 1896. Reprint, Park Forest, Ill.: Prairie School Press, 1966.

Morley, Judy Mattivi. *Historic Preservation and the Imagined West: Albuquerque, Denver, and Seattle.* Lawrence, Kans.: University Press of Kansas, 2006.

Mulder, William, and A. Russell Mortensen, eds. *Among the Mormons: Historic Accounts by Contemporary Observers.* New York: Alfred A. Knopf, 1958.

Mulvey, Christopher. *Anglo-American Landscapes: A Study of Nineteenth-Century Anglo-American Travel Literature.* Cambridge: Cambridge University Press, 1983.

Mumford, Lewis. *The Brown Decades: A Study of the Arts in America, 1865–1895.* New York: Harcourt, Brace, 1931.

Nash, Gerald D. *Creating the West: Historical Interpretations 1890–1990.* Albuquerque: University of New Mexico Press, 1991.

Nee, Victor G., and Brett de Bary Nee. *Longtime Californ': A Documentary Study of an American Chinatown.* 1972. Reprint, Stanford: Stanford University Press, 1986.

Nye, David E. *American Technological Sublime.* Cambridge, Mass.: MIT Press, 1996.

———. *Narratives and Spaces: Technology and the Construction of American Culture.* New York: Columbia University Press, 1997.

Olsen, Donald. *The City As a Work of Art.* New Haven, Conn.: Yale University Press, 1986.

Pascoe, Peggy. *Relations of Rescue: The Search for Female Moral Authority in the American West, 1874–1939.* New York: Oxford University Press, 1990.

Pomeroy, Earl. *In Search of the Golden West: The Tourist in Western America.* 1957. Reprint, Lincoln: University of Nebraska Press, 1990.

———. *The Pacific Slope: A History of California, Oregon, Washington, Idaho, Utah, and Nevada.* Lincoln: University of Nebraska Press, 1965.

Powers, Laura Bride. *The Story of the Old Missions of California: Their Establishment, Progress and Decay.* San Francisco: Wm. Doxey, 1893.

Pred, Allan, and Michael John Watts. *Reworking Modernity: Capitalisms and Symbolic Discontent.* New Brunswick, N.J.: Rutgers University Press, 1992.

Pritchard, Annette, Nigel Morgan, Irena Ateljevic, and Candice Harris, eds. "Editors' Introduction: Tourism, Gender, Embodiment, and Experience." In *Tourism and Gender: Embodiment, Sensuality, and Experience,* 1–9. Wallingford, U.K.: CAB International, 2007.

Rainey, Sue. *Creating Picturesque America: Monument to the Natural and Cultural Landscape.* Nashville, Tenn.: Vanderbilt University Press, 1994.

Rapson, Richard. *Britons View America: Travel Commentary, 1860–1935.* Seattle: University of Washington Press, 1971.

Rast, Raymond W. "The Cultural Politics of Tourism in San Francisco's Chinatown, 1882–1917." *Pacific Historical Review* 76, no. 1: 29–60.

Raycraft, Mary Beth. "Introduction: A Parisienne's Adventures in Chicago: Discoveries and Consequences." In *A Parisienne in Chicago: Impressions of the World's Columbian Exposition,* by Mme Léon Grandin, xvii–xliv. Urbana: University of Illinois Press, 2010.

Reps, John W. *Cities of the American West: A History of Frontier Urban Planning.* Princeton, N.J.: Princeton University Press, 1979.

———. *Cities on Stone: Nineteenth Century Lithograph Images of the Urban West.* Fort Worth, Tex.: Amon Carter Museum, 1976.

———. *The Forgotten Frontier: Urban Planning in the American West before 1890.* Columbia: University of Missouri Press, 1981.

———. *Views and Viewmakers of Urban America: Lithographs of Towns and Cities in the United States and Canada, Notes on the Artists and Publishers, and a Union Catalog of their Work, 1825–1925.* Columbia: University of Missouri Press, 1984.

Ritzker, George, and Allan Liska. "'McDisneyization' and 'Post-Tourism.'" In *Touring Cultures: Transformations of Travel and Theory,* edited by Chris Rojek and John Urry, 96–109. London: Routledge, 1997.

Rothman, Hal. *Devil's Bargains: Tourism in the Twentieth-Century American West.* Lawrence: University Press of Kansas, 1998.

Ryan, Mary. *Women in Public: Between Banners and Ballots, 1825–1880.* Baltimore: Johns Hopkins University Press, 1989.

Rydell, Robert. *All the World's a Fair: Visions of Empire at American International Expositions.* Chicago: University of Chicago Press, 1984.

Said, Edward. *Orientalism.* London: Routledge & Kegan Paul, 1978.

Sandmeyer, Elmer Clarence. *The Anti-Chinese Movement in California.* Urbana: University of Illinois Press, 1973.

Schivelbusch, Wolfgang. *The Railway Journey: The Industrialization of Time and Space in the 19th Century.* Berkeley: University of California Press, 1977.

Schlissel, Lillian. *Women's Diaries of the Westward Journey.* New York: Schocken Books, 1982.

Schneider, Robert A. "The Postmodern City from an Early Modern Perspective." *American History Review* 105, no. 5 (December 2000): 1671–72.

Schwarzer, Mitchell. "Architecture and Mass Tourism." In *Architourism: Authentic, Escapist, Exotic, Spectacular,* edited by Joan Ockman and Salomon Frausto, 12–33. Munich: Prestel Verlag, 2005.

Sears, John. *Sacred Places: American Tourist Attractions in the Nineteenth Century.* New York: Oxford University Press, 1989.

Secrest, Clark. *Hell's Belles: Prostitution, Vice, and Crime in Early Denver.* Rev. ed. Boulder: University Press of Colorado, 2002.

Shaffer, Marguerite. *See America First: Tourism and National Identity, 1880–1940.* Washington, D.C.: Smithsonian Institution Press, 2001.

Simmel, Georg. "The Metropolis and Mental Life." In *The Sociology of Georg Simmel,* translated by Kurt H. Wolff, 409–24. New York: Free Press, 1950.

Siry, Joseph M. *Carson Pirie Scott: Louis Sullivan and the Chicago Department Store.* Chicago: University of Chicago Press, 1988.

———. *The Chicago Auditorium Building: Adler and Sullivan's Architecture and the City.* Chicago: University of Chicago Press, 2002.

Smith, Carl S. *Chicago and the American Literary Imagination, 1880–1920.* Chicago: University of Chicago Press, 1984.

Smith, Henry Nash. *Virgin Land: The American West As Symbol and Myth.* 1950. Reprint, Cambridge, Mass: Harvard University Press, 1970.

Smith, James R. *San Francisco's Lost Landmarks.* Sanger, Calif.: Word Dancer Press, 2005.

Smith, Ryan K. "Viewpoint: Building Stories: Narrative Prospects for Vernacular Architecture Studies." *Buildings & Landscapes* 18, no. 2 (Fall 2011): 1–14.

Smith, Valene, ed. *Hosts and Guests: The Anthropology of Tourism.* 2nd. ed. Philadelphia: University of Pennsylvania Press, 1989.

Snow, Edwina Jo. "British Travelers View the Saints: 1847–1877." *BYU Studies* 31, no. 2 (Spring 1991): 63–81.

Solnit, Rebecca. *River of Shadows: Eadweard Muybridge and the Technological Wild West.* New York: Penguin Books, 2003.

Spears, Timothy B. *Chicago Dreaming: Midwesterners and the City, 1871–1919.* Chicago: University of Chicago Press, 2005.

Spence, Clark, ed. *The American West: A Source Book.* New York: Thomas Y. Crowell, 1966.

Stanonis, Anthony. *Creating the Big Easy: New Orleans and the Emergence of Modern Tourism, 1918–1945.* Athens: University of Georgia Press, 2006.

Stieber, Nancy. "Architecture between Disciplines." *Journal of the Society of Architectural Historians* 62, no. 2 (June 2003): 176–77.

Stowe, William W. *Going Abroad: European Travel in Nineteenth-Century American Culture.* Princeton, N.J.: Princeton University Press, 1994.

Taylor, Nicholas. "The Awful Sublimity of the Victorian City: Its Aesthetic and Architectural Origins." In *The Victorian City: Images and Realities,* edited by H. J. Dyos and Michael Wolff, 431–47. London: Routledge & Kegan Paul, 1973.

Tchen, John Kuo Wei. *Genthe's Photographs of San Francisco's Old Chinatown.* New York: Dover Publications, 1984.

———. *New York before Chinatown: Orientalism and the Shaping of American Culture 1776–1882.* Baltimore: Johns Hopkins University Press, 1999.

Towner, John. "Approaches to Tourism History." *Annals of Tourism Research* 15, no. 1 (1988): 47–62.

Trachtenberg, Alan. *The Incorporation of America: Society in the Gilded Age.* New York: Hill & Wang, 1982.

Truettner, William. "Ideology and Image: Justifying Westward Expansion." In *The West As America: Reinterpreting Images of the Frontier, 1820–1920,* edited by William Truettner, 27–53. Washington, D.C.: National Museum of American Art, 1991.

Turner, Frederick Jackson. "The Significance of the Frontier in American History." In *The Frontier in American History*, 1–38. New York: Henry Holt, 1921.

Upton, Dell. *Another City: Urban Life and Urban Spaces in the New American Republic*. New Haven, Conn.: Yale University Press, 2008.

———. "Architectural History or Landscape History?" *Journal of Architectural Education* 44, no. 4 (1992): 195–99.

———. *Architecture in the United States*. Oxford: Oxford University Press, 1998

———. "The City As Material Culture." In *The Art and Mystery of Historical Archaeology: Essays in Honor of James Deetz*, edited by Anne Elizabeth Yentsch and Mary C. Beaudry, 51–74. Boca Raton, Fla.: CRC Press, 1992.

———. "Inventing the Metropolis: Civilization and Urbanity in Antebellum New York." In *Art and the Empire City: New York, 1825–1861*, edited by Catherine Hoover Voorsanger and John K. Howat, 3–45. New York: Metropolitan Museum of Art, 2000.

———. "Pattern Books and Professionalism: Aspects of the Transformation of Domestic Architecture in America, 1800–1860." *Winterthur Portfolio* 19 (1984): 107–50.

Urry, John. "Regazing on the Tourist Gaze." In *Tourism Revisited: International Colloquium of Architecture and Cities #2*, edited by David Vanderburgh and Hilde Heynen, 19–28. Brussels: Network for Theory, History, and Criticism of Architecture, 2007.

———. "Sensing the City." In *The Tourist City*, edited by Dennis R. Judd and Susan S. Fainstein, 71–86. New Haven, Conn.: Yale University Press, 1999.

———. *The Tourist Gaze: Leisure and Travel in Contemporary Societies*. London: Sage Publications, 1985.

van Leeuwen, Thomas A. P. *The Skyward Trend of Thought: The Metaphysics of the American Skyscraper*. Cambridge, Mass.: MIT Press, 1988.

Van Orman, Richard A. "San Francisco: Hotel City of the West." In *Reflections of Western Historians*, edited by John Alexander Carrol, 3–18. Tucson: University of Arizona Press, 1969.

Veijola, Solie, and Eeva Jokinen. "The Body in Tourism." *Theory, Culture and Society* 11, no. 3 (1994): 125–51.

Verdoia, Ken, and Richard Firmage. *Utah: The Struggle for Statehood*. Salt Lake City: University of Utah Press, 1996.

Vertovec, Steven, and Robin Cohen. "Introduction: Conceiving Cosmopolitanism." In *Conceiving Cosmopolitanism: Theory, Context, and Practice*, edited by Vertrovec and Cohen, 1–22. Oxford: Oxford University Press, 2002.

Wade, Louise Carroll. "Meatpacking." In *Encyclopedia of Chicago*, edited by Janice L. Reiff, Ann Durkin Keating, and James R. Grossman, Chicago: Chicago History Museum, Newberry Library, and Northwestern University, 2004. www.encyclopedia.chicago history.org/pages/804.html.

Wade, Richard. *The Urban Frontier: The Rise of Western Cities, 1790–1830*. Cambridge, Mass.: Harvard University Press, 1959.

Walker, Richard. "Another Round of Globalization in San Francisco." *Urban Geography* 17, no. 1 (1996): 60–94.

Walker, Ronald W., David J. Whittaker, and James B. Allen. *Mormon History*. Urbana: University of Illinois Press, 2001.

Walkowitz, Judith. *City of Dreadful Delight: Narratives of Sexual Danger in Late-Victorian London.* Chicago: University of Chicago Press, 1992.

Weber, Adna Ferrin. *The Growth of Cities in the Nineteenth Century: A Study in Statistics.* New York: Columbia University, 1899.

White, Hayden. *Tropics of Discourse: Essays in Cultural Criticism.* Baltimore: Johns Hopkins University Press, 1978.

White, Morton, and Lucia White. *The Intellectual Versus the City: From Thomas Jefferson to Frank Lloyd Wright.* Cambridge, Mass.: Harvard University Press, 1962.

White, Richard. *It's Your Misfortune and None of My Own: A History of the American West.* Norman: University of Oklahoma Press, 1991.

———. "Race Relations in the American West." *Western Historical Quarterly* 38, no. 3 (1986): 396–416.

———. *Railroaded: The Transcontinentals and the Making of Modern America.* New York: W. W. Norton, 2011.

Wiebe, Robert. *The Search for Order, 1877–1920.* New York: Hill & Wang, 1967.

Williams, Rosalind. *Notes on the Underground: An Essay on Technology, Society, and the Imagination.* Cambridge, Mass.: MIT Press, 1990.

Willis, Carol. *Form Follows Finance: Skyscrapers and Skylines in New York and Chicago.* New York: Princeton Architectural Press, 1995.

Withey, Lynne. *Grand Tours and Cook's Tours: A History of Leisure Travel, 1750 to 1915.* New York: William Morrow, 1997.

Wolner, Edward W. "Chicago's Fraternity Temples: The Origins of Skyscraper Rhetoric and the First of the World's Tallest Office Buildings." In *The American Skyscraper: Cultural Histories,* edited by Roberta Moudry, 98–119. Cambridge: Cambridge University Press, 2005.

———. *Henry Ives Cobb's Chicago.* Chicago: University of Chicago Press, 2011.

Wrobel, David. *Promised Lands: Promotion, Memory, and the Creation of the American West.* Lawrence: University Press of Kansas, 2002.

———. "The World in the West: Friedrich Gerstäcker, Richard Francis Burton, and Isabella Bird on the Nineteenth-Century Frontier." *Montana: The Magazine of Western History* 58, no. 1 (Spring 2008): 26, 97n1.

Wrobel, David M., and Patrick T. Long, eds. *Seeing and Being Seen: Tourism in the American West.* Lawrence: University Press of Kansas, 2001.

Zunz, Olivier. *Making America Corporate: 1870–1920.* Chicago: University of Chicago Press, 1990.

Index

Page numbers in italics indicate illustrations.

Abroad and at Home: Practical Hints for Tourists (Phillips), 101
Adair, Cornelia, 132
Adams, Emma, 39
Addison, Joseph, 46
Adler, Dankmar, 123, 125, 127
adventurers, in West, 11
advertisements, 47, *68*. *See also* billboards and signs
aerial views, 49, 50, *56*, 142–43
African Americans, 165, 170
Aitken, James, 82–83, 99, 142
Album of Salt Lake City, Utah (Dwyer), 139
Alexander II (czar), 229n81
Alexis, Russian grand duke of, 94, 97, 229n81, 230n93
Alta California (newspaper), 66
American Indians. *See* Native Americans
American Life (Rousiers), 19
American West. *See* West, the
America Revisited (Sala), 104
"America's Switzerland," 45, 223n6
Angell, Truman Sr., 138
anonymity, 37
architecture: and boosterism, 108–109, 113, 115, 122–23; characteristics of, 109,

114, 164; in Chicago, 115, 121, 123; and civilization, 129, 156; Cliff House as, 119–20; in Denver, 113, 134, 136, 169, 231n5; in downtowns, 120; Ferree on, 231n7; as fine art, 113–14; Grandin on, 117; and Great Fire of 1871, 115; in guidebooks, 113; insubstantial nature of, 134; and Loop, 115; Medley on, 110; and metal frames, 131; modernization of, 109; of Mormon Tabernacle, 141; of Native Americans, 63–64; and nature, 136; Pierrepont on, 110–11; Price on, 110; Ralph on, 121; Robinson on, 111; in Salt Lake City, 136; in San Francisco, 110–11, 144, 145, 151, 231n5; and tourists, 109–10, 116–17, 134, 151, 231n7; and urbanism, 16, 116–21; in West, 115–16, 134, 156. *See also* balloon frames; brick buildings; built environment; Egyptian architecture; Gothic architecture; Greek architecture; *specific buildings*
Arnold, Matthew, 113
art and artists: Addison on, 46; characteristics of, 164; Jenney on, 115; and nature, 46; skyscrapers as, 125; and urbanism, 46; *urbs in horto* by, 49

Assembly Hall, 139
Atchison, Topeka, and Santa Fe Railroad,
    34. *See also* railroads
atriums, 3
Auditorium Building, 61, 125–26, *127,*
    131–32
Aurora, Colorado, 54
automobiles, 205
Avery, Benjamin Parke, 153

Baedeker, Karl, 54
Baldwin Hotel, 148
balloon frames, 133–34, 232n11. *See also*
    architecture
Barbary Coast, 158–59
Barneby, W. Henry, 81, 181–82
Barton, Harry Scott, 103–104
Bates, James Hale, 135, 178, 195
Baumann, Edward, 128
bay windows, 152. *See also* architecture
Beadle, Charles, 33
Beauties of California (Griswold), 183
"Ben Butler" (seal), 58
Berkeley Lake, 54
Bickham, William Denison, 85, 171
Bierstadt, Albert, 32
billboards and signs, 90, 91. *See also*
    advertisements
Bird, Isabella Lucy, 31, 171
bird's-eye views, 49, 50, *56,* 142–43
bison, 30
Bitter Cry of Outcast London, The
    (Mearns), 38
Blackall, Charles, 123
black persons, 165, 170
Blake, Mary, 90
blasé outlook, defined, 28
blood atonement, 173, 177. *See also*
    Mormons
Blouet, Léon Paul, 28, 104
Board of Trade, 61, 133
Boddam-Whetham, John W., 90, 92, 194
Bonwick, James, 143, 152, 180
boosterism: and architecture, 108–109, 113,
    115, 122–23; on billboards and signs,
    91; and bird's-eye views, 50; and built
    environment, 108–109; and Cham-

ber of Commerce Building, 128; and
change, 65, 66; characteristics of, 71;
and Chicago, 54, 71, 78, 122–23; and
Chinese community, 186–88, 189,
196, 199; and civilization, 112, 113, 115;
and cosmopolitanism, 160, 164, 165,
173–74; defined, 222n2; and Denver,
54, 61–62, 135, 168–69, 170–71; and
diversity, 161–62, 166; and Ensign Peak,
201; and exaggeration, 55–56; and fire
and police protection, 115; and Golden
Gate Park, 59; and Great Fire of 1871,
92; and history, 63; and hotels, 147; and
infrastructure, 115; and interior design,
118; and lawlessness, 31; and Masonic
Temple, 126; and modernization, 28,
29–30, 36, 42, 122; and nativism, 45;
and nature, 41–42, 43–45, 46, 69; and
Palace Hotel, 150; and parks, 51, 119;
and photography, 49; and railroads,
78; and residential districts, 133; and
Rocky Mountains, 61–62; and Salt
Lake City, 95–96, 106, 173–74; and Salt
Lake Theater, 139; and San Francisco,
58, 60, 62, 144, 146–47; and skyscrapers,
125; and technological advancements,
63; and tourists, 45; and transportation, 115; and Union Stock Yards, 103;
and urbanism, 29, 39, 45–46, 47; and
Walker House, 139; and West, 66–67.
See also guidebooks
bordellos and prostitution, 187, 208
boulevards, 51–52, 53, 118, 119
Bourbonnaud, Louise, 212
bow windows, 152. *See also* architecture
branch lines, 25, 34. *See also specific railroads*
breweries, 96
brick buildings, 134–35. *See also*
    architecture
Bridges, DeWitt C., 73
Bright, Anne Mathilda, 100–101, 167
Broadway Theater, 135
built environment: and boosterism,
    108–109; in Chicago, 72; and Chinese
    community, 155–56, 190–91, 195; and
    civilization, 113, 134; defined, 109; in
    Denver, 134; and nature, 143; Pidgeon

on, 108; in Salt Lake City, 58, 108, 140–41, 142–43; in San Francisco, 110, 144–156; and tourists, 109–10, 111, 118, 120, 195; and urbanism, 11–12. *See also* architecture

Burke, Edmund, 44

Burke, William Henry, 126

Burnham, Daniel Hudson, 3, 123, 129

business travelers, 237n2. *See also* tourists

cable cars, 62, 78, 81

California As It Is (San Francisco Call), 144

California: For Health, Pleasure, and Residence (Nordhoff), 31, 191–92

California Illustrated (Boruck), 183–84

California Illustrated: Including a Trip through Yellowstone Park (Warren), 147

"California Zephyr" (train), 208. *See also* railroads

Campbell, J. F., 94, 99–100

Cannon, George Q., 174

Capitol Hill, 54

Carbutt, Mary Rhodes: on cable cars, 81; on Chinese community, 193; on Denver, 136; on Golden Gate Park, 119; on Oakland, 80

cartoon, *35*

Celestials. *See* Chinese community

cemeteries, 51. *See also specific cemeteries*

Central Pacific Railroad, 7, *8–9*, 25, 34. *See also* railroads

Chamberlain, William, 56

Chamber of Commerce Building, 128

Chard, Thomas, 193

Checker-Board Guide to Chicago (guidebook), 64

Chesbrough, Ellis Sylvester, 98

Cheyenne. *See* Levee District

Chicago, Illinois: Adams on, 39; African Americans in, 165; architecture in, 115, 121, 123, 130; attractions of, 205; Blackall on, 123; Boddam-Whetham on, 92; and boosterism, 54, 71, 78, 122–23; boulevards in, 53; Bourbonnaud on, 212; Bright on, 100–101, 167; built environment in, 72; as bully, 100; and Burnham, 123; cable cars in, 78;

Campbell on, 94; civilization in, 117, 121; and Cleveland, 52; and Cobb, 123; complexities and contradictions in, 87, 94–95, 99, 100, 130; cosmopolitanism in, 166; Cotton on, 78, 100, 168; Dewar on, 83; diversity in, 161, 164–67, 168; Dugard on, 167; elevated trains in, 78; energy of, 88, 89, 92; and entertainment panoramas, 67; expectoration in, 233n63; fires and firefighters in, 95; Flinn on, 63; freshwater distribution in, 98–99; as garden city, 53, 90, 101; Giacosa on, 100; Gladden on, 35; grain elevators in, 23, 97, *99;* Grandin on, 100, 117, 167; Great Fire of, 6; Greenwood on, 61; ground transportation in, 34–35; growth of, 6, 10, 22, 39; in guidebooks, 4, 98, 222n4; guides in, 26; Hesse-Wartegg on, 101; and history, 66, 67; Holand on, 72; hotels in, 94; house moving in, 92; infrastructure of, 90, 91–92; and Jenney, 52, 123; and Joliet, 64–65; Jones on, 39, 87–88, 115; Kent on, 101; Kipling on, 102; and Lake Michigan, 74; languages in, 165, 167; lawlessness of, 31, 35; Leng on, 70; Levee District in, 167, 208, 238n25; Lewis on, 94–95, 168; Lucy on, 89; as manufacturing community, 97; and Marquette, 64–65; Marshall in, 26; and McCormick, 22; McElrath on, 101; Medley on, 94; Merewether on, 66; Metropolitan Correctional Center in, 208; modernization of, 23, 39–40; Mohr on, 87; multisensory experiences of, 79; Naylor on, 78; and Olmsted, 52; oppressiveness of, 100–102; parks in, 52, 119; and the past, 63; Pfeiffer on, 31; Phillips on, 101; Pidgeon on, 92; pollution in, 23; population of, 22; and railroads, 25, 34, 78; Ralph on, 88; Raycraft on, 167–68; reconstruction of, 66; Roberts on, 89; Robinson on, 77, 168; and Root, 123; and Sable, 64; skyscrapers in, 3, 4, 13, 35, 120, 121–134; Smiles on, 91; streetcars in, 78, 88; and Sullivan, 123; tourists in, *35,* 101; and trade, 23;

Chicago, Illinois (continued)
    Treseder on, 4–5, 200; Turland on, 89;
    Union Stock Yards in, 23, 26, 102–104;
    urbanism vs. nature in, 6; and Vaux, 52;
    Ward on, 77–78, 95, 204; Warner on,
    101; weather conditions in, 101, 222n4;
    as West, 7; and World's Columbian
    Exposition, 35; Zehme on, 39
Chicago and Its Environs (Schick), 165
Chicago by Day and Night: The Pleasure
    Seekers Guide to the Paris of America
    (Vynne), 167
Chicago Illustrated (souvenir book), 64
Chicago River, 23, 99
Chicago School of Architecture, 124
Chicago: The Marvelous City of the West
    (Flinn): architecture in, 122, 123; cos-
    mopolitanism in, 165; Masonic Temple
    in, 4; Palmer House in, 132; skyscrapers
    in, 125
Chicago Tribune (newspaper), cartoon in, 35
Chicago Water Tower, 97, 209
Chinese community: Bates on, 195;
    Bickham on, 171; Boddam-Whetham
    on, 194; and boosterism, 186–88, 189,
    196, 199; boundaries of, 241n98; and
    built environment, 155–56, 190–91,
    195; Carbutt on, 193; characteristics of,
    210–11; Chard on, 193; and civilization,
    155; complexities and contradictions in,
    155–56; contributions of, 12; and cos-
    mopolitanism, 185, 188; dangers of, 189;
    in Denver, 170, 171; as deviant popula-
    tion, 187; Dewar on, 193; discrimina-
    tion against, 156, 170, 187, 192–93;
    economic competition in, 195; exoti-
    cism of, 12, 188–89; Green on, 193;
    growth of, 185, 186, 189–190, 241n100;
    in guidebooks, 162, 188–89, 193; and
    guides, 26; Harper on, 197; Hendrix
    on, 195; immigration to, 186; Jackson
    on, 198; Jones on, 195; joss houses in,
    191; Lee on, 197; Leslie on, 198; Lucy
    on, 171; Marshall on, 195; as Mongo-
    lians, 165, 166; opium dens in, 190; as
    "other," 16, 155; payment received by,
    185–86; Pidgeon on, 171, 197; praise

for, 194–95, 196, 197, 199; Price on,
    194–95; prostitution in, 187; quarantin-
    ing of, 185; and race, 156; remaking of,
    206; Robinson on, 193; in Salt Lake
    City, 240n77; in San Francisco, 6, 12,
    16, 36, 146, 155, 185–86, 189, 196, 210,
    211, 241n98; and sensationalism, 189;
    as slum, 155; slumming in, 187; Smith
    on, 195, 197; Strong on, 192; theaters in,
    191; and tourists, 26, 155–56, 187, 188,
    193–94, 196, 197–99; Vivian on, 194;
    Wilde on, 197; Wills on, 186–87, 197;
    work ethic of, 16
Chinese Exclusion Act (1882), 186
Christos (Thorvaldsen), 210
Church, John H. C., 176
Churchill, Caroline, 175
Church of Jesus Christ of Latter-Day
    Saints. See Mormons
Cincinnati, Ohio, 21, 219n7
cities. See urbanism; specific cities
City Creek Center, 206
City Park, 54
civilization: and architecture, 129, 133, 156;
    Arnold on, 113; and boosterism, 112,
    113, 115; and boulevards, 118; and built
    environment, 113, 134; in Chicago,
    117, 121; and Chinese community,
    155; defined, 111–12; and downtowns,
    120; and guidebooks, 114; and Mis-
    sion San Francisco de Asis, 155; and
    Palace Hotel, 148; and parks, 118; and
    Salt Lake City, 136, 138, 139; in San
    Francisco, 120, 144, 147; and stock
    exchanges, 151; and tourists, 151; and
    urbanism, 112–13; in West, 112, 156; and
    Zion's Co-operative Mercantile Insti-
    tution, 140. See also cosmopolitanism
Clark, Susie: on Mormons, 175; on Mor-
    mon Tabernacle, 141; on Oakland, 73;
    on Salt Lake City, 180; on San Fran-
    cisco, 73; on streetcars, 82
Clarkson, Banyer, 184
classes, intermingling of, 119
Cleveland, H. W. S., 52
Cliff House, 58, 119–20, 213, 214
Cobb, Henry Ives, 123

Codman, John, 25–26, 179
Cody, William "Buffalo Bill," 30–31
Col. A. Andrews "Diamond Palace," 29
Colorado Cities and Places (guidebook), 135
Colorado Hand-Book, The: Denver and Its Outings (Stone), 55
Colorado Springs, Colorado, 55
Columbian Exposition, 4, 10, 13, 35
Cone, Mary, 58
Cook's California Excursions (Cook), 32
Cosmopolitan Hotel, 148, 157–58, 237n1, 237n2
cosmopolitanism: and boosterism, 160, 164, 165, 173–74; characteristics of, 159–60; in Chicago, 166; and Chinese community, 185, 188; and Cosmopolitan Hotel, 157–58; defined, 160; and Denver, 168–69; and diversity, 159, 160–61, 179, 183; Leng on, 184–85; and Levee District, 167; and Mormons, 174; and "other," 164; and ports, 164; and Salt Lake City, 173–74, 178, 179, 181; and San Francisco, 182, 183, 184–85, 199; and tourists, 160; and urbanism, 16. *See also* civilization
Cotton, L. de, 78, 100, 168
Crest of the Continent, The: A Record of a Summer's Railroad Ramble through the Rocky Mountains (Ingersoll), 168–69
crickets, 23
crowds, 71, 89
culture, 26–27, 55, 162. *See also* civilization; cosmopolitanism

daguerreotypes. *See* photography
Denver, Colorado: African Americans in, 170; Alexis on, 97; architecture in, 113, 134, 136, 169, 231n5; attractions of, 205; Bates on, 135; Bickham on, 85; Bird on, 31, 171; bird's-eye views of, *56;* and boosterism, 54, 61–62, 135, 168–69, 170–71; bordello district of, 208; brick buildings in, 134–35; built environment in, 134; Carbutt on, 136; Chinese community in, 170, 171; complexities and contradictions in, 36, 87; and cosmopolitanism, 168–69; culture in,

55; diversity in, 170, 171; economy of, 169; energy of, 85, 86, 87; fires in, 65–66, 134; as fountain of youth, 41; as garden city, 56; geographical location of, 169; Gilpin on, 169; growth of, 10; in guidebooks, 54, 55, 134; health in, 41, 44, 55, 56, 85; improvements to, 54–55; Ingersoll on, 36, 135; Johnson on, 85, 87; and Kansas Pacific Railroad, 222n43; Kingsley on, 39; Larimer Street in, *86;* lawlessness in, 31, 65; Lee on, 136; Lower Downtown area of, 239n42; Lucy on, 85; Marshall on, 85; Mead on, 135; modernization of, 36, 39–40; and nature, 6, 55, 136; Pidgeon on, 85, 171; poor persons in, 170; Ralph on, 85; reconstruction of, 65–66, 134; and Rocky Mountains, 35–36, 55, *56,* 61, 74, 85, 136; Rousiers on, 206; Sanders on, 41, 44; segregation in, 170; smelting in, 230n93; Stone on, 54–55; and tourists, 25, 35–36, 170–71; urbanism of, 6, 23, 65; Western Union Telegraph Company on, 29; Whitman on, 36, 75–76; as Wild West, 170
Denver Ale Company, 97, 230n93
Denver: By Pen and Picture (guidebook), 29
Denver Pacific Railroad, 25. *See also* railroads
Deseret Woolen Mills, 96
developers, 124–25
deviant populations, 172, 187
Dewar, Thomas, 83, 130, 148–49, 193
discrimination, 37, 156, 170, 192–93
diseases, 37
diversity: and boosterism, 161–62, 166; and chaos, 168; in Chicago, 161, 164–67, 168; Clarkson on, 184; colorfulness of, 162; and compartmentalization, 168; and cosmopolitanism, 159, 160–61, 179, 183; and culture, 162; in Denver, 170, 171; Greeley on, 237n10; among Mormons, 177–78; and Mormons, 161; and "other," 162; in Salt Lake City, 161, 179, 181; in San Francisco, 161, 182–83, 184, 185; and sensationalism, 162–63; and tourists, 71; of West, 200, 237n10

"dominant individualism," 32
downtowns, 120. *See also* urbanism; *specific cities*
Drexel Boulevard, 53
Dugard, Marie, 167
Dwinell, M., 176
Dwyer, James, 139

earthquakes, 65, 92, 95, 145–46
Egyptian architecture, 116. *See also* architecture
Eldridge, Mr., 177
elevated trains, 78, 88
elevation changes, 8–9. *See also* railroads
elevators: in Cosmopolitan Hotel, 157–58; in Masonic Temple, 3–4; in Siegel, Cooper and Company Building, 128; Treseder on, 3, 4, 7, 203
elites, 15–16, 220n14. *See also* boosterism
Endowment House, 139
Engels, Friedrich, 21
engineering processes, 12–13
Enlightenment, 46
Ensign Peak, 62, 142, 201, 202
entertainment panoramas, 67–68
environmental destruction, 76–77
Equitable Building, 62
ethnic diversity. *See* diversity
Europe, tourists in, 221n23
Evanston, Illinois, 53
exceptionalism, 26
Excursion to Colorado, California, and the Yosemite Valley, An (Jenkins), 44, 183
exoticism, 188–89
expectoration, 233n63

factories and factory tours, 13, 96
Faithfull, Emily, 49
Falk, Alfred, 82, 153
Farquharson, David, 157
Ferree, Barr, 231n7
ferries, 25, 60
Ferro, Giovanni Vigna dal, 180
fires and firefighters: and boosterism, 115; in Chicago, 95; in Denver, 65–66, 134; in San Francisco, 65, 95, 145; and

urbanism, 37. *See also* Great Fire of 1871
Five Months Fine Weather in Canada, Western U.S., and Mexico (Carbutt), 119
Flinn, John J., 63
Folsom, William, 137, 140
Fort Douglas, Utah, 62
frames, balloon, 133–34, 232n11. *See also* architecture
frames, metal, 130, 131, 146. *See also* architecture
France, government of, 19–20
Frenzeny, Paul, engraving by, *196*
freshwater distribution, 84, 98–100
"Frontier Thesis," 32

Galena and Chicago Union Railroad, 22–23. *See also* railroads
garden cities: Chicago as, 53, 90, 101; Denver as, 56; Salt Lake City as, 57; and tourists, 72–73; in West, 52–60
"Garden of the Gods," 55
Gassaway, Frank Harrison, 227n11
Gaynor, John P., 148
"General Sherman" (seal), 58
Gentiles, 174, 180, 181. *See also* Mormons
Germania Smelting and Refining Works, 96
Geysers, 33
Giacosa, Giuseppe, 89, 100
Gilpin, William, 169
Gladden, Washington, 35
Glazier, Willard, 98
Golden Gate Park, 59–60, 62, 119
gold rush, 144–45
Gothic architecture, 116. *See also* architecture
Graceland Cemetery, 53. *See also* cemeteries
grain elevators: and Chicago, 23, 70, 97, *99;* construction of, 98; Leng on, 70; as observatories, 97; Pidgeon on, 98; Robertson on, 97; and tourists, 13; Vivian on, 97
Grand Boulevard, 53
Grand Canyon, 34

Grandin, Mme. Léon, 88–89, 100, 117, 167

Grand Northern Hotel, 61. *See also* hotels

Grand Tour of Europe, 7, 27, 63

Grant Bros.' Livery and Transfer Company, *68*

Great Fire of 1871: and Alexis, 94; and architecture, 115; and boosterism, 92; Campbell on, 94; and Chicago Water Tower, 209; and entertainment panoramas, 67; and history, 66; Lewis on, 94–95; rebuilding after, 6, 65, 70–71, 88, 94, 121, 129–30; and Sienkiewicz, 130; and tourists, 93–94. *See also* Chicago, Illinois; fires and firefighters

Great Salt Lake, 57–58

Greek architecture, 116. *See also* architecture

Greeley, Horace, 237n10

Green, Frank, 193

Greenwood, Thomas, 61

Griffin, Sir Henry Lepel, 102

Gripenberg, Alexandra, 175

Grow, Henry, 137–38

Guangdong Province, China, 189. *See also* Chinese community

guidebooks: advertisements in, 47; architecture in, 113; Assembly Hall in, 139; Aurora in, 54; by Baedeker, 54; Baldwin Hotel in, 148; Barbary Coast in, 159; Berkeley Lake in, 54; Board of Trade in, 133; boulevards in, 51–52; Capitol Hill in, 54; Chicago in, 4, 98, 222n4; Chinese community in, 162, 188–89, 191, 193; City Park in, 54; and civilization, 114; Colorado Springs in, 55; contents of, 5, 43; Cosmopolitan Hotel in, 148; Denver in, 54, 55, 134; Drexel Boulevard in, 53; Endowment House in, 139; Ensign Peak in, 62; Evanston in, 53; examples of, 43; freshwater distribution in, 98; "Garden of the Gods" in, 55; Graceland Cemetery in, 53; Grand Boulevard in, 53; Great Salt Lake in, 57–58; health in, 43; history in, 64; hotels in, 117–18; industrial areas in, 47–48; joss houses in, 192; Lake Shore Drive in, 53; Lick House in, 147–48; Lincoln Park in, 53; Manitou Springs in, 55; Masonic Temple in, 4; Mission San Francisco de Asis in, 154; Mormons in, 57; and nature, 15; Nob Hill mansions in, 151; Oakland in, 79; Oakwood Boulevard in, 53; Occidental Hotel in, 148; Palace Hotel in, 148; parks in, 51; pleasure drives in, 51–52; Porter's Mineral Baths and Springs in, 54; Pullman in, 53–54; Salt Lake City in, 57, 62, 65, 137; San Francisco in, 36, 58–59, 65; Sloan Lake in, 54; South Park in, 54; as "strangers' guides," 47; suburbs in, 52; and urbanism, 15. *See also* boosterism; *specific guidebooks*

Guide Book to San Francisco (Hittell): art in, 118; Chinese theaters in, 191; diversity in, 183; parks and roads in, 51; U.S. Mint in, 149

guides, 26

Guide to San Francisco and Vicinity (Doxey), 147, 148, 154

Guillemard, Arthur, 150–51

Hall, William Hammond, 59

Hand Book of Winter Resorts (D. Appleton and Company), 55

Hardy, Iza Duffus, 84, 140–41

Harper, Harriet, 153, 182, 197

Harper's Weekly (magazine), 19–20, 131

harvesting, 22

hawkers, 80. *See also* hotels

Haymarket Affair, 37

health: in Denver, 41, 44, 55, 56, 85; in guidebooks, 43; and Salt Lake City, 57; and West, 43

health seekers. *See* tourists

"Heathen Chinee, The" (Harte), 192

Hendrix, E. R.: on Chinese community, 195; on Mormons, 175; on Palace Hotel, 149, 150; on San Francisco, 79

Hesse-Wartegg, Ernst von, 101

high-rises. *See* skyscrapers

Historical Souvenir of San Francisco (Heininger), 67–68

Holand, Hjalmar, 72
Holly Water Works, 97
Holton, E. D., 142, 177
Hopkins, Mark, 49
Horrors of the Mongolian Settlement (Raymond), 189, 190
Hotel del Monte, 33–34
hotels: and boosterism, 147; characteristics of, 164; in Chicago, 94; in guidebooks, 117–18; and hawkers, 80; and Medley, 94; observatories in, 118; and railroads, 78; rebuilding of, 94; in Salt Lake City, 143; in San Francisco, 147–48, 182, 185, 235n120; and tourists, 43, 132, 235n120; and urbanism, 149
houses, moving of, 92, *93*
How the Other Half Lives (Riis), 38
Hudson, T. S., 92
Huehl, Harris W., 128
Hutchings, James, 148

Illinois and Michigan Canal, 22–23
Illinois Central Railroad grain-storage facilities, 61. *See also* grain elevators
illnesses, 37
Illustrated Hand Book and Guide to Chicago and the World's Columbian Exposition (Schneyer), 52, 53
immigrants, 160, 182, 184, 186
Independence, Missouri, 57
Indians. *See* Native Americans
industrial areas, 47–48
industrialization, 13, 21, 26, 71. *See also* modernization
infrastructure, 90, 91–92, 115
Ingersoll, Ernest, 36, 135
In Search of the Golden West (Pomeroy), 222n40
interior design, 117, 118, 126
Irish-American Workingmen's Party of California, 186

Jackson, Helen Hunt, 153, 198
Jackson, William Henry, 48–49
Jackson Park, 52–53
Jenney, William le Baron, 52, 115, 123

Jesus Christ of Latter-Day Saints, Church of. *See* Mormons
Johnson, Matthew, 83, 144, 178
Johnson, Osmun, 85, 87
Joliet, Louis, 64–65
Jones, Harry: on Chicago, 39, 87–88, 115; on Chinese community, 195; on San Francisco, 92, 185
joss houses, 191, 192, 197
Joyaux, Georges J., 104
"Just Arrived in Chicago—Trying to See the Tops of Buildings" (cartoon), *35*

Kansas Pacific Railroad, 25, 222n43. *See also* railroads
Kant, Immanuel, 44
Kent, Henry Brainard, 101, 136–37, 175
Kingsbury, Joseph C., 69
King's Handbook of the United States (guidebook), 47–48, 55, 125–26, 135
Kingsley, Rose Georgina, 39, 193
Kipling, Rudyard, 102, 132, 149, 176

labor unions, 37, 186
Lake Michigan, 74
Lake Shore Drive, 53
landscape. *See* nature
landscape architects, 50–51
Larimer Street, *86*
Latter-Day Saints. *See* Mormons
lawlessness, 31, 35, 65. *See also* mythologizing
Lee, S. M., 136, 151, 197
Leng, John: on Board of Trade, 133; on Chicago, 70; on cosmopolitanism, 184–85; on grain elevators, 70; on infrastructure, 90; on San Francisco, 90, 184–85; on U.S. Mint, 149–50
Leslie, Miriam, 146, 198
Lessing, Julius, 133–34
Levee District, 167, 208, 238n25
Lewis, Charles E., 94–95, 98–99, 168
Lick House, 147–48
Lights and Shades in San Francisco (Lloyd), 163, 189, 190
Limerick, Patricia, 172
Lincoln Park, 53

lithographers, 49
Lone Mountain Cemetery, 58. *See also* cemeteries
Loop, 35, 89, 115
Lower Downtown area, 239n42
Lucy, Henry: on billboards and signs, 90; on Chicago, 89, 90; on Chinese community, 171; on crowds, 89; on Denver, 85; on earthquakes, 92; on San Francisco, 82, 92; on Union Stock Yards, 102, 231n115
Ludlow, Fitz Hugh, 176

machinery, exhibits of, 13
manifest destiny, 76
Manitou Springs, Colorado, 55
Manning, Samuel, 142, 144
mansions, Nob Hill, 151, 153
manufacturing communities, 96–97
Market Street, *150*
Marquette, Jacques, 64–65
Marshall, Charles, 180
Marshall, W. G.: on billboards and signs, 91; in Chicago, 26; on Chinese community, 195; on Denver, 85; on industrialization, 26; on Mormons, 179; on Mormon Temple, 141; on Salt Lake City, 143; on San Francisco, 91
Marvels of the New West (Thayer), 169–70
Marx, Karl, 21
Masonic Temple, *129;* acclaim for, 126; atrium of, 3; and boosterism, 126; and Burke, 126; and Burnham, 129; characteristics of, 4, 126, 129; designers of, 3; dimensions of, 4; elevators in, 3–4; guidebooks on, 4; interior design of, 126–27; as observatory, 61; and Pretyman, 126; purposes of, 127; and Root, 129; technological advancements of, 4; Treseder on, 3, 4, 7, 17; views from, 3, 4
mass production, 49. *See also* industrialization
May, Karl, 31
McClintock, A. H., 140, 142
McCormick, Cyrus, 22

McElrath, Thomson P., 76, 101, 227n15
Mead, Solomon: on Denver, 135; on Mormons, 176; on Mormon Temple, 142; on U.S. Mint, 150; on West, 199
mechanization, 37, 77. *See also* industrialization
Medley, George, 94
Medley, Julius, 110
Merewether, Henry Alworth, 66, 84, 146, 178
metal frames, 130, 131, 146. *See also* architecture
"Metropolis and Mental Life, The" (Simmel), 28
Metropolitan Correctional Center, 208
Metropolitan Life Unveiled; or, The Mysteries and Miseries of America's Great Cities (Buel), 173
Michigan Central and Michigan Southern Railroad, 25. *See also* railroads
miners and mining, 30, 75–76, 96, 180
Mission San Francisco de Asis (Mission Dolores), 153–55
modernization: and anonymity, 37; of architecture, 109; attractiveness of, 20; and boosterism, 28, 29–30, 36, 42, 122; of Chicago, 23, 39–40; of Cincinnati, 21; of Denver, 36, 39–40; effects of, 13, 20, 21–22, 28, 37; of industrial areas, 48; and Mission San Francisco de Asis, 154; and nature, 42, 62; and photography, 66; and pollution, 37; and progress, 28, 29–30; and racial discrimination, 37; Ralph on, 20; Rousiers on, 20; of Salt Lake City, 39–40; of San Francisco, 39–40; and tourists, 12, 13, 21–22, 26, 34; and urbanism, 14, 37; in West, 12, 13, 14, 20–29, 34; of wheat harvesting, 22. *See also* industrialization
Mohr, Nicolaus, 87
Mongolians. *See* Chinese community
Monterey, California, 33–34
Moran, Thomas, 32
"Mormon" Metropolis, The: An Illustrated Guide to Salt Lake City and Its Environs (guidebook), *68,* 106, 138, 173

Mormons: Bates on, 178; and blood atonement, 173, 177; Churchill on, 175; Church on, 176; Clark on, 175; contributions of, 12; conversion to, 178; and cosmopolitanism, 174; criticism of, 172–73, 174–76; as deviant population, 172, 187; diversity among, 161, 177–78; Dwinell on, 176; exoticism of, 12; foreign-born members of, 177–78; and Gentiles, 174; Gripenberg on, 175; in guidebooks, 57; and guides, 26; Hendrix on, 175; history of, 65; Johnson on, 178; Kent on, 175; and Kipling, 176; Limerick on, 172; Ludlow on, 176; Marshall on, 179; Mead on, 176; Merewether on, 178; polygamy of, 172, 173, 174–76, 178; population of, 6; Preston on, 176; Rice on, 175–76; Richards on, 176; Robinson on, 172, 177; Ryland on, 178; in Salt Lake City, 12, 16, 23, 65, 95–96, 136, 172; Todd on, 178; Topsöe on, 175; and tourists, 26, 36, 136, 139, 172, 173, 174–75, 177; women as, 175, 176; work ethic of, 16
Mormon Tabernacle, *107*, 108, 137–38, 141
Mormon Temple, *107;* and Angell, 138; construction of, 137, 138–39, 141–42; and Dwyer, 139; Manning on, 142; Marshall on, 141; Mead on, 142; Pidgeon on, 108; and tourists, 141; and Young, 138
mountains. *See* Rocky Mountains; Sierra Nevadas; Wasatch Mountains
Muirhead, James Fullarton, 59–60, 135–36, 151, 152
multisensory experiences: of Chicago, 79; of Oakland, 79, 80; of San Francisco, 79, 80–81, 82; of tourists, 15, 72; in urbanism, 72; in West, 15
Muybridge, Eadweard, 48–49
mythologizing: characteristics of, 30; and Cody, 30–31; of West, 6, 20, 22, 29–34. *See also* lawlessness

Native Americans: architectural ruins of, 63–64; and Barneby, 181–82; decimation of, 30, 32; discrediting of, 154; history of, 63–64; on reservations, 30, 32; as savages, 64; and tourists, 32. *See also* mythologizing
nativism, 37, 45
natural gas wells, 76
nature: Addison on, 46; and architecture, 136; and art, 46; and boosterism, 41–42, 43–45, 46, 69; and boulevards, 119; and built environment, 143; and Central Pacific Railroad, 34; and Denver, 55, 136; and Enlightenment, 46; and Golden Gate Park, 59–60; and guidebooks, 15; inaccessibility of, 33–34; and interior design, 117; and mechanization, 77; and modernization, 42, 62; and morality, 46; and parks, 119; and picturesque, 46; and Salt Lake City, 96, 143; and San Francisco, 58–59, 74; and technological advancements, 76; and tourists, 14, 21, 29, 32, 39, 46; and Union Pacific Railroad, 34; and urbanism, 14–15, 42, 46, 50, 69, 74; and West, 14, 30, 32, 39, 219n6
Naylor, Robert Anderton, 78, 88
newspapers, 164. *See also specific newspapers*
New York Stock Exchange, 221n29
Niagara Falls, New York, 7
nighttime illumination, 13
Nob Hill, 62
Nob Hill mansions, 151, 153
nonfictional urban sensationalism, defined, 238n15
Northern Pacific Railroad, 34. *See also* railroads
nostalgia, 65

Oakland, Alameda, and Berkeley Ferry Building, 228n29
Oakland, California: Carbutt on, 80; Clark on, 73; ferries and steamers departing from, 25, 60; in guidebooks, 79; multisensory experiences of, 79, 80
Oakland Mole, 243n11
Oakwood Boulevard, 53
obelisk, 202
observatories, 62, 97, 118
Occidental Hotel, 148. *See also* hotels

O'Farrell, Jasper, 145
Ohlone Indians, 154. *See also* Native
    Americans
"Old Shatterhand," 31
Olmsted, Frederick Law, 51, 52–53, 59
opium dens, 190, 193. *See also* Chinese
    community
O'Rell, Max, 28, 104
Orton, William, 29, 221n29
Osdel, John van, 132
"other," 16, 155, 162, 163–64
*Our Great West: A Study of the Present
    Conditions and Future Possibilities of the
    New Commonwealths and Capitals of the
    United States* (Ralph), 18, 19
overcrowding, 21
oversubsidization, 13. *See also* railroads

Pacific Ocean, 58
Pacific Tourist, The (Williams), 44, 57, 134
"Painted Ladies," 152. *See also* residential
    districts
Palace Hotel, 148–49, *150*
Palmer House, 132
Panic of 1873, 220n16
panoramas, 49, 56
Parallel (ship), 120
Park Branch Line, 34. *See also* railroads
parks: advantages of, 119; and boosterism,
    51, 119; in Chicago, 52, 119; and civili-
    zation, 118; by Cleveland, 52; construc-
    tion of, 51; entertainment in, 119; in
    guidebooks, 51; by Jenney, 52; location
    of, 118–19; and nature, 119; by Olmsted,
    52; in San Francisco, 60, 225n50; and
    tourists, 119; and urbanism, 119; by
    Vaux, 52
pastoral, the, 48, 51
persecution, 187. *See also* Chinese com-
    munity; racial discrimination
Pfeiffer, Emily, 31, 37–38
Philadelphia, Pennsylvania, 28
Phillips, David L., 155
Phillips, Morris, 84, 101, 131
photography, 49, 66
picturesque, the: and nature, 46; and Olm-
    sted, 51; and photography, 49; theories

of, 46; and urbanism, 45–52, 60, 74;
    and Vaux, 51
Picturesque America (D. Appleton and Com-
    pany), 223n9
Pidgeon, Daniel: on balloon frames, 134;
    on built environment, 108; on Chicago,
    92; on Chinese community, 171, 197;
    on Denver, 85, 171; on grain elevators,
    98; on Mormon Tabernacle, 108; on
    Mormon Temple, 108; on Salt Lake
    City, 107–108; on San Francisco, 184
Pierrepont, Edward, 84, 110–11, 132,
    232n11
Pike's Peak, 62
"Plain Language from Truthful James"
    (Harte), 192
plat, of Salt Lake City, 201
plat, of Zion, 57
pleasure drives, 51–52
pleasure seekers. *See* tourists
police and police protection, 115
pollution, 21, 23, 37
polygamy, 172, 173, 174–76, 178. *See also*
    Mormons
*Polygamy; or, The Mysteries and Crimes of
    Mormonism* (Beadle), 173
polygonal building, 67–68
poor persons, 37, 170. *See also* slums
Porter's Mineral Baths and Springs, 54
ports, 164
Preston, William, 144, 176
Pretyman, William, 126
Price, M. Philips, 110, 194–95
prisons, 220n6
promotional materials. *See* boosterism;
    guidebooks
Prospect Hill, 62
prostitution and bordellos, 187, 208
Pullman, George, 204
Pullman, Illinois, 23, 53–54, 203–204

quarantining, 185. *See also* Chinese
    community

race, 156
racial discrimination, 37, 156, 170, 192–93
Rae, William F., 73

railroads: and boosterism, 78; and Chicago, 78; costliness of, 10, 219n8; and hotels, 78; oversubsidization of, 13; price wars of, 10; and Pullman, 23; and sublime, 74–75; and tourists, 13; across United States, *8–9, 24* and World's Columbian Exposition, 10. *See also specific railroads*
Ralph, Julian: on architecture, 121; on Chicago, 88; on Denver, 85; and *Harper's Magazine,* 19–20; on modernization, 20; on San Francisco, 184; on skyscrapers, 128; on streetcars, 88; on West, 18
Ralston, William, 148
Raycraft, Mary Beth, 167–68
Raymond and Whitcomb Company, 10
Ready Reference Guide to Chicago and the World's Columbian Exposition (A. N. Marquis and Company), 43–44, 52, 103
religion, 238n16. *See also* Mormons
Remington, Frederic, 30
reservations, 30, 32. *See also* Native Americans
residential districts, 133, 143, 151–53. *See also* suburbs
resorts, 41–42, 57, 58–59
Reynolds, John, 82
Rice, Harvey: on Mormons, 175–76; on Mormon Tabernacle, 141; on San Francisco, 82, 146, 185
Richards, Mary Bradshaw, 176, 180
Richardson, Albert D., 95, 158
Roberts, Morley, 89, 184
Robertson, W. F. and William, 25, 80–81, 97, 155
Robinson, Phil: on architecture, 111; on Chicago, 77, 168; on Chinese community, 193; on Mormons, 172, 177; on Salt Lake City, 172; on San Francisco, 73, 111
Rochefoucauld-Liancourt, F. A. F. de La, 27
Rocky Mountains: as "America's Switzerland," 45; and boosterism, 61–62; and Denver, 35–36, 55, *56,* 61, 74, 85, 136
"Rocky Mountain Scenery" (Chamberlain), 56
Root, John Wellborn, 3, 123, 129
Rousiers, Paul de, 19–20, 23, 132, 206

rush hour, 83, 89
Russel, Nicholas, 80, 83
Russell, Charles, 30
Russian Hill, 62
Ryland, Walter P., 178, 212

Sable, Jean Baptiste Pointe du, 64
Sacramento, California, 25
Sala, George Augustus, 110, 179
saloons, 180, 181
Salt Lake City, Utah, *107, 181;* Aitken on, 142; architecture in, 136, 144; attractions of, 205; bird's-eye views of, 142–43; Bonwick on, 143, 180; and boosterism, 95–96, 106–107, 173–74; breweries in, 96; built environment of, 58, 108, 140–41, 142–43; Chinese community in, 240n77; *Christos* in, 210; City Creek Center in, 206; and civilization, 106, 107, 136, 138, 139; Clark on, 180; Codman on, 179; complexities and contradictions in, 84; and cosmopolitanism, 173–74, 178, 179, 181–82; Deseret Woolen Mills in, 96; diversity in, 161, 179, 181–82; energy of, 179; and Ensign Peak, 142; factories in, 96; Ferro on, 180; and Fort Douglas, 62, 208–209; freshwater channels in, 84; as garden city, 57; Gentiles in, 180, 181; growth of, 10, 23, 179–80, 181; in guidebooks, 57, 62, 65, 137; Hardy on, 84, 140–41; and health, 57; hotels in, 143; Johnson on, 83, 144; Kent on, 136–37; and Kingsbury, 69; Manning on, 144; as manufacturing community, 96–97; Marshall on, 143, 180; McClintock on, 140; McElrath on, 76; Merewether on, 84; and mining, 96, 180; modernization of, 39–40; Mormons in, 6, 12, 16, 23, 65, 95–96, 136, 172; and nature, 6, 96, 143; oddity of, 141; Phillips on, 84; Pidgeon on, 107–108; Pierrepont on, 84; plat of Zion of, 57; Preston on, 144; residential districts of, 143; as resort, 57; Richards on, 180; Robinson on, 172; Ryland on, 212; Sala on, 179; saloons in, 180, 181; Sanders on, 143; Temple

Square in, 137; and tourists, 25, 36, 96, 171–72, 173; tours in, *68;* Travers on, 143; urbanism in, 6; and Utah Central Railroad, 96; and Wasatch Mountains, 57, 62, 74; weather conditions in, 84; Wills on, 171–72

Salt Lake Theater, 139

Sanders, Sue A. Pike, 41, 44, 62, 143

San Francisco, California: Adams on, 39; Aitken on, 82–83; architecture in, 110–11, 144, 145, 146, 151, 152, 231n5; attractions of, 205; Avery on, 153; Beadle on, 33; billboards and signs in, 90, 91; Blake on, 90; Boddam-Whetham on, 90; Bonwick on, 152; and boosterism, 58, 60, 62, 144, 146–47; Bridges on, 73; built environment in, 110, 144–56; cable cars in, 62, 81, 209–10; chaos of, 145; Chinese community in, 6, 12, 16, 36, 146, 155, 185–86, 189, *196,* 210, *211,* 241n98; civilization in, 120, 144, 147; Clark on, 73; Clarkson on, 184; Cliff House in, 36, 213; Col. A. Andrews "Diamond Palace" in, 29; complexities and contradictions in, 36–37, 79, 146; Cone on, 58; and cosmopolitanism, 182, 183, 184–85, 199; decay in, 153–54; diversity in, 161, 182–83, 184, 185; earthquakes in, 65, 95, 145–46; energy of, 92; and entertainment panoramas, 67–68; European nature of, 207; Falk on, 82, 153; and ferries, 60; fires and firefighters in, 65, 95, 145; and Geysers, 33; and gold rush, 144–45; grid plan of, 145; growth of, 10, 66, 144; in guidebooks, 36, 58–59, 65; Harper on, 153, 182; Hendrix on, 79; history of, 65; hotels in, 147–48, 182, 185, 235n120; house moving in, 92, *93;* Hudson on, 92, 152; immigrants in, 182, 184; infrastructure of, 90; Jones on, 92, 185; lawlessness in, 65; Leng on, 90, 184–85; Leslie on, 146; Lucy on, 82, 92; Marshall on, 91; Merewether on, 146; modernization of, 39–40; Muirhead on, 152; multisensory experiences of, 79, 80–81, 82; and nature, 6, 58–59, 74, 153; nostalgia in, 65; parks in, 60, 225n50; Pfeiffer on, 37–38; Pidgeon on, 184; Pierrepont on, 110–11; popularity of, 217n1; population of, 22; Rae on, 73; Ralph on, 184; reputation of, 147; residential districts in, 36, 151–53; as resort, 58–59; Rice on, 82, 146, 185; Richardson on, 95; Roberts on, 184; Robertson on, 80–81; Robinson on, 73, 111; Russel on, 80, 83; Sala on, 110; Seal Rocks in, 212, 214–15; slums in, 155; Smiles on, 145; Stevenson on, 36–37, 95, 153; stock exchanges in, 150; streetcars in, 81–82; topography of, 153; tourists in, 36; transitory nature of, 111; Travers on, 79; and urbanism, 6, 23, 59, 65; Walworth on, 212; Wills on, 82; Workingman's Party in, 37; and Yosemite, 33

San Francisco Album (Fardon), 223n15

San Francisco Chronicle (newspaper), 59

Savage, Charles R., 48–49

"savage" natives, 11, 14, 30. *See also* mythologizing; Native Americans

seals and Seal Rocks: and Cliff House, 58, 120, 213; in San Francisco, 212, 214–15

segregation, 170

seismic activity, 65, 92, 145–46

sensationalism, 163, 189

Sharon, William, 148

sicknesses, 37

Siegel, Cooper and Company Building, 128

Sienkiewicz, Henry, 130

Sierra Nevadas, 45

signs and billboards, 90, 91. *See also* advertisements

Simmel, Georg, 28

skyscrapers: as art, 13, 125; and boosterism, 125; in Chicago, 13, 35, 120, 121–34; dangers of, 130–31; design of, 124; and developers, 124–25; Dewar on, 130; *Harper's Weekly* on, 131; isolated nature of, 124; names of, 125; Phillips on, 131; public purpose of, 128; Ralph on, 128; reactions to, 122; Stead on, 130; and tourists, 13, 121, 122, 128, 132

sleeper cars, 7. *See also* railroads
Sloan Lake, 54
slumming, 187. *See also* tourists
slums, 155. *See also* poor persons
smelting, 227n15, 230n93
Smiles, Samuel, 83, 91, 145
Smith, Joseph, 57
Smith, Mrs. J. Gregory, 195, 197
Smith, William, 177
Solano (ferry), 227n26. *See also* ferries
South Park, 54
Souvenir Album of 1891: City of Denver Colo
    (Barbot), 113
stagecoaches, 25
State Street, *129*
Stead, William P., 130
steamers, 25
steel frames, 130, 131, 146. *See also*
    architecture
stereographs, 49–50, 223n17
Stevenson, Robert Louis, 36–37, 95, 153
St. Louis, Missouri, 219n7
stock exchanges, 150–51
stockyards. *See* Union Stock Yards
Stone, W. G. M., 54–55
"strangers' guides," 47. *See also* guidebooks
streetcars, 78, 81–82, 88–89
Strong, George Templeton, 192
sublime, the: Burke on, 44; characteristics
    of, 75; Kant on, 44; and mining, 75;
    and railroads, 74–75; Taylor on, 75; and
    tourists, 76; and urbanism, 72–77; West
    as, 44, 74; Williams on, 44
suburbs, 52. *See also* residential districts
Sullivan, Louis, 123, 125, 127
Sutro Heights, 60, 62

Taber, Isaiah West, 49
Tacoma Building, 61
Taylor, Benjamin F., 75
Taylor, John, 177
Taylor, Obid, 140
technological advancements, 12–13, 63,
    76–77, 157–58. *See also specific techno-*
    logical advancements
Telegraph Hill, 62, 153
temblors, 65, 92, 95, 145–46

Temple Square, 137
theaters, 139, 191
Thomas, Julia, 177
Thomas Cook and Son, 10, 27
Tocqueville, Alexis de, 220n6
Todd, John, 178
Topsöe, Vilhelm, 175
tourists: and architecture, 109–10, 116–17,
    133, 134, 151, 231n7; and automobiles,
    205; and Board of Trade, 133; and
    boosterism, 7, 45; and boulevards, 119;
    and built environment, 109–10, 111,
    118, 120, 195; and cable cars, 62; and
    Cannon, 174; in Chicago, *35,* 101; and
    Chinese community, 26, 155–56, 187,
    188, 191, 193–94, *196,* 197–99; and
    Cincinnati, 219n7; and civilization, 151;
    and cosmopolitanism, 160; and crowds,
    71; democratization of, 10; in Denver,
    25, 35–36, 170–71; and engineering
    processes, 12–13; and ethnic diversity,
    71; in Europe, 27, 221n23; and garden
    cities, 72–73; and geography, 22; and
    grain elevators, 13; and Grand Tour
    of Europe, 27; and Great Fire of 1871,
    93–94; and history, 68–69; and hotels,
    43, 132, 235n120; and industrializa-
    tion, 71; labels for, 219n13; and Levee
    District, 167; and mining, 75, 96; and
    Mission San Francisco de Asis, 154–55;
    and modernization, 12, 13, 21–22, 26,
    34; and Mormons, 26, 36, 136, 139,
    172, 173, 174–75, 177; and Mormon
    Temple, 141; multisensory experiences
    of, 11, 15, 72; and Native Americans,
    32; and nature, 14, 21, 29, 32, 39, 46;
    and Niagara Falls, 7; number of, 13–14;
    and opium dens, 190; and parks, 119;
    patterns of, 14; in Pullman, 53–54, 203;
    and railroads, 13, 33; in Salt Lake City,
    25, 36, 96, 171–72, 173; in San Fran-
    cisco, 36; and "savage" natives, 14; and
    skyscrapers, 13, 121, 122, 132; and ste-
    reographs, 49–50; and St. Louis, 219n7;
    and sublime, 76; and Sutro Heights,
    60; and technological advancements,
    12–13; and tranportation, 89; and trans-

continental railroads, 33; and unfair labor practices, 13; and urbanism, 11–12, 26, 71, 207–208; and vehicular traffic, 71; and West, 6, 10, 21, 29, 200, 205; women as, 219n5; and Young, 174

Tourist's Guide Book to Denver (Woodbury), 135

tours: of factories, 13; by Kingsbury, 68, 69; in Salt Lake City, 68; of Union Stock Yards, 102; to Yellowstone, 53

touters, 80. *See also* hotels

trade, 22–23

traffic, vehicular, 71

transcontinental railroad: bird's-eye views of, *24,* 25; cities along, 34; Codman on, 25–26; completion of, 12; and destinations, 33; importance of, 7; and tourists, 33

Trans-continental Tourist (Crofutt), 159

transportation, 89, 115. *See also specific types of transportation*

travelers. *See* tourists

Travers, W. T. Locke, 79, 143

Treseder, Mable: on Chicago, 4–5, 200; on elevators, 3, 4, 7, 203; on Masonic Temple, 3, 4, 7, 17; on Siegel, Cooper and Company Building, 128

Turland, Ephraim, 89, 99

Turner, Frederick Jackson, 32

Twain, Mark, 237n1

Underground Railroad, 165. *See also* African Americans

unfair labor practices, 13, 21

Union Depot, 135

Union Pacific Railroad, 7, *8–9,* 25, 34. *See also* railroads

unions, 37, 186

Union Stock Yards: Barton on, 103–104; Blouet on, 104; and boosterism, 103; in Chicago, 23, 26, *48,* 102–104; cruelty in, 103–104; Griffin on, 102; Joyaux on, 104; Lucy on, 102, 231n115; tours of, 26, 102

University of Denver, 135

Upchurch, J. J., 62, 192; and Pike's Peak, 62

urban boosters. *See* boosterism

urbanism: and architecture, 16, 116–21; and art, 46; bird's-eye views of, 46, 50; and boosterism, 29, 39, 45–46, 47; and built environment, 11–12, 37; and Chamber of Commerce Building, 128; chaos of, 46–47; characteristics of, 16–17; and civilization, 15–16, 112–13; complexities and contradictions in, 74; and cosmopolitanism, 16, 162; and Denver, 23, 65; and diseases, 37; and efficiency, 46–47; and elites, 15–16; and entertainment, 119; and fires, 37; and Golden Gate Park, 59; growth of, 37; and guidebooks, 15; and hotels, 149; idealization of, 49; and Jackson, 49; and labor unions, 37; literature about, 38; maturity of, 47; and modernization, 14, 37; multisensory experiences in, 72; and Muybridge, 49; and nativism, 37; and nature, 14–15, 42, 46, 50, 69, 74; and observatories, 61; orderliness of, 48; and parks, 119; and pastoral, 48, 51; and picturesque, 45–52, 60, 74; and poverty, 37; and progress, 46–47; readability of, 47; and San Francisco, 23, 65; and Savage, 49; and sublime, 72–77; and Taber, 49; and tourists, 11–12, 26, 71, 207–208; and Watkins, 49; and West, 6, 14, 15, 25, 207, 213, 215; and working conditions, 37; and zoning, 47. *See also specific cities*

urbs in horto, defined, 49; by lithographers, 49

U.S. Mint, 149–50

Utah Central Railroad, 25, 96, 174. *See also* railroads

Vaux, Calvert, 51, 52

vice districts, 167. *See also* bordellos and prostitution; Levee District

"Victorians," 152. *See also* residential districts

Views of Utah and Tourists' Guide (Savage), 62

visitors. *See* tourists

Vivian, Henry Hussey, 97–98, 194

Walker, W. S., 149

Walker House, 139

Walworth, Ellen, 212
Ward, Martindale C., 77–78, 95, 132, 204
Warner, Charles Dudley, 101
Wasatch Mountains, 57, 62, 74
Water Tower, Chicago, 97, 209
waterworks. *See* freshwater distribution
Watkins, Carleton, 48–49
weather conditions, 43, 84, 101, 222n4. *See also specific cities*
wells, 76
Wells, Emiline, 177
West, the: architecture in, 115–16, 134, 156; authenticity of, 207; bison in, 30; Blouet on, 28; and boosterism, 6, 66–67; and civilization, 112, 156; complexities and contradictions in, 73–74; culture in, 26–27; diversity in, 161, 200, 237n10; "dominant individualism" in, 32; Egyptian architecture in, 116; engineering processes in, 12–13; exceptionalism of, 26; garden cities in, 52–60; geographical boundaries of, 220n12; Gothic architecture in, 116; and Grand Tour of Europe, 7; Greek architecture in, 116; Greeley on, 237n10; and health, 43; and history, 63; landscapes of, 7; lawlessness of, 30, 31; Mead on, 199; miners in, 30; modernization of, 12, 13, 14, 20–29, 34; multisensory experiences in, 15; mythologizing of, 6, 20, 22, 29–34; and nature, 14, 30, 32, 39, 44, 219n6; and the past, 63–69, 115–16; population growth in, 10; Ralph on, 18; and religion, 238n16; as resort destination, 41–42; Rousiers on, 19; rural in, 22; "savage" natives in, 11, 30; and sublime, 44, 74; technological advancements in, 12–13; and tourists, 5–6, 10, 21, 29, 200, 205; unexpectedness in, 205; and urbanism, 6, 14, 15, 22, 25, 32, 207, 213, 215; weather conditions in, 43; "wild" adventurers in, 11. *See also specific cities*
Western Union Telegraph Company, 29
wheat harvesting, 22
Whitman, Walt, 36, 75–76
Wilde, Oscar, 100, 197
Wild West, 170. *See also* West, the
Williams, Henry T., 44
Wills, Mary, 82, 171–72, 186–87, 197
windows, 152. *See also* architecture
women, 175, 176, 219n5
Woodruff, Wilson, 173
Woodward's Gardens, 60
work ethic, 16
Workingman's Party, 37
World's Columbian Exposition, 4, 10, 13, 35
World's Fair Chicago 1893 Souvenir Illustrated (guidebook), 126, 128

Yellowstone, 34, 44, 53
Yosemite, 33, 44, 227n11
Young, Brigham, 96, 138, 174

Zehme, Friedrich Wilhelm Heinrich, 39
Zion's Co-operative Mercantile Institution (ZCMI), 140, 142
zoning, 47